TORAH IN THE MOUTH

Torah in the Mouth

WRITING AND ORAL TRADITION
IN PALESTINIAN JUDAISM
200 BCE–400 CE

Martin S. Jaffee

OXFORD

UNIVERSITY PRESS

2001

OXFORD
UNIVERSITY PRESS

Oxford   New York
Athens   Auckland   Bangkok   Bogotá   Buenos Aires   Calcutta
Cape Town   Chennai   Dar es Salaam   Delhi   Florence   Hong Kong   Istanbul
Karachi   Kuala Lumpur   Madrid   Melbourne   Mexico City   Mumbai
Nairobi   Paris   Shanghai   Singapore   Taipei   Tokyo   Toronto   Warsaw

and associated companies in
Berlin   Ibadan

Published by Oxford University Press, Inc.,
198 Madison Avenue, New York, New York 10016

Oxford is a registered trademark of Oxford University Press

Library of Congress Cataloging-in-Publication Data
Jaffee, Martin S.
Torah in the mouth : writing and oral tradition in Palestinian Judaism, 200 BCE–400 CE
/ Martin S. Jaffee.
p. cm.
Includes bibliographical references.
ISBN 0-19-514067-2
1. Judaism—History—Post-exilic period, 586 B.C.–210 A.D.
2. Judaism—History—Talmudic period, 10–425.   3. Tradition (Judaism)—History of
doctrines.   4. Rabbinical literature—History and criticism.   I. Title.
BM176 .J35 2000
296'.09'014—dc21   00-028485

9 8 7 6 5 4 3 2 1
Printed in the United States of America
on acid-free paper

For
Nisan Barukh b. Avraham Jaffee
truly his brother's keeper

Preface

The seeds for this study were sown during my graduate studies in the late 1970s. It was then that I first read, through the critical lens of Jacob Neusner's monumental achievement, the great studies of Birger Gerhardsson on Jewish and Christian oral tradition. The seeds germinated for the first half decade of my postgraduate professorial career as I began to reflect upon the literary character of texts I had translated and commented upon in a series of rather narrow and — as the justifiably few readers of those studies might agree — ultimately arid exercises. It was only in the late 1980s, after a chance encounter with Werner Kelber's marvelous study of oral tradition in the early Christian communities, that I learned of the enormous, and continually growing, scholarship on oral literature and tradition that had emerged since Gerhardsson and Neusner had made their contributions to the field.

It took me the entire decade of the 1990s to absorb this scholarship, to catch up with its diverse reverberations in the various fields of classical and biblical studies, and to find my own particular way of bringing it to bear upon the interpretation of the rabbinic theme of Torah in the Mouth. The resulting study — this book — is both the result and a kind of record of this game of catch-up.

The second and largest part of the book — the part devoted to the rabbinic tradition per se — has at its core a series of my essays published in various venues from 1991 to 1998. These have been thoroughly revised, rethought, and expanded in light of what I have learned since. The first part of the book, which discusses the shape of oral tradition in the Second Temple period, was written most recently — for the explicit purpose of contextualizing the rabbinic portion of the study. As I got down to work, I realized that if I did not deal with the question of oral tradition in Second Temple Judaism in a paragraph, it would require at least 150 typescript pages. I made the choice of writing the 150 pages.

In the course of teaching myself a body of scholarship which was by no means my intellectual patrimony, it soon dawned upon me that I had found the theme that would make of my accumulated rabbinic studies a genuine thesis about the history of oral tradition in early Judaism — namely, while Second Temple Jewish scribal culture had a rich oral-literary culture, it had as yet formulated no ideological self-consciousness about it. What we find in the rabbinic conception of Torah in the Mouth, accordingly, is the conjoining of an oral-literary culture rooted in the Second Temple period with a decidedly recent rabbinic ideology that explained the relation of that culture to prestigious written Scriptures and the human Sages who served as the guardians of tradition. Just how recently that ideology had emerged, under what cultural constraints, and for what purposes are all matters that I have attempted to clarify in the second part of the study.

Readers will soon notice that the argument of the book is built upon successive close readings of translated texts. I am responsible for the translations of all texts from the Dead Sea Scrolls and rabbinic literature. Translations of the Hebrew Bible and New Testament generally follow the Jewish Publication Society Tanakh and the Revised Standard Version respectively, although I have taken liberties where I felt it necessary to highlight a particular interpretive possibility. Citations from other Second Temple period Jewish literature or from Greco-Roman literature generally follow standard translations and these sources are identified in the notes where appropriate.

In translitering Hebrew, Aramaic, and Greek material I have tried to accommodate scientific accuracy and the reader's convenience. Greek transliterations attempt nothing more than to reproduce the Greek sounds with appropriate symbols of the Latin alphabet. Hebrew and Aramaic are a bit more complicated. Here I have used two systems. Sometimes I reproduce only the consonantal text using a rather standard system of transliteration, where ' = 'aleph, ' = 'ayin, ḥ = ḥet, ṭ = ṭet, k = kaf, s = samekh, ṣ = tzadi, q = quf, š = shin, and ś = sin. At other times, I transliterate in accord with modern spoken Hebrew. Thus, *mitzvah* renders *mṣwh*, *halakhah* renders *hlkh*, *divrei soferim* renders *dbry swprym*, and so forth.

Acknowledgments

While this work does include some previously published material, the vast bulk of the writing and revision took place between the summers of 1998 and 1999. During that period I was the beneficiary of a fellowship from the National Endowment for the Humanities, which freed me from the classroom and enabled me to spend virtually every working day in my study. I wish to acknowledge the generosity of the NEH in supporting my work. It would never have appeared without the support of that remarkable institution.

The beginning of the writing also coincided with my appointment as the Samuel and Althea Stroum Professor of Jewish Studies at the University of Washington. Mr. and Mrs. Stroum have been wonderful supporters of Jewish Studies at the university and have been particularly generous to me personally. I wish to thank them here for their support. May this volume give them some pleasure and a sense of significant return on their investment in my career.

During the years in which this study germinated, I have of course benefitted enormously from numerous conversations with colleagues around the world on various topics connected with it. Those whose criticisms and questions have taught me the most include Professors Albert Baumgarten (Bar-Ilan University), Marc Bregman (HUC-JIR, Jerusalem), Yaakov Elman (Yeshiva University), John Miles Foley (University of Missouri, Columbus), Steven Fraade (Yale University), Robert Goldenberg (SUNY, Stony Brook), Catherine Hezser (The Free University of Berlin), and David Stern (University of Pennsylvania). In addition, I owe great thanks to two younger scholars, Professors Elizabeth Shanks Alexander (University of Virginia; Ph.D., Yale, 1998) and David Nelson (Washington University; Ph.D., HUC-JIR, Cincinnati, 1999). Both risked their academic necks by incorporating my developing work into their own dissertation studies of orality in rabbinic tradition, and honored me by the invitation to serve as an outside advisor on their dissertation committees.

Ms. Cynthia Read, executive editor for religion at Oxford University Press, sent my manuscript to two readers, both of whom — I was gratified to learn — were enthusiastic about the study. I inadvertently discovered the identity of one of them, Professor Richard Sarason. It was from him that I took my first courses in midrash as a graduate student at Brown University. Professor Sarason was kind enough to send on his heavily annotated copy of my manuscript, marked up as carefully as I remembered him marking my graduate papers. I have responded to virtually all of his suggestions regarding my argument and textual analyses (and hope I have finally learned when to use "it's"). He read my manuscript with care and integrity—including the dense notes—sparing me many embarassments. I thank him dearly for his generous act of *gemilut ḥasadim*. I feel privileged that a teacher who helped guide my first faltering steps as a scholar ultimately had a hand in the culmination of a project that has been very dear to my heart.

My colleagues in the Comparative Religion and Jewish Studies programs of the Jackson School of International Studies of the University of Washington have been very supportive of my work since I arrived here in 1987. I must single out two for special thanks. First, the Director of the Jackson School from 1995 to 2000, Professor Jere Bacharach, has been extraordinarily resourceful in employing clever bureaucratic subterfuges to buy time for me to write. His efforts often made the difference between a summer in the classroom teaching an introduction to Western Religions or one enclosed in my study, puzzling out the problems that became this book. Second, throughout most of the decade in which I worked on this study, I enjoyed the ear and mind of my talmudic study partner, Professor Hillel Kieval (now, alas, of Washington University in St. Louis). In our weekly poring over the talmudic page, Hillel forced me over and over to refine my "oral hermeneutic" of the text in a way that helped it transcend my own intuitions and to become communicable to a critical mind. The Talmud, in an alliterative reference to a tradition of the common folk, exclaims, "Give me a study partner or give me death!" (B. Taanit 23a). Thanks to Hillel, I know what this means.

During the time I have lived in Seattle I have been blessed by the emotional and spiritual support of its warm Jewish community. I can't possibly acknowledge everyone in this space, but I cannot leave unnamed two people who have loomed very large in my life as I thought about Torah in the Mouth. First, Rabbi Sholem Ber Levitin, Northwest Regional Director of Chabad-Lubavitch, has been a steadfast confidant to me and my family during many hard times. More important, as a living bearer of the fruits of a contemporary master–disciple relationship in Torah, he has taught me what to look for as I thought about the past. Second, I must mention my dearest friend and study partner, Mr. Jason Kintzer, whose emotional and spiritual support during the year of this writing in particular has in many ways kept me whole. I cannot hope to have a better friend.

Of all those named above, there are many to whom I might, with justice, have dedicated this book. The dedication, however, goes to my brother, Mr. Nisan Jaffee. He is more than a brother and more than a friend. Between us the timely arch of a brow or the gesture of a hand bespeaks years of shared memories and draws howls of laughter, much to the befuddlement of our families. I have no way of describing what his companionship means to me, both in matters of simple human solidarity and in terms of spiritual direction. My life in the past several years has been turbulent: marred by the death of my beloved mother, Belle Jaffee, just as I began to write this study; by my own progressing illness; and by other family tragedies—in all, not a life conducive to the writing of books. That I have, with Heaven's help, produced this one is due largely to my brother's love, encouragement, and unfailing kindness to me and mine. He truly exemplifies the Hillelite imperative to be "among the disciples of Aharon, loving peace, pursuing peace, loving God's creatures, and bringing them near to Torah" (Avot 1:12)

Seattle, Washington   Martin S. Jaffee
The Seventh Day of Chanukkah
The New Moon of Tevet, 5760
10 *December,* 1999

Contents

TORAH IN THE MOUTH

Introduction

The Problem of Rabbinic Oral Tradition

It is best to begin, as always, with a text. In the Babylonian Talmud, which, since its redaction (sometime between the sixth and eighth centuries of the Common Era), has functioned as a kind of Summa of rabbinic law and theology, we find the following etiological account of rabbinic methods of transmitting oral tradition (B. Eruvin 54b):[1]

> Our Masters repeated this tradition: How is the Repeated Tradition arranged [for transmission]?
>
> Moshe learned it from the mouth of the Omnipotent. Aharon entered and Moshe repeated for him his chapter. Aharon retired and sat toward the left of Moshe. [Aharon's] sons [Elazar and Itamar] entered and Moshe repeated for them their chapter. His sons retired, Elazar sitting to the right of Moshe and Itamar to the left of Aharon.
>
> Rabbi Yehudah says: Aharon always remained at the right of Moshe.
>
> The Elders entered and Moshe repeated for them their chapter. The Elders retired. All the nation entered and Moshe repeated for them their chapter. The result is that Aharon acquired four [repetitions], his sons acquired three, the Elders acquired two, and all the nation acquired one.
>
> Then Moshe retired and Aharon repeated for them his chapter. Then Aharon retired and his sons repeated for them their chapter. Then his sons retired and the Elders repeated for them their chapter. The result is that all acquired four [repetitions].
>
> On this basis said Rabbi Eliezer: A person is obliged to repeat traditions to his disciples four times.
>
> And this follows logically: Just as Aharon learned from the mouth of Moshe, and Moshe learned from the mouth of the Omnipotent, doesn't it follow that mere mortals who learn from mere mortals should do so as well?
>
> Rabbi Aqiva says: Where do we learn that a person is obliged to repeat for his disciples [indefinitely] until they learn? For it is said: "And teach it to the children of Israel" (Dt. 31:19).

3

And where do we learn [to teach it] until it is fluent in their mouths [as memorized text]? For it is said: "And place it in their mouths" (Dt. 31:19).

And where do we learn that he is obliged to show him [other] perspectives [on the memorized text]? For it is said: "Now these are the rulings that you should present before them" (Ex. 21:1).

The talmudic comment on this text goes on to raise a number of pragmatic questions about the protocol of pedagogy—including the claim that at least one disciple of Rabbi Pereda (the Talmud protects the disciple's identity by failing to mention his name, though we are encouraged to sympathize with his harried master) required 400 repetitions to master his Repeated Tradition! But we have seen enough to begin our own discussion.

Before us is the most detailed account in the rabbinic literature of both the methodology for teaching the contents of rabbinic oral tradition and the historical claim that this methodology originated with Moses' reception from God of the fundamentals of the oral tradition. Our attention should be drawn to a number of points. First, the introduction to the text ("Our Masters repeated this tradition") is a common talmudic formula that indicates a citation from oral tradition transmitted by the Tannaim—the Sages who preceded the talmudic masters. It tells us that what we are about to learn is an ancient text transmitted faithfully over many generations by word of mouth. In this case, of course, the citation formula itself certifies the very claim that the text makes about the faithfulness and antiquity of the tradition. The tradition "repeated by our Masters" itself explains the grounds for trust in the tradition's reliability.

The cited text identifies its own genre. That genre is *mšnh* (vocalized, in all probablity, as *mishnah*).[2] This noun, formed from a root (*šnh*) meaning to "repeat," bears the sense of tradition repeated and memorized. It also denotes a particular collection of such traditions often referred to in the Talmud titularly as Mishnah, a compilation ascribed to the editorial activity of Rabbi Yehudah the Patriarch. His work is likely to have been completed sometime at the dawn of the third century CE. But our text's *mšnh* is not a reference to that compilation, for the Mishnah of Rabbi Yehudah records no direct sayings of Moses and certainly no "chapters" with Moses, Aaron, or Joshua as their tradents. Rather it refers to the broader tradition of repeated learning of which the Mishnah is a particular condensation. I render *mšnh*, therefore, as Repeated Tradition—precisely as the text describes it. *Mšnh* is both a text and a textual process; a tradition of learning from which discrete textual formulations emerge.

The text wants to know: how was the Repeated Tradition taught? We learn that it was taught by the student's listening to the words of a teacher and repeating his words. We also learn—particularly from the comments attributed to Rabbis Eliezer and Aqiva, which suggest that our text may have circulated at least as early as the first third of the second century CE—that the pedagogical model established in the Sinaitic generation is precisely the basis for rabbinic instruction in the present generation. Sages today teach their disciples precisely as the Blessed Holy One taught Israel through Moses.

The content of the tradition given to Moses may no longer have been preserved in its original form—after all, we no longer have the words given to Moses, transmitted to Aaron and, thence, to all the people. The Talmud explains in another place that much was forgotten in the trauma following Moses' death and had to be reconstructed by logical inference, the original words having been lost (B. Temurah 15b–16a). The point, however, is that the tradition surviving among the Sages is transmitted in the original way—by patient repetition, from master to disciple, from mouth to ear, and from ear to memory, without the intervention of a written text. This teaching is thoroughly oral; in the parlance of the Talmud and other early rabbinic writings, it is Oral Torah (*twrh šb'l ph*)[3] or, as I prefer to render it—Torah in the Mouth.

Now, as it happens, for at least a thousand years the traditions of Torah in the Mouth have been memorized from written texts.[4] Later in this book I will argue that written recensions of Oral Torah existed as early as the third century CE, not much later than the era represented by teachers such as Rabbi Aqiva and Rabbi Eliezer, and certainly well before the historical moment at which the anonymous composers of this section of Babylonian rabbinic tradition chose to adduce the text just cited as a precedent for their own oral pedagogy.

I would like, therefore, to call attention to another text, more recent in origin. It is the composition of an esteemed scholar of medieval European literature, Franz Bäuml. He has thought deeply about the processes by which orally composed poetic traditions found their way into written compositions that preserved the traits of orally transmitted traditions out of which they emerged. Of course, the texts upon which Bäuml works, such as the *Song of Roland*, are in no sense analogous in genre to those produced by ancient rabbis. But something suggested by Bäuml has stuck in my mind for many years. In a way, this book is the result of my effort to explore its implications for my own understanding of rabbinic literature.

Bäuml is interested in the formulaic, repetitive style of oral-traditional poetry, its reliance upon sterotypical literary forms. On the one hand, written versions of such oral-traditional poetry betray their dependence upon the oral-performative setting in which the unwritten versions had their social being prior to having been written down. On the other, the act of writing introduces its own changes into the character of the oral text. Not only does it wrest the text from its social matrix of performance, fixing a living and constantly shifting text into a much less malleable form. More important, it changes the nature of the oral tradition that continues to surround and mediate the written text to its audience.

This is what Bäuml has to say about the problem. I cite his text extensively, omitting certain parts that are less directly relevant here:

> The mechanism of oral transmission, which is the basis for stereotypical formulation on the lexical and thematic levels, does not cease to function in the transmission of texts like the *Chanson de Roland* or the *Niebelungenlied* merely because they have become written and their formerly oral formulism has become a matter of style. . . . *In such instances one must distinguish between the functions of stereotypical devices in the processes of oral and written composition, transmission, and reception* [italics added]. In each process these devices can have a mechanical and a referential function. In the processes of oral-epic composition, performance, and reception, they are essential mechanisms for the composition and simultaneous performance of the text, as well as for its reception and retention. They are also culturally essential references to the tradition they formulate and transmit. In the

process of oral-formulaic written composition they play no essential mechanical part, but they necessarily have a referential role: they refer to a specific (oral) type of text and thus represent the convention which determines the composition of the written text. Once this written text is formulaically composed, there is no longer any option to the function of its stereotypical devices as mechanisms in its performance and reception. Whether the text is read aloud, recited from memory, or read silently, its formulism mechanically affects its performance; it aids recitation from memory, conditions reading by its repetitiveness, and serves the retention of the text in the memory. . . . *But whatever the mechanical role of formulism in performance and reception may be, its referential function is clear: the written formulaic text inescapably refers the receiver to the oral-formulaic tradition, provided only that he is familiar with its attributes. In referring to the oral tradition, the written text fictionalizes it. Since the one is given a role to play within the other, since oral formulae in the garb of writing refer to "orality" within the written tradition, the oral tradition becomes an implicit fictional "character" of literacy* [italics added].[5]

In my photocopy of this article, the portions here italicized are heavily marked and annotated. What has struck me is not just the obvious point—in the first italicized passage—that the compositional methods that enable the oral composer to offer a smooth, spontaneous recitation function somewhat differently for the one who composes from the oral-performative tradition for written transmission. It is, rather, Bäuml's final observation that I have returned to over and over, turning it this way and that, to find what I could within it.

The point, as I have understood it, is that the oral-performative tradition, once it is imitated in writing, is in some sense alienated from itself, the written text reconstructing the oral tradition as an objective cultural presence now discernible to its audience in a way never seen so clearly before. Oral tradition exists, that is, as an unperceived reality, calling no particular attention to itself until, because of whatever social factors might have led to the transmission of oral literature in written form, the tradition finds itself reproduced as written text. It discovers its "orality," as it were, by gazing at its face in the mirror of the written text. Henceforward, even as the oral tradition continues, even as the written version itself pursues its literary career as an orally performed and aurally experienced cultural possession, the oral tradition is never the same. It has become a commodity, an element of exchange, in the shaping of culture, more or less valuable in the shifting constellation of a given society's literary universe.

In this book I try to explore Bäuml's insight as a frame of reference for understanding the nature and history of oral-performative literary tradition in ancient Judaism. For a variety of reasons—most of them connected to the limitations of my own scholarly competence and energies—I have circumscribed my frame of reference to Palestinian Judaism from the last centuries of the Second Temple period to the period by which the compilation of the Palestinian Talmud is conventionally said to have been more or less completed. Following my understanding of Bäuml's point, I have conceived the study as a kind of description of Palestinian Jewish oral tradition coming, if one could speak this way, to consciousness of itself.

The book begins, in part I, with a study of what I call the "scribal culture" of late Second Temple Judaism, a culture rich in oral traditions that circulated in connec-

tion with the transmission of written texts of Scripture, but one that (I argue) was
virtually innocent of self-consciousness regarding the orality of tradition. Oral tradition existed, but it wasn't much thought about. Jewish scribes and literary tradents
transmitted the substance of tradition by word of mouth as well as in writing. They
mined a rich vein of orally mediated themes, stories, and norms without expending
much energy thinking about it all as a "tradition" with its own coherent borders and
content.

Part II is devoted to the evidence of the surviving rabbinic literature, all of which
is written. The emergence of oral tradition in Judaism to explicit ideological self-
consciousness as Torah in the Mouth is, I argue, embedded in the social matrix of rabbinic discipleship training, the characteristic forms of which were worked out in Palestine. Exported, as it were, to Babylonia in the same centuries, this social matrix continued
to nourish Babylonian ideological formulations of oral tradition. We have seen a marvelous example in the text from B. Eruvin 54b, one of the great written fictionaliza-
tions, in Bäuml's sense, of oral tradition in all of rabbinic literature. Interesting as the
Babylonian material is, however, I am not sure that it does much more than iron out
a few details of conceptions first worked out by Palestinian masters in their third- and
fourth-century Galilean study groups. I won't argue this point here and will leave it to
reviewers to demonstrate why I should have taken the story further.[6]

This study will exploit a number of theoretical perspectives and delve into a variety
of quite different sorts of written literature in order to make its point. But the thematic coherence of the whole project is, I hope, discernible in two threads of inquiry
woven throughout. Everywhere I am concerned with discerning (1) ways in which
oral means of performing texts in public gatherings (and the types of public involved
in those gatherings) affected the transmission of the written versions of those texts,
and (2) ways in which the orally mediated interpretive traditions associated with
written texts became perceptible as cultural realities "outside of" the texts themselves
and thus required some sort of ideological legitimation in relation to the written texts.[7]

I confess disappointment that I cannot point to a specific "cause" that might
explain, in sociological or hermeneutical terms, precisely why the cultural phenomenon of oral tradition, essentially invisible to Second Temple scribes as an object of
reflection, stood at the very center of the later rabbinic community's self-definition.
I think I can, however, explain in a minimal sense why the fictionalization of rabbinic oral tradition as Torah in the Mouth proved so crucial to the developing social
systems surrounding the rabbinic masters of the third century and beyond. The answer, I shall argue, has much to do with a larger struggle, within the early Byzantine
culture in which later Galilean masters participated, over the relative primacy of the
Sacred Book or its Expounder in the spiritual formation of literate intellectuals. But
we shall delay that discussion for its moment.

Oral-Literary Tradition, Oral-Performative Tradition, and Text-Interpretive Tradition

Throughout this study I shall make repeated reference to the three terms enumerated in the heading to this section. For the sake of clarity, let me explain them briefly
here. By *oral-literary tradition* I mean nothing more theoretically profound than the

handy definition proposed by O. Anderson for "oral literature" in general: "those verbal products of a culture which have pretensions beyond everyday speech."[8] An "oral-literary tradition" exists wherever such verbal products with pretensions beyond ordinary speech are cultivated for preservation and sharing in public settings.

The existence of an oral-literary tradition does not require an absence of literacy or writing. Distinct cultures can and do preserve a written literary tradition that is quite distinct from its oral-literary tradition. The traditions function at different registers of the overall culture and need not intersect, although it is quite common for written literary tradition to have an enhanced prestige over the oral, the latter defined as "folk culture."[9]

An oral-literary tradition exists in and through its public performances. Thus the *oral-performative tradition* is the sum of performative strategies through which oral-literary tradition is summoned from memory and delivered in diverse public settings.[10] In cultures without a written literature, the oral-performative tradition is, of course, the only setting for the sharing and embellishment of literary tradition. But there is more to oral-performative tradition than what is embodied in nonliterate societies. That is, cultures that preserve their texts in hand-copied manuscripts also transmit such texts primarily in and through an oral-performative tradition.

Prior to the introduction of the printing press, as we shall see, texts in manuscript were routinely shared in oral-performative settings. "Reading" was primarily a social activity in which a declaimer delivered the written text to its audience. In such settings, the oral-performative tradition included not only the recitation of the written text, but also the inflections of voice, gesture, and interpretive amplification through which the performer gave audible life to the script. In the culture of Second Temple Jewish scribal groups, oral-performative tradition was a common medium for sharing written texts. This was true as well in later rabbinic circles, surely as far as the reading of canonical scriptures is concerned. At issue in much of this book is the degree to which this practice applied to the textual traditions designated as Torah in the Mouth. Was the oral-performative tradition of *mšnh* grounded in the performative presentation of texts that had been set down in written form? I will argue that in all likelihood it was.

Finally, by the term *text-interpretive tradition* I mean a body of interpretive understandings that arise from multiple performances of a text (written or oral). They come to be so closely associated with public renderings of a text as to constitute its self-evident meaning. As a tradition, the text-interpretive material exists in the memories of both the textual performers and their auditors. The public readers deploy the text selectively in light of their judgment of their audiences' capacities, while audiences supply it in their reception of the reading.[11]

No text-interpretive tradition will ever be thoroughly exhausted in a single textual performance; rather, more or less of it will be rendered explicit according to circumstances. When (and if) text-interpretive traditions reach written compositions, however, they often tend to be exhaustive in their scope. Also they may generate further text-interpretive tradition to clarify their own obscurities. The rabbinic literature in general is one of the great monuments of text-interpretive tradition that continually folds back upon itself in an indefinitely sustained process of textual amplification that reaches no natural closure as long as the interpretive communities that transmit the texts remain intact.

The Theoretical Program of This Study

If these key terms are clear, I can now explain in greater detail the aim of this study. First, I hope to contribute a bit more discipline to the academic discussion of the nature and antiquity of rabbinic Oral Torah. This matter has long suffered from confusion, which is generated in part by lack of clarity regarding the distinct elements of oral tradition just identified. Let me now reconfigure these three elements in a slightly different conceptual structure.

Fundamental to all that follows is the theoretical commitment to distinguish within Palestinian Judaism three distinct, albeit interrelated, dimensions of oral-literary tradition as they would apply cross-culturally. These are (1) *the textual substance of the tradition* (i.e., the oral-literary tradition per se, or the heritage of oral texts); (2) *the social settings in which the texts are composed, stored, and transmitted* (i.e., the institutional settings of the oral-performative and text-interpretive traditions); and (3) *the ideological system by which the texts and their social settings are represented within the culture.*[12]

The key reason for drawing these distinctions is that doing so permits the possibility of distinguishing the praxis of oral tradition (i.e., its compositional, transmissional, and performative elements) from the ideological constructions that frame the cultural meaning of that praxis. That is, in Bäuml's terms: the way in which oral tradition is "fictionalized," or represented to its audience as a cultural possession, has a social history of its own, distinct from that of the verbal substance transmitted within the tradition or that of the social institutions within which the tradition is performed. The literary substance and performative dimensions of an oral-literary tradition have one sort of life; the theoretical legitimations of the tradition as a distinctive cultural possession have quite another.

These distinctions are often blurred by students of rabbinic oral tradition in particular who seek to puzzle out the connections between Second Temple Jewish oral tradition and the rabbinic tradition of Torah in the Mouth.[13] Many scholars, in my judgment, have tended to confuse the general contents of oral-literary tradition in Judaism (surely a phenomenon as old, in some cases, as ancient Israelite culture) with the rabbinic representation of this material as Torah in the Mouth (which, even on the most generous reading of the sources, may have emerged as a technical term no earlier than the turn of the Common Era).[14] We will see later in this study, for example, that rabbinic literature preserves many echoes of literary themes preserved in writings from the Second Temple period; but it does not follow that the perpetuation of some Second Temple text-interpretive traditions in rabbinic literature implies a similar antiquity for either the specific oral-performative tradition of the Sages or the substance of their oral-literary tradition. Simply put, Second Temple scribal communities certainly had their oral-literary traditions and text-interpretive traditions, and they mediated them in oral-performative traditions of various kinds. But all of this does not add up to the essential continuity of rabbinic Torah in the Mouth with all that went before it. Lacking is the crucial element of ideological self-consciousness.

Let us restate this point by clarifying the relationships that link these three analytically distinct aspects of tradition of orally transmitted literature. The sine qua non of any oral-literary tradition is, obviously, the substance and form of the texts preserved by a given society and selected for continued transmission. With the exception of orally transmitted folktales, which seem to obey rather consistent thematic and structural principles across many cultures,[15] other orally transmitted literary genres are rather more idiosyncratic in their themes and degree of linguistic fixity.[16]

The second necessary condition for an oral-literary tradition is the complex of social practices — the oral-performative tradition — that governs production and transmission of the texts. Distinct from textual substance, this aspect of oral tradition comprises the institutionalized, conventional settings for sharing the traditional texts or reiterating them in various sorts of performance.[17] Any oral-literary tradition must have both of these aspects to survive, since the tradition is by definition the sum of its texts and the processes that transmit them. Without a transmitting community the texts would die, and without the texts the community would have no collective memory.

In contrast, the third aspect of oral tradition — the ideological — is not necessary to its existence. It emerges only in settings in which the distinction between written and oral-literary tradition has become crucial to some sort of social undertaking that distinguishes the bearers of the oral tradition from those who do not bear it. This needn't always be the case. But in historical societies as diverse as those that produced the Indian Vedas and modern Balkan oral epic, bearers of the oral tradition will develop a set of ideological formulations through which they conceive its relationship to other, especially written, elements of their literary culture. In doing so, they will also be thinking about the relationship of their own community to others with whom they share some common elements of literary tradition. The resultant ideological formations will constitute part of the rationale for sustaining the particular life of the community, even as they explain and defend the distinctive orality of the tradition.[18]

In the literary culture of classical Rabbinic Judaism, the concept of Torah in the Mouth corresponds to this third, ideological, aspect of oral tradition. It emerged as the dominant ideological trope through which rabbinic Sages grasped the social meaning of the performative and interpretive dimensions of their oral-literary tradition. Conceived as Torah in the Mouth, the actual texts transmitted as oral tradition — the oral-literary tradition mentioned earlier — were correlated for theological, hermeneutical, and jurisprudential purposes with the written Scriptures inherited by the Sages from earlier Judaism and shared with other Jews (and, increasingly, Christians) beyond the rabbinic social orbit. As Torah in the Mouth, the second aspect of rabbinic oral-literary tradition — its text-creating and text-performative process — was constructed as the embodiment of a generations-long series of transmissions that linked contemporary tradents and performers to ancient founders. By establishing a link to past generations, however, the ideological construction of Torah in the Mouth also enforced a separation in the present — from other Jews and Christians who shared Scripture but who were ignorant of, or denied, the legitimacy of the rabbinic text-interpretive tradition that claimed to provide Scripture's exhaustive explanation.

The Structure of Argument

This study is, accordingly, an extended reflection upon the relationship of ideologies of orality to the material and social foundations of textual practices in Palestinian Judaism during the centuries in question. Part I, focusing entirely on the Second Temple period, unfolds in three chapters.

The first attempts to describe the nature of literacy in the Second Temple period and the role of oral-performative and text-interpretive traditions in particular within a broadly sketched representation of "scribal culture." The chapter's main conclusion is that, to the degree that scribal groups were aware of orality as a cultural form for the transmission of literary tradition, they ascribed ideological value to it only as the original form of the sacred book. That is, the oral moment of tradition was perceived as the dictation of the book to the first scribe. By contrast, the orality of the traditions that mediated the results of writing—what we have called the oral-literary, oral-performative, and text-interpretive traditions—were of relatively little interest to Jewish scribes. I suspect that the explanation is simple: where Scripture itself had not yet achieved textual uniformity as a cultural icon, social divisions focused upon the textual tradition embodied in the book rather than upon the traditions of its exposition.

Chapters 2 and 3 illustrate and amplify this point in reference, first, to the scribal community that seems responsible for at least some of the Dead Sea Scrolls and, second, to that other well-studied scribally oriented community of textual exegetes, the Pharisees of late Second Temple times. These chapters find little reason to assume the existence during this period of any articulate ideological formations of oral-literary tradition as a distinctive Judaic cultural possession. It was the oral delivery of the sacred book itself that served as the focus of ideological reflection. In light of the common view that the idea of Oral Torah is distinctively Pharisaic, it will be necessary to look rather closely at the evidence usually adduced for this view.

Part II is composed of four chapters that turn exclusively to the problem of the rabbinic construction of oral-literary, oral-performative, and text-interpretive tradition as Torah in the Mouth. Chapters 4 and 5 focus upon the earliest compilations of rabbinic literature, the Tannaitic compilations routinely regarded as reflecting traditions formulated from the late Second Temple period through the late second century CE. These chapters explore the degree to which this literature conceives of its roots in essentially oral processes of transmission, and they chart the diverse ideological constructs by which this orality was understood.

I agree with other scholars that the conception of Torah in the Mouth emerges first in this literature, although I will quibble with some who see it as having existed in nascent rabbinic culture since the earliest decades of that community's formation in the Yavnean academy. Even by the third century, we shall see, it hardly constituted a universally accepted conception within this early literary corpus. Chapter 6 illustrates why. There I offer close textual studies of various texts in the Mishnah and the Tosefta that, to my mind, offer the strong suggestion that the compilation of these foundation texts of Torah in the Mouth were made possible by the technology of pen, ink, and writing surface. An oral-literary tradition among the Tannaim there certainly was; but its relation to surviving texts such as the Mishnah remains to be understood.

This is, I think, a curious result. In the Tannaitic material we find for the first time in Palestinian Judaism all three aspects of an ideologically self-conscious oral-literary tradition: orally transmitted texts, specific settings and procedures of transmission, and an ideological trope that explains the significance of the entire oral-traditional enterprise in terms of a primordial revelation co-original with that of what is now called the Torah in Script (*twrh šbktb*). And precisely here we find evidence that the very texts regarded as embodying this oral-literary tradition were preserved (by whom and by how many we cannot know) in written recensions.

Finally, chapter 7—the summation of the rabbinic part of the inquiry—reflects extensively upon this curiosity. It asks how the generation that received this substantial heritage of Tannaitic textual material—the third- and fourth-century masters of oral tradition responsible for the Palestinian Talmud and great Amoraic compilations of scriptural exegesis—made its own sense of a Torah in the Mouth that had been written down in manuscript. The classical form of the concept of Torah in the Mouth, I suggest, is associated with a broad redefinition of the authority of the Palestinian rabbinic master in shaping not only the intellectual life, but also the emotional and religious sensibilities of his disciples. It is bound up, moreover, with the attempts of such masters to distinguish the discipline of rabbinic discipleship from that of other highly articulate Greco-Roman discipleship communities just then coming to dominate the intellectual and religious landscape of early Byzantine Palestine.

Offered in part II, then, is a set of reflections upon the social role of writing and oral performance of written texts in a society that, as a matter of ideological principle, came to deny that the written sources of its oral-performative tradition exist. In the epilog, chapter 8, I will offer my own estimate of what this denial might tell us about the relationship of Torah to its textual representations in classical Rabbinic Judaism.

PART ONE

ORAL TRADITION AND
SECOND TEMPLE SCRIBALISM
*The Spoken Word and Ideologies
of the Book*

1

Social Settings of Literacy and Scribal Orality

Oral/Aural Literacy in Second Temple Judaism

Palestinian Jewish society of the last centuries of the Second Temple period was, like others in the Greco-Roman world, intimately familiar with the written word. Writing—in Greek as well as the native Hebrew and Aramaic—was employed in a variety of economic functions and legal instruments across various social strata.[1] In markets and town squares, legends on coins and seals proclaimed propaganda on behalf of regional minting cities and contenders for political hegemony.[2] Complex works of literature—historical, legal, ethical, hymnodic, and even novelistic—were composed and circulated.[3] Social movements of various kinds embraced ancient, revered books as symbols of identity and authenticity and used the written word polemically to position themselves in relation to each other along a spectrum of explosive social and religious questions.[4] There was even enough of a literary public in the country's three languages to sustain efforts to render important Hebrew texts into Greek and Aramaic.[5]

But, for all its literacy, this was not a "bookish" society of the type that has existed in the modern world since the development of mass-produced, printed literature.[6] For one thing, the group of people who could actually compose, transcribe, and communicate the contents of written compositions—whether brief letters or lengthy literary works—was quite small in relation to the society as a whole.[7] Such skills were regarded as esoteric professional acquisitions rather than a general cultural patrimony. Persons possessing them were, for the most part, members of elite scribal guilds associated with official institutions of palace, law court, and temple. Outside such groups, the ability to write was routinely limited to elementary forms of record-keeping. For most people, reading was a matter of retrieving and utilizing the information of such records.[8]

Except for those trained in technical scribal schools, individuals did not usually have equal facility in writing, composition, and reading. The capacity to decipher, for example, a simple written receipt recording a land transaction didn't always imply a person's ability to read a literary work, copy a written text, or transcribe one from oral dictation. It therefore remains an open question as to how many habitual readers of, for example, business records or legal contracts could master the more complex writings that circulated among the literarily productive cultural elites.

One consequence of this socially stratified character of literacy in Second Temple Judaism is that the consumption of a literary text was not commonly a matter of an individual reader communing silently with a text in a moment of privacy, as in modern times. Such acts of reading for pleasure, for information, or for personal enrichment—the common experiences in literate societies since the sixteenth-century invention of the mass-produced book—were exceedingly rare as a cultural pattern.[9] Part of the reason is that books, expensive and time-consuming to produce and copy by hand, were themselves primarily objects of the official, rather than the domestic, domain. In addition, inscribed objects in general, and books in particular, commonly functioned as ritual objects whose iconic significance transcended that of the information they preserved.[10] This last observation is a point to which we shall return shortly.

We observe for the moment, however, that the scarcity of books, and the sacral aura that commonly surrounded them, help us to grasp another aspect of Second Temple literary culture: the social distribution of book collection. Large collections of books were not found in private homes, and there is only slender literary evidence (and virtually no uncontroversial physical evidence) of institutionalized libraries accessible to a broad public of readers. Rather, collections of literature may have been created in connection with ideologically self-conscious religious or cultic communities, such as the ruling priestly groups associated with the Jerusalem Temple or dissident communities of the kind that stood behind at least some of the Dead Sea Scrolls.[11]

In contrast to governmental archives devoted to preserving written records concerning official acts, these collections of books were not storage bins for documents that would be read only to the degree that their information was of instrumental value. Rather, the collections were specialized in focus, preserving primarily those materials that, precisely because they figured prominently in the ideological program of its users, would be consulted repeatedly, their texts often memorized and their values internalized in the context of public instruction.[12]

Even in such ideologically articulate circles, where sophisticated literacy could be assumed for most members, there was commonly a distance between the physical book and its audience. An important impediment to the simple perusal of a book's contents was the form of the book itself. The codex—with its coveniently leafable pages bound into a pamphlet at the spine—would not revolutionize literary culture and information retrieval in the Roman Empire until well into the second century CE. For Palestinian Jews of the Second Temple period, as for anyone else of that time, books were preserved on sheets of papyrus or treated leather bound end to end into scrolls of varying length. Long books made for long, heavy scrolls.[13]

As a result, unless one wanted to read a book from beginning to end in one or a series of sittings, the scroll was virtually useless as a handy source of information. One might have to scroll many yards through a text to consult a particular passage. Accordingly, the most effective use of the scroll for information retrieval was available only to people—scribes themselves or others closely associated with textual performance—who were so familiar with the text that they would know more or less where in the scroll to find what they needed.[14]

In other words, those best able to use the scroll for what we might call "informational" purposes would be people who in a basic sense already knew its contents through approximate memorization. The text was as much a fact of their memory as it was a physical object. This point was well articulated by M. Martin long ago and it is worth quoting him at length:[15]

> The primary function of a scribe . . . is that of one whose work consists in transcribing a text by his own hand. I use the word transcribe deliberately. The scribe may, in effect, perform his professional work in one of three ways, or by a combination of one or two or all three of them. He may, on the one hand, copy out his text by eye having beside him the exemplar to be transcribed. This method relies on the purely visual medium and the regular split-second effort of memory with or without oral repetition of what he is transcribing. On the other hand, he may transcribe his text from dictation. This method relies on the purely aural medium and aural memory with perhaps again some oral repetition of what has just been read to him for transcription. Or, as a third way, he may transcribe his text from memory. And here we must remark that our modern conception of memory has been modelled and seriously affected by the advent, difffusion, general use and plenty of the printed word. The medium in this third method is far more delicate and liable to error and subjective affection than the other two. The scribe's memory may be a predominantly aural one or it may be predominantly a visual one, or it may be an audio-visual one, and depending on its character, the errors and subjective affections of his work will follow suit. But it is true that if we were to conceive of a hierarchy in scribal proficiency dedicated to the transcription of sacred books and writings more or less canonically . . . fixed in their number and text, we would certainly place in the first place as a master-scribe the one who through skill and practice in his profession not only possessed a fine handwriting but could also be expected to transcribe by rote the sacred books or treasured writings whose transcription constituted his professional calling. I say, were we to conceive such a hierarchy, because the ancient powers of memory and retention are things which we can with difficulty represent to ourselves.

It is, of course, impossible at this historical distance to estimate the percentage of a given literary community that, following Martin's model, would have mastered most of its books in memory. It is even more precarious to guess how closely memory approximated written versions. But it is likely that the material form of the scroll encouraged readers to view it as a mnemonic safety device—a storage system for texts already held substantially in the memory—rather than a reference source of information outside the reader's knowledge.

Earlier I alluded briefly to another consequence of the form of the scroll upon the way it was read. With the exception of scribes actually engaged in book production and copying, the reading of books was commonly connected to ritualized, public ceremonies rather than private study. For most people, and for most of the time, a book was a commodity that one "heard" through the medium of another human voice; "reading" was the activity of declaiming a text before an audience in a social performance approaching the gravity of ceremonial ritual.[16] The book was a locus of power and authority far more than information. It was precisely its power that made the information worth attending to. And its authority was manifested publicly in and through the human voice—often that of an officially appointed communal teacher—that sounded out the text's words and expounded its mysteries.[17]

All that has been described here should remind us that, in the time and place at hand, the characteristic organs of the literary life were the mouth and the ear, and its main textual reservoir was the memory. Literary culture was commonly delivered orally and received aurally, the memory serving as the connector between mouth and ear. The intervention of the eye and the hand was confined largely to creating the necessary material foundation for literary preservation. What was true for the process of communicating and sharing literary texts held true as well for the activities of their composition.

Precisely because texts were composed under the assumption that they would be read in the setting of oral performance, their compositional styles drew deeply upon habits of speech and rhetorical traditions that had their living matrix in oral communication.[18] Yet it is virtually impossible now for a modern reader—even one lucky enough to be holding the physical remnant of a Second Temple scribal manuscript from the Judean desert—to penetrate the written surface of such texts to recover the actual oral discourses behind them. Even a text composed orally for the purpose of written preservation stands at an esthetic distance from the actual speech of oral communication, for literary diction in any form is not simply "talking," even though it might seek to place speeches in the mouths of literary characters.[19] Nevertheless, as literary ethnographers have impressively shown, it is quite possible to retrieve the oral-literary registers—reflected in stylized diction, speech patterns, and rhetorical conventions—that nourished the writings that emerge from cultures of the manuscript.[20]

The oral/aural setting of Second Temple literary culture contributed to one other aspect of the book that needs to be considered here: a given book normally circulated in a variety of textual forms, some longer and some shorter, one copy distinct in a variety of ways from any other.[21] The line between the authorial creator of a book, its scribal copyists, and its interpretive audience was a rather blurry one and was often crossed in ways no longer retrievable by literary criticism of the surviving texts. To the degree that a book *was* its oral declamation and aural appropriation (rather than its mere material copy), the manuscript substrate of the book often bore the influence of the performative contexts in which it was shared.[22]

Scribal additions to manuscripts were not always set aside in marginalia to distinguish them from the "original." The marginal notations recording orthographic and other textual peculiarities of a canonically fixed document would not appear in Jewish Bibles for nearly a millennium. Rather, as is true of many types of orally transmitted literature, the "original" text did not mean the "first" version that came from the mouth or the pen of the author. In functional terms, the "original" text meant the version whose words reached the audience at a given performative reading.[23] Accordingly, additions to the manuscript text were incorporated through copying into the next version of the text in an incremental process of textual transformation. The desire to reproduce faithful copies surely explains the remarkable stability of the most prestigious texts, such as the Torah of Moses. Yet the substantial evidence of textual variation suggests the presence of a tacit scribal assumption that a faithful copy might well include interpretive material that clarified the author's thought in addition to the author's actual words. The scribe's judgment about what the author had meant, in other words, was legitimately included in the record of what, according to the manuscript tradition, he had said.

Under these conditions, the "correct" text of a book was linked to the social boundaries of the community that preserved it. That community would harbor and reproduce its particular manuscript traditions.[24] These would overlap in many ways with the traditions of other communities who happened to have preserved the same book, but there would also be important local differences. These might extend from differences in the spelling of particular words to variations in the sequence of particular passages and, in some cases, major disparities of content.[25] Such variations were common in the texts of precisely those works that moderns — accepting as a fact of nature the textual fixity of the printed Bible — would expect to be preserved most carefully in textually uniform copies. Only at the very end of the Second Temple period — and more specifically in the decades leading up to the bar Kosiva rebellion of 132–135 — does there seem to have been some desire to overcome the textual pluriformity of books regarded by most ancient Jews as part of the "sacred writings" delivered to Moses, David, and other ancient prophets of Israel.

Students of those Dead Sea Scrolls that preserve literary works now incorporated into the Jewish scriptural canon have discerned, among a wide range of text types, a family of texts that conforms in many ways to the canonical versions (the so-called "Masoretic Text") transmitted in later Rabbinic Judaism.[26] It is not clear which scribal community sponsored such text types or whether such incipient textual uniformity reflects a consensus among a number of socially distinct communities. But the very appearance of a uniform textual tradition for key literary classics testifies to a transforming moment in the history of Second Temple Judaism.[27]

The canonizing activities that extended not only to defining lists of approved books but to the authorization of specific textual traditions signal a profound change in the perception of the book among literate Palestinian Jews. The ideological consequences of this change, as will be seen at length in part II of this study, would not be fully developed until the flowering of the rabbinic movement in the third century CE. But already at the end of the first century, the relatively open border between written texts and their orally governed cultural life, between what the words of the text said and what they might mean, had begun to close. In the literary culture under formation in the wake of the destruction of the Second Temple, the book — especially the portions ascribed to Moses or his prophetic heirs — was equated increasingly with its written version rather than with the event of its interpretive performance. As the fixed, uniform text of Scripture became a cultural icon, scribes were increasingly hesitant to fold the results of the oral-performative interpretations of the text into its manuscript tradition. Accordingly the interpreted meaning of the literary text, the substance of its oral life, was perceived as something extraneous to it. No longer the omnipresent — hence invisible — environment in which written literature took shape and was transmitted, the oral tradition that mediated the meaning of the book was becoming an object with a reality of its own, seen as something distinct from the book.

In this sense, the oral-performative literary life of Second Temple scribal culture is the foundation of what would later emerge in ideological garb among the rabbinic Sages as Torah in the Mouth, an oral tradition represented as a primordial and necessary complement to a canonical corpus of sacred writings fixed forever at the moment of their original delivery to the prophet from whose pen the text had come. But it must be stressed that, *during the Second Temple period itself,* there is little evidence for reflection upon text-interpretive or oral-performative tradition as a reality independent of the books they brought to life. It was, rather, the book itself that dominated the attention of those who produced and circulated it. For the present, then, it is best to focus more sharply upon the social setting of Second Temple Judaic literary culture in which the oral and aural dimensions of the written word were taken for granted. There too we shall find some ideological conceptions of the oral word; but they are of a rather different nature than those produced in the early centuries of the post-Temple reconstruction of Jewish literary culture under the guidance of rabbinic Sages.

Scribalism and the Oral Origins of the Book

We should begin with the literati themselves, the scribes to whose activity we owe so much of the literary evidence of Second Temple Judaism. The English word "scribe" normally renders a number of Semitic, Greek, and Latin terms that span a wide range of meaning. These include the Hebrew term *sofer* and its Aramaic equivalent, *safar,* Greek terms such as *grammateus* and *grammatikos,* and the Latin *libellarius* (*liblarios* in Greek and *lavlar* in Hebrew). Depending on context, most of these terms can refer to a range of positions or professions in which literacy is a critical requirement, such as bureaucrats associated with official institutions, accountants, notaries, teachers of literacy skills, and finally, full-fledged transmitters and composers of legal, historical, or sapiential tradition.[28]

For most of the Second Temple period, the primary employer of various sorts of literary scribes was the Jerusalem Temple itself, which served as the political and economic, as well as the cultic, center of the country. Under the administration of a succession of High Priests from the time of the Persian restoration until its destruction in 70 CE,[29] the operation of the Temple in its various roles depended upon its scribal infrastructure. It is surprising, then, how little information about scribes, their training, and their duties is transmitted in the literature of the period.[30]

The earliest allusion to the existence of scribal schools in Jerusalem comes from the first quarter of the second century BCE in the writings of Yeshua ben Eliezer ben Sira. Toward the end of his collection of proverbs and hymns, this prominent scribe invites prospective seekers of wisdom to "take up lodging in the house of instruction" (Sira 51:23).[31] In light of the author's praise of the piety, learning, and social prominence of the scribe (*sofer/grammateus*: Sira 38:24–39:11), it is likely that his "house of instruction" denotes a setting for scribal education that included not only the skills of literacy, but a program of incorporating the knowledge of texts into a rigorous personal discipline. The scribe was not merely a recorder of texts but, to a genuine degree, an embodiment of their values.

It is impossible to know the degree to which Yeshua ben Eliezer's school was typical of his era or whether his high ideals for scribal education were shared beyond his own circle,[32] yet it is no great leap of faith to assume that institutions of technical scribal training stretched back to the Persian period. Jerusalem, with the restored Temple at its core, had been the main administrative center of Jewish Palestine since the latter portion of the sixth century BCE. Convenience alone would have dictated that most scribal training occur in and around the capital.[33]

Scribes who served communities beyond Jerusalem or who were connected to institutions other than the Temple would necessarily have been trained in technical skills identical to those taught in Jerusalem: the preparation of writing surfaces and inks, as well as other aspects of bookcraft. It is also likely that scribal textual training, both in Jerusalem and elsewhere, would have included mastery of key legal and historical writings (such as the Torah of Moses and the core of the later prophetic canon) that underwrote the political legitimacy of the Temple and its priesthood. Unfortunately, outside of the writings of Yeshua ben Eliezer, no such curricula survive, either for Temple-employed scribes or for those who might have served in outlying areas.[34]

Yet the existence of many texts from the mid-second century BCE and onward that severely criticize the Hasmonean (non-Tzadokite) High Priestly establishment—especially the dissident "Tzadokite" writings found in some of the Qumran scrolls—force the conclusion that, at least from that period, literary scribes worked in a variety of settings beyond the Temple administrative system and its elite culture.[35] Employing genres such as law,[36] visionary writings,[37] history,[38] and hymnody[39] that shaped the work of Temple literary scribes, dissident scribes cultivated a kind of "revisionist tradition" which called into question the legitimacy of the established Hasmonean legal and political order.

Such political or theological objections to the Hasmonean Temple state do not entitle us to assume that the dissidents were themselves anti-priestly in outlook or nonpriestly in familial origins. The genealogical connections of Jerusalem's Temple scribes to priestly families cannot be assumed. But even if a scribal career was not limited to men of priestly lineage, it was likely an important avenue of employment for priests not directly connected to the lineage of the High Priestly families.[40] An earlier tendency of historians to posit the existence of a large number of "lay scribes" serving the needs and political-religious interests of a nonpriestly urban middle class, and establishing themselves in competition with official priestly teaching authority, has for some time come under criticism.[41] The existence of lay scribes serving at the levels of the notary, as accountants, or as private tutors to the children of wealth is by no means out of the question, but a significant nonpriestly literary community beyond the reach of Temple authorities, and functioning as an independent center of literary or intellectual tradition among a growing class of urbanized intellectuals, is difficult to account for in economic terms.

The community that appears to have occupied the Qumran site more or less continuously from the early Hasmonean period until shortly after the rebellion against Rome of 66 CE was decidedly not an example of such a class. This was not, first of all, a "lay" community. Whatever its actual demographic composition, it was—as the next chapter will show—ideologically committed to priestly norms and literary traditions. Moreover, through the pooling of resources as a requisite of membership, it was able to support its scribal members through its own internal economy. Beyond such voluntary associations of highly committed individuals, it would have been possible to sustain the livelihood of a large professional lay-scribal class only in major urban centers with a market for books. But such a market is hard to assume in Second Temple Judea outside of Jerusalem itself or, perhaps, of Sepphoris in the Galilee.[42]

A market for books requires two conditions: the wealth to purchase them and the need to own them. The wealth may have been available in the small pockets of Palestinian Jewish urbanization, but we have already seen that the need for private copies of books is the product of a type of literate environment that would not emerge in Palestine for some time. It is precarious, therefore, to link the economic viability of lay-scribalism to the book trade.

A possible alternative, some have suggested, is that lay-scribes may have been supported as teachers in schools. On this model, a socially and intellectually prominent class of lay-scribes might have been employed in schools that competed with Temple or priestly authorities over the interpretation of common traditional texts. The problem is that there is little reliable evidence for the existence of a widespread system of education in the Second Temple period, even among the prosperous urban merchants or landed gentry.

References to synagogues as places dedicated to study of Torah imply no more than popular public reading and preaching/teaching associated with Sabbath and festival celebrations, not the sustained tutoring required for public instruction in literary tradition.[43] And literary mentions of a widespread Second Temple school system that might have employed scribal teachers on a significant scale are, as Goodblatt has observed, almost entirely confined to the rabbinic literature of a much later period.[44] It appears, then, that education in literacy of any sort outside of professional scribal training remained socially confined to the private household, where it was managed by older family members or hired tutors.

We are left with the impression that the extension of a genuine literary culture was socially confined to the Temple scribal administration, a small nonscribal urban elite, and dissident, scribally trained groups who stood in political opposition to the Hasmonean state.[45] In other words, scribal literary culture was largely a phenomenon associated with priests or those trained in priestly milieus, whose economic existence was sustained by ideologically committed sociopolitical communities. It was not a "popular" culture. The bulk of the surviving writings of the period corroborates this conclusion, both those texts now included in the canon of the Hebrew Scriptures and those that eventually ceased to be copied and circulated in rabbinic communities.

As Morton Smith pointed out some time ago, the texts now incorporated into the scriptural canon of Judaism constitute the record of a Second Temple cultic community centered in Jerusalem.[46] With some notable exceptions,[47] virtually the entire canon of Hebrew Scriptures offers perspectives on the origins of the Temple cult and its officiants, the nature of cultic conduct, or events leading to the cult's catastrophic termination and the consequences thereof for the ongoing life of Israel. However varied the constituent traditions of the Hebrew canon might be, they are knit together in a very tight priestly weave. There are many different scenarios for

imagining the gradual emergence of this canon and explaining its ideological coherence, but crucial to virtually all of them is the role of scribal composers and transmitters of individual books and gradually expanding subcanonical collections of books
emanating directly or indirectly from the Temple.[48]

Precious little is known, on the other hand, about the social settings of much of
the Second Temple literature that ultimately dropped from the canonical traditions
of later rabbinic Judaism. Nevertheless, much of this literature, especially texts exploiting the apocalyptic genre, is preoccupied with issues surrounding the Temple
and its priestly guardians. It is likewise dotted with suggestive scribal images. The
Testament of Levi, an apocalyptic work of the second century BCE, is ascribed to the
progenitor of the priestly lineage. This work draws an explicit link between priestly
status and the cultivation of scribal skills: "Teach your children letters . . . so that they
might have understanding throughout all their lives as they ceaselessly read the Law
of God" (13:2–3).[49] A roughly contemporary text, the Book of Jubilees, confirms the
connections of Levi's descendants to the world of the scribe, describing how a dying
Jacob "gave all his books and his father's books to Levi, his son, so that he might preserve them and renew them for his sons until this day" (45:15).[50] Apparent here, as in
the canonical corpus defined by later Judaism, is a discernible connection between
the texts transmitted within literary tradition and the social setting of priestly scribalism.

It appears that attempts to define the social identity of scribes from the content
of their texts ultimately yields a few generalities, but little more. There is, however,
a nearly universal rhetorical trait of all these texts, crossing virtually all genres, that
does illuminate the nature of scribal literary culture wherever it appeared: scribes
rarely took credit for the creation of their literary works. Instead, they generally observed scrupulous authorial anonymity, couching their compositions in the form of
pseudepigraphic ascription to famous figures from the past.[51] Especially in writings
designed to engage polemically matters of public concern, scribal compositions were
cast as depositories of texts dictated long ago to a primordial scribal ancestor[52] and
transmitted and amplified through the ages as communal possessions held in a kind
of literary trust for the present generation.[53] As will shortly be seen, this characteristic rhetoric of anonymity, and its literary correlate of pseudepigrapy, are crucial clues
for interpreting the way scribal communities grasped the relationship between written books and oral communication.

Virtually any heroic figure from the past could serve as a scribal ancestor/au-
thor. Enoch, the obscure antedeluvian father of Methuselah (Gen. 5:21–24), was
known by the third century BCE to have been a "scribe of righteousness" (1 Enoch
12:4) who ascended to Heaven to become the transcriber of angelic petitions (1 Enoch
13:4–7). Characteristically, upon his death he transmitted to Methuselah his scribal
heritage: "And now, my son Methuselah, I recount to you and write down for you: I
have revealed everything to you and have given you books about all these things. Keep
. . . the books from the hand of your father, that you may pass (them) on to the generations of eternity" (1 Enoch 82:1; cf. Jubilees 7:38–39).[54] Presumably, the readers
of the substantial and chronologically diverse Enochic literature believed their own
copies to preserve, with the amplifications of ensuing tradition, the original dictation from heavenly angel, to Enoch, to Methuselah.[55]

Moses, of course, was said to have written down what he heard from the God of Israel at Sinai and at other moments in order to produce the Torah of Moses (Ex. 24:4, Num. 33:2, Dt. 31:9, 22). The second-century BCE composers and transmitters of the book of Jubilees merely supplemented the record by preserving what had also been dictated to Moses by a heavenly messenger in the same Sinaitic setting: "And the angel of the presence spoke to Moses by the word of the Lord saying, 'Write the whole account of creation, that in six days the Lord God completed all his work and all that he created'" (2:1).[56] Moses recorded as asked; his scribal descendants transmitted what he had committed to their care, as they transcribed his book from the dictation of a reader or directly from a manuscript exemplar.

The image of scribal transmission of the book from original dictation is ubiquitous. Testaments conveyed on the deathbeds of the sons of Jacob were portrayed as having been transmitted orally to them and preserved in scribal copies.[57] Another founding hero, Ezra, symbolized the perfect blending of priestly lineage and scribal craft (Ezra 7:1–6; cf. Neh.8:1–8). He too was a transmitter of written words first heard audibly. A late first-century CE apocalypse in his name, identified in apocryphal canons as 4 Ezra, offers remarkably vivid descriptions of his scribal activities in receiving illuminations and auditions from the transmundane world, transcribing them in books, and passing them on to instruct future decoders of their visions. It may be helpful to pause to consider them for a moment.

The historical setting constructed by the narrator is the devastation following the destruction of the Solomonic Temple and the burning of the Torah. At this moment of crisis, Ezra petitions God to convey upon him the spirit of prophecy so that the scribe might "write everything that has happened in the world from the beginning, the things which were written in your Law, that men may be able to find the path, and that those who wish to live in the last days may live" (4 Ezra 14:22).[58] Then God replies:

> Prepare for yourself many writing tablets, and take with you Sarea, Dabria, Selemia, Ethanus, and Asiel—these five, because they are trained to write rapidly, and you shall come here and I will light in your heart the lamp of understanding, which shall not be put out until what you are about to write is finished. (14:23–25)

Ezra prepares for revelation as he would for the copying of a book, readying his materials and hiring copyists skilled in rapidly reducing to text what their ears have received. But note too the particular role of the lamp of understanding placed in the scribal heart. This passage is as clear a confession as can be found that, in the conception of the scribe, his own writing came from beyond him in a state of illuminated intelligence.

The literary result of this illumination is worth a moment of attention. According to the narrator:

> [T]he Most High gave understanding to the five men, and by turns they wrote what was dictated, in characters which they did not know. They sat forty days, and wrote during the daytime, and ate their bread at night. . . . And when the forty days were ended, the Most High spoke to me, saying, 'Make public the twenty-four books that you wrote first and let the worthy and the unworthy read

them; but keep the seventy that were written last, in order to give them to the wise among your people. (14:42–47)

This passage draws unmistakably on an ancient and well-known legend regarding the scribal inspiration that produced the Septuagint, the Greek translation of the Torah. Yet it makes a different point.

Proponents of the Septuagint, such as the Alexandrian allegorist Philo, were satisfied to praise the authoritative status of this translation of the Torah of Moses by calling attention to the miraculous circumstance of its origins (Philo, *Life of Moses* 2:37):[59]

> Sitting [on the island of Pharos] in seclusion with none present save the elements of nature, earth, water, air, heaven, the genesis of which was to be the first theme of their sacred revelation, for the laws begin with the story of the world's creation, they became as it were possessed, and, under inspiration, wrote, not each several scribe something different, but the same word for word, as though dictated to each by an invisible prompter.

Our late first-century Palestinian scribe is, by contrast, rather more ambitious. His reference to forty days and nights unmistakenly calling upon Sinaitic imagery, he describes Ezra and his companions as a renewed vehicle of revelation, their work validating a full scriptural canon of twenty-four books.[60] And not only this: our scribe claims to transmit a far larger corpus of inspired writings destined for only the illuminated scribal worthies of every generation.

In passages such as these, the reality of scribal work has become the basis for authenticating the content of the scribally composed and transmitted book. The composer of 4 Ezra shows the tight linkage of the rhetoric of literary authenticity in Second Temple literary culture to the archetypical scribal method of copying from oral dictation. The book originated from an author's voice and extended that authorial voice in writing through the mediation of a scribal copyist. The messenger who read out the contents of the book made present in his voice the persona of the author. When the author was portrayed as a figure inhabiting the heavenly world, and when that author communicated to a human medium, the resulting text could be represented as a prophetic product, a revelation. The original scribe, who "received" the book from its transmundane author, was the prophet, and the scribes who transmitted his work continued the chain of representing his persona as their texts were passed on and read as pregnant messages.

The humility of the scribal pseudepigrapher, who accepted no personal responsibility for the contents of works transmitted as tradition, is the humility of the ventriloquist. A voice whose owner is hidden behind the image of a venerable literary persona can say things otherwise best left unstated on one's own authority. Thus the actual practice of scribal dictation, familiar everywhere as a fact of life, became a rhetorical convention verifying the authenticity of the written message. The representation of the visionary moment of illuminated dictation announced that a particular scribal work was worthy of sustained and serious attention. It had come, after all, not from the scribe, but from the transmundane author.

This last observation enables us to complete our understanding of the oral dimension of scribal literacy in the Second Temple period. At a practical level, we have seen, the orality of scribal texts must be located in the simple logistics of book-life in a culture of the manuscript. Scribal works, trading upon the rhythms of the world of literary speech, exploited orally grounded rhetorical conventions of composition and diction. The handwritten book's lack of genuine closure and the absence of standard copies for all but the most widely known works, ensured that the copying and transmission of texts made ample room for the interpretive intervention of the scribe. Finally, the resulting written work was normally shared in performative settings and experienced as an aural phenomenon.

But more crucially, as a matter of literary conception, the image of the professional scribe copying his text from the oral dictation of the real author established the connection of all texts to a primordial setting of oral communication. The original book was represented as having been dictated and recorded in the process of its commission to writing. Every public reading, therefore, was a rehearing, a restoration of the book to its pristine moment of oral origin, and a new occasion to recopy the dictated text, if only in the scroll of memory. "Listen, Baruch, to this word," wrote an early second-century CE pseudepigrapher, adopting the persona of Jeremiah's scribe, "and write down in the memory of your heart all that you shall learn" (2 Bar. 50:1).[61]

Summary

We may now review some of the basic perspectives of the discussion of the nature of scribal culture in Second Temple Judaism and its relation to oral-performative literary tradition. This culture was rooted in the work of scribal professionals who, if they were not employed in Temple administration, would normally have received a training similar to those who were. The literature they cultivated was deeply rooted in their own institutional and social settings, and knowledge of most of it circulated primarily within those communities. Where it extended beyond scribal communities, literary culture was mediated primarily through the official Temple cultic system or unofficial, occasional public functions perhaps associated with ritualized readings of classic texts in the emerging institution of the synagogue.

In this culture, the very definition of "reading" included the oral pronouncement of the text in public audition—its oral-performative tradition. This fact about the dissemination of any book also shaped the way the origins of prophetic books in particular were imagined. A stream of speech was posited at the moment of the prophetic book's first delivery into script. Imagined on the model of scribal dictation, the book was held to emerge as an author/composer delivered the text fully formed to the scribal copyist/transmitter entrusted with its effective communication to further audiences.

An act of oral delivery, that is to say, was posited not only as the origin of a book, but as the guarantee of its authenticity. Nevertheless, the malleability that its oral life conferred upon the written text—in its various performative renderings, its expansions and contractions in diverse copies—went all but unnoticed. The book's authenticity was guaranteed by the image of its oral delivery to the first scribe, and this authenticity of origins enabled the text to accommodate a remarkable fluidity in the course of its manuscript transmission and performative history. The book was the message heard, grasped as the restoration to speech of the original message. That its meaning depended upon an ongoing text-interpretive tradition of orally mediated reinscription and renewed exposition went, it seems, virtually unnoticed. As will be seen, the silence of the most articulate Second Temple scribal groups regarding the existence and nature of oral tradition—whether in association with written texts or independent of them—is virtually total.

2

Performative Reading
and Text Interpretation at Qumran

The Visibility of Unwritten Tradition

In chapter 1, we stumbled upon an important observation. A technological fact of manuscript culture—that books were commonly composed and transcribed by dictation to a scribe—had become for at least some Second Temple scribal communities a trope in which nothing less than the communication of humans with the divine order could be figured. By constructing narratives in which primordial scribal ancestors heard and transcribed the words of God or his angels, Judean scribes of the second century BCE and later expressed their own convictions of having received words original to the transmundane world from which prophecy ultimately had come.

Consider for a moment the notion that the prophetic book in particular originated in a moment of transmundane audition analogous to the scribal recording of a human author's literary dictation. This scribal assimilation of the oral moment of mundane literary origins to the otherworldly flash of revelatory illumination cast a long shadow upon the socially structured, oral-traditional environment in which the transmission and communication of the book were steeped. The malleability of the physical copy of the book as it passed through a series of scribal copyists, the performative conventions that rendered the aurally received book available and intelligible to audiences beyond the scribal professionals themselves, the fund of text-interpretive traditions that lodged in multiple memories and enabled common understandings of the written text's meaning—all these aspects of the oral culture that shaped the literary history of the written book were virtually invisible to such communities despite (or perhaps because of) their very pervasiveness.

The pioneering scholar of primitive Christian oral tradition, Werner Kelber, has captured this invisibility of the ubiquitous in a provocative metaphor. He likens oral-performative literary tradition to a biosphere, an all-but-invisible environment of intertextual associations and ready-to-hand interpretive tropes that serves as the condition for the meaning of written texts, yet which cannot be reduced to their linguistic contents. "Tradition in this encompassing sense," he argues, is a circumambient contextuality or biosphere in which speaker and hearers live. It includes texts and experiences transmitted through or derived from texts. But it is anything but reducible to intertextuality. Tradition in this broadest sense is largely an invisible nexus of references and identities from which people draw sustenance, in which they live, and in relation to which they make sense of their lives.[1]

The result, as we observed in chapter 1, is the widespread perception of identity between the inscribed book and the interpretive performance tradition in which the book's public meanings are proclaimed and absorbed.

These perceptions of identity of the book with its text-interpretive tradition could be challenged, of course, only where communities preserving the same book found themselves at interpretive odds over its meaning. At that moment, the invisible "biosphere" of textual meaning would become markedly clear, forcing a retreat to the inscribed text "in itself" to arbitrate the conflict of interpretations. It is precisely in this manner that some communities of Palestinian Jews, who cultivated a rich engagement with books and the oral-performative traditions of their exposition, did indeed come to draw important distinctions between the contents of books, confined to the written text, and what now emerged as supplementary text-interpretive traditions that escaped written preservation even as they continued to explain what was written.

The well-attested, ideologically charged sectarianism of Second Temple Jewish social elites—so superbly documented recently by Albert Baumgarten[2]—expressed itself largely through conflict about the proper interpretation of prestigious texts regarded as a heritage from the ancient past. Such scribal communities clearly recognized the distinctions between written books and their interpretive traditions. They had then to explain (or, in the case of intercommunal antagonisms, to deny) the authority of orally mediated interpretive traditions that circulated in association with venerable writings. It is important, then, to direct attention toward some of the instances in which communities of learning reflected upon the authority of text-interpretive tradition as a body of knowledge related to, but distinct from, the scribally authorized book.

The sources for exploring the matter are, paradoxically, too rich and too poor. As Michael Fishbane has shown with particular throughness and brilliance, the entire canonical corpus of Hebrew Scripture testifies to manifold ways in which texts committed to manuscript were shaped by their passage through the prism of orally mediated interpretive tradition.[3] Scribes may not have been formally endowed by institutional fiat with the authority to interpretively improve the texts that passed through their hands, but they certainly did so—under the assumption, apparently, that this was their commission.

Similarly, numerous students of the Second Temple literature have shown how richly the images and ideas of the canonical Scriptures informed the diverse literary productions that laid claim to prophetic authority during the period. Here too the extensive reframings of well-known narrative traditions and interpretive revisions of legal traditions dotting this literature are undertaken without ideological justification, as if such revisioning were a natural, inevitable aspect of literary life.[4] The ubiquitous fact that interpretive traditions generated in social settings of oral exchange served as the transformative medium of written texts does not, however, disclose the ideological systems by which the interpreters grasped the authority of their own interpretive acts. Nor, in fact, does it tell us if they paid particular attention to the authorization of oral tradition at all.

This is precisely where our evidence is poor. It is often quite difficult to summon up clear pictures of the social groups that carried and developed various literary traditions. Nor do Second Temple writings always permit glimpses of the meanings such groups might have ascribed to the oral or written status of the media that bore into the future results of their literary-interpretive activity. For example, there are no texts deriving from the Second Temple period, in which writers defend the oral-performative interpretive tradition of their communities by appealing to the tradition's very unwritten form as the principle of its authority to govern the meaning of scriptural writings.

In order to illustrate the dimensions of this silence about the authority of orally mediated traditions of textual performance and interpretation, it is necessary to focus the discussion in this and the next chapter upon two well-studied groups. Each appears to have developed at least implicitly recognized conceptions of the authority of the interpretive traditions that stood at the heart of its communal engagement with written texts. But neither resorted—as far as the evidence can be pushed—to the polemical strategy that will emerge among rabbinic Sages by the third century CE: namely, that the authority of communal understandings of key writings is guaranteed by the exclusively oral medium in which those understandings are preserved.

We have already encountered the first group in the discussion of Second Temple scribalism. The community associated episodically with the Qumran site from Hasmonean times on through the war of 66–73 CE may have had some connection to the Essenes, an apparently ascetic fellowship mentioned by a number of ancient ethnographers and historians of Second Temple Jewry.[5] For the past half century, however, all historical reconstructions of the Qumran group must be built upon writings, secreted in caves throughout the Dead Sea wilderness during the war of 66–73 CE, which preserve some living connection to the traditions generated within the community. The main task in this chapter will be to identify and reflect upon the conceptions of the authority of written texts and their oral-performative transmission that may be recovered from these writings. I will indicate as well how these representations of various modalities of interpretive tradition may point to attitudes that enjoyed a wide currency within the group for much of its history.

The next chapter will devote sustained attention to a second well-known Second Temple community of textual interpreters, the Pharisees. This group represents a peculiarly complex problem for anyone attempting to reconstruct the nature of its ideological universe. Unlike the Qumran community, whose world can be explored in some detail on the basis of its own literary remains, the Pharisees are known entirely from writings produced by more or less partisan observers. As scholars now universally recognize, it is necessary to grasp the interests of these observers—whether neutral or hostile—in order to evaluate the pictures of the Pharisees they preserve. Accordingly, when we reach the discussion of Pharisaic tradition in chapter 3 we will pay particular attention to how the perspectives of these literary witnesses my have affected what we have received.

The Qumran Yahad and Its Text-Interpretive Tradition

After a half century of intense study, the scrolls found in the vicinity of Khirbet Qumran from 1947 through the early 1950s continue to raise controversy. Among well-trained scholars there remain some who continue to deny that the site was in fact the center of any sort of sectarian community.[6] Among the majority who accept the view that Qumran served as a sectarian settlement, there is continued debate concerning the identity of the group. The early equation of the sect with the Essenes continues to enjoy strong consensual support, but there is increasing appreciation of some significant and long-noted disparities between the ancient literary images of the Essenes and the material and textual evidence from Qumran.[7]

The questions about the identity of the group also touch upon the interpretation of the literary texts from the various caves. Which texts are to be interpreted as reflecting the views and practices of the Qumran community, and which are reflective of larger religious currents in Second Temple Palestine? To what degree is it possible to assume that the mere availability of a text in the Qumran cache indicates the community's acceptance of some or all of its central ideas? The present study offers no opportunity to treat these questions at length.

I shall refer to the group alternatively as the "Yahad" or the "Tzadokites," since both terms cluster together in a number of crucial works. In choosing these terms, I intend to make as minimalistic a stand as possible on the sect's possible identification with the Essenes or other voluntary religious associations known from other Second Temple sources. The term, *yhd* ("Community"), appearing principally in the Damascus Covenant (CD),[8] the Community Rule (1QS),[9] and several *pesher* compositions,[10] clearly is a self-designation employed by the community. Many of these same texts highlight the role of a priestly group known as the "Sons of Tzadok" (*bny sdwq*) as authoritative communal figures, or of a priestly teacher, the "Righteous Teacher" (*mwrh hsdq*), as a historical founder. Thus the sense of historical connectedness to the Tzadokite priestly family appearing prominently in the eschatological priesthood imagined by the exiled prophet Ezekiel (Ezek. 40:46, 43:19, 44:15, 48:11), and in the priestly lineage of the post-exilic priest-scribe Ezra (Ezra 7:1–2), played some sort of central role in the Yahad's self-understanding.[11]

Our discussion here focuses on two primary matters. The first concerns the nature of the social situations in which the Tzadokite community gathered around common texts for study and the sorts of teaching authority enjoyed by those who expounded texts. The second question concerns the subject matter of textual study. Which texts were placed at the center of collective concern, and how did the community understand the authority of the learning that issued from collective textual study?

These questions have been raised in numerous forms by scholars of the Qumran literature. My own conclusions are deeply indebted to the studies of Joseph Baumgarten,[12] Steven Fraade,[13] Lawrence Schiffman,[14] and Shmaryahu Talmon[15] in particular. The purpose of revisiting this matter here is not to bring previously unnoticed material to the discussion or to offer dramatic reinterpretations of well-known materials. Rather, in reviewing some well-studied texts from a commonly accepted critical vantage, I hope to stress the significance of a single observation.

It is clear that the Yahad was deeply engaged in the oral-performative transmission of written texts and shared a rich tradition of orally mediated understandings of such texts. Moreover, embodiment of this accumulation of written and oral tradition in the form of concrete behavioral norms was taken as a sign of full participation in the community. *It is striking, therefore, that this heritage of text and interpretation was not designated by any term denoting "tradition" at all. Indeed, little of it—beyond the writings regarded as Scripture stemming from primordial prophecy— seems to have been perceived as something received from the distant past or handed down by a succession of authoritative tradents.*[16] To be sure, it was orally delivered and aurally received, transmitted through teachers in a public setting of oral instruction. But it did not depend for its authority upon guarantees of sound transmission over vast stretches of time. Rather, its authority rested upon the confidence that it was disclosed in contemporary moments of illumination, gifts of prophecy secured by current communal leaders. And its record was most likely transmitted in writings that themselves became the subjects of further interpretive activity, rather than in oral traditions beyond the range of written preservation.

The Study Session of the Community

The most important single representation of textual study in the Tzadokite corpus serves as the hermeneutical basis upon which to interpret other sources. This is the passage from the Community Rule that mandates the public study of the Torah and an associated body of learned tradition among a deputation of leaders known as the Community Council (*'ṣt hyḥd*) (1QS 6:6–8):

> And let there not be lacking [*w'l ymš*], in a place where the ten are [*'šr yhyw šm h'śrh*],[17] a man expounding the Torah [*'yš dwrš btwrh*] day and night,/ on the proper relations of a man with his fellow [*'l ypwt 'yš lr'hw*].[18]
>
> And the Many [*whrbym*] shall diligently spend a third of all the nights of the year reciting the Book [*lqrw' bspr*], expounding the Ruling [*ldrwš mšpṭ*],/ and offering benedictions communally [*lbrk byḥd*].[19]

The passage contains a number of puzzles that need to be confronted before the questions of concern to us here can be brought to it. Those most important to us are, unfortunately, hidden by the very act of translation.

The first puzzle concerns the relationship between the two rulings I have rendered as separate paragraphs. Does CD prescribe a single study community presided over by one interpreter, or is the study session of the Many construed as an event distinct from that undertaken "where the ten are"? If the underlying Hebrew rulings are read conjunctively, with the second intended to amplify the implications of the first, then the "man expounding the Torah" would preside over the Many in nightly study.[20] But the Hebrew also supports a disjunctive reading, such that the first rule applies to the "man expounding the Torah" in a community quorum of ten and the second describes a separate gathering of the Many.[21]

Are there grounds for reaching a decision about how the relation between these two rulings was interpreted at Qumran?[22] A close parallel to this passage, preserved in the medieval copy of the Damascus Covenant (CD 13:2–4), offers some help:

And in a place of ten [*wbmqwm 'šrh*], let there not lack a priestly man learned in the book of Hagi. According to his dictates ['*l pyhw*]/ shall all be governed.[23]

But if [*w'm*] he is not learned in all these, and a man of the Levites is learned/ in them, then the lot shall fall to all the members of the Camp to conduct themselves according to his dictates.

We will discuss the reference to the book of Hagi momentarily. As for the rulings themselves, the first (CD 13:2–3) establishes that a quorum of community members should be presided over by a teaching priest whose directives should be followed. The second (CD 13:3–4) offers a contrast to its predecessor. Its introductory *vav* ("but") works disjunctively to point out that, failing the absence of a learned priest, a Levite or other person may determine matters involving the application of communal law.[24]

Can CD 13:2–4 instruct us how to read 1QS 6:6–8? Perhaps so, since it appears that the two passages share a similar pattern: a general rule followed by an addendum that addresses a situation uncovered by the original ruling. If so, the *vav* that introduces 1QS 6:7–8 should be rendered disjunctively as "but." On this reading, the rule indicates that the sessions presided over by the "expounder of the Torah" (1QS 6:6–7) are distinct from the study sessions of the "Many." Accordingly, 1QS 6:6–7 offers the simple requirement that any representation of the Community Council numbering ten have among it a learned person capable of instruction in authoritative texts. Let us, then, deal with it on its own before moving on to its companion.

The ruling is not as clear as we might like regarding the content of textual study in the quorum it prescribes. The fundamental subject of study is the "Torah." Yet, as we have seen, the parallel at CD refers to the "book of Hagi." The identity of this book is something of a controversy in Qumran scholarship,[25] but we cannot pass judgment on this problem here. I observe only that even if we take 1QS's "Torah" to be the unadorned scroll of the Mosaic Torah, the passage does not describe a simple recitation of the text. The verb, *dwrš*, suggests interpretive explication of some sort.[26] And, given the context of rules for collective gatherings in which this passage appears, it seems clear that this interpretive explication is an act of instruction rather than a private activity of the expounder.

What remains unclear is the status of the expounder: on what authority does he teach? CD, of course, insists on his priestly status, even though the continuation of that text allows for nonpriestly leadership. Moreover, the immediately preceding rule in 1QS 6:5–6 describes a meal in which "the priest shall stretch forth his hand" to bless the bread and wine on behalf of the diners. But it is unlikely, in the present context, that 1QS 6:6 carries forward this description of a priestly prerogative. Just two lines above this ruling is another:

And in every place in which there are ten men of the Community Council, let there not be lacking from among them a priestly man. And each man shall sit before him in accord with his status. And thus shall they be asked for their counsel on any matter. (1QS 6:3–4)

Described here is a meeting of some sort of governing body in which a priest presides. The language of 1QS 6:6—"in a place where the ten are"—refers back to 1QS 6:3–4, treating the meal rule of 1QS 6:5–6 as an interjection. The point is that when there are ten members of the Council gathered, one of them (whether or not he is a priest) must engage the others in Torah study. This surely is the likely motive behind 1QS 6:6's reformulation of CD's "priestly man" [*'yš khn*] as "a man expounding the Torah" [*'yš dwrš btwrh*].

1QS 6:6–7, then, mandates an act of study when a small quorum of the communal leadership gathers together. An official gathering of ten communal leaders constitutes a "community" in miniature, empowered to conduct its internal business on behalf of the "Many."[27] The ruling, however, provides no explicit reason why this deputation must engage in textual study by virtue of its having convened. 1QS 6:7–8 may provide an indirect explanation for this requirement. It clearly specifies that the community as a whole, the "Many," is required to engage in a perpetual ritualized engagement with authoritative texts. The study activity of the gathered Council, therefore, may be conceived as a replication of that of the collective. Precisely as the Community Council convenes, constituting thereby a body distinct from the community as a whole, it reconstitutes its connection to the whole by replicating its central ritual act of study. In short, the Council must study precisely because it is a deputation of the Many, and the Many is itself a community of study.

We may now focus more fully on this communal act described at 1QS 6:7–8, since it is so fundamental to the ethos of the Tzadokite community. The Many is required to establish a nightly study-watch throughout the year, comprised of three activities: reading, exposition, and benediction.[28] Our first observation is that textual study is represented as a collective act incumbent upon the entire community. We may assume that individuals could and did study texts on their own — certainly scribes would have done so in the course of their production and transmission of texts. But this passage specifies that the community as a whole should ideally be devoted to continual textual study over and above any private engagement with textual learning.

The study session described here is more than an occasion for spreading familiarity with the contents of authoritative books and traditions. Rather, the session of the Many seems to have been understood as a setting for occasional disclosures or revelations that were then transmitted as part of the community's fund of separatist knowledge.[29] It is important to recall in this context a common metaphorical distinction, woven throughout the discourse of CD and 1QS in particular, between knowledge that is "hidden" (*nstr*) and that which is "disclosed" (*nglh*).[30]

As in the following passage, this distinction coincides with the social boundary between the Yahad and the rest of Israel. The entrant into the community:

> must take upon himself, through a binding oath, to return to the Torah of Moses, according to all that has been commanded;/ with a full heart and soul to all that has been disclosed concerning it [*kkwl hnglh mmnh*] to the Sons of Tzadok, the priests [*lbny šdwq hkwhnym*],[31] the guardians of the covenant and the expounders of His will. (1QS 5:8–9)

Here the penitent returns to the covenant of Israel through an act of assent to the particular reading of that covenant current in the Yahad. From this perspective, the setting of study described in 1QS 6:7–8 is the context for the generation and dissemination of such disclosures of the hidden. That is, the knowledge transmitted in the study session of the Many constituted the fund of prophetic disclosures that enabled its participants ritually to draw and reinforce the social boundary that distinquished the Yahad from Israel in general.

The knowledge defining this boundary, apparently, was constituted by the social norms of the Tzadokite community, deemed always to have emerged from the study of authoritative texts under the guidance of illuminated teachers. 1QS 8:15's interpretation of Is. 40:3 seems to refer precisely to such a setting of occasional disclosures of new implications in the text of Torah. Explicating the prophetic injunction to "prepare the way of the Lord in the wilderness, make straight in the desert a highway for our God," the text defines the acts of preparation and straightening as follows:

> This refers to the exposition of the Torah [*mdrš htwrh*] which He committed into the hand of Moses to do, in accordance with all that is disclosed from time to time[32] [*kkwl hnglh 't b't*: cf. 1QS 9:13], and which the Prophets disclosed through His holy spirit.

What is disclosed in periodic intervals of collective illumination becomes part of the reigning ethos of the community, shaping behavior in accord with specific norms.

There is one final dimension of the exposition of the Ruling that needs consideration. We have already observed that the recitation of the Book and exposition of the Ruling are part of a larger performance that includes the recitation of benedictions. The conjunction of public study accompanied by benedictions suggests, as Fraade has pointed out, that the nightly rhythm of study was conceived as a liturgical activity, a performance that ritualized the transmission of textual knowledge conceived on the model of a sacrificial offering.[33] The sounds of the uttered words constituted a transaction between the human community and Heaven even as the communication of textual knowledge bound the group into a common discipline. In deference, perhaps, to the actual ongoing sacrificial cult in the Jerusalem Temple, the Tzadokite study-sacrifice was timed for the night, when the Jerusalem altar was inactive. Thus textual study, while sacrificial in character, did not compete with the sacrificial system mandated in the Torah and conducted, as far as the Tzadokites seemed to have held, by a flawed priesthood; it supplemented that system and, perhaps, made up for its subversion by the sitting Hasmonean priestly regime.

This sacrificial interpretation of the Yahad's study-watch sheds some light upon another enigmatic passage (1QS 9:3–5), which, in line with later rabbinic conceptions, has often been taken as a reference to the atoning effects of prayer:[34]

> When there comes to be in Israel, in accord with all these principles, a foundation for the holy spirit in eternal truth, they shall bring atonement for wanton guilt and sinful transgression, and restore the Land to favor without the flesh of whole offerings or sacrificial fats. *And the offering of the lips through the Ruling* [*wtrwmt śptym lmšpt*] *will be as a sweet aroma of righteousness,*[35] and those who perfect their way will be like a freely given offering in that time.

The italicized passage intertextually recalls Hos. 14:3's prediction that "words" will one day achieve the effects of sacrifice. Redeployed in the setting of the Yahad, the prophet is now understood to predict that it is nothing less than the oral utterances of communal study of the Ruling that will in the future atone for Israel's historical transgressions.

The final issue before us concerns the actual method of the textual study depicted in 1QS 6:6–8 and other relevant passages. Note first of all the distinction in 1QS 6:7–8 in particular between verbs denoting kinds of study and their direct objects. The rule prescribes an act of "recitation" (*qr'*) appropriate to the Book and an act of "exposition" (*drš*) appropriate to the Ruling. While it is clear that the recitation of the Book is preliminary to the exposition of the Ruling, the relationship of the two acts remains unspecified. Is the Ruling exegetically derived from the Book, or is it an independent textual entity in its own right? In either event, is the Ruling a written document or an orally transmitted compendium of some sort?

The key to interpreting this exposition of the Ruling lies in the term, *mšpṭ*, which stands behind the translation "Ruling." As Schiffman has pointed out, *mishpat* is a technical term in CD and 1QS, denoting behavioral prescriptions particular to the community.[36] The Ruling, on this reading, is in some sense the preserved record of the periodic disclosure of things "hidden" from all Israel and "disclosed" to the Yahad in their collective textual studies[37] "according to the Ruling of each time" (*lmšpṭ 't w't*: CD 12:20).

But the specific textual procedure that constitutes the act of "expounding the Ruling" is tantalizingly vague. It is possible that before us is an exegetical activity that generates from the Torah itself, as a kind of midrashic application, a normative prescription for explicitly communal behavior.[38] The general disinterest of Qumranic texts, however, in using the literary form of exegesis to link communal rules to laws from the Torah mitigates against this interpretation.[39] Alternatively, it is also possible that the exposition of the Ruling is an exegetical inquiry into a text other than the Torah. That is, the Ruling is a source of teaching in its own right, and "expounding" it is a matter of applying and extending the Ruling itself.[40] The evidence of successive revisions of sectarian regulations within CD and 1QS, noted by J. Baumgarten and S. Metso in particular, lends support to the latter interpretation.[41] It seems likely, then, that this passage assumes the existence of an authoritative body of written texts related to, but separate from, the laws encoded in the Torah. It is the corpus of inner-communal "disclosures," rather than the unadorned scriptural text itself, that undergirds the specific form of life that distinguishes members of the community from those beyond its perimeter.

Oral Performance, Prophetic Presence, and Written Record

Even among those who doubt that Qumran served as a site for an industrious project of text composition,[42] the sources before us show that the oral presentation of written texts and the orally mediated transmission of the text-interpretive tradition played a key role in the common life of the community. The interpretive study of texts was not confined to priestly leaders or scribal professionals. Rather, it extended beyond them to become part of the ethos of the collective. While a small minority of the community would have mastered all the scribal skills, the entire group aspired to a degree of textual knowledge appropriate to scribes. Moreover, the results of textual exposition—particularly as it intersected with and found social embodiment in the behavioral norms applicable within the community—were intended for rapid dissemination throughout the group by designated teachers, priestly and nonpriestly alike.

The passages we have examined describe a twofold textual foundation lying at the basis of collective study: the recitation of the Book and the exposition of the Ruling. The precise nature of this recitation and exposition, and the identity of their textual objects, is impossible to identify with much certainty. Whether the Book (or the book of Hagi) is synonymous with the canonical Torah of Moses or not, the text is represented as being publicly read forth as the basis of a secondary discourse. This secondary discourse, the exposition of the Ruling, seems to have been the foundation of innovative application of the texts of the Book. But this application was not represented as exegesis, even of a prophetically inspired sort (as in the *pesher* texts). Rather, it was represented as a prophetic delivery itself, a divine disclosure delivered to a teacher.

Both sources of instruction — the Book and the Ruling — are represented as having been delivered orally and received aurally in public session. But while the written character of the Book is certain, matters are vaguer regarding the Ruling. The Ruling is nowhere referred to specifically as a written source. Nevertheless, the weight of Qumran scholarship warrants the conclusion that the Ruling was composed and transmitted in writing, its remnants preserved in the various interpretations of biblical laws and sectarian rulings found in the very documents we have examined. This picture coincides with that drawn by Byrskog of the interrelation of written and oral/aural media in the preservation and transmission of the other major focus of qumranian literary tradition preserved in the *pesher* literature. "The written traditions from the Righteous Teacher," he argues, "were not devoid of oral and aural functions within the transmission process. The written means used for carrying the traditions related to aural means for conveying them."[43] Authorized knowledge may have circulated widely through oral means, but the decisive authority of that knowledge was linked inevitably to written texts — to the Book and the Ruling, where communal discipline was at stake; to the *pesharim* and other texts, where collective self-understanding was the issue.[44]

Summary

Despite the many unsolved problems we have considered, the material from Qumran yields an inescapable conclusion with regard to our central question about the authority of the orally performed traditions of reading and exposition that circulated within the textual study sessions of the Yahad. Text-interpretive tradition — the cumulative results of multiple textual readings built up over time in the memories of the community's members — was received not as tradition transmitted from the past, but as ongoing revelation continuing into the present. While delivered orally in the context of textual study, it appears to have been routinely compiled, reformulated, and transmitted in written compositions that themselves were subjected to oral-performative exposition. There is no suggestion in any of the Yahad-related materials, however, that the group assigned authoritative status to an unwritten body of collective tradition on the specific grounds that it had been orally mediated through ancient tradition. While oral teaching was clearly the norm — people acted "in accord with the dictates" ('*l py*) of selected teachers and heard the pronouncements of the expounders of the Torah — the authority of the teaching appears to have been connected inextricably to that of the writings from which it originated. And the definitive expression of its authority was found not in its oral nature, but rather in the fact of its having been itself inscribed on the leaves of scrolls.

From this perspective, the Yahad's engagement with written texts is wholly continuous with those common among the broader scribal communities discussed in chapter 1. In those communities the authoritative oral moment of textual tradition, in itself authorizing further explicative teachings, was located at the origins of the book, in a disclosive moment of authorial illumination. The contents of the oral-literary tradition that had escaped written form was not perceived at all as an entity distinct from the book; rather, it was carried along within the orbit of the written text itself, as the performative tradition of its public exposition.

What distinguished the Yahad from other Second Temple literary circles was one simple fact: while the scribal progenitors of such venerable texts as the Torah of Moses, the Enochic works, or Jubilees located the origins of their revelations in the distant past, the Yahad regarded itself as blessed to have such prophets in its very midst. Delivered with prophetic authority, the living traditions of the community were perceived not as supplements to prophetic books, but as divine disclosures themselves. As such, they were recorded in written texts, upon which alone all other forms of unwritten tradition would find their attenuated authority. How was it different, we may now wonder, among those other formidable opponents of the Yahad and its text-interpretive traditions—the Second Temple Pharisees?

3

The Media of Pharisaic
Text-Interpretive Tradition

The Problem of the Sources

A standard, indispensable scholarly handbook on the history of Judaism in Second Temple and early post-Temple times states as common knowledge the following claim about Pharisaic Judaism. "Needless to say, according to the Pharisaic outlook not only the written Torah was binding; but also the exegesis and supplementation, known as the 'oral Torah,' provided by the scribes."[1] This "needless to say" disguises a complex problem. This chapter, taking up a debate current among historians of early Judaism, will call into serious question arguments that the rabbinic conception of text-interpretive tradition as a primordial revelation of an Oral Torah originates in the pre-70 circles of the Pharisees.[2]

The point, to be precise, is that the sources of information on Pharisaism and its traditions of textual interpretation surely suggest a high degree of Pharisaic pride in possessing an ancient tradition of authoritative interpretations of the Torah's laws in particular. But the sources offer little evidence upon which to identify among the Pharisees an ideological commitment to preserving a text-interpretive tradition in an exclusively oral-performative medium. That is to say, Pharisaic ideas regarding the oral origins of the prestigious book are likely to have been similar to those we found current among other scribal communities of Second Temple Palestine (see chapter 1). But the extent to which they were equally committed to the oral origins or exlusively oral transmission of non-scriptural traditions is, on the basis of available sources, impossible to surmise.

Let us, then, take a look at the sources. All of them are at a second remove from the Pharisees themselves. There is not a single text from the Second Temple period that can sustain for long the argument that it was composed by a Pharisee for the purpose of expressing a Pharisaic point of view.[3] In contrast to the state of affairs among the Yahad, whose textual practices and conceptions of text-interpretive tradition can be explored through the study of texts produced or used within the community, any historical representation of the Pharisees' social system, Pharisaic practices, or the

Pharisaic thought-world is entirely dependent upon secondhand reports that come from a variety of witnesses. Each witness approaches description of the group from a particular point of view.

Surviving accounts of the Pharisees, written by authors presumed to have had at least superficial contact with them, come from four quarters. The earliest of these observers are the composers of at least some of the Qumranian scrolls that exhibit signs of Tzadokite origin. While the Pharisees are never mentioned explicitly by name anywhere in the Qumran corpus, most scholars assume that they are alluded to as the "Expounders of Smooth Things" (*dwršy hhlqwt*), mentioned by the composers of the Damascus Covenant, the Thanksgiving Scroll, the *pesharim* to the books of Isaiah and Nahum, and a few other texts found in the Qumran caves.[4] The antagonism toward them on the part of the Qumranian writings suggests that the Yahad came into political conflict with Pharisees at various points during the Hasmonean period. But the highly coded historical allusions are sufficiently veiled to make precise identification of the historical contexts and issues a precarious matter.

Texts from the late first century CE comprise a second body of evidence about the Pharisees. Epistolary writings and hagiographical compositions preserved by early Christian communities in the names of the apostle Paul and the four evangelists have figured prominently in critical reconstructions of Pharisaism as it might have existed in the early middle first century CE. So too the historical writings of the foremost ancient historian of the Jews, Flavius Josephus (né Yosef b. Matityahu), are routinely mined for information about the earlier Pharisees of the Hasmonean and Herodian periods. While historians cannot work around these texts or dismiss their testimony, it is also difficult to know exactly how to move behind them to the Pharisaic reality they describe.

Aside from two enigmatic passages in the letters of Paul, information about the Pharisees in early Christian literature comes primarily from the canonical Gospels, whose Pharisees serve largely as literary foils for the heroic character of Jesus. The evangelists completed their work during the last third of the first century CE, and their interest in the Pharisees—confined to the group's relationship to Jesus during the years of his ministry and, to a lesser degree, the response of Pharisees to the post-Easter activities of his disciples and apostles—is shaped largely by the rhetorical concerns of Christian proclamation. Historians, therefore, continue to puzzle over how much the Gospels' composers may project onto the context of the first third of the first century an antagonism that might be historically more pertinent to the tensions between Jewish-Christian or Gentile-Christian communities with other Jewish groups of the latter third of the century, including those from which rabbinism ultimately emerged.

The third source, Josephus, offers the bulk of his discussion of the Pharisees in his two principal historical writings, the Jewish War (composed by about 78 CE) and the Jewish Antiquities (a product of the mid-90s). In each he accords them central roles in the politics of the Hasmonean era, particularly during the reigns of John Hyrcanus (ruled 134–103 BCE), Alexander Jannaeus (ruled 103–76 BCE), and Alexandra Salome (ruled 76–67 BCE). Some of Josephus' sources of information regarding the Pharisees seem to go back to the lost writings of the Herodian court historian, Nicolaus of Damascus, and so may represent more or less contemporary accounts.[5] In a third work, moreover, Josephus claims to have studied with some care the Pharisaic philosophy of his own day (Life 12).[6]

This combination of primary literary sources and personal acquaintance has led many historians to place a great deal of confidence in the Josephan picture of the Pharisees. But it is increasingly understood that Josephus shaped his literary sources with relative freedom as he composed his historical writings, and that his various accounts of the Pharisees are influenced by his own concerns to present an intelligible view of Palestinian Jewry to his largely non-Jewish readership. It is, then, no simple matter to distinguish "historical fact" from "literary representation" in Josephus' accounts of the Pharisees.[7]

Finally, the most recently composed body of sources regarding the Pharisees are those that dot the classical rabbinic corpus of late Roman, early Byzantine, and Sassanian times. These are among the most difficult to use. It is most likely that at least some Pharisees were included in the post-70 coalition of scribal scholars, priests, and administrative officers whose early-third-century CE heirs had begun to form the early literary traditions of rabbinic Judaism.[8] But the rabbinic literature of the third to sixth centuries is itself not much interested in Pharisaism as a historical phenomenon. The earliest rabbinic compilations, such as the Mishnah and associated compendia, do at times link some rabbinic traditions to teachers who may well have been Pharisees. But we shall see that depictions of Pharisaism as a coherent social movement are few and unsystematically drawn. Moreover, it will become clear that texts making the strongest claims of the filiation of rabbinism with Pharisaism are rather late in the development of rabbinic tradition, occuring exclusively in the Babylonian Talmud,[9] compiled in its extant form perhaps as recently as the sixth to seventh centuries.

Any attempt to discuss ideological conceptions of text-interpretive tradition among the Pharisees as an exclusively oral possession must, therefore, be alert to the difficulties posed by our best sources. Let us, then, turn to each type of source in sequence, asking how it depicts the nature of Pharisaic interpretive tradition. Only after such a survey will we be able to ask whether a coherent picture emerges from the various representations.

The Qumran Literature

As was mentioned earlier, all knowledge of the Yahad's perception of Hasmonean-period Pharisees depends upon a slim set of references to enemies of the group known as "Expounders of Smooth Things." Two interpretive issues are intertwined in reading the Qumran sources on this matter. The first is the basis upon which the Expounders can be identified as a group more or less identical to those Pharisees known, primarily through Josephus, to have been involved in Hasmonean court politics. The second issue concerns the name "Expounders of Smooth Things" itself. What are the Smooth Things expounded and why do they so antagonize the authors of these texts? We shall see that the common identification of the Expounders as Pharisees seems nearly incontrovertible. But there are grounds for being skeptical that the identification of the Smooth Things tells us as much about Hasmonean Pharisaic tradition as many scholars have wished to claim.

In most of the settings in which the Expounders appear, the context clearly presents them as some sort of organized group that high-handedly violates the Yahad's own sense of covenantal law and misleads the larger community of Israel. Thus the prophetic vision of the destruction of Nineveh (Nah. 3:7) is interpreted as follows: "Its explanation [concerns] the Expounders/ of Smooth Things, whose counsel ['ṣh] shall perish and whose assembly [knst] shall be dispersed, and they will no longer persist in misleading [the] community, and the Innocent/ will no longer support their counsel" (4QpNah, fr. 3–4, 3:6–7).[10]

At least two passages, moreover, suggest some sort of focused violence directed by the Expounders toward the Yahad. For example, the Damascus Covenant's opening homily about Israel's waywardness reports upon the rise of a "Man of Mockery" ('yš hlṣwn) who "sprinkled upon Israel from the waters of the Lie" (CD 1:14–15). In consequence, "they expounded Smooth Things and chose illusions [mhtlwt] and speculated/ about loopholes [prṣwt] . . . / and caused the covenant to be transgressed and the statute to be abrogated. And they ganged up against the soul of the righteous, and despised in their souls all who walked/ in perfection. And they pursued them with the sword and relished conflict among the people" (CD 1:18–21; cf. 1QHodayot 2:31–32).

In general, references to the Expounders are enmeshed in symbolic references that are difficult to decode, and the previous examples are no exception. They do not give much help in identifying what might have been the origins of focused violence against the Yahad on the part of its opponents. Yet on the basis of one specific reference, the Yahad's mysterious opponents may be narrowed down to a group of Jerusalemites who invited a certain "Demetrius, King of Greece" to establish himself as ruler in Jerusalem (4QpNah, fr. 3–4, 1:2).[11]

This allusion is illuminated by an incident described by Josephus (War 1:92–98, Antiquities 13:377–383), usually dated to 88 BCE. Disgusted with the policies of the Hasmonean Priest-King, Alexander Jannaeus, his opponents (unnamed in Josephus' account) invited the Seleucid ruler, Demetrius III Eukeres, to oust the Hasmonean dynast. Ultimately Alexander prevailed, but in revenge he executed 800 of his opponents. After Alexander's own death in 76 BCE, Josephus portrays newly empowered Pharisees as taking vengeance upon those of Alexander's advisors who had executed the 800 (War 1:113, Antiquities 13:410–415). In the context of the Josephan report, it is difficult to avoid the conclusion that the Expounders of Smooth Things of the Nahum *pesher* encodes a reference to a Pharisaic group. Presumably, they engaged in some sort of reprisals against members of the Yahad who, whatever their feelings about Alexander Jannaeus, had opposed a coup d'etat that involved a Gentile ruler dominating Jerusalem.[12]

In addition to the political dispute that resulted in the Yahad's conflict with the Pharisees, there appear to have been other errors of the Pharisees that drew the enmity of the Yahad. We have seen that CD 1:18 denounces Jews who, "expounding Smooth Things," also "speculated about loopholes" in the Torah of Israel. The nature of this exposition, and the very meaning of "Smooth Things," is the nub of the interpretive problem. Most likely, as some English translators of the term dwršy hhlqwt have suggested, the term refers to a tendency to seek "easy interpretations" of covenantal law.[13]

It is likely, then, that the Smooth Things are a reference to interpretive judgments about the application of covenantal law which conflict with the revelations disclosed to the Yahad in the nightly vigils of study referred to in the previous chapter. On this reading, the Pharisees are represented as a group that ignores the Yahad's specific revelations and insists on interpreting certain matters of covenantal law in light of its own traditions. Obviously, the precise way in which the Pharisees might have interpreted the origin, nature, and authority of such traditions is a matter of great interest.

Some scholars have proposed that the term "Expounders of Smooth Things" contains information that can answer this question. Specifically, "Smooth Things" (*ḥlqwt*, vocalized as *ḥalaqot*) is understood as a wordplay on the term *hlkwt* (vocalized as *halakhot*).[14] The latter is commonly used in rabbinic literature of the third century and later to designate rabbinically sponsored rulings that carry the authority of binding tradition. According to scholars pursuing this interpretation, the phrase "Expounders of Smooth Things" is a punning reference to the Pharisaic practice of expounding rulings on the basis of traditional, orally transmitted law. This practice, presumably, yielded results that conflicted with the prophetically inspired "hidden things" of the Yahad.

If this view could be established, there would indeed be grounds to suggest that the idea of an authoritative, orally transmitted legal tradition mediated through scriptural interpretation was a key element of Pharisaic ideology at least as early as the first century BCE. It would suggest, moreover, a genuinely early Second Temple period lineage for what eventually emerges in third-century rabbinic culture as "Torah in the Mouth" stemming from Sinai. This is an intriguing suggestion, but it depends upon a tissue of highly speculative assumptions.

The term *halakhah* appears nowhere in the Qumranian corpus, nor is it attested in any surviving Jewish literature of the Second Temple period. Its earliest appearances are in the Mishnah and related rabbinic literature of the third century CE and later. As we shall see in chapter 4, the term *halakhah* (and its plural, *halakhot*) bears a number of nuanced meanings, not all of them implying that *halakhot* are exegetically generated. Many rabbinic traditions, in fact, deny the scriptural foundations of substantial bodies of halakhic tradition. This fact constitutes the first objection to the claim that the qumranian *ḥlqwt* provides the earliest attestation of the rabbinic concept of *halakhah* as an orally transmitted tradition of laws derived from scriptural exegesis but not explicitly contained in the Torah. Such a claim selects only one range of attested meanings for historical retrojection beyond rabbinic usage back to the Pharisees. Even if the term *halakhah* could be of demonstrably Pharisaic coinage, it would not be possible on the basis of the term *ḥlqwt* alone to infer precisely which range of rabbinic meanings could be imputed to the Pharisaic enemies of the Yahad.[15]

But the most important criticism of the idea that the Yahad's references to *ḥlqwt* satirize Pharisaic *hlkwt* is the observation that the term *ḥlqwt* is not itself of Qumranian coinage. Rather, it enters Qumranian terminology from scriptural antecedents. This is no secret to students of the Qumran scrolls, but its significance is normally underappreciated. The most crucial passage comes from Is. 30:10. Here the prophet denounces the defiant among Israel who refused to listen to the Torah of God and "who said to the Seers: Do not see! and to the Visionaries: Do not envision for us in honesty! Speak to us Smooth Things [*hlqwt*], envision Illusions [*mhtlwt*]!" The conjunction of *hlqwt* and *mhtlwt*, Smooth Things and Illusions, stands directly behind CD 1:18's complaint regarding some of Israel's seduction by the Man of Lies (see above), and serves as the intertextual reference point for CD's use of the term "expounding Smooth Things." We learn that Pharisaic teachings are equated with self-serving lies and illusory principles—but know nothing about the nature of their derivation or authority.

A second example of how the scriptural text informs the Qumranian terminology comes from the fragmentary *pesher* to the book of Isaiah itself. The pesharist's comment on Is. 30:10 has unfortunately been lost, but the following point appears in conjunction with a contiguous verse that promises "swift shall your pursuers be" (Is. 30:16): "Its explanation concerns the End of Days with regard to the Ex[pounders] of Smooth Things/ who are in Jerusalem . . ." (4QpIsa^c, fr. 23, 2:10–11). While the larger point has been lost in the damaged text, it seems clear that the proximity of Is. 30:10's "speak to us Smooth Things" finds its intertextual echo in the passage before us.[16]

In both of these cases, the argument can be made that the Qumranian reference to Expounders of Smooth Things exemplifies the larger tendency of the *pesher* genre to read the Yahad's historical experience against the background of scriptural images.[17] But it is doubtful that we can press the term too far for clues as to the nature of Pharisaic oral-interpretive tradition. Indeed, the intertextual context of Is. 30:10 suggests, rather, that *the pesharist viewed Pharisaic legal tradition not as false exegesis, but as false prophecy.* It is a tantalizing coincidence that *hlqwt* blends euphoneously with a term first attested in the rabbinic literature of the third century CE. But we should hesitate in concluding that we have found the earliest evidence of a Pharisaic ideological commitment to orally transmitted legal-interpretive tradition.

Our survey thus far has come up with relatively slim results. It is likely that the phrase "Expounders of Smooth Things" is indeed a reference to the Pharisaic group that came into conflict with the Yahad over political affairs during the reign of Alexander Jannaeus. It also seems clear that, from the Yahad's point of view, Pharisaic faults included not only political treason, but a more fundamental rejection of the legal prescriptions revealed to Israel in the study vigils at Qumran. Pharisaic life—as the Yahad perceived it, at least—was, by contrast, governed by reference to "easy expositions" of the Torah and a penchant for finding "loopholes." But if we appreciate the shaky grounds for accepting the facile equation of *hlqwt* and *hlkwt*, the crucial question of how the Pharisees understood the origin and authority of their text-interpretive tradition remains unanswered in the Qumran sources.

Early Christian Literature

In contrast to the allusive and vague references to the Pharisees in the literature of the Yahad, the Pharisees of the earliest Christian writings are drawn in clear, bold strokes. Along with Sadducees and scribes, the Pharisees appear in each of the canonical Gospels (and in Acts) as leading figures in the Galilean and Jerusalemite communities in which Jesus of Nazareth and his earliest followers found their audiences. There is no opportunity here to mount a comprehensive survey of the diverse pictures of Pharisaism found in early Christian writings. Nor can we go into detail on the question of how specific portrayals of the Pharisees in relation to Jesus might be shaped by a growing recognition among the increasingly Gentile churches of the latter part of the first century that commitment to the messiahship of Jesus entailed estrangement from the communities of ethnic Judaism. Rather, we will move briefly through the various chronological strata of the early Christian literature and focus on specific textual moments that promise some insight into the nature of first-century Pharisaic interpretive tradition, at least as it appeared to those for whom all Judaic tradition had come to its culmination in the career and teaching of Jesus.

The earliest Christian sources in which Pharisees play a role are frustratingly silent about the question of Pharisaic tradition. The apostle Paul's letter to the Philippian church, written during the middle 50s, is the earliest text written by a believer in Jesus' messianic identity to mention Pharisees. Here, in portraying his own *bona fides* as a genuine Jew who has reason for confidence in his relationship with the God of Israel, Paul portrays himself in the famous formulation: "circumcised on the eighth day, of the people of Israel, of the tribe of Benjamin, a Hebrew born of Hebrews; as to the law a Pharisee [*kata nomon pharisaios*], as to zeal a persecutor of the church, as to righteousness under the law blameless" (Phil. 3:5–7).[18]

The doctrinal content of Paul's self-identification as a Pharisee was amplified in Christian tradition to include beliefs regarding the resurrection of the dead (e.g., Acts 23:6–10) that are obliquely confirmed in Josephan portrayals of the group (e.g., War 2:163, Antiquities 18:14). But here in Paul's own words the significance appears narrower. Paul simply points out that his pursuit of covenantal piety conforms to legal norms espoused by the Pharisees. He offers nothing, however, by way of an explanation of the specific content of those norms, their authority, or their relation to the revealed prescriptions of Scripture.[19]

There is one other Pauline passage that might illumine Paul's situation to a degree. In his letter to a community in Galatia, also datable to the mid-50s, Paul has another occasion to remind his readers of his knowledge of Judaism. The passage is of great interest, for it uses the criterion of revelation (*apokalupseos*) to distinguish Paul's preaching from all other teaching about Christ (Gal. 1:11–16):

> For I would have you know, brethren, that the gospel which was preached by me
> is not man's gospel. For I did not receive it from man, nor was I taught it, but it
> came through a revelation of Jesus Christ. For you have heard of my former life in
> Judaism, how I persecuted the church of God violently and tried to destroy it; and
> I advanced in Judaism beyond many of my own age among my people, so extemely
> zealous was I for the traditions of my fathers [*patrikon mou paradoseon*].[20] But when
> he who had set me apart before I was born, had called me through his grace, was
> pleased to reveal his Son to me, in order that I might preach him among the Gentiles, I did not confer with flesh and blood.

Here Paul subsumes the Judaic "traditions of my fathers" under a larger category of humanly generated tradition that includes the teachings of other apostles about Christ.

Paul makes no explicit equation of his former Judaic traditions with specifically Pharisaic norms, but it is tempting indeed to read his allusion here in light of his Pharisaic self-identification in Philippians. The result is that, from Paul's new postrevelation perspective, his Pharisaic tradition appears to have been, even in full respect to its antiquity, merely a human construction. But this idea is of little help in determining how the Pharisaism known to Paul might have represented the source of whatever traditions it transmitted. Perhaps by showing Pharisaic tradition to be "human-all-too-human" Paul is satirizing a Pharisaic claim to possess a divinely disclosed text-interpretive tradition akin to that found in the prologue to the third century rabbinic tractate, Avot 1:1ff (of which, more later, particularly in chapter 4). But this notion is purely speculative and cannot enter into a description of the Pharisaic conception of tradition known to Paul. In sum, Paul's writings help us little in our efforts to learn about the sorts of authority enjoyed by Pharisaic interpretive tradition or the degree to which it was, as a *matter of principle*, transmitted independently of written texts.

The second source of early Christian tradition about the Pharisees, more or less contemporaneous with the Pauline corpus, is the hypothetical source of memorable sayings ascribed primarily to John the Baptizer and Jesus, known to New Testament scholarship as "Q."[21] Broadly speaking, this source is claimed to underlie those parallel passages of the Gospels of Matthew and Luke that have no parallel in Mark. The Pharisees make only occasional appearances in passages that draw upon Q, and in all but one case they figure only in the redactional language supplied by the Matthean editor rather than in the logion itself. These references, accordingly, are not part of the original Q tradition at all, but rather are the contribution of the Matthean gospel tradition.

For example, John the Baptizer's condemnation of the "brood of vipers" is directed against Sadducees and Pharisees in Mat. 3:7–12 but to "the multitudes" in Luke 3:7–9. In the story of the exorcism of the demoniac, similarly, the crowd's skeptical comments are ascribed to the Pharisees in Matthew's two versions (Mat. 9:32–34, 12:22–28), whereas Luke places them in the mouths of "some of the people" (Luke 11:14–15). The same distinction occurs in Mat. 12:38–42 ("Pharisees")/Luke 11:16 ("others") where a request for Jesus to perform a sign draws his condemnation of "an evil generation." This equivocation in the earliest layer of the eventual gospel tradition about the precise antagonists besetting John and Jesus should make us cautious in drawing any inferences about Pharisees from these passages. In any case none of them is relevant to our interest in Pharisaic concepts of tradition.

The only passage of Q that refers to Pharisees within quoted logia is found in Q 11:42, within the extended condemnations of Pharisaic faults woven throughout Jesus' speeches in Mat. 23:1–36/Luke 11:39–52.[22] Here too there are suggestive differences in the way Q is shaped in the transmitted Gospel texts. The formulaic phrase "Woe to you, scribes and Pharisees, hypocrites!" which inaugurates each condemnation in Matthew, is absent in the Lukan parallels. Luke, for its part, confines its opprobrium to Pharisees alone (omitting scribes, who play no role in Luke's narrative framework) and neglects the explicit charge of hypocrisy (although Pharisaic hypocrisy is surely the point throughout).

Q 11:42 and its accompanying material, in any case, make no specific mention of Pharisaic tradition per se. Nor do its references to such practices as cleansing cups or tithing herbs necessarily distinguish these practices as central to or distinctive of Pharisaic tradition. The point is not that Pharisees, contrary to other Jews, purify their utensils or tithe mint and cumin; rather it is that they do this while "neglecting the weightier matters of the law" (Mat. 23:23) or, in the Lukan version, "the love of God" (Luke 11:42). Ultimately, then, the Q tradition is no more helpful than the Pauline corpus in illuminating the character of Pharisaic tradition in the first half of the first century CE.

Moving to the next stage in the formation of the emerging Christian gospel tradition, represented by the synoptic Gospels of Mark, Matthew, and Luke, we find ourselves planted firmly in the latter third of the first century.[23] The composition of the Gospel of Mark is usually dated to sometime after the mid-60s of the first century, with Matthew and Luke following in the 80s and 90s. Here the sparseness of Q's testimony about the Pharisees is overcome by a plethora of overlapping and, at times, competing representations of the Pharisees as being among the most persistent antagonists of Jesus' person and message. The full range of images has been the subject of frequent discussion and will not detain us here. From the perspective of our interest in the nature of Pharisaic tradition, however, one particular passage, paralleled in Mat. 15:1–20 and Mark 7:1–23, is of singular importance.

The unit begins with Jesus' criticism of the preoccupation of scribes and Pharisees with hand-washing before meals (Mat. 15:1–2/Mark 7:1–5), a theme explored as well in the Q materials underlying Mat. 23 and Luke 11 (see above). In the present setting, Jesus goes on to a broader charge, reminiscent of Paul's statements in Gal. 1:14, that Pharisaic practices in general replace divine commandments with human conventions (Mat. 15:3–9/Mark 7:6–13). He concludes by redefining defilement as that which is found in the human heart rather than absorbed from material agents such as food (Mat. 15:10–20/Mark 7:14–23). The parallel versions differ slightly in the sequence of logia and their precise formulation. Each pericope, moreover, has its own emphasis, containing material not found in its companion. Since the Markan version focuses more squarely on our own interests here, we will use it as the basis of this discussion.

The most relevant portion extends from Mark 7:1–13 (Mat. 15:1–9):

1. (7:1–2) Now when the Pharisees gathered together to him, with some of the scribes, who had come from Jerusalem,/ they saw that some of his disciples ate with hands defiled, that is, unwashed.
2. (7:3–4) For the Pharisees, and all the Jews, do not eat unless they wash their hands, observing the tradition of the elders [*paradosin ton presbuteron*]; and when they come from the market place, they do not eat unless they purify themselves; and there are many other traditions [*parelabon*] that they observe, the washing of cups and pots and vessels of bronze.
3. (7:5) And the Pharisees and the scribes asked him, "Why do your disciples not live [*peripatousin*] according to the tradition of the elders, but eat with hands defiled?"
   (7:6–8) And he said to them, "Well did Isaiah prophesy of you hypocrites as it is written (Is. 29:13):
   'this people honors me with their lips, but their heart is far from me;/
   in vain do they worship me, teaching as doctrines the precepts of men'
   [*entalmata anthropon*]/.
   You leave the commandment of God, and hold fast the tradition of men."

4. (7:9–13) And he said to them, "You have a fine way of rejecting the commandment [*entelon*] of God, in order to keep your tradition [*paradosin*]! For Moses said, 'Honor your father and your mother [Ex. 20:12, Dt. 5:16]'; and 'He who speaks evil of father and mother, let him surely die [Ex. 21:16, Lev. 20:9]'; but you say, 'If a man tells his father or his mother, What you would have gained from me is Corban (that is, given to God) — then he is no longer permitted to do anything for his father or mother,' thus making void the word of God through your tradition [*paradosei*] which you hand on [*paredokate*]. And many such things you do."

Sections 1 and 3 are an original literary unity into which 2 has been interpolated as a parenthetic ethnographic guide to Pharisaic ritual practice.[24] Section 4 amplifies the concluding point of 3, that Pharisaic tradition contravenes the divine will.

Let us focus on key points of interest in sections 2–4 in sequence. As A. Baumgarten has observed, 2's key terms for tradition, *paradosin* and *parebelon*, correspond respectively to the acts of passing on and receiving something from the past. These echo the Hebrew roots *msr* and *qbl* that play a key role in the later Mishnah's representation of the linkage of rabbinic tradition to Mosaic origins (M. Avot 1:1ff.).[25] Mark here identifies hand-washing as an element of this larger tradition received from the ancestors. Later rabbinic tradition also links traditions about ritual hand-washing at mealtimes to the first-century disciples of Hillel and Shammai (M. Berakhot 8:2–3, T. Berakhot 5:26–27).[26] So it is at least possible that — if this interpolated passage stems from a late moment in the development of Mark's textual tradition — it might reflect terminology for the transmission of tradition that was current in some Jewish circles in the latter portion of the first century CE or after.

The question, however, is whether in Mark's view this tradition is distinctive to the Pharisees. "All the Jews," after all, follow this custom.[27] So it is not clear at this point that the Pharisaic challenge to Jesus' disciples is based on specifically Pharisaic custom or, to the contrary, accuses the disciples of ignoring the traditions of Israel in general.[28] Section 3 resolves this matter. Jesus' ascription of Is. 29:13's "people" (LXX: *laos*; MT: '*m*) to his Pharisaic opponents leaves no doubt that, in Mark's mind, whether or not the Pharisees originated the ritual of hand-washing, it is their tradition alone that has elevated a human convention to the level of a divine commandment. The quotation from Scripture is a close paraphrase of the Septuagint, which also contrasts divinely originating *didaskalias* ("doctrines") with mere human "precepts" (*entalmata*: cf. MT: *mṣwt 'nšym*). It is impossible to know whether late first-century Pharisees claimed divine origins for their customs, but it is clear that Mark understands their loyalty to their traditions as defiance of God's own commandments.

Another important element of section 3 is the very question posed by the Pharisees to Jesus. As is commonly pointed out, the verb *peripatousin* is best rendered as "walking" or "conducting oneself," in this case in accord with the tradition of the elders. It is likely that some form of the Hebrew root *hlk* underlies this expression. The reflexive form is well attested in the Hebrew Bible (e.g., Gen. 6:9, 17:1, 24:40; Ps. 26:3; Is. 38:3/2 Kings 20:3) and Qumran (e.g., 1QS 3:20–21, 4:15, CD 12:22, 20:6) as a description of a comprehensive pattern of behavior, for good or ill. And certainly, we stand here close to the semantic range covered by the term *halakhah* in later rabbinic texts. At the very least, then, this passage conveys the sense that, among Pharisees, ancient traditions were revered as part of an all-embracing pattern of life. It may constitute, as well, the earliest indirect attestation of the term *halakhah* in the sense it ultimately bore in later rabbinic literature.

Section 4 reinforces the images of its predecessor, adding more fuel to the fire. The contrast between divine norms (*entelon*) and Pharisaic tradition (*paradosin*) echoes the vocabulary of LXX Is. 29:13, showing how Pharisaic customs regarding vows permit violations of the divine commandment to honor parents. It is precarious to assert that, in this highly polemical passage, Mark has gotten Pharisaic custom entirely straight. Later rabbinic laws of vows, in contrast to Mark's representation, incorporate a mechanism for absolving oneself from any vows that entail violations of biblical commandments.[29] Indeed the specific instance of the absolution of a vow involving dishonor of parents is addressed at M. Nedarim 9:1. It is impossible, obviously, to surmise the Pharisaic situation. But Mark's representation of the term "Corban" as central to the language of oaths is reflected in Josephus and early rabbinic literature as well.[30] While we might suspect Mark of exaggerating the extent to which vows would have been made in order to circumvent scriptural commands, the text is clearly in touch with genuine Palestinian Jewish practice, both within and beyond the Pharisaic orbit.

To summarize the conclusions about what can be learned from early Christian literary sources regarding the conception of text-interpretive authority among the Pharisees of the mid-late first century CE: Paul, Q, and the synoptic traditions concur that a salient trait of first- century Judaism in general was comformity to an ancestral tradition of norms that govern behavior. Paul *may* view this adherence to tradition as distinctive to Pharisaism, but Q's single reference represents it as a characteristic of Jewish piety in general. The synoptic tradition represented in Matthew and Mark moves well beyond both Paul and Q in defining Pharisaism substantially as loyalty to a distinctive ancestral tradition that in some sense can supersede specific biblical laws. But the synoptics are less interested in the details of this tradition than in showing how it blinds the Pharisees to the teaching and person of Jesus.

These results, obviously, leave many questions unanswered. Was Pharisaic ancestral custom anchored in a text-interpretive tradition? The sources make no particular reference to text-interpretive practices among Pharisees, although we do find the charge that the tradition can do violence to scriptural norms. If not textually rooted in scriptural interpretation, was the tradition perceived as independent of Scripture but in some sense equally important? Christian sources give us little basis upon which to judge. How was the authority of Pharisaic tradition conceived by those who submitted to it? The synoptics represent its authority as grounded in ancestral usage rather than in the personal authority of the teacher. This idea seems convincing, but in light of the concern of the Gospels to highlight the charismatic authority of Jesus over against that of tradition, it is possible that Phaisaic traditionalism may be overstated as well.[31] Therefore we cannot entirely discount the role of charismatic teaching authority, of a kind we earlier noticed at Qumran, within Pharisaic circles.[32]

Finally, and most germane to our concerns here: early Christian sources tell us precious little about the specific content of Pharisaic text-interpretive tradition and nothing about the *form*—oral, written, or some combination of each—in which it might have been transmitted. That is, if Christian sources of the first century were our only source of knowledge about Pharisaic tradition, it is unlikely that we would suspect that it was privileged as a purely oral tradition uncontaminated by the written word. There may be more to say on this last subject after a survey of the representation of Pharisaism in the most exhaustive first-century source on the nature of Second Temple Jewish society.

The Writings of Josephus

The extant writings of Flavius Josephus are among the most important and well-studied sources for the history of the Jews during the Second Temple period. His discussions of the Pharisees, in particular, woven throughout writings produced over the course of the last two decades of the first century CE, form the basis of virtually all academic accounts of the nature of Pharisaism prior to the first century.[33] In his various accounts of Pharisaic involvement in Judean politics during the Hasmonean dynasty, during the reign of Herod, and in the last decades prior to the war against Rome, Josephus consistently portrays the Pharisees as a disciplined political group promoting as part of its program a scrupulous adherence to ancestral Jewish tradition anchored in the laws of Moses.[34] Unfortunately, he shares virtually nothing about the particulars of this tradition. Were Josephus our only source for Pharisaic customs, for example, we would know nothing about the Pharisaic hand-washing and tithing that otherwise looms so large in the Gospels. While somewhat more forthcoming about the ideological justifications of Pharisaic tradition and its relation to larger Pharisaic political goals, Josephus' statements remain frustratingly vague and difficult to interpret with finality. Nevertheless, the confluence of Josephus and the Gospel accounts on the conjunction of Pharisaic legal expertise and traditionalism is an important fact.

We cannot in this space survey all of Josephus' reports. Instead we will focus principally on a single passage, Antiquities 13:295–298,[35] which has often served as the hermeneutical foundation for interpreting other Josephan reports about the nature and authority of text-interpretive tradition among the Pharisees. Unparalleled in Josephus' earlier work, War, it portrays the Pharisees as a group already in existence during the reign of John Hyrcanus (134–103 BCE), the first Hasmonean ruler to hold the title of High Priest and King.

Josephus' report assumes an excellent working relationship between John Hyrcanus and the Pharisees at the outset of his reign and attempts to explain how the relationship soured. The setting for the Josephan narrative is a celebratory meal in which Hyrcanus, described as "one of [the Pharisees'] disciples . . . and greatly loved by them" (Antiquities 13:289),[36] gathers his Pharisaic allies around him. In response to the king's invitation for advice about how he might perfect his reign, a Pharisee named Eleazar points out a flaw in Hyrcanus' lineage that, according to Lev. 21:14, would disqualify him for the High Priesthood. In the ensuing embarassment, a Sadducean opponent of the Pharisees, Jonathan, takes advantage of the situation to curry favor with the discomfited king (Antiquities 13:296–297):

> And Jonathan exacerbated his anger greatly and achieved the following result: he induced Hyrcanus to join the party of the Sadducees, to abandon the Pharisees, to

repeal the ordinances [*nomima*] that they had established among the people, and to punish those who observed these ordinances.

For our purposes, the crucial part of this passage is the suggestion that Pharisees possessed ordinances that they believed ought to apply to all Jews beyond the Pharisaic community per se. Indeed, it appears that the primary motive for Pharisaic involvement with the Hasmonean court was to influence the king to institutionalize their ordinances as the law of the land. Presumably, it was precisely these that were revoked with Hyrcanus' defection to the Sadducees.

Josephus' account now continues with a brief, but famous, explanation of the nature of these "ordinances" (Antiquities 13: 297–298):

> [T]he Pharisees passed on to the people certain ordinances [*nomima*] from a succession of fathers [*ex pateron diadoches*], which are not written down [*anagegraphtai*] in the laws [*nomois*] of Moses. For this reason the party of the Sadducees dismisses these ordinances, averring that one need only recognize the written ordinances [*nomima ta gegrammena*], whereas those from the tradition of the fathers [*paradoseos ton pateron*] need not be observed.

This passage is a notorious intepretive crux among Josephus scholars.

Many have proposed that this account of the differences between Pharisees and Sadducees demonstrates that a fully developed concept of orally transmitted, unwritten law received from Sinai stands behind the Josephan references to "ordinances from a succession of fathers, which are not written down in the laws of Moses."[37] That is, the rabbinic concept of Torah in the Mouth—if not the specific terminology—would be fully in place by the mid-second century BCE. Others have pointed out that Josephus' reference to laws not written in Scripture need not imply that the laws were as a matter of principle transmitted orally—only that they constituted an acknowledged tradition supplemental to scriptural law.[38] The implication of this position is, of course, that the link between rabbinic Oral Torah and the Pharisaic "tradition of the fathers" remains undemonstrated.

With the recent work of Steve Mason, this dispute appears to have been decisively resolved. Mason has combed the Josephan oeuvre for other appearances of the key terms that appear in this passage (*nomima, anagrapho, oi pateres, paradosis, diadoche*).[39] On this basis he concludes that the present passage "says nothing whatsoever about the question whether the Pharisees actually transmitted their teachings orally or in writing. . . . Josephus has nothing to say about the matter. His point is that the Pharisaic ordinances were not part of the written Law of Moses and that for this reason they were rejected by the Sadducees."[40]

Once Antiquities 13:297–298 is removed from consideration as a source of evidence for Pharisaic conceptions of oral-performative tradition of textual interpretation or legal rulings, there are no other Josephan reports that raise any suggestion that the authority of Pharisaic text-interpretative tradition depended either on a theory of Mosaic origins or on an explicit commitment to oral preservation alone. Josephus' accounts of Pharisaic success in winning the ear of Queen Alexandra Salome after the death of her husband, Alexander Jannaeus, tell us what we already know. The Pharisees were "exact exponents of the laws" (*tous nomos akribesteron*) of the country (War 1:110–111), determining them in accord with the "traditions of their fathers" (*pateroan paradosin*: Antiquities 13:408). The characterization of the Pharisees as diligent legal interpreters appears as well in Josephus' well-known ethnography of the Essene, Sadducean, and Pharisaic "philosophies" (War, 2:162, Antiquities 18:12), while their "extremely precise adherence to the ancestral heritage" (*exakribosei mega pronoun tou patrioi*) during the Herodian period is noted at Antiquities 17:41.

In sum, the Josephan account of the Pharisaic text-interpretive tradition tells us about how the Pharisees proposed to disseminate its legal norms, but nothing about literary substance or form. Josephus shows only that the Pharisees—whether vying for influence in the courts of John Hyrcanus, Alexander Jannaeus, Alexandra Salome, or Herod—pursued a single-minded effort to establish the results of their own traditions of painstaking interpretation of ancestral law as the official program of the state. In this, of course, they are no different from Josephus' Sadducees or the anonymous writer of the Qumranian "Halakhic Letter," who, attempting to win the ear of a reigning Hasmonean king with regard to a series of legal disputes affecting access to the Temple, begs him to "reflect upon all this and pray for Him to correct/ your counsel and to remove from you evil plans and the promptings of Belial/ so that you may rejoice at the end of time, as you discover that some of our words are true" (4QMMT C:28–30).[41]

The Rabbinic Literature

Turning now to the rabbinic representations of Pharisaic tradition, we recall the earlier caveat against assuming too readily a simple preservation of Pharisaic materials in rabbinic sources. At the same time, it is only fair to acknowledge a few stubborn facts that suggest some sort of key link between the Pharisees and the later rabbinic Sages. One is the matter of Gamaliel, mentioned in Acts 5:34–42 as a Pharisaic leader and in Acts 22:3 as Paul's guide to Pharisaic teachings. A "Rabban Gamaliel the Elder"[42] figures prominently in rabbinic literature as an early first-century Sage, a skeptic regarding priestly (perhaps Sadducean) observance of purity regulations (T. Avodah Zarah 3:10), and an influential transmitter of ancient tradition. So here is one Second Temple period Sage who is recalled outside of the rabbinic tradition as a Pharisee and whose image in rabbinic tradition fits the profile of a Pharisee—a person expert in an ancestral legal tradition who distances himself from the official Temple priesthood.[43]

Further tantalizing correspondences between figures valorized in rabbinic tradition as leading Sages and identified outside of that tradition as Pharisees are supplied by Josephus. The "Simon, son of Gamaliel" mentioned by Josephus as "a native of Jerusalem, of a very illustrious family, and of the sect of the Pharisees, who have the reputation of being unrivalled experts in their country's laws" (Life 190–191) is surely identical to the Sage known in rabbinic tradition as Rabban Shimon b. Gamaliel. There he is recalled as a figure in the mid-first-century succession of leadership who, on at least one occasion, acknowledged his opposition to Sadducean practices regarding laws of the Sabbath rest (M. Eruvin 6:2).[44] While he is not explicitly identified in rabbinic sources as a Pharisee, the memory of his conflict with a Sadducee supports the clear Josephan claim about his party affiliation.

Second, but less compelling, is Josephus' reference to the Pharisees Pollion and Samaias (Antiquities 15:370–371), who came into conflict with Herod. It is tantalizing to see here garbled references to the shadowy "pair," Shemaiah and Avtalion, mentioned in M. Avot 1:10, or perhaps to the famous first-century shapers of rabbinic legal tradition Hillel and Shammai, whom M. Avot 1:12 names as having received the traditions of Shemaiah and Avtalion. All of these figures overlap with the Herodian period, and there is an undeniable euphony of names. Nevertheless, Neusner's judgment is probably wisest: "efforts to fill in the gaps by identifying Shemaiah and Avtalion with Pollion the Pharisee and his disciple Samaias of Josephus . . . have little in their favor, apart from the approximate similarity of the names of Shamaiah and Samaias."[45]

It is beyond serious doubt, then, that there was some participation of Pharisees in the shaping of what ultimately became second- and third-century rabbinism. But this participation does not of itself give us much confidence that rabbinic traditions offer reliable pictures of any aspect of Pharisaism. This difficulty is particularly true regarding the authority of tradition, which played such a crucial role in the promulgation and spread of rabbinic teaching from the third century and onward. At issue is not merely the historical difficulty of attempting to describe the pre-70 forms of ideas and institutions first attested in rabbinic texts of the third century and later; there is also the very basic question of names. A crucial problem in using the rabbinic literature for insight into any aspect of pre-70 Pharisaism is that it is rarely clear which, if any, of the various coherent groups mentioned in these sources are in fact identical to the Pharisees we met in Josephus or the early Christian writings.[46]

In rabbinic literature, the most common collective term for figures perceived as members of the rabbinic community of learning is the Hebrew word "Sages" (*ḥkmym*). When referring to the pre-70 forbears of the rabbinic movement of the second to sixth centuries, this term dominates as well.[47] The only text, for example, that explicitly identifies Pharisees (*prwšym*) as *ḥkmym* is a passage, cited as a Tannaitic tradition, appearing for the first time in the Babylonian Talmud in the mouth of the fourth-century Pumbeditan Sage Abbaye (B. Qiddushin 66a).[48] This text is also commonly cited to prove the antiquity of an orally mediated interpretive tradition among the Second Temple Pharisees.[49] It is therefore, despite its relatively late entry into the rabbinic literary tradition, a useful point of entry for our discussion.

The story is a rabbinic version of the incident reported in Josephus, Antiquities 13:288–297, that led to John Hyrcanus' persecution of the Pharisees. In the Talmud, however, the incident is located in the reign of Hyrcanus' son and successor, Alexander Jannaeus, who appears in this account as "Yannai the King."[50] This and other discrepancies between the Josephan and talmudic story needn't detain us, for our point is not to solve the literary-traditional puzzles presented by these two accounts.[51] Let us rather focus on the representation of the Pharisees in the talmudic account.

In celebration of a military victory, Yannai gathers together "all the Sages of Israel" for a feast. One Elazar b. Poirah, whose motivation remains unclear, urges the king to raise the question of the legitimacy of his service as High Priest, insinuating that "the hearts of the Pharisees are set against you." In response, an "elder [*zqn*], Yehudah b. Gedidiah," brings to light the rumor of Yannai's mother's captive status. The rumor is disproven and "the Sages of Israel departed" in bitter circumstances. Within this brief story, the terms "Sages," "elder," and "Pharisees" all appear in close proximity and are virtual synonyms. Clearly the narrator sees no crucial distinctions among them.

Let us take a brief look at the conclusion of the Tannaitic narrative (1, 3), follow-ing the departure of the Sages. Note in particular the interpolated comment of the fourth-century Pumbeditan Sage Rav Nahman b. Yitzhak (2):

> 1. [Yannai the King asked Elazar:] What shall I do? [Elazar replied:] If you take my advice, crush them! [Replied Yannai the King:] But the Torah—what will become of it [if its teachers are destroyed]? [Replied Elazar:] Look—it is bound and stored in the corner! Whoever wants to learn may come and learn!
>> 2. Said Rav Nahman b. Yitzhak: Immediately a spirit of heresy entered [Yannai the King], for he should have said: The Written Torah will fare well, but what will become of the Oral Torah?
> 3. Now immediately the evil burst forth through Elazar b. Poirah and he killed all the Sages of Israel. And the world was devastated until Shimon b. Shetah arose and restored the Torah to its former status.[52]

Yannai the King (1) worries about the fate of Torah instruction in Israel if he exacts his vengeance against the Sages/Pharisees, but his worries are allayed by Elazar. If they are eliminated, points out Elazar, the text will survive as other expounders—presumably more to his liking—come to replace the Sages. The Pharisees/Sages are destroyed until another hero of Torah, Shimon b. Shetah, arises to restore Torah learning among the people (3).

The contrasts between the putatively Tannaitic material of units 1 and 3 and the Amoraic interpolation of 2 are important. The Pharisees/Sages of the Tannaitic nar-rative are represented as teachers of "Torah," expounders of a holy text. Rav Nahman, however, reads the narrative through a fourth-century lens thoroughly colored by Amoraic conceptions of the exclusively oral transmission of rabbinic tradition. He is astounded that Yannai the King expresses no concern for the preservation of the unwritten Torah and he can attribute this carelessness only to theological deviance. Clearly, it is Rav Nahman, not the Tannaitic narrator, who regards the Pharisees/Sages as bearers of a tradition of orally transmitted exposition of the Torah.

It is notoriously precarious to assign dates to traditions internal to rabbinic compi-lations, as the compositional and transmissional processes of the rabbinic literature remain imperfectly understood. And this passage is no exception. But there are a few clues to guide us in suggesting an earliest point for the circulation of its key assump-tion that the Sages of old are in some sense identical to the ancient Pharisees.

The narrative, I have pointed out, is first attested by a fourth-century Sage, Abbaye. While it is represented as originating in early Tannaitic tradition, it appears in none of the earlier compilations of Tannaitic material. Indeed, rabbinic tradition preserves no stories about the reign of Yannai the King until he is linked to the career of Shimon b. Shetah in a Tannaitic narrative cited in the Palestinian Talmud by the mid-third-century Sage Rabbi Yirmiya b. Abba (Y. Berakhot 7:2, 11b/Y. Nazir 5:3, 54b).[53] So it would seem that a third-century date for the present form of this narrative would be possible. Also pointing toward a third-century point of origin is the absence from the body of the text of any mention of an orally transmitted Torah. This is the contribution of a later, fourth-century, glossator—Rav Nahman. While the substance of the story—the origin of the conflict between Pharisees and a Hasmonean ruler—is certainly ancient, as Baumgarten has shown, the narrative identification of Pharisees and Sages cannot be projected earlier than the third century CE. In all, our passage is a very poor foundation upon which to build a case either for the antiquity of the connection between Pharisees and Sages or for the development among Pharisees of an ideological commitment to the transmission of an exclusively oral tradition of textual interpretation.

The general lack of rabbinic interest in drawing historical connections between Pharisaic and rabbinic intellectual lineages is surprising, given the great value assigned in the Mishnah and all later rabbinic compilations to delineating patterns of intellectual tradition through chains of transmission (e.g., M. Avot 1:1ff.). It is therefore curious that, while there are a number of rabbinic texts that refer to Pharisees as an identifiable Second Temple community, there is little suggestion in them that the transmitters of these texts found here references to their own immediate predecessors. We can confine ourselves, for present purposes, to the Tannaitic compilations that most probably contain traditions formulated from the second through the early third centuries.[54]

The most important of these, because it is commonly read as proof of rabbinic continuity with the Pharisees, is found in M. Yadayim 4:6–7. The passage records a series of disputes between Pharisees and Sadducees[55] regarding matters of law for which the Torah provides no explicit ruling:

1. (M. Yad.4:6) Sadducees say: We challenge you, Pharisees! For you rule: "The sacred writings render the hands unclean, but the Homeric books do not render the hands unclean."[56]
2. Said Rabban Yohanan b. Zakkai: And have we only this against the Pharisees? Behold, they rule: "The bones of an ass are clean, but the bones of Yohanan the High Priest are unclean!"[57]
    3. [The Sadducees] replied: According to their preciousness is their uncleanness, so that a person will not turn the bones of his father and mother into spoons!

    He replied: So, too, regarding the sacred writings—in accordance with their value is their uncleanness. But the Homeric books, which have no value—they do not render the hands unclean.
4. (M. Yad.4:7) Sadducees say: We challenge you, Pharisees! For you declare clean the spout of liquid.[58]
5. Pharisees say: We challenge you, Sadducees! For you declare clean a stream of water flowing from a cemetery![59]
6. Sadducees say: We challenge you, Pharisees! For you rule: "My ox and my ass that have caused damage—we are obliged for compensation [as at Ex. 21:35]; but my male or female slave who has caused damage—we are exempt from compensation."[60]
    7. But consider: concerning my ox and my ass, upon which I'm obliged to perform no commandments, I am still obliged for damage they cause; doesn't it follow, concerning my male and female slave, upon whom I'm indeed obliged to perform commandments, that I should be obliged for damage they cause?

    They replied: No! If you raise the case of my ox or my ass, which have no power of intention, will you also persist regarding my male or female slave, who indeed have the power of intention? For if I abuse him, he may go and torch another's harvest, and I would be obliged for compensation.

On the basis of purely literary-formulaic considerations, the passage consists of two distinct elements. A list (1–2 + 4–6) governed by a distinctive compositional formula (X say: We challenge you, Y, because of Z) has been supplemented by explanatory material (3, 7). This formal distinction between the compositional elements corresponds to an interesting distinction in viewpoint as well.

In the core list, Pharisees and Sadducees are set against each other with no explicit suggestion as to which party the composer favors. Indeed, there may even be a hint of preference for the Sadducean positions: an important Sage of the early Yavnean period, Rabban Yohanan b. Zakkai, weighs in against the Pharisees with his own complaint (2), and the Sadducees fire the last salvo (6). The supplements to this core list, however, reorient the entire point. The interchange between Rabban Yohanan and Sadducees at 3 now shows his statement at 2 to have been ironic: he in fact agrees with the Pharisees on the capacity of Scriptures to defile the hands, and he bases his view on a principle that the Sadducees themselves are made to articulate: "preciousness" and the capacity to defile are integrally connected. Similarly, the debate between Sadducees and Pharisees at 7 results in a Pharisaic victory grounded in the power of logic.[61]

As I have already pointed out, it is dangerous to attempt to date the "composition" of any compositional unit in the rabbinic corpus. But insofar as the legal positions ascribed here to the Pharisees tend to be adopted in other Mishnaic passages, it seems likely that M. Yadayim 4:6–7 (+8) reached its present form during the late second-century or early third-century decades that witnessed the overall compositional work that yielded the Mishnah. Its core list, however, is likely to be older. How much older, it is impossible to say. At least two of these disputed issues (2, 4) are attested in the Qumranian Halakhic Letter (4QMMT B:22–23, 55–58) to have separated its writer from a dominant Jewish party in the second century BCE.[62] So even if we cannot date the formulation of the core list that early, it surely preserves memories that emerge very early in the historiography of legal Jewish disputation.

What appears to have happened is that a pre-70 catalogue of Pharisaic–Sadducean disputes, represented at least in part by our core list, has been preserved in the rabbinic Mishnah. Its preservation, however, came at the price of editorial modifications that shift the original emphasis of the tradition. What began as a neutral or mildly pro-Sadducean list of disputes was reconstructed into an example of legal reasoning that aligns the Pharisaic views more closely to the legal positions taken in the later rabbinic tradition.

M. Yadayim 4:6–7 confirms many details about Pharisees that we have noticed elsewhere. First, it corroborates the Josephan picture of the Pharisees and Sadducees as groups in legal conflict. It also confirms the picture—of 4QMMT and the Gospels—that purity served as a point of contention among interpreters of scriptural law in late Second Temple times. It even testifies that certain elements of Second Temple Pharisaic legal tradition played a formative role in the shaping of the Mishnah's representation of its own halakhic tradition. *But M. Yadayim 4:6–7 does not confirm that the literary framers of this third-century* CE *tractate, believed themselves to be descendants of the Pharisees.* The Mishnah's concern is to establish the ancient lineage of legal principles and reasoning, through the mediation of a genuine rabbinic hero, Rabban Yohanan b. Zakkai (e.g., M. Avot 2:8, M. Rosh Hashannah 4:1–4, T. Parah

3:8), who is himself never identified as a Pharisee, even though he is made to speak on their behalf. But it shows little interest in creating the impression of communal continuity and identity between pre-70 Pharisees and third-century Sages.

The passages we have just examined constitute the strongest evidence for simple social continuity between Pharisaism and rabbinism. Even so, the case for such continuity is a weak one. The earliest rabbinic identification of Pharisees and Sages can be assigned to a source cited no earlier than fourth century CE Pumbedita (B. Qiddushin 66a), whereas a classic, early portrayal of Pharisaic–Sadducean conflict (M. Yadayim 4:6–7) shows only that some elements of Pharisaic legal tradition were embraced by the Mishnaic editors. But neither the Tannaitic foundation of B. Qiddushin 66a nor M. Yadayim 4:6–7 knows anything about the exclusively oral transmission of Pharisaic interpretive tradition.

Let us examine one last passage that often appears in attempts to link the third-century Sages to pre-70 Pharisaic communities.[63] When we meet a group in the Mishnah and Tosefta that corresponds most closely to the Gospels' portrayal of Pharisaic obsession with tithing, hand-washing and other concerns involving cleanness, we find them referred to not as "Pharisees," but as "Associates" (*ḥbrym*). The richest source for this group is found in T. Demai 2:2–3:9, some form of which probably underlies the extremely truncated presentation of the rules for joining the Association (*ḥbrwt*) adumbrated in M. Demai 2:2–3.[64] The Tosefta offers a compendious collection of rulings regarding requirements for admission into Associate status, the conduct expected of Associates, and the nature of Associates' relationships with Jews, including family members who may not be members of the Association.

T. Demai 2:2 and M. Demai 2:3 offer rather different criteria for defining the primary obligations of the Associate.[65] They agree, however, that the discipline of the Associate is defined in contrast to the practices of the *'m h'rṣ* (vocalized as *am ha-aretz*). This term, in its distinctively rabbinic meaning, is best rendered as "an undisciplined Jew." It refers primarily to Jews whose ignorance or carelessness regarding rabbinic disciplines of tithing behavior and ritual cleanness places their food under suspicion of being untithed or ritually unfit for consumption.

In this vein, T. Dem. 2:2 holds that the Associate

> shall not offer heave-offering and tithes to an undisciplined Jew [of priestly lineage]; and he shall not prepare clean foods in the presence of [*'ṣl*][66] an undisciplined Jew [of common lineage]; and he shall eat his non-sanctified food in conditions of cleanness.

The Mishnah, for its part, specifies that the Associate

> does not sell wet or dry [produce] to an undisciplined Jew [of priestly or common lineage]; and he does not purchase wet [produce] from him; and he does not accept the hospitality of the undisciplined Jew; and he does not receive him [in the Associate's home] while [such a Jew] is wearing his own clothing.

It is not the differences, but the convergences that concern us here. For both texts the Associate's responsibility is twofold: (1) to ensure that he does not aid the undisciplined Jew in consuming untithed produce or in rendering food ritually unclean, and (2) to ensure that he is personally untainted by the uncleanness common among undisciplined Jews.

The Tosefta assumes that such undisciplined Jews are found throughout the social hierarchy, from the priesthood down to the peasantry. Therefore the undisciplined Jew is not merely an ignorant or unlettered Jew; he could be a priest learned in priestly lore who neglected the specific practices prescribed for the Association. The surprising aspect of the Tosefta's discussion is that, despite the restrictions against close association with undisciplined Jews, the boundary between the Associates and such Jews is fairly permeable. As the Tosefta's catalogue of rules unfolds, it soon becomes clear that undisciplined Jews are assumed to be able to take trustworthy vows of conforming to practices of the Association (T. Demai 2:3, 2:5), upon which point, presumably, they enter the same period of training incumbent upon other initiates (T. Demai 2:10–12). It is taken for granted, moreover, that Associates may live in households with undisciplined Jews, either blood relatives or apprentices (T. Demai 2:15–19, 3:5, 3:9). And most surprisingly, it is even understood that Associates and undisciplined Jews might, under the proper circumstances, join together at times of rejoicing over food and drink (T. Demai 3:6–8), as long as proper precautions have been taken to ensure the ritual fitness of the refreshment.

There are many obvious similarities between the Mishnaic and Toseftan descriptions of the Association and the early Christian description of Pharisaism. It is tempting, following Chaim Rabin, to suppose that the term "Association" was used by Pharisees among themselves to describe initiates into their own inner circle.[67] Yet even if we grant the possiblity that the Association is nothing other than a Pharisaic fellowship, some cautionary points must be made.

First, the Toseftan and Mishnaic materials are ambiguous about the relationship between members of the Association and the group known as Sages. Among the composers and transmitters of this material, the groups were seen as overlapping but not identical. In the Mishnah, for example, the mid-second-century authority Rabbi Yehudah includes among his own requirements for membership in the Association the proviso that the applicant "has served [the Sages] in the House of Study" (M. Demai 2:3). From his point of view, then, participation in the collective life of learning among the Sages should be part of the training for Association membership. But at this point not all Associates have come under the umbrella of the Sages. He would like to remedy that situation. Significantly, the Mishnah represents the anonymous disputants of Rabbi Yehudah as disagreeing with him regarding this criterion: "They said to him: These [additional criteria, including service in the House of Study] are not part of the procedure [for membership]" (M. Demai 2:3). While Rabbi Yehudah would knit the Association more tightly to the group of Sages, his colleagues argue for a greater distinction between the two groups.

The Tosefta, for its part, seems closer to the position staked out in the Mishnah by Rabbi Yehudah, even though he is not cited in its discussion (T. Dem. 2:13):

1. One who comes to accept upon himself the discipline of an Associate—even if he is a disciple of a Sage [*tlmyd ḥkm*],[68] he must state his acceptance [through a verbal formula].
2. But a Sage [*ḥkm*][69] who holds a place in the learning community (*yšybh*) need not state his acceptance, for he already did so when he took his place.
3. Abba Shaul says: Also: a disciple of a Sage needn't state his acceptance. Furthermore, others can declare their acceptance before him![70]

The three rulings explore the contrast between the situation of the disciple of the Sage and the Sage himself regarding membership in the Association. The assumption is that the Association is a group which Sages and their disciples may join. Rulings 1 and 2 point out that the Sage, by virtue of his teaching role, is granted automatic entry into the Association, while disciples are required to make a formal declaration of intent to abide by the Association's discipline. Abba Shaul (3), a late first- to early second-century figure, dissents from the first ruling, granting the disciple equal status with the Sage regarding membership.

The Mishnaic and Toseftan passages indicate that the relationship between the Association and the Sages was a live issue from about the turn of the second century (Abba Shaul) into its second half (Rabbi Yehudah), a generation or so after Pharisaism had ceased to exist as a distinct political and religious community in Jewish Palestine. Surely this is not a stretch of time so vast as to totally confuse memories of late Second Temple sectarian fellowships. Yet if the Association of the Mishnah and the Tosefta ultimately had its roots in Second Temple Pharisaism, neither the Mishnah nor the Tosefta assumes that Pharisaic Associates were by virtue of that fact also Sages. Indeed, if anything, we detect a tendency to conceptually disinguish the Association from the Sages as the second century continues.[71]

Finally, and most germane to the larger purpose of this chapter, is the utter absence from these descriptions of the Association's discipline of any mention of the source of its rules or the nature of their authority. The foundation of the Association's tithing and purity rulings are never linked to any specific biblical source or ascribed to the authority of an orally preserved legal tradition. Moreover, the texts are vague on so crucial a matter as whether the Associate's discipline stems from the traditions cultivated by the Sages or stands substantially independent of that tradition. If the Sages are a society distinct from the Associates, it is at least plausible to suppose that they linked themselves to divergent lines of tradition. The very capacity of our texts to imagine a distinction between the Sages and the Associates suggests, in fact, that the sources of the Association's discipline were conceived to be independent of the larger tradition cultivated among the Sages. The Sages of the Mishnah, in short, did not imagine their intellectual or communitarian ancestors to have been Pharisaic participants in the Association.

This negative result regarding the primary focus of this study has further implications as well. Neusner's studies of the history of Mishnaic law showed, long ago, the root of many rabbinic legal ideas in prerabbinic and conceivably Pharisaic milieus.[72] It is futile to argue against some degree of continuity between the substance of Pharisaic legal and text-interpretive tradition and the substance of rabbinic halakhic thought in its earliest periods. But the continuities of substance, however suggestive they might be, are not evidence for continuities of social identity between the two communities. On the basis of rabbinic sources, it is impossible to show that the Sages had a long-standing historical understanding of their own roots in ancient Pharisaic communities.

Indeed, were such an understanding current in the second and third centuries, we might have expected it to be cultivated by Palestinian Sages under Roman hegemony as yet further evidence of their connection to a prestigious pre-70 community discussed in the widely read works of Josephus. The absence of such memories in the Mishnah and the Tosefta suggests that it was simply not a significant element in the larger rabbinic image of the past—or at least that such memories were deemed unworthy of preservation.

We have noted, however, that such connections begin to be cultivated in the Tannaitic and Amoraic traditions preserved in the Babylonian Talmud, bypassing the earlier Palestinian Talmud. It is indeed likely that the editors of the latter, working as they did under Christian political domination in late fourth-century Palestine, would have had little incentive to develop or cultivate memories of Pharisaic connections that had slender basis in the received traditions of the Mishnah and its associated texts. But Babylonian Sages living among Christians in a society governed by Zoroastrians may well have found some value in exploiting Christian perceptions that the Sages were heirs of the Pharisees, just as they enjoyed circulating unflattering stories about Jesus.[73] In any case, the Talmud Bavli's interest in either Jesus or the Pharisees is so slim that anti-Christian polemic hardly serves as the sole explanation for their circulation. Ultimately the Babylonian traditions linking Sages to Pharisees do not yield to a simplistic ideological explanation. And these traditions have little bearing at all on the historical question of rabbinic origins.

Summary

This chapter has examined a variety of sources often cited as evidence for a Pharisaic ideological commitment to the transmission of an orally preserved and transmitted text-interpretive tradition. In each case, the sources have proven to be far more ambiguous than many historians have commonly represented them. Clearly, Pharisees preserved customary practices, including a ritualized concern for preservation of purity, that they conceived to be mandated in the Torah of Moses.[74] Such may be said of the Yahad as well, who, as we saw in the previous chapter, grounded the authority of communal disciplinary rules in prophecy rather than in ancestral oral tradition.[75]

In contrast to the Yahad, there is little doubt that such customary practices were transmitted in Pharisaism with the understanding that their authority was grounded neither in the exegetical brilliance of living teachers nor in the inspired utterings of contemporary prophets. Rather, their authority was vested in the venerable traditions of ancient teachers received from the past and transmitted with accuracy into the future. Here the Pharisees may indeed have had some disputes with the prophetic self-understandings of their Qumranian contemporaries. We may surmise, moreover, given what seems to be virtually universal practice among other scribal communities of Second Temple times, that Pharisaic scribes and their students had a memorized fluency in the scriptural text as well as an extensive mastery of the orally mediated text-interpretive traditions in which it was carried. Presumably, they expounded the scriptural text in oral settings of instruction as did all other Jewish groups.

So, like any scribal community of the Second Temple period, the Pharisees would have borne their scriptural texts within a rich tapestry of oral-performative interpretive tradition. But did the Pharisees—in contradistinction to every other scribal community of Second Temple Jewish Palestine—hesitate to write down the results of such instruction or otherwise insist that the results had always been transmitted orally since Mosaic times and must so remain? Our only surviving reporters with a plausible claim to personal knowledge of first-century Pharisaism—the apostle Paul and the historian Josephus—say nothing about this. And none of the sources before us has suggested that anyone held this view of the Pharisaic conception of tradition earlier than the third or fourth century CE, when rabbinic masters of the Oral Torah began to find their own institution mirrored in images of the ancient past.

The most we can say is that the Pharisees, like other Second Temple communities invested in scribal practices, are likely to have enjoyed a richly oral and aural experience of written texts, particularly those of Scripture. But unlike the case of the Yahad, whose own writings have revealed clues about the actual study practices that mediated textual knowledge, there is nothing produced within Pharisaism that might guide us to a richer knowledge of this crucial community's experience of its own text-interpretive tradition—and, I must add, nothing produced by interested bystanders.

At the close of this first section of this study, a single point should be emphasized. Wherever we look in the scribal communities of Second Temple Judaism in Palestine, we find a busy engagement with sophisticated written works of epic scope, and a richly developed heritage of interpretive insight and orally mediated tradition. We find reading practices linked closely to public ceremony and instruction in which oral communication was the primary medium of textual knowledge. But we find virtually no shred of interest in the orality of the oral-performative literary tradition as such. As we saw in chapter 1, the human voice was linked ideologically to the prophetic or divine origins of great books, establishing the authority of the contemporaries who mediated that primordial, authorizing voice in their performative recitations. But where tradition was perceived at all, its oral character went unregistered. For such Jews, Torah was orally delivered and aurally received, communicated from mouth to ear in syllables laid forth in written works. But there was as yet no "Torah in the Mouth."

PART TWO

ORAL TRADITION
AND EARLY RABBINISM
*The Spoken Word in an Ideology
of Tradition*

4

Tannaitic Tradition as
an Object of Rabbinic Reflection

The End of Scribalism and the Emergence of Tradition

A century and a half elapsed between the Roman defeat of Palestinian Jewry in 73 and the compilation of the earliest rabbinic literary texts in the early third century. Two major wars—the rebellion of 66–73 and the bid for renewed independence in 132–135—along with their attendant economic and demographic dislocations had radically changed the face of Palestinian Jewry.

First-century Palestinian Jewish society had been centered in Judea, its climate of opinion shaped by such contending groups as priestly and scribal elites, cultic societies of the sort represented by the Yahad and Pharisees, and politicized followers of one or another messianic claimant. But the third century offered a different picture. The depopulation of Judea encouraged richer Jewish settlement in the Galilean hills, expanding urban life in what had once been a cultural backwater.[1] The later efflorescence of Palestinian Jewish culture reflected in rabbinic literature and other archeological evidence was, however, still in its nascent period.

Intellectual and cultural elites had yet to fill the vacuum left by the departure of traditional shapers of thought. Priestly families seem to have retained influential social positions for a time, despite the loss of their primary cultic function.[2] But High Priests and Sadducees were by now the stuff of garbled historical memory. Similarly, Pharisees survived as hazy figures in narratives of antiquity, while the Yahad had all but vanished in the collective recollection of the past. Most influential followers of the Messiah, Jesus, had come to define themselves as a community beyond Judaism. Scribes, however, remained as copiers of scriptural texts and the necessary documents of public life. They served large settlements of Jews centrally located in the Galilee of the Land of Israel and throughout Mesopotamia. And among them were small circles of wisdom teachers and their disciples, whose titular use of a common form of respectful address, *rabbi* (*rby*, "my Master"), would ultimately distinguish them from other sectors of Jewish society.[3]

Precisely the way in which the rabbinic movement formed within the power vacuum of post-70 Jewish Palestine, the social composition of the groups who collectively came to call themselves Sages, the identities of the figures who played a central role in the formation of the rabbinic community—all these are subjects of continual speculation among historians of early Judaism.[4] I shall not contribute to this speculation here, but there is one small point that we must observe, since it has a central bearing upon the particular way in which the earliest rabbinic literary sources portray the oral-performative tradition cultivated among the Sages.

The destruction of Jerusalem meant, among other things, the end of the central focus of scribal literary culture in Jewish Palestine. The scribal profession, of course, had long been pursued beyond the framework of the Temple economy and education, as the scribal activity in the Yahad attests. Nevertheless, as long as the Temple stood, it remained a fundamental hub of scribal culture, in terms of which dissident groups marked their ideological differences through articulate scribal productions. The destruction of the Temple did not put an end to scribal culture: the social functions of scribes beyond the copying of books, such as notarial services, ensured their continued usefulness and thus the continuity of a professional identity. But the close association of scribal skills with priestly birth or service to priestly communities and their ideologies seems to have been sundered. The Second Temple period's common literary representation of the scribe—as the effective voice of the ancient prophets recorded in the texts of ancient revealed books—fell into decline. It was replaced by a more mundane appreciation of the scribe as a technician performing an essential, but ultimately mundane service.[5]

Scholars have long observed in the earliest rabbinic literature a marked decline in the religious status accorded the priesthood.[6] That this fate befell the scribe as well seems to have been overlooked. Rabbinic traditions compiled by the early third century know of some Sages who are scribes,[7] and on rare occasion even refer to the Sages collectively as scribes.[8] But whatever role professional scribes might have played in the formative decades of the rabbinic community, by the early third century they seem to stand at the outskirts of the rabbinic group rather than at the institutional or ideological center. This marginality is captured in the trenchant observation of M. Sotah 9:15: "Since the day of the destruction of the Sanctified House the Sages declined to the level of scribes and the scribes to the level of clerks."

The point is crucial, for it may have something to do with the characteristic ideological shift that distinquishes Second Temple scribal groups—whether the Yahad, the Pharisees, or the as yet unidentified groups behind the Enochic and related literatures—from the rabbinic communities of the third century. The difference concerns perceptions of the role of oral communication in the genesis and transmission of literary tradition. The scribal literati of Second Temple times, we saw, found the oral life of written texts ideologically meaningful only when reflecting upon the *origins* of the works they themselves composed, copied, and taught. Interpretive tradition per se—the oral-performative matrix of textual communication and explication— was nearly invisible to them as an object of reflective thought.

By contrast, the figures whose opinions are formulated for transmission in the earliest rabbinic texts seem to have been intensely aware of possessing a comprehensive, orally mediated textual tradition containing, among other things, norms that affected the smallest patterns of daily life. That this tradition was found most immediately in the instructions of Sages rather than in written books was taken for granted.

In association with this assumption about the oral means of transmitting authoritative tradition, the figures of priest and scribe, who dominated Second Temple images of legitimate literary tradents, recede from view as principal transmitters of tradition. They are replaced by the image of the Sage, whose authority is grounded not in his scribal skills or his priestly genealogy, but rather in his mastery of wisdom heard from a chain of masters.

Within two and a half centuries of the end of the Second Temple period—surely by the latter quarter of the third century—rabbinic scholars had developed the essential outlines of their conceptions of Torah in Script and Torah in the Mouth.[9] Unlike their predecessors in Second Temple scribal milieus, these Sages had developed a clear distinction between the written sources of textual study and the oral-literary tradition within which the texts were interpreted and the results themselves framed for preservation in a distinctive oral-performative tradition.

The chapters in part II of this study explore aspects of this emergence to ideological explicitness. Chapters 4 and 5, for the most part, focus on the foundations of an ideology of oral tradition in the earliest surviving jurisprudential and historiographic materials preserved within the rabbinic literary record. The focus is on the literature ascribed in the Talmuds to the Tannaim, the "repeaters of tradition" who lived from the late first century BCE to the early third century CE.[10]

First and most important among the Tannaitic sources is the Mishnah, the earliest compilation of rabbinic legal thought, edited in Palestine at the turn of the third century.[11] The Tosefta, a Palestinian companion to the Mishnah, will also figure in this discussion.[12] We shall consult as well a number of Palestinian biblical commentaries (*midrashim*)—commonly regarded as representing Tannaitic opinion—which offer models of early rabbinic text-interpretive tradition in explicit association with the text of the Mosaic Torah, particularly the books of Exodus (Mekhilta of Rabbi Ishmael), Leviticus (Sifra), Numbers, and Deuteronomy (Sifre).[13]

This literature offers a rich, if unsystematic, testimony to the ways in which early rabbinic Sages formulated their awareness of possessing an oral-literary tradition that was at once textually distinct from Scripture yet in some sense definitive of its meaning. It provides as well the basic outlines of how the legal aspects of that oral-literary tradition were perceived by the Sages as constituting the textual foundation of an oral-performative tradition of its own.

The Repeated Tradition as Oral-Literary Tradition

The Tannaitic literature everywhere assumes a simple dichotomy regarding the communication of religiously authoritative knowledge.[14] Knowledge recorded in scriptural texts is "recited" (*qr'*), that is, it is read aloud by sounding out the cues from a written text before the reader's eyes.[15] The resulting recitation is *mqr'* (*miqra*), a term that, by extension, comes to designate the entire tradition of Scripture—"that which is recited [in public instruction as divine teaching]." The rabbinic practice of "reading" is thus wholly continuous with the oral-performative textual delivery familiar from Second Temple scribalism.

The distinction of rabbinic culture from earlier forms of scribal culture becomes evident from the way in which Sages conceived of the text-interpretive tradition that mediated the orally performed scriptural text. Interpretive tradition received by a Sage from his own teacher and transmitted to a disciple is "repeated" (*šnh*) on the basis of what has been "heard" (*šm'*) in association with the written text.[16] That is, knowledge surrounding the scriptural text is a mnemonically managed tradition, reported aloud from memory without any reference to a written source. There is, in this representation at least, no written record to verify the truth of a report, other than the general consensus of tradents regarding what has been transmitted.[17]

The consequences of publicly defying the accepted tradition of "what has been heard" are well described in the deathbed advice of Aqavya b. Mehalelel, a Sage recalled as opposing the consensus of Sages on certain disputed matters (M. Eduyyot 5:7):

> At the hour of his death he said to his son: My son, retract four teachings I used to offer.
> He replied: Why didn't you retract them [earlier] yourself?
> He replied: I heard from the mouth of the majority and they [my opponents] heard from the mouth of the majority. I insisted on what I heard and they insisted on what they heard. But you have heard from an individual and from the multitude. It is best to leave the teachings of an individual and to hold fast to the teachings of the multitude.

Aqavya could not adduce a source to verify his position over against the majority. In the absence of a written textual record, it was the consensus of collective memory that defined the authentic contour of the transmitted tradition over against the insistence of an individual.

In parallelism with the case of Scripture, the repetition of what has been heard and transmitted in collective memory is represented by the nominal form of the crucial root. In this case, *šnh* yields *mšnh* (*mishnah*), "repeated tradition." Such repeated tradition seems to have been conceived not as excerpted from documentary compilations, but rather as teachings associated with specific Sages, or anonymous tradents, who transmitted them as discrete logia. The following formulation, explaining the emendation of a teacher's version of a rule in light of another transmitted version, is typical (M. San. 3:4): "Said Rabbi Yose: This is the repeated tradition [*mšnt*] of Rabbi Aqiva, but the earlier repeated tradition [*mšnh r'šwnh*] was formulated as follows. . . ." Here *mšnh* does not refer to a formal document with a title—"the" Mishnah—but rather to a discrete transmission of information stemming from a person rather than from an objectively available compilation of oral or written texts.[18]

By the mid third century, however, matters had become more complex. The term "repeated tradition" came often to denote not merely a report about a certain matter, but more commonly a collection or compilation of such reports, a work of relatively circumscribed compass, that is, the Mishnah.[19] The Talmuds know of more than one compilation of traditions that circulated with this title,[20] but it is clear that the compilation ascribed to the editorial work of Rabbi Yehudah b. Shimon b. Gamaliel, whose reign as patriarch extended from the late-second to the early-third centuries, ultimately took pride of place in emerging curricula of rabbinic study. Thus the sixth chapter of M. Avot, universally understood to be a late, post-Tannaitic addition, begins: "Sages repeated the following traditions in the idiom of the Mishnah" (M. Avot 6:1).[21]

This terminological shift is itself an important moment in the history of rabbinic tradition, but for the present it is sufficient to note that transmissions of repeated tradition, either as discrete logia or in the form of publicly circulated redactions, are assumed to be orally delivered, aurally received, and managed within the memory. The principal distinction between the repeated tradition of *mšnh* and the oral-performative interpretation of Scripture lies in the textual basis itself. Scripture is pronounced verbatim from a written copy. Rabbinic teaching, including the inherited interpretations of Scripture, is retained in the memory, which serves as the record for the performance of the text. Both texts are orally delivered in the act of one's mastering and communicating them; they differ only in their material form.

In the sources compiled in received texts of the Mishnah and its rather more extensive Toseftan version, there is no question that mastery of the repeated tradition constituted the sine qua non of rabbinic discipleship, for it is precisely the mastery of that tradition through service to a Sage that distinguished disciples from other Jews. One could "hear" the tradition only from someone who had himself heard it from his own teacher. Nevertheless, mastery of both sorts of tradition—the scriptural book and the repeated words of Sages—was regarded as necessary for participation in the rabbinic community of learning:

> Whoever possesses Scripture [*mqr'*], repeated tradition [*mšnh*], and a worldly skill will not quickly sin. . . . But whoever does not possess Scripture, repeated tradition, and a worldly skill has no place in civilized society. (M. Qid. 1:11)

While repeated tradition held pride of place, it was founded on the prior oral mastery of scriptural texts, without which the substance of the repeated tradition remained intellectually unintelligible and morally inaccessible.

This latter point is stressed in a remarkable text which, while not formally in the Mishnaic-Toseftan stream of literary tradition, appears to have been strongly influenced by it in its formative outlines. In Avot de-Rabbi Natan's version of the Hillelite teaching of M. Avot 1:13, the following amplification appears (A12):[22]

> One who fails to serve the Sages is worthy of death. How so?
> An incident concerning a certain person of Bet Ramah who held himself to a high level of piety: Rabban Yohanan b. Zakkai sent to him a certain disciple to investigate him.
> He went and found him taking oil and placing it upon a[n earthenware] stove-range and then taking it from the stove-range and pouring it into his cooking.
> [The disciple] said to him: What are you doing?
> He replied: I am [behaving as][23] a High Priest who eats his heave offering in a state of purity!
> [The disciple] asked: This stove-range—is it in a state of impurity or purity?
> He replied: Do we have a case in the Torah in which a stove-range can become unclean? Rather it speaks of an unclean oven, for it is said [of an earthen vessel]: "everything inside it shall be unclean" (Lev.11:33) [and we don't put things inside a stove-range]!
> [The disciple] replied: Just as the Torah has spoken about an oven that has become unclean, so has it spoken of a stove-range that has become unclean, for it is said: "Everything on which the carcass of any of them falls shall be unclean: an oven or stove-range shall be smashed" (Lev.11:35)!

[The disciple] continued: If this is how you conduct yourself, you've never eaten food in purity for a single day of your life!

Here the unfortunate pietist has misunderstood one scriptural text and overlooked another, with grave consequences for his efforts to live at a high standard of cultic purity. What has led to his imperfect grasp of the simple text of Scripture? His failure to see the scriptural commandment embodied in the practice of an authoritative teacher. The point of the tale is that, while the text of Scripture is certainly there for all to read, it is understood only in the context of the teaching of the Sage whose repeated teachings bring the written text to life.

A toseftan passage nicely illustrates the distinction between "reciting" Scripture and "repeating" *mšnh* as well as the status equavalence of the recited and repeated curricula as sources of religious knowledge. At issue is a person who has suffered a form of bodily discharge that normally conveys a degree of impurity that, in the time of the Temple, would have barred the person from entering the sacred precincts. In the present era, shall the impurity disqualify the victim from uttering holy words during the period of contamination? The text distinguishes between persons whose impurity is insufficient to disqualify them from sacred study and those whose status is too virulent to permit the utterance of holy words (T. Berakhot 2:12):

1. A male with a genital discharge, and a female with a genital discharge, and the menstruant, and the parturient are permitted to *recite from* [*lqrwt b-*] the Torah, the Prophets, or from the Writings and to *repeat from* [*lšnwt b-*] repeated tradition [*mšnh*], from exegetical tradition [*mdrš*], from halakhic tradition [*hlkh*], and from homiletical tradition ['*gdh*]—but those with a seminal discharge are prohibited from all of these.
2. Rabbi Yose says: But [the person with the discharge] may repeat his customary halakhic traditions, as long as he does not amplify the repeated tradition [but merely sets it forth verbally].

We shall not be detained here by the text's surprising assumption—surpressed in later versions of the passage—that women would be reciting from Scripture or repeating rabbinic traditions.[24] The point here is that the Toseftan tradition assumes a rather reified curriculum of rabbinic learning, all of which is mastered in some sense through verbal repetition, and all of which should not be sounded through unclean lips.

While it is not clear precisely how this passage draws its distinctions between, say, repeated tradition [*mšnh*] on the one hand and halakhic tradition [*hlkh*] on the other (especially unit 2), it is certain that both are subsumed under the nonscriptural category of learning that is the unique domain of the Sage. What seems to concern Rabbi Yose is that the person with the emission should be excluded from the fullest participation in the life of learning until his impurity is cleansed. Thus he might repeat his traditions, but he may not engage in dialectical explanation of the details.

The specific verbal details, in fact, seem to have been important. While the occasional claim that Sages memorized their teacher's words and reported them verbatim is without real foundation,[25] it seems clear that the shapers of Mishnaic and Toseftan traditions valued the ability to report repeated traditions in relatively fixed verbal formulas.[26] As is clear from the following example, involving the early second-century circle surrounding Rabbi Aqiva, disputes about legal substance could at times be grounded in divergencies in the memorization of formulaic patterns of speech. At issue is a detail of the Second Temple sacrificial cult, about which there was apparently no eyewitness testimony.

When deputations of priests from local villages were called up for rotation in the Temple sacrificial cult, local townspeople would recite the Torah in their villages in correspondence to selected moments of the Temple service, while others would travel to Jerusalem with the priests to act as witnesses to the offerings. At issue in the present passage is the precise wording of a repeated tradition regarding variations of the activities of the nonpriestly delegation.

All authorities have mastered a list of at least three liturgical activities (the singing of the Hallel psalms, the Additional Sacrificial Offering, and the Wood Offering) at which no delegation of nonpriests need be present. These activities serve as fixed terms for the list. Rabbi Aqiva and ben Azzai differ, however, on precisely how the qualifiers of these terms are attached (M. Taanit 4:4):

1. Every day in which Hallel is recited—there is no delegation of witnesses [reciting Scripture] at the [time of the] Dawn Sacrifice.
2. [And on days requiring] the Additional Offering—there is no [delegation] at the Gate-Closing;
3. [and on days requiring] the Wood Offering—there is no [delegation] at the Afternoon Sacrifice: the words of Rabbi Aqiva.
4. Said to him ben Azzai: This is how Rabbi Yehoshua would repeat it— "The Additional Offering— *there is no [delegation] at the Afternoon Service;* the Wood Offering— *there is no [delegation] at the Gate-Closing.*"
5. Rabbi Aqiva then began to repeat in accord with ben Azzai.

The core issue is at units 2–3 versus 4. Both Rabbi Aqiva and ben Azzai (a student of Rabbi Yehoshua) agree that tradition transmits a ruling that a certain delegation is abandoned on days in which the Additional Offering and the Wood Offering are made. But the two Sages have transposed the specific facts of the matter. Rabbi Aqiva has memorized the pattern:

Additional Offering—Gate-Closing
Wood Offering—Afternoon.

Ben Azzai, by contrast, has preserved the order of the protases but reversed the apodoses:

Additional Offering—Afternoon
Wood Offering—Gate-Closing.

It is unclear from the Mishnah whether Rabbi Aqiva concedes to his colleague on logical grounds or because his memory has been corrected. His response, nevertheless, is to revise his own version of the tradition and to henceforward repeat it in Rabbi Yehoshua's formulation so that the correct version might be transmitted.

There are other passages as well in which the correction of memory leads to the revision of that which is thereafter repeated as tradition.[27] Thus the colleagues of Isi the Babylonian are portrayed as requesting him to recite repeatedly certain traditions of his teacher in order to correct a doubtful teaching that has contaminated the tradition (T. Zevahim 2:17). Sages, we find, could even be imagined as requiring their disciples to remind them of their own teachings. According to M. Ohalot 16:4, a person who has examined a graveyard for contaminating corpse matter and found none remains in a presumption of purity sufficient to enable him to eat food preserved in a state of sanctification. The Tosefta adds a supplementary narrative (T. Ahilut 16:8):

> 1. Rabban Yohanan ben Zakkai's students asked of him: One who has examined—
>   shall he eat [without purification]?
>
>   He replied: He doesn't eat.
>
>   They said to him: But you taught us that he eats!
>
>   He replied: Well said! A thing which my own hands did and my own eyes saw,
>   that I nevertheless forgot—it is all the more appropriate that [I should recall it]
>   now that my ears have heard it!
> 2. It is not that he didn't know! Rather he wanted to arouse his students. . . .
> 3. Rabbi Yehoshua says: One who repeats traditions but does not labor [to master
>   their content] is like a man who sows but does not reap; and one who learns
>   *torah* and forgets is like a woman who gives birth and buries.
> 4. Rabbi Aqiva says: Sing me constantly! Sing!

This passage is of remarkable interest for its attitudes toward memorization. First of all, (1) Rabban Yohanan's disciples remember what he himself, despite his own actions in accord with his teachings, has forgotten. I cannot explain why it would seem plausible that Rabban Yohanan had forgotten "what his own hands did and his own eyes saw," but it is significant that the appropriate jog to his memory is hearing his own words repeated to him by his students. We are asked to understand that the experience of hearing his own teaching reported to him sets in motion a train of associations that help him reconstruct the experiences upon which his original ruling was proffered.

The spectacle of a Sage forgetting his own words, however, is too much for the final tradent of this story, who has blunted its force with the disclaimer at 2 and the apostrophe to memorization at 3. These stress the importance of memorizing and mastering one's traditions. In the concluding contribution, Rabbi Aqiva speaks in the name of the Repeated Tradition itself, beseeching its human tradents to incorporate it in their memories through song.[28]

This point needn't be belabored any further. At the foundation of the earliest rabbinic compilations stands the assumption that literary traditions distinctive to the rabbinic community are passed on in the medium of speech, from Sage to disciple. They are mastered in memory through private reiteration and performed publicly in the process of being reported and examined. These traditions are already framed as generic entities, with a distinctive taxonomy. Aggadic traditions, conveying their points through narrative, are juxtaposed with halakhic traditions that specify forms of behavior. Text-interpretive traditions, conceptualized as *midrash*, are distinguished from *halakhah*, conveyed in an oral-performative tradition of its own. Let us move further, then, and flesh out some relevant distinctions within the oral-performative tradition of *halakhah* in particular.

Halakhah as a Modality of Tradition

The term *mishnah* is only the most comprehensive label for a series of subcategories or tradition genres which often overlap in their range of reference.[29] Our brief glance at T. Berakhot 2:12 above showed one example, and we will see more before long. It is surprising, then, that terms corresponding most nearly to the Latin *traditio* and its cognates in other Indo-European languages are rare, and their usage corresponds only partially to the semantic range of the English. Substantive nouns such as *msrt* (*masoret*: "that which is passed on")[30] and *qblh* (*qabbalah*: "that which is received")[31] are scarce and of restricted semantic range. The verbal forms of these roots—"to hand on" (*msr*) or "to receive" (*qbl*)—are more common and appear in the frequently cited passage of M. Avot 1:1ff that defines the rabbinic chain of learned tradition stemming from Moses. We shall soon note a few other instructive examples.

While nouns formed of roots meaning "to transmit" or "to receive" have their place in the Tannaitic lexicon of tradition, a far more prominent place is reserved for a noun derived from the root *hlk*, to go or walk. This is the term *halakhah*, usually rendered in translation as "law."[32] This rendering is not entirely inappropriate, but neither is it unproblematic. For the moment, it is enough to observe that *halakhah* has a much broader usage within the Mishnah and Tosefta in particular, a usage that indeed proves instructive for this study.

For example, M. Gittin 6:7 records the opinion, in the name of Rabbi Meir, that a man who appoints three agents to deliver a bill of divorce to his wife thereby bestows upon them the status of a court. Unlike mere agents, they are now empowered to delegate the writing of the document to another person. There is a problem, however, since the tradition according to Rabbi Meir differs from other formulations on the same subject that circulate within the community:

1. Now this *halakhah* [of Rabbi Meir's] was brought by Rabbi Haninah of Ono when he was released from prison: I have received [*qbl*] [as tradition] that one who says before three: "Give a bill of divorce to my wife"—they may appoint others to write it, since he has constituted them as a court.

2. Said Rabbi Yose: We reply to our messenger—We too have received [*qbl*] [as tradition] that even if he said before the High Court in Jerusalem: "Give a bill of divorce to my wife"—they must learn to write it and then deliver it.

Halakhah here is used in a manner analogous to the term *mšnh*, which we explored at M. Taanit 4:4. It is a report, orally delivered, of a legal norm which is received by the reporter as tradition (*qbl*) from an authoritative source (here unspecified) and then transmitted. It is possible, as in the present instance, to have conflicting reports, and these must be adjudicated. Unlike ben Azzai's challenge to Rabbi Aqiva (M. Taanit 4:4), Rabbi Yose's response to Rabbi Haninah is not really about which version of a shared traditional text has been correctly memorized and transmitted. Rather, at stake here is a question of larger theoretical approaches that, stemming from different masters, have come into conflict in the discourse of their disciples.[33]

One way of dismissing apparent conflicts among transmitted rulings from different sources highlights the degree to which the formulators of Mishnaic and Toseftan traditions conceived of *halakhah* as a datum passed on within the medium of oral-performative tradition. A valid objection to the authority of a halakhic report is a claim that it is based upon a misunderstanding of the spoken word by one of its transmitters. As in the following interchange, such a claim yields an effort to reconstruct the original halakhic report by identifying the element within it that misled the tradent who transmitted it from his teacher (M. Ohalot 16:1; cf. T. Ahilut 15:12):

1. All movable tools [that overshadow a corpse] convey the uncleanness [of the corpse] when [their diameter equals] the thickness of a cattle prod.
2. Said R. Tarfon: May I cut off the lives of my children if this is anything but a mangled *halakhah!* For the one who heard [*hšwm'*] it heard [*sm'*] and erred, as follows:
3. The farmhand carrying a cattle prod on his shoulder, and one end overshadowed a grave—they declared it unclean [*tm'whw*] under the rule of tools that overshadow a corpse.
4. Said Rabbi Aqiva: I can correct this in a way which preserves the words of Sages, as follows:
5. All movable tools [that overshadow a corpse] convey the uncleanness to the person who carries them by the thickness of a cattle prod, and upon themselves by any amount, and upon other persons by the width of a square handbreadth.

According to Rabbi Tarfon (2), the anonymous ruling at 1 is grounded in an incorrect inference drawn from an improperly understood case (3). The issue is a complex matter of the capacity of a round object, such as a cattle prod, to contract uncleanness from overshadowing the contaminating remnant of a corpse and to convey it to humans and other utensils through contact with them or by overshadowing them.

Spelling out the problem will help us to understand Rabbi Tarfon's objection and Rabbi Aqiva's response. A fundamental postulate of early rabbinic thought on uncleanness is that a tent containing an olive's bulk of corpse matter conveys the uncleanness of the corpse matter to other objects in the tent (M. Ohalot 2:1). Throughout this body of thought, a "tent" is understood metaphorically as any surface that measures a handbreadth square and overshadows the requisite measure of corpse matter (M. Ohalot 3:6–7). The metaphor can even extend to round objects, such as a pillar lying on the ground, if they create an overhang of at least one handsbreadth over the corpse matter (M. Ohalot 12:6).[34]

This is all assumed at ruling 1 and is now applied to nonstationary objects. The movable cattle prod can function as tentlike conveyer of uncleanness if it is the thickness of a handbreadth. Thus, if one end of the prod overshadows corpse matter, utensils passing under the other end will contract uncleanness. Rabbi Tarfon's objection (2) is based upon his utter rejection of the idea that a relatively slender object can serve as a tent. In reply, he offers a case that, in his view, offers a sound view of the law (3).

The latter ruling is not about the capacity of the cattle prod to convey uncleanness to other objects, but only about its ability to become contaminated itself from overshadowing. The crucial but ambiguous phrase *tm'whw* ("they declared it unclean") has been mistakenly interpreted in reference to the worker, insofar as the pronominal suffix *hw* can refer equally to the porter or the prod. For Rabbi Tarfon, a perfectly acceptable proposition about the capacity of a round, slender, moving object to contract uncleanness from a corpse beneath it has been "mangled" to produce the false inference that the same object can convey uncleanness to other items beneath it, including the worker.

Rabbi Aqiva's contribution is to propose a new general theory of the transmission of uncleanness by movable objects. His theory (5) incorporates ruling 1 within its scope while accounting for Rabbi Tarfon's case at 3. The elegance of the solution is not our concern. We observe only that both Rabbi Tarfon and Rabbi Aqiva assume an oral milieu for the transmission of 3 and acknowledge that errors of interpretation grounded in the oral transmission of knowledge are conceivable. They differ only regarding whether ruling 1 is such an error.

It is clear, then, that the term *halakhah* commonly refers to an orally transmitted report concerned with normative behavior in a particular sphere of activity. To this we may now add a second and related usage which is even more prevalent. Throughout the Tannaitic literature, in context after context, *halakhah* refers not only to discrete logia relating cases or principles, but also to the *entire complex of norms* deemed active within the community of the Sages.

Consider the following discussion, which alludes to the penchant of tradition transmitters for preserving contradictory opinions about halakhic norms in the literary form of disputes between particular Sages (M. Eduyyot 1:5–6):

1. Now, [insofar as the *halakhah* is determined only in accord with the majority of Sages] why are minority opinions mentioned where there are majority opinions?

   So that, should a court agree with a minority opinion, it may rely on it in its own deliberations,[35] for a court is unable to overrule the opinion of a fellow court unless it exceeds the latter in wisdom and number. . . .

2. Said R. Yehudah: If so, why are minority opinions mentioned among the majority for nought? So that if a person says "So have I received" [*qbl*], one may reply "You [only] heard [*šm'*] so-and-so's [minority] opinion."

As far as this discussion is concerned, halakhic *traditions*—reports about specific norms or practices—serve as the basis for the construction of a halakhic *tradition*—a systematic corpus of normative rulings. But not all *traditions* are equally effective in structuring the ongoing life of the community as an embodiment of its effective *tradition*. Rather, it is necessary to convene a body of halakhic tradents in order to determine which traditions are to become socially operative and which are to remain a passive possession of the community, preserved only as materials for pure learning.[36]

It is in this usage that the connotation of *halakhah* passes almost seamlessly from "tradition" to its usual rendering, "law," such as a body of conventional rules and procedures deemed normative by a majority of Sages: "One accepts [*šwm'yn*: literally, "hears"] this [view], for he spoke in accordance with the *halakhah*" (M. Peah 4:1–2); "If this is *halakhah*, then we'll accept it, but if it is a result of logical inference, one may demur" (M. Keritot 3:9); or, ubiquitously, "And the *halakhah* is in accord with his views." In such cases, a halakhic report is acceptable because it conforms to a preexisting, collectively maintained corpus of norms. But as soon as we recognize that *halakhah*, in addition to its sense as "tradition," routinely bears the sense of "law," we must immediately ask: What kind of law?[37]

Halakhah as a Modality of Law

Surprisingly, the term *halakhah* appears hardly at all in that major division of the Mishnah, the Order of Damages, which is concerned with the judicial and legislative institutions of Israel. Further, in the Mishnah as a whole, I find no cases in which the Jerusalem High Court (Sanhedrin) of the Second Temple period, which the Mishnah portrays as a rabbinic institution combining judicial and legislative functions, is said to have legislated a *halakhah*.[38] Rather, legislation has its own distinctive terminology: courts or individual Sages "establish" or "ordain" (*tqn*)[39] this or that practice (e.g., M. Rosh Hashannah 4:1–4, M. Sheqalim 7:5–7); they "decree" (*gzr*) that such and such a procedure must be enacted or that public fasts must be held (e.g., M. Yadayim 4:3, M. Taanit 3:6). Similarly, where the High Court recommends a course of action based upon its interpretation of scriptural commandments, it issues its results as a *hwr'h*, a "teaching" or "instruction," not as a *halakhah* (e.g., M. Horayot 1:1).

This representation of the situation prior to the destruction of Jerusalem in 70 CE is consistent with that drawn of judicial procedure after the reconstitution of the Sanhedrin at Yavneh in the following decades. Sages and courts are still depicted as instituting normative practices and promulgating decrees, but the legal utterances that formulate these norms are not identified as *halakhah*. Rather, in the context of judicial procedure *halakhah* represents a question brought to the court's attention for a ruling.

Precisely this notion of *halakhah* is discernible when one compares parallel formulations of a court case transmitted in the Mishnah and the Tosefta. M. Parah 7:6 records a ruling concerning the extent to which a particular act performed in the course of a purification ritual might impair the rite's effectiveness. The ruling is glossed as follows:

> This went [*hlk*] to Yavneh on three successive Festivals [for evaluation]. And on the third Festival they declared [the result] suitable [not as a permanent practice, but only] as a temporary measure [*hwr't š'h*].

Note the Tosefta's version at T. Parah 7:4:

> In regard to this *halakhah* did the residents of Asya[40] go up to Yavneh on three successive Festivals. And on the third Festival [etc.].

The Tosefta's parallel rendering of the Mishnaic tradition adds two pieces of information lacking in the Mishnah. First, it identifies the party, "the residents of Asya," that brought the Mishnah's case to the attention of the Yavnean Sages. More important from our perspective, it discloses a fundamental conception of the status of cases brought before the court. The conception lies in the assonance of the Mishnah's operative verb, "went" (vocalized as *halakh*), and the Tosefta's identification of *halakhah* as the item placed at the court's discretion.

We cannot reconstruct the literary history of these parallel versions. It is possible that the Toseftan tradent, hearing the Mishnah's *halakh*, subconsciously filled in the details with the appropriate noun. It is equally possible that the Toseftan report is the basis of a Mishnaic abbreviation.[41] In either tradition-historical scenario, the fact remains that the Tosefta clearly understands by *halakhah* a problem requiring judicial attention, rather than a judicial pronouncment; it is a fact used in the court's deliberation, not a statement of the court's establishing the law.

Another usage of *halakhah* in a judicial setting will add yet further texture to the Mishnah's sense of the term's legal character. The example comes from one of the rare appearances of the *halakhah* in the Order of Damages itself. Tractate Sanhedrin, which discusses the constitution of the judicial system, the jurisdictional powers of various types of courts, legal process, and so on, concludes with a list of capital crimes and appropriate methods of execution.

Among those subjected to execution by strangulation is a prophet who, in Scripture's terms, "presumes to speak in My name an oracle that I did not command him to utter, or who speaks in the name of other gods" (Dt.18:20). Of him M. Sanhedrin 11:6 reports:

> One who prophesies in the name of [a god honored by] an alien cult and says: "Thus said the [god of the] alien cult"—even if he agreed with the *halakhah* to declare as polluted that which is [in fact] polluted or to declare as pure that which is pure [—he shall be executed by strangulation].

The point of interest here is that the law broken by the prophet is that of Scripture, which prohibits delivering oracles in Israel in the name of foreign gods. The Mishnah simply adds that such prophecy is a capital crime even if the actual message is in entire conformity with *halakhah*.

Halakhah in this passage refers to the particular traditions of the Sages about ritual pollution, discussed in great detail in the Order of Purities. The stricture against pseudo-prophecy for which one may be punished is not a *halakhah*, it is a biblically grounded commandment (*mṣwh*, vocalized *mitzvah*). One can break a commandment even by teaching a unanimously held *halakhah*—if one ascribes it to a foreign god rather than to the authority of the Sages. So where the Mishnah has an opportunity in its discussion of civil and criminal law to refer to *halakhah*, it means not a law enforceable by judicial sanction, but a verbal tradition about a custom or practice that can come under the scrutiny of the court—in short, a matter that must be addressed by a legal authority in order to pronounce the law.[42]

It is, in fact, among the narrative materials of the Tosefta that we find the richest depiction of the wide range of contexts in which issues of halakhic interest are reviewed, discussed, and declared binding. All of these are portrayed as oral, face-to-face encounters in which written texts have no role. Among them are mealtime discussions akin to philosophical symposia,[43] conversations between Sages and disciples during travel,[44] formal oral-performative recitations of tradition,[45] conflict situations between a Sage and a rabbinic or nonrabbinic opponent,[46] official judicial deliberations,[47] and the like. In many of these, the narrative suggests that conflicting halakhic opinions can be resolved by the ad hoc decisions of Sages in the absence of any formal deliberations, which decisions are then passed on as binding practice, *halakhah*.

Thus, T. Berakhot 1:4 reports the following incident involving two Sages of the Yavnean Academy, active during the first third of the second century CE until the Bar Kosiva rebellion of 132–135. The Toseftan text is deeply intertwined with a parallel Mishnaic report (M. Berakhot 1:3) regarding the posture for reciting the scrip-

tural passages known in rabbinic tradition as the Shema, and it adds the following
(T. Berakhot 1:4):

1. A report concerning Rabbi Ishmael and Rabbi Eleazar b. Azariah, who were
   tarrying in a certain place:
2. Now, Rabbi Ishmael was reclining and Rabbi Eleazar b. Azariah was upright.
   When the time for the recitation of the *Shema* arrived, R. Ishmael arose [to recite
   it standing], while Rabbi Eleazar b. Azariah reclined [to recite it reclining].
       Said Rabbi Ishmael: What is this, Eleazar? He replied: Ishmael, my brother,
   . . . I, who had been upright, reclined [so as to recite in the appropriate posture],
   while you, who had been reclining, arose [for the same reason].
       He replied: You reclined in order to carry out the views of the House of
   Shammai, while I arose in order to carry out the views of the House of Hillel.
3. Another version [of Rabbi Ishmael's reply]: So that the disciples shouldn't see
   [both of us reclining to recite] and enact the *halakhah* permanently in accord
   with your views!

The glossator's comment, section 3, is instructive: the actions of Sages are presumed
to reflect halakhic norms received from their teachers. Where there is a conflict of
such norms, however, yet where two Sages are observed to accord with one of the
conflicting versions, disciples will determine normative practice in the future in
accord with the precedent of the Sages' actions.

Sages, then, determine the *halakhah* by their acts, and disciples pass that deter-
mination into custom. There is no question here of institutional adjudication or
formal judicial legislation. No consultation of a written text intervenes between the
perception of a legal issue and its authoritative resolution. Rather the rendering of
the halakhic decision is as simple as a bodily action. Its representation in the medium of spoken narrative transmits its legal force as an abiding element of the oral-
performative tradition.

But matters are not always so clear-cut. In addition to reports of halakhic deter-
mination set in informal settings, the Tosefta, unlike the Mishnah, portrays the promulgation of *halakhah* as a judicial activity of the High Court. The richest picture
of the halakhic tradition in legal dress comes from an extended account of the procedure for clarifying an obscure halakhic question. It is reported in the name of Rabbi
Yose b. Halafta, a Sage central to the reconstitution of the rabbinic movement, in
about 140 in the Galilean town of Usha, after the failure of bar Kosiva.

In the mid-second century, from the perspective afforded by a recent, catastrophic
war that witnessed the deaths of important teachers, the procedure of the ancient
Sanhedrin was recalled rather nostalgically as follows (T. Sanhedrin 7:1/Hagigah 2:9;
cf. M. Sanhedrin 11:2):[48]

1. In the early days there were no disputes in Israel. Rather the Court of Seventy
   [judges] was in the [Temple's] Chamber of Hewn Stone, and the other courts
   of twenty-three were in the towns of the Land of Israel. Two courts of three each
   were in Jerusalem—one on the Temple Mount and one on the Rampart.
2. If one party [to a dispute] required a [ruling of] *halakhah*,[49] he would go to the
   court of his town. . . . If they had heard [a tradition on the question], they would
   tell them. If not he and the senior member among them would come to the
   court on the Temple Mount. If they had heard, they would tell them. If not,

both parties would come to the court on the Rampart. If they had heard, they
would tell them. If not, both parties would come to the court in the Chamber
of Hewn Stone. . . .

3. The *halakhah*[50] was asked. If they had heard, they would tell them. But if not,
they would call a vote. If those who declared for uncleanness were in the majority, they declared for uncleanness; if those who declared for cleanness were in
the majority, they declared for cleanness.

4. From there would *halakhah* go forth and become publicized in Israel.

5. Upon the proliferation of disciples of Shammai and Hillel who had not attended
[their Masters] as fully as necessary, disputes increased in Israel, and two Torahs
emerged.[51]

Clearly, the High Court is represented as a mixture of a legislative and judicial body,
capable of applying received *halakhah* even as it may pass it into legislation. But what
is the nature of this *halakhah*? It is remarkably consonant with the picture we have
described above on the basis of the Mishnah.

First, as in M. Ohalot 16:1, it is an orally transmitted datum of tradition, about which
one has either "heard" or not (2). Second, as in M. Eduyyot 1:5–6, it may be a rational
decision subject to argument and the consent of the majority (3). Finally (3), as in
M. Parah 7:6 and M. Sanhedrin 11:6, it is represented here in reference not to civil or
criminal law, but as a ritual matter: in this case a question of whether an unspecified
person or object has been polluted by a source of uncleanness which would impose the
need for a ritual of purification. The image of Sages deliberating about the "pure and
the polluted" is something of a trope which sums up the Sages' acts of deliberation. It
should not be pressed too hard in order to exclude matters of criminal or civil law from
the purview of halakhic tradition. The choice of this particular trope, however, is instructive. For even where we find an explicit attempt to place the halakhic process in
the context of legislative and judicial institutions—the court system—the subject matter of that process is not imagined as a question of, say, guilt or innocence, financial
liability or freedom from liability; rather, at issue is a fine point of cultic procedure.

Thus the most explicit linkage of *halakhah* with Israelite institutions of social
regulation reveals both that *halakhah* may include laws within its overall structure
but that its structure is not defined per se as law. Even where *halakhah* may become
"law," it is also, and perhaps primarily, "tradition" of a unique kind. It is tradition
received and self-consciously created within the circles of the Sages, whether that
circle is the relatively informal companionship of masters and disciples or the highest legislative and judicial institutions of the Land of Israel. What is primary in the
creation of *halakhah* is the act or orally transmitted opinion of the Sage; the social
or institutional setting of that act or utterance is immaterial for evaluating its authority as a customary norm. With this last observation in mind, we are prepared to ask
the next logical question: precisely how does the early rabbinic literature imagine
the role of its Sages in the production of oral-literary tradition and its application?[52]

The Sage as a *Halakhic* Source

This question brings us into confrontation, first of all, with the figure of Moses himself, the archetypal legislator. The Mishnah transmits a story about a day when de-

liberations in the House of Study yielded a decision, unwarranted by scriptural law, to impose tithing obligations upon produce grown by Jews in the Transjordanian territories of Ammon and Moab. Rabbi Eliezer b. Hyrcanus, an important figure in the early Yavnean period, is reported to have greeted the ruling with the following remark (M. Yadayim 4:3):

> "The mystery of the Lord is with those who fear Him, and His covenant shall inform them" (Ps.25:14)! Go and tell the Sages: Do not mistrust your decision! For I have received a tradition [*qbl*] from Rabban Yohanan b. Zakkai, who heard it [*šm'*] from his Master, who heard it from his Master ultimately as a *halakhah* of Moses from Sinai that Ammon and Moab separate the Poor Tithe in the Sabbatical Year![53]

The extension of scriptural tithing law promulgated by the contemporary community of Sages here finds its authority in the fact that it restores a halakhic institution of Moses, the first convener of an Israelite court,[54] and conforms to a continuous tradition passed down from the Prophet to Eliezer's own teacher, Rabban Yohanan b. Zakkai.

This and a handful of other Mishnaic and Toseftan references to *halakhot* transmitted from the time Moses stood on Sinai have often been taken to prove that early Tannaitic masters linked the entire halakhic tradition to Mosaic authority.[55] But this is unlikely. The episodic references to such Mosaic *halakhot* (e.g., M. Eduyyot 8:7, M. Peah 2:6, T. Sukkah 3:1) in the earliest rabbinic compilations deal with minor issues within the larger structure of halakhic thought. Neither the Mishnah nor the Tosefta claims Mosaic warrant on behalf of entire corpora of laws which, central to much of the Mishnah's own program, are nevertheless unattributed to ancient authorities. So the Mishnah's designation of a norm as a *halakhah* originating with Moses himself, and passed on unchanged within the tradition of the Sages, serves no identifiable polemical or jurisprudential agenda regarding the halakhic tradition as such. The most we can learn from it is that, from the Mishnah's own perspective, all but three of its innumerable traditions are post-Mosaic.

Indeed, the Mishnah and Tosefta find little need to locate rabbinic halakhic traditions in the distant past. With the exception of a single reference to a practice initiated by unnamed prophets (M. Megillah 3:5), the Mishnah identifies no *halakhah* from the pre-exilic period at all. Similarly, it attributes virtually nothing to anyone who might have lived from the time of the exiled Judeans' return to their land under Cyrus in 539 BCE until the beginning of the Hasomonean period, about 150 BCE, when traditions ascribed to the shadowy "Pairs" begin to emerge (e.g., M. Hagigah 2:2; cf. M. Avot 1:4–12). The earliest named figures routinely represented as passing on halakhic materials as oral-literary tradition are Hillel and Shammai, contemporaries who were active toward the end of the first century BCE and on into the first CE, and whose disciples are routinely assigned opposing views in halakhic controversies.

For the most part, then, it is certain that, as far as the tradents behind Mishnaic and Toseftan traditions are concerned, the bulk of the oral-literary tradition of halakhic norms is conceived to be of rather recent vintage, promulgated by teachers whose disciples — or whose disciple's disciples — could still be consulted for details. The testimony to this point of view must be teased out of the relatively few passages that describe the social settings of halakhic creation, but they yield a consistent picture nonetheless.

In one instance, for example, a series of reports concerning the proper observance of the Sabbath is explained as follows (T. Shabbat 1:16; cf. M. Shabbat 1:4):[56]

1. These are among the *halakhot* which they proclaimed in the upper room of Hananiah b. Hezekiah b. Gurion when they went up to visit him.
2. They counted a quorum and the Shammaites outnumbered the Hillelites, and on that very day they decreed [*gzrw*] eighteen edicts.
3. And that day was as bitter for Israel as the day on which the Golden Calf was prepared.

This account of halakhic legislation, set prior to the destruction of the Temple in 70, is rather different from that offered by the Tosefta's account of the High Court's deliberations (T. Sanhedrin 7:1/Hagigah 2:9 above). The occasion for promulgating the *halakhot* is portrayed as a kind of halakhic power grab; it is circumstantial and ad hoc rather than the action of an officially designated institution. The Sages happened to be in a particular spot and a vote was taken to the advantage of the Shammaite school of tradition. Despite the circumstances of their promulgation, however, the decrees remain legitimate as halakhic norms. It is not force itself as a creator of halakhic norms that troubles the Tosefta (3); rather it is the fact that it was wielded by the wrong party. Even so, the result remains a valid act of halakhic legislation regardless of its circumstances.

The Toseftan redaction of Tannaitic tradition is, in most respects, similar to the Mishnah in regarding halakhic tradition as a relatively recent creation, punctuated by more or less severe and frequent mid-course corrections. On the question of the antiquity and authority of the halakhic tradition, Toseftan material thoroughly confirms the Mishnah's view (exclusive, perhaps, of the polemical case of M. Avot) that the bulk of that tradition is a recent contribution of the Sages stemming from Hillel, Shammai, and their disciples. T. Eduyyot 1:1's account of the first efforts to compile an organized corpus of Sages' teachings is instructive:

1. When Sages gathered at the Vineyard at Yavneh they said: in the future a person might seek a teaching among the [Sages'] words of *torah* and not find it, among the words of the scribes and not find it, for it is said (Amos 8:11–12): ". . . They shall wander from sea to sea and from North to East, and they shall run hither and yon to seek the word of YHWH, but they shall not find it."
2. "the word of YHWH"—this refers to prophecy.
3. "the word of YHWH"—this refers to the End.
4. "the word of YHWH"—this means that no teaching of the [Sages'] words of *torah* cohere with each other.
5. [Thereupon, Sages] said: Let us begin with [the traditions] of Hillel and Shammai.

The Yavneans (1), according to this account, anticipate a future in which Sages' teachings will be forgotten; but their effort to organize them for preservation reveals the shallowness of their own historical memory (4–5). Nothing goes back before the Herodian period in which Hillel and Shammai thrived.

T. Eduyot's inadvertant confession regarding the rather recent roots of halakhic memory is confirmed in other Toseftan historical recollections. Of Mosaic *halakhot*, for example, the Tosefta preserves only two, one dependent upon the account of

M. Yadayim 4:3 (T. Yadayim 2:16), the other concerning the celebration of the Festival of Booths in the Herodian Temple (T. Sukkah 3:1).[57] To be sure, Toseftan historiographical material—unlike the Mishnah—ascribes a few rulings of a halakhic character to biblical heroes or figures who lived prior to the Roman occupation of Palestine. Thus authoritative acts of legislation regarding priestly service in the Temple are ascribed in one passage to Moses, Samuel, and David (T. Taaniyot 3:2), while Shimon b. Shetah, a hero located by rabbinic tradition in the reign of Alexander Jannaeus (see chapter 3), is said to have instituted on behalf of women an important modification regarding the marriage contract (T. Ketubot 12:1). With the exception of these few instances, however, the Tosefta confirms the impression received from the Mishnah. While some few halakhic norms may indeed have great antiquity, the *halakhah* itself, conceived as a total body of tradition now preserved in the Sages' teachings, is the product of the recent past.

The Tosefta, in fact, differs markedly from the Mishnah in only one crucial respect: its tradents are far more willing than the Mishnah's compilers to identify conflict and struggle for power as factors in halakhic legislation. We noted earlier the way in which M. Shabbat 1:4's rather benign discription of the events in Hananiah b. Hezekiah's upper room is configured as a tragedy in T. Shabbat 1:16. This picture of halakhic power politics prior to the destruction of the Temple is redrawn in the figures of post-70 authorities as well. Of the important Yavnean Sages, Rabbi Eliezer b. Hyrcanus (T. Niddah 1:5) and Rabban Gamaliel II (T. Taaniyot 2:5), the Tosefta reports attempts after their deaths to reverse their halakhic decisions. The report concerning Gamaliel, who presided over the High Court at Yavneh, is especially revealing (T. Taaniyot 2:5):

1. As long as Rabban Gamaliel lived, the *halakhah* was practiced in accordance with his views. After the death of Rabban Gamaliel, Rabbi Yehoshua tried to nullify his views.
2. Rabbi Yohanan b. Nuri rose to his feet and said: May I observe that the body follows the head! As long as Rabban Gamaliel lived, the *halakhah* was practiced in accordance with his views; now that he is dead you attempt to nullify his views?
3. Said Rabbi Yehoshua to him: Shall we not concede to you? Let us establish the *halakhah* in accordance with Rabban Gamaliel!
4. And not a soul questioned the matter.

This passage assumes that the precise forms of halakhic practice in a given generation are anchored in the authority of a single individual, the head of the Court (1). At the same time, after the death of such an authority, it is possible to reconsider those views and to alter the norms by which the tradition is placed into effect within the community. In the present instance, of course, the attempt to nullify Rabban Gamaliel's halakhic decisions fails (2–4), but the course of action is in principle conceivable.

Halakhah, in other words, may be tradition, but it is tradition subject to change and fluctuation in its specific implementation. This is so precisely because it is grounded in the personal authority of human beings. As relations of power among the Sages shift, so too the precise forms of embodying halakhic tradition in communal or private practice are likely to shift as well.

Summary

Both the Mishnah and the Tosefta agree in their assumption that the substance of halakhic tradition is transmitted by word of mouth, from teacher to disciple, as an orally managed body of knowledge. But this is not precisely equivalent to what first-century accounts of the Palestinian Jewish scene knew as Pharisaic "ancestral tradition." The crucial distinction is obvious: the rabbinic compilations routinely portray the halakhic tradition as relatively recent in vintage—from Hasmonean-Herodian rather than Mosaic-Prophetic times—and subject to marked alteration of its content and application. It is a tradition the shape of which is governed not by the weight of the past, but rather by the creative impact of powerful personalities within the various institutions under rabbinic control.

To be sure, some few elements in the overall tradition are attributed to ancient legislators, such as Moses. But the example of Moses serves only to legitimate the Sage himself as an originator of halakhic tradition, not merely its exponent. Just as the Sage is the recipient of the tradition, having heard it from his teacher, he is also the molder of it, for his intellectual ingenuity and political instincts permit him to shape the collective embodiment of halakhic tradition in accord with his own vision. There is nothing he can innovate that is not, if he has the power to impose it, capable of entering tradition; there are few applications of tradition that are not, to a greater or lesser degree, alterations in its current.

It remains to be pointed out, however, that within the Mishnah itself the conception of *halakhah* as a tradition constituted by its own innovative applications under the authority of the Sages appears to be problematic. The problem is simple and predictable: if the Sages' cumulative tradition of halakhic judgments is authoritative in Israel, what is the ultimate foundation of this authority apart from the power of the Sages to impose it? In what way are the patterns of halakhic tradition connected to the abiding and unchanging patterns of Judaic covenantal life inscribed in the texts of the Torah of Moses? In the Sages' wrestling with this issue we shall find the seeds of what ultimately became the fully developed conception of two complementary, equally binding revelations, each mediated by a distinctive oral-performative tradition—the one grounded in inscriptions upon a a scroll and the other inscribed solely in the memory.

5

The Ideological Construction
of Torah in the Mouth

Torah—Mosaic and Rabbinic

The best-known example of the claim that all rabbinic teaching stems from a Mosaic source is, of course, the opening unit of the Mishnah's tractate Avot (1:1–2:8).[1] Beginning with Moses, who "received (*qbl*) *torah* from Sinai and passed it on (*msr*) to Yehoshua" (M. Avot 1:1), the compiler of this list of teachers and their teachings links the words of successive Sages into a chain of tradition spanning the First and Second Temple periods, covering the post-70 period of reconstruction under the disciples of Hillel and Rabban Yohanan b. Zakkai, and culminating with the early third-century CE patriarch Rabban Gamaliel III, the son of the illustrious patriarch Rabbi Yehudah. This compendium of wise sayings, amplified with the gnomic utterances of numerous Tannaitic masters—from the famous Rabbi Aqiva to the obscure ben Bag Bag—enjoyed wide circulation in rabbinic circles. Recognized as an effective apologia defending the continuity of rabbinic teachings with the teaching of Israel's greatest prophet, the collection as a whole was included by the close of the sixth century within the larger curriculum of learning that came to be identified as the Mishnah per se.[2] Like other Mishnaic tractates, Avot also circulated in an expanded, Tosefta-like compilation ascribed to Rabbi Natan.[3]

Not all modern scholars have resisted the tendency to see in Avot's chain of tradition an allusion to a fully developed concept of a dual, written and oral, revelation.[4] But the fact remains that M. Avot does not yet speak of the Sinaitic origins of Torah in Script and Torah in the Mouth, but only of *torah*. M. Avot does not, therefore, offer a defense of the idea that the Mishnah or the Oral Torah originates with Moses. Rather it extols the traditionality of rabbinic teachings, linking their authority to the greatest possible source of authority. In S. Fraade's trenchant formulation, "disciples of sages, through their engaged study and hence interpretation of this text, might be empowered to view the very activity of their study as part of an unbroken, living chain of Torah and tradition extending back to and deriving from Sinai, with themselves as the latest links."[5]

M. Avot's use of the term *torah* in particular—without the definite article that would denote Scripture—to indicate the teaching that Sages receive from Moses is not accidental or ill-considered. Its roots go back to Second Temple usage and scriptural sources, in which, complementing explicit divine revelation, *torah* can refer as well to "received tradition passed on most explicitly by teachers."[6] There is an implicit, if unexplained, connection between *torah* and what Sages call *hatorah*, "the Torah" of Moses. In order to get a better sense of the connotations of Avot's usage of *torah*, and to gauge the relationship of *torah* to the Torah of Moses on the one hand and to the rabbinic text-interpretive and oral-performative traditions on the other, we should survey some other illuminating materials from the early rabbinic corpus.

Text-Interpretive Tradition as the "Essence of Torah"

As was pointed out in chapter 4, the Mishnah recognizes as a matter of course a distinction between the divine commandments found in the Torah of Moses, which it calls *mṣwt* (*mitzvot*), and the patterns of life mandated by the various formulations of halakhic tradition. The former, it was assumed, emerged organically from the Mosaic Torah itself. God's commandments might have required clarification by the ongoing project of text-interpretive tradition cultivated in rabbinic circles, but those commandments had no taint of human construction. The halakhic tradition, by contrast, emerged beyond the boundaries of scriptural interpretation. Its foundation lay in the teachings associated with the names of important Sages that were transmitted in oral-performative settings of instruction. A pressing jurisprudential problem, therefore, was to clarify the relationship between these two distinct sources of norms, to establish hierarchies of authority by which sources within the system might be evaluated.

The matter is addressed most explicitly in a well-known observation about the relationship between the Sages' oral-performative tradition of *halakhah* and scriptural commands. This observation appears in two textually related versions, one in the Mishnah and the other in the Tosefta. Since they are complementary, we shall examine each on its own, beginning with the text of M. Hagigah 1:8:[7]

1. [The Sages's power to effect] the release of vows flutters in the air with nothing [in Scripture] to rely upon.
2. The *halakhot* of the Sabbath, pilgrimage offerings, and sacrilege are like mountains hung by a hair, with little Scripture and many *halakhot*.
3. [The *halakhot*] of judicial procedure, sacrifice, cleanness and uncleanness, and forbidden consanguinity have something [in Scripture] upon which to rely.
4. And they are indeed (*hn hn*)[8] the essence of *torah*.

This is hardly an exhaustive list of halakhic themes laid out in comparison to their scriptural bases. The Tosefta, in fact, will try to correct this. Nevertheless, the point is made: rabbinic legal tradition as a whole can be likened to a pyramid. At its apex stand halakhic norms entirely unencumbered by scriptural foundations (1). Their authority rests upon the wisdom of the Sages themselves, transmitted with accuracy through the oral-performative tradition. At its base lie norms with "something in

Scripture on which to rely" (3), those in which rabbinic norms most explicitly engage the text-interpretive tradition associated with public study of the Mosaic Torah. Between the extremes are located traditions that have only tenuous connections to scriptural sources.

Now, this is an impressive admission. The text-interpretive tradition associated with Scripture and the oral-performative tradition of *halakhah*, in this view, are distinct. They are complementary and intersecting, but the authority of the latter is not grounded in its being derived from the former.[9] Of even greater interest, however, is the glossator's comment (4). In a phrase that is tantalizing in its ambiguity—"the essence of *torah*"—he employs the term *torah* as a synthetic category that encompasses in its purview both halakhic judgments of Sages and scripturally grounded textual interpretations.

A contextual reading suggests, as David Weiss-Halivni has pointed out, that the "essence of *torah*" refers simply to the *halakhot* enumerated at unit 3.[10] Thus the "essence of *torah*" is that body of oral-literary tradition as a whole in which the rabbinic oral-performative tradition, *halakhah*, enjoys the firmest foundations in the text-interpretive traditions associated with the Torah of Moses. In other words, where *halakhah* most clearly emerges directly from scriptural exegesis, there one finds the fundamental core of *torah*.[11] That being said, it is important to pay attention to its clear implication: whether or not rabbinic *halakhah* is well grounded in the text-interpretive tradition associated with the recitation of Mosaic texts, it nevertheless enjoys the status of *torah*, authoritative teaching.[12]

A more pointed expression of the Mishnah's claim appears in the Tosefta's version of our passage, recorded in parallel renderings at T. Hagigah 1:9 and T. Eruvin 8:23–24. The literary relationship of the Toseftan text to its Mishnaic counterpart is a complex one, although it seems clear that the Tosefta offers a rather clumsily pieced-together expansion of the Mishnaic text. To highlight the Mishnah–Tosefta relationship, I have rendered passages unique to the Toseftan tradition in italics and intruded my own brief observations at crucial junctures.

In the version preserved in T. Hagigah 1:9, the Tosefta reads:[13]

1. [The Sages' power to effect] the release of vows flutters in the air with nothing [in Scripture] to rely upon (= M. Hag. 1:8.1).
2. *Rather, the Sage releases [one from a vow] in accordance with his own wisdom:*

The Tosefta's addition stresses what is implicit in the Mishnah. In the nullification of vows, the Sage acts on his own authority without any reliance upon the warrant of text-interpretive tradition. The Tosefta continues:

3. The *halakhot* of the Sabbath, pilgrimage offerings, and sacrilege are like mountains hung by a hair, with little Scripture and many *halakhot* (= M. Hag. 1:8.2).
4. *They have nothing to rely upon. . . .*[14]

The Tosefta is again more expansive than the Mishnah, but now redundantly and infelicitously. If the release of vows (1) has "nothing to rely upon," the relatively more firmly connected themes of 3 should do better. But instead, the Toseftan tradent (4) has simply repeated the judgment made at 1. Now the Tosefta adds:

5. [The *halakhot* of] judicial procedure, sacrifice, cleanness and uncleanness, and forbidden consanguinity (= M. Hag.1:8.3).

6. —*and in addition to these, vows for substitute valuation [of persons and sacrificial beasts], sanctifications, and [Temple] dedications—have much Scripture and many midrash and* halakhot.

7. They have something upon which to rely (= M. Hag.1:8.3).

Unit 6 is interpolated into the Mishnaic citation (5 + 7), adding four halakhic themes to the Mishnah's list and emphasizing the contrast between these and the themes of unit 3. While the latter have "little Scripture and many *halakhot*," the former are rich in Scripture that has generated a substantial body of rabbinic text-interpretive tradition (*midrash*) and oral-performative legal tradition (*halakhot*). They should have more than "something upon which to rely," but the tradent seems content to preserve the mishnaic formulation.

In any event, the real point comes at the end:

8. *Abba Yose b. Hanan says: "These eight topics of torah are the essence of the* halakhot (/M. Hag.1:8.4).

Abba Yose's enumeration of eight topics of *torah* confirms that, in his view, the "essence of the *halakhot*" are those topics in which both the results of scriptural interpretation and rabbinic oral-performative *halakhah* are well represented.

We must ask: is there a significant distinction to be drawn between the Mishnah's reference to the "essence of *torah*" and the Tosefta's formulation: "these topics of *torah* are the essence of the *halakhot*"? In both cases the point is similar: the core of authoritative legal tradition is found where law is most deeply imbedded in scriptural interpretation. But this should not obscure the fact that, in the Tosefta, *torah* and *halakhah* have been profoundly transvalued. In *torah*, for the Tosefta, the teachings of Moses in Scripture and those of the Sages' oral-performative tradition each have their place. But the most authoritative core—the "essence of the *halakhot*"— is constituted by rabbinic traditions that exhibit the clearest scriptural warrant. *Halakhah*, in other words, has been resignified and emptied of its fundamental independence from scriptural interpretation.

We have here been alerted to a fundamental tension in Tannaitic thinking about the relation of text-interpretive tradition associated with Scripture and the oral-performative tradition transmitted by Sages as legal norms independent of the Mosaic Torah. The concept of *torah* mediates this tension. It has made room for the co-existence of Scripture and rabbinic tradition within a comprehensive body of authoritative learning that transcends both. The text-interpretive tradition associated with the recitation of Scripture here emerges as the symbolic center of rabbinic conceptions of *torah*. The Tosefta testifies that the effort to synthesize the two sources of *torah*—the Mosaic book and the halakhic oral tradition—has become a matter of pressing ideological concern.[15]

Oral-Performative Tradition as a Modality of Revelation

The Mishnaic and Toseftan material we have examined claims a wide range of relationships between halakhic norms and scriptural commandments. But the claim is scarcely exemplified in these compilations, for they are rather poor in concrete examples of scriptural interpretation. The key testimony to the complex rabbinic project of weaving the halakhic traditions of the Sages into the fabric of scriptural law is found chiefly among collections of Tannaitic biblical exegesis. These appear to have begun their compositional history around the middle of the third century and survive as detailed compendia organized around the heart of the Mosaic Torah—the legal portions of Exodus, Leviticus, Numbers, and Deuteronomy. Within them we have the most explicit representations of how rabbinic readers of the scriptural text grasped that text through the prism of the oral-performative tradition of recitation and explication that gave it voice.[16]

This is not the place, however, to mount a comprehensive study of the ways in which early rabbinic biblical exegesis folds back into the text rabbinic norms and practices now enshrined in the traditions of the Mishnah and the Tosefta.[17] We can, however, scan some examples of a small but ideologically significant body of texts that make a scant appearance in the Mishnah and the Tosefta[18] but that proliferate within the extra-Mishnaic collections of Tannaitic biblical exegesis and, later, the Talmuds. For reasons that will soon become clear, I shall refer to these texts as "curriculum pericopes."

Like other examples of midrashic exegesis, the curriculum pericope quite easily elides the distinctions between the scriptural word and rabbinic tradition. But it is much bolder in its attempt to demonstrate that the very genres of the comprehensive rabbinic oral-literary tradition (and not only its text-interpretive results) are anticipated in the revelation to Moses. Accordingly, these pericopes normally select scriptural clauses in which two or more synonyms for divine instruction appear. The exegetical discourse then relates each of these synonyms to one of the intellectual operations or literary genres characteristic of the rabbinic curriculum. The result is a hermeneutical procedure in which scriptural terms are systematically resignified and reconfigured so as to anticipate and define the rabbinic taxonomy of traditional learning.

Normally, elements of the scriptural lexicon are linked to such rabbinic terms as *halakhah*, *midrash*, and *aggadah* (broadly, ethical maxims). Other common terms include *divrei soferim* (scribal rulings), *talmud* (legal dialectic), *mishnah* (recitation of traditions), *gezerot* (edicts), and other technical terms for rabbinic learning. We have seen that such a taxonomic interest in the modalities of tradition is already part of the intellectual equipment of the Mishnah and the Tosefta. The point of the curriculum pericope is simply to provide such a taxonomy of tradition with a scriptural genealogy. It embodies as exegetical discourse the ideological claim that the rabbinic curriculum of study is in some sense included in the revelation to Moses.

An important example occurs in Mekhilta de-Rabbi Ishmael to Exodus 15:26. In this verse, the children of Israel have just crossed the Sea of Reeds and are suffering from thirst three days into their wilderness wandering. Responding to the people's murmuring, Moses miraculously sweetens the bitter waters of Marah and takes the opportunity to impose a covenant promise upon Israel (Ex.15:26):

> And he said: If you will indeed listen to the voice of YHWH your God, and do what is upright in his sight, and lend your ears to his commandments, and observe

all his laws, then I will not send upon you all the plagues which I sent upon Egypt, for I am YHWH, who heals you.

Observe the Mekhilta's refraction of the verse:

1. "To the voice of YHWH your God"—these are the Ten Commandments, given from mouth to mouth in ten utterances.
2. "And do what is upright in his sight"—this refers to the sublime *aggadot* which resound in the ears of every person.
3. "And lend your ears to his commandments"—this refers to the *gezerot*.
4. "And observe all his laws"—this refers to the *halakhot*.[19]

The creator of this set of correspondences assumes that the various scriptural references correspond to elements of rabbinical learning (2–4), each of which is held to be continuous with the initial moments of revelation (1). Of particular interest is the linkage of scriptural laws and rabbinic *halakhah* (4). This decision is clearly inflected by the Mishnaic and Toseftan estimate of *halakhah* as a traditional legal structure. At the same time, however, it furthers the argument—mounted specifically at T. Hagigah 1:9 and M. Hagigah 1:8—that *halakhah*, as an oral-performative tradition, is in some sense reducible to the interpretive construction of the implications of revealed commandments. The independence of halakhic tradition from scriptural foundations—taken for granted in most Mishnaic and Toseftan settings—is here deftly undermined by stipulating an identity between the Sinaitic laws and the halakhic corpus.

The tradent of the Mekhilta's exegesis has narrowed the rather wide semantic band along which the term *halakhah* moves in the Mishnah and the Tosefta. In the latter, the weight of emphasis rests upon the relatively recent origins of halakhic discourse in the circles of Sages; but now the minor theme of the Mosaic origins of some halakhic norms has come to dominate. If we are to read the Mekhilta's exegetical elaborations of Scripture contextually into the pre-Sinaitic situation described in the scriptural verse itself, the exegete's argument is that the covenant promise at Marah was in fact made in the name of the revelation that was to follow, a revelation that included not only the Mosaic Torah but the oral-performative halakhic tradition that would define its relevance to Israelite covenant life.

While there is no reason to assume that the editors of the Mehkilta have any direct hand in the creation of other compilations of rabbinic legal exegesis, we find a remarkable uniformity of opinion throughout the other collections regarding the relation of the rabbinic curriculum in general, and the halakhic element in particular, to elements of revelation. Throughout these documents, creators of curriculum pericopes take great pains to insist that all aspects of rabbinic oral-literary tradition—exegetical or otherwise—have their ultimate derivation from revelation.

Another example, this from the Sifra to Leviticus, must speak for a diverse range of material. Here is God's cautionary statement to Aaron at the entrance to the Tent of Meeting after the death of his two sons, who had offered "strange fire" upon the altar (Lev.10:10–11):

This is an eternal law throughout your generations, to distinguish between the holy and the profane, between the unclean and the clean, and to guide the children of Israel in all the laws which YHWH spoke through Moses

Note the rendering of this verse in Sifra Shemini, par.1:9:

1. "to distinguish between the holy and the profane"—this refers to vows for substitute valuation ['*rkyn*: cf. Lev.27 and M. Arakhin].
2. "between the unclean and the clean"—this refers to the laws of pollution and
   purification [e.g., Lev. 11–15 and the Mishnah's Order of Purities].
3. "and to guide the children of Israel"—this refers to Sages' judicial rulings [*hwr'wt*:
   cf. Lev.4 and M. Horayot].
4. "in all the laws"—this refers to the *midrashot*.
5. "which God spoke"—this refers to the *halakhot*.
6. "through Moses"—this refers to Scripture.

Units 1–3 link the verse's various topical rubrics to the corresponding topic in the
rabbinic tradition of learning. Thus, for example, the injunction to distinguish between the profane and the holy, which is given no concrete qualification in Scripture, is linked to a particular subtheme in the Mishnah's general treatment of the
principles of sanctification—rules governing how one estimates the monetary value
of one's person, cattle, and so on so as to sanctify the equivalent value in money to
the Temple. Shared by each of the three topics chosen by the exegete at 1–3 is the
fact that for each an ample body of Mishnaic material on the topic corresponds to
a relatively rich scriptural foundation as well. These are not, that is, examples of
halakhot which have "nothing to rely upon."

Units 4–6, however, are of most importance for us. The reference to "laws" is
linked to rabbinic text-interpretive tradition associated with scriptural law (*midrash*),
God's speech is interpreted as a reference to the oral-performative halakhic tradition,
and Moses' role is summed up as the writing of Scripture. Here a decisive move has
been made. The *halakhah* is no longer merely rabbinic tradition or an element, with
Scripture, in a larger body of *torah*. Rather, it is tradition which comes from the mouth
of God.[20]

In sum: the Tannaitic midrashic literature has no unanimity regarding the precise equivalence of *halakhah* to one or another scriptural term. But there is no doubt
whatever that, in its view, halakhic tradition, along with the entire spectrum of rabbinic learning, is to be included with Scripture itself as part of the original revelation
to Israel. In a formulation found now in Sifre to Deuteronomy 32:2, par. 306:

> Just as the same rain falls upon trees and gives to each a distinctive flavor—vines
> in accord with their nature, olives in accord with their nature, figs in accord with
> their nature—so too are words of *torah* all one—yet they contain [the distinct char-
> acteristics of] Scripture, mishnah, halakhot, and *aggadot*.

The theological reconceptualization of *halakhah* from human oral-performative
tradition to the very speech of God is essentially complete. Indeed, from the perspective of the curriculum pericope, it is a small step to the classical legitimation of
halakhic authority found in the conception of the Written and Oral Torah.

That tentative step, in fact, takes place within the Tannaitic midrashic compilations themselves. Here, once in Sifre to Deuteronomy Dt. 33:10, par. 351, and once in
Sifra Behuqotai (to Lev.26:46), a conventional scriptural reference to divine teachings
in the plural (*twrwt*) yields the same midrashic response: "This teaches that two Torahs
were given to Israel, one by mouth and one in script." A brief comparison of these two

passages will enable us to conclude our tracing of the diverse conceptions of halakhic origins and authority that remain in tension within the Tannaitic materials.

In Moses' final blessing of the tribes of Israel prior to his death, he offers a charge to the priestly tribe of Levi: "They shall teach your judgments to Jacob and your Torah [*twrtk*] to Israel" (MT Dt.33:10). As L. Finkelstein has noted,[21] the midrashic response at Sifre to Deuteronomy, par. 351, assumes a small change in the vocalization of *twrtk* to yield "your Torahs" (*twrwtyk*):

1. "And your Torahs to Israel"—this teaches that two Torahs were given to Israel, one by mouth (*bph*) and one in script (*bktb*).
2. Agnitos the Hegemon asked Rabban Gamaliel, saying to him: How many Torahs were given to Israel? He replied: Two—one by mouth [*bph*] and one in script [*bktb*].

The extant biblical texts uniformly attest the singular form of Torah. Accordingly, the *midrash*ist (1) is most likely bringing his conception of two Torahs to the text rather than reasoning toward it from a textual cue.[22] The brief narrative at 2 links the idea to an early Tannaitic authority, probably the Yavnean Rabban Gamaliel II.[23] Here, in a post-Mishnaic compilation of Tannaitic exegetical tradition, is our first attempt to assign the idea of two revealed sources of Torah, one written and one in writing, to a rabbinic Sage.

The point did not remained unchallenged. A midrashic compilation roughly contemporary with Sifre, the Sifra to Leviticus, preserves an important curriculum pericope of the type we have already examined. The scriptural text is Lev. 26:46: "These are the statutes, the judgments, and the Torahs [*twrwt*] which YHWH established between himself and the people Israel on Mount Sinai by the hand of Moses." The *midrash*ist, more fortunate than his colleague in Sifre Deuteronomy 351, has the advantage of a scriptural source that speaks of Torah in the plural. His resignification of the entire series of legal terms follows accordingly (Sifra, Behuqotai, par. 8:12):

1. "The statutes"—these are the exegetical traditions [*mdršwt*].

   "the judgments"—these are the rules of judicial procedure [*dynym*].

   "the Torahs"—this teaches that two Torahs were given to Israel, one in script [*bktb*] and one orally [*b'l ph*].
      2. Said Rabbi Aqiva: Now did Israel have only two Torahs?! Indeed, weren't many Torahs given to Israel? "This is the Torah of the Whole Offering" [Lev. 6:2], "This is the Torah of the Meal Offering" [Lev. 6:7], "This is the Torah of the Guilt Offering" [Lev. 7:1], "This is the Torah of the Peace Offering" [Lev. 7:11], "This is the Torah when a person dies in a tent" [Num. 19:14].
3. "Which YHWH established between himself and the people Israel"—Moses was privileged to mediate between Israel and their Father in Heaven.
4. "on Mount Sinai by the hand of Moses"—this teaches that the Torah was given with all its *halakhot*, details, and explanations through Moses on Mount Sinai.

Units 1 + 3–4 are more explicit than other pericope in linking all of rabbinic oral-performative tradition—including *halakhot*—to Sinaitic revelation as part of *an orally delivered* Torah complementing the one written in Scripture. But note the important intrusion attributed to Rabbi Aqiva (2). Citing the frequent scriptural usage of *twrh* to mean a body of topically delimited instruction, he dismantles the exegetical assertion of unit 1 into an absurdity. Whatever the authority of the Oral Torah might be, it requires no support from scriptural exegetes.

The text from Sifra shows that, even in the latest strata of the Tannaitic corpus, the emerging conception of rabbinic tradition as an element of revelation is far from secure. The prestigious figure of Rabbi Aqiva himself is marshalled as a critic of ideological excesses mounted on its behalf. But it has made its appearance as one among a number of competing models by which Sages sought to root their distinctive tradition—halakhic learning—solidly in the soil of the revelation upon which Israel's covenantal existence is grounded. For the third-century tradents of Tannaitic midrashic learning, the oral-performative tradition in which halakhic norms are carried is no longer represented as it routinely appears in the materials of the Mishnah and the Tosefta—as the result of human ingenuity working in spheres beyond the range of Scripture. Rather, it is portrayed as an epiphenomenon of the same processes that produce Scripture. Like the Mishnah's *halakhah*, that of the Tosefta and the midrashic compilations is the effective source of traditional learning by which Israel maintains the continuity of its life with the commandments of Scripture. But unlike anything in the Mishnaic and Toseftan swath of traditional halakhic discourse, the midrashic representations of rabbinic text-interpretive tradition have begun to collapse the distinction between divine words and traditions transmitted within human institutions. Whatever is legitimately incorporated into the rabbinic tradition of learning is by that very fact connected in some way to the heritage of Sinai.

Halakhah, Words of the Scribes, and Sinaitic Tradition

There is one final aspect of this process that deserves our attention: the way in which early rabbinic legal theorists located *halakhah* in relation to other sources of legal norms that tradition had identified as originating beyond the explicit sense of Scripture. The most important of these are identified in the Tannaitic compilations as the "words of the scribes" (*dbry swprym*; vocalized *divrei soferim*).[24] Like *halakhah* itself, *divrei soferim* has more than a single connotation in early rabbinic jurisprudential and historical reflection. Subtle shifts in the term's signification as it passes through the tradental groups who compiled the Mishnah and the Tosefta will provide yet another example of the tendency of rabbinic theorists of the middle to late third century to assimilate more and more of the inherited extrascriptural oral-performative tradition to revelation itself.[25]

In the Mishnah, the distinction between *halakhah* and *divrei soferim* as sources of tradition is drawn most clearly by reference to a third source of norms, the Mosaic Torah itself (*hatorah*). This point is clear on the basis of the one place in the Mishnah (paralleled in Sifra Emor, par. 10:11) in which scribal opinion is explicitly juxtaposed with *halakhah* (M. Orlah 3:9):

1. New grain [of the spring harvest] is forbidden [for consumption prior to the offering of the first sheaf] anywhere [in the Land and in the Exile] on the basis of the Torah [Lev. 23:10–15].
2. But [the prohibition of] foreskin-fruit[26] [Lev. 19:23] [in the Exile] is *halakhah*.
3. And seed of diverse kinds [Lev. 19:19 and Dt. 22:9–11] [is prohibited from being sown together even in the Exile] on the basis of *divrei soferim*.

The Mishnah recognizes an apparently troubling legal fact: rabbinic tradition applies to diaspora Jews certain agricultural prohibitions that, at least from a superficial reading of the Torah, should apply only in the Land of Israel. On what authority do these extensions rest? The answer is supplied by reference to the three distinct sources of authoritative legal tradition.

The Mishnah grounds the diaspora prohibition against new grain in the language of the Torah itself (1). Lev. 23:10–15 is clear that the offering of the first sheaf is to be taken from the produce of the Land of Israel. But in a concluding coda, Lev. 23:15 prohibits the consumption "in all of your dwellings" of any produce prior to the removal of the sheaf. On the basis of this specification, the Sages' text-interpretive tradition stipulates that the intent of the prohibition is to cover any area of Jewish settlement, including lands of the Exile. Since the inference can be directly linked to a scriptural source, the resulting prohibition is regarded as part of the intended sense of the ruling: it is "from the Torah."[27]

The basis of the diaspora prohibitions against foreskin-fruit and the sowing of diverse kinds are acknowledged to have a more attentuated foundation in the Torah. In the case of foreskin-fruit, Scripture does not forbid such fruit "in all your dwellings." Presumably, then, the Mishnaic prohibition stands on the authority of the Sages' oral-performative tradition rather than explicit scriptural language as mediated within traditions of text-interpretation. We are not surprised, therefore, to learn that it is, as the Mishnah states, *halakhah* (2).

The surprise comes in ruling 3. Like the Torah's prohibition against foreskin-fruit, that against sowing diverse kinds of seeds in the same field is not modified by any reference to "all your dwellings." Accordingly, the Mishnah acknowledges that the extension of the prohibition to the diaspora is founded in the traditional norms rather than in the Torah. But instead of seeing the expected reference to halakhic tradition, we are directed to "words of the scribes."

What is at stake in the assumed distinction between *halakhah* and words of the scribes? M. Orlah 3:9 itself provides no explicit explanation of this distinction nor of its implications regarding the relative authority of each legal source. Amoraic authorities of the third century were themselves puzzled by the matter, offering divergent solutions.[28] Both *halakhah* and words of the scribes clearly constitute sources of legal guidance. Are the sources, however, distinct in origin but equal in authority? Or is there a distinction to be made in their authorities as well?

Traditions reflected in the Mishnah and Tosefta, unfortunately, nowhere address this point explicitly, but some inferences are nevertheless possible. The first observation we can make is that there is an important difference in the way *halakhah* and *divrei soferim* are assumed in the Mishnah to correlate with scriptural commandments. As we saw in chapter 4, the Mishnah and Tosefta commonly understand halakhic dicta to constitute a source of legal material not merely supplementary to Scripture, but genuinely definitive of its application.[29] As authoritative tradition, halakhic norms established by the Sages govern the embodiment of the scriptural code, even if, in M. Hagigah 1:8's vivid image, they "flutter in the air" or "hang by a hair," and despite the acknowledgment that the "essence of the *halakhot*" (T. Hagigah 1:9) lies precisely where Scripture and *halakhah* are most deeply intertwined.

Matters are not as simple in the case of teachings attributed to scribal authority. In the handful of rulings identified as such in the Tannaitic literature, scribal teachings, like many halakhic dicta, appear to constitute legal views supplementary to those of Scripture. Thus they share with halakhic norms an origin beyond the range of text-interpretive tradition per se. They are not "from the Torah." But at this point the resemblance of scribal teaching to halakhic tradition ends. In all Mishnaic contexts it is quite clear that, unlike norms identified as *halakhah, divrei soferim* play an essentially contingent role in the overall legal structure.[30]

Thus, in the crucial domain of contamination and purification, M. Tohorot 4:7 lists a series of "doubtful cases in which Sages declared [that a potential source of contamination is] clean." Among these are "a case of doubt regarding [sources of contamination identified by] the words of scribes." The implication is spelled out at M. Tohorot 4:11:

1. [Here is a] case of doubt [identified by] the words of scribes:
2. He ate foods [deemed] unclean [by scribal authority],[31] drank liquids [deemed] unclean [by scribal authority],[32] his head and most of his body entered drawn water, or three logs of drawn water fell upon his head and most of his body[33]— doubt in such cases is ruled clean.
3. But a matter involving a primal source of uncleanness, and it is [defined as such] by the words of the scribes—doubt in such cases is ruled unclean.

What is at issue here in the Mishnah? A person suffering any of the mishaps identified in unit 2 is deemed unclean on the basis of scribal tradition. The practical impact is that such a person will render unfit for priestly consumption any priestly offerings he happens to touch (M. Zabim 5:12).

The Mishnah now rules that if there is a doubt that the person has actually become contaminated, or a doubt whether he has engaged in an effective purification procedure, it is possible to rule leniently and to declare the person clean. By contrast, a person suspected—but not proven—to suffer a scripturally grounded state of uncleanness would remain in the presumption of uncleanness. The reason for leniency in the scribal case is that these extensions of the Torah's definition of uncleanness are sponsored solely by scribal authority. Matters are different, however, at ruling 3. The scribes might stand behind the designation of, for example, congealed soil beneath a corpse (M. Ohalot 3:5)[34] as conveying the uncleanness of the corpse itself. But because of the extreme implications of corpse contamination, the Mishnah permits a doubt in this instance to be judged strictly as unclean.

This discussion exemplifies the conception of the legal authority of scribal tradition that was assumed by the shapers of the Mishnaic tradition. It is roughly analogous to the halakhic teaching of an individual that has not been accepted as a normative halakhic ruling by the majority of Sages. That is, it survives only as an element in the tradition of learning (e.g., M. Eduyot 1:5, discussed in chapter 4). It functions as a source placed in the hands of Sages to apply or overrule in accordance with their own judgment. Scribal rulings are transmitted within the oral-performative tradition as material for halakhic reflection and can be applied with the full sanction of halakhic tradition if circumstances so require. But they do not in themselves have the authority of a binding tradition or legal rule.

We can now bring this point to bear upon the interpretation of M. Orlah 3:9, the issue that generated the inquiry. It would appear that M. Orlah 3:9's ruling regarding foreskin-fruit, identified as a *halakhah*, would enjoy a firmer legal foundation than the scribal proscription against sowing diverse kinds in the diaspora. Thus the distinction between *halakhah* and scribal tradition is symptomatic of a broader hierarchy of extrascriptural norms implied in Mishnaic jurisprudence. At the top are rabbinic norms, borne in the text-interpretive tradition associated with the Mosaic Torah, that are defined as the plain implication of scriptural language (*min hatorah*, "from the Torah"). Below them are rabbinic oral-performative traditions, based in logical reasoning, preserved independently of the text-interpretive tradition's construction of the Torah's language (*halakhah*). Lower still are scribal teachings (*divrei soferim*), which are accorded normative status only when accepted by Sages into the larger structure of halakhic norms.

This hierarchy is strikingly similar to that we found in M. Hagigah 1:8, with the addition of scribal teachings to the bottom of the pyramid of authority. As we shall now learn, however, the Mishnah's carefully drawn distinctions between the halakhic tradition and scribal learning was not to enjoy much resonance in the developing jurisprudence of the rabbinic community. One reason, perhaps, is the logical anomaly of the status of scribal teachings. If they are traditions that can be applied at the option of a Sage, what distinguishes them from minority halakhic opinions, such as those discussed at M. Eduyyot 1:5, that are preserved in memory even though they do not function as binding norms? I know of no discussion of this problem in the Tannaitic compilations, but it is quite clear that later heirs of the Mishnaic literary heritage recognized the problem. They solved it, moreover, with remarkable elegance — by eliding the distinction between halakhic norms and scribal teachings altogether. In those strands of Tannaitic tradition that began to assimilate halakhic norms into the original Sinaitic revelation, we find a corresponding assimilation of scribal teachings to the status of halakhic tradition.

The hermeneutical activity that underlay and supported such new constructions of the shape of tradition is not difficult to trace. The most illustrative example concerns not Moses, but another hero of ancient Judaism, Abraham, the first human to acknowledge the God of Israel. Traditions already included in the Mishnah assume that Abraham, despite having lived many generations before Moses, had already been a follower of the laws delivered on Sinai to God's greatest prophet.

M Qiddushin 4:14 offers a brief exegetical inference drawn from Gen. 26:5. After commenting on this passage, I will point out how its resonances are heard and transmitted in the Tosefta. The Mishnah states:

> We find that Father Avraham observed the Torah [*hatorah*] in its entirety before it was given, as it is said: "Since Abraham obeyed my voice, and kept my observances, commandments, statutes and my teachings [*torotai*]. (Gen. 26:5)

Abraham's obedience to the Torah prior to its revelation, asserted in the introduction to the paragraph, is implied by the scriptural text itself, which lists a series of virtual synonyms for divine law as testimony to Abraham's obedience to God. The Mishnah therefore offers little beyond a restatement of the scriptural claim. At best it highlights for a rabbinic audience the centrality of Abraham as a model of obedience—hardly an original or controversial thought in ancient Judaism.[35]

Later appropriations of this reading of Gen. 26:5, however, take their points of departure from a detail of the verse which seems to hold little interest for the framer of the Mishnaic passage. This is the appearance of the word *torah* in its plural form, "my teachings" (*torotai*). We already noted in chapter 4 that the plural form of *torah* served as a scriptural hook upon which to hang the emergent conception of an Oral and Written Torah in Sifra to Leviticus and Sifre to Deuteronomy. The Tosefta, for its part, charts a different direction. Insofar as the two main Tosefta manuscripts unpack the meaning of the plural form of *torah* in significantly different ways, we shall take a look at both.

MS. Vienna's version of T. Qid. 5:21 says of Abraham:[36]

> 1. And the Omnipresent blessed him in his old age more than in his youth. And why so? For he enacted the Torah even before it came, as it is said: "Since Abraham obeyed my voice . . . and my *torot*."
> 2. "My *torah*" is not stated; rather, "my *torot*." This teaches that the interpretations [*t'my*] of the Torah and all its specifications [*dqdwqyh*] were revealed to him.

Compare MS Erfurt's version of the exegetical play of unit 2:[37]

> "My *torah*" is not stated; rather, "my *torot*." This teaches that the words of the Torah and the words of the scribes were revealed to him.

The Tosefta's attention, like that of the tradents of materials such as those we reviewed at Sifre Deuteronomy 351 and Sifra Behuqotai, is drawn to the implications of the plural form of *torah*. For each tradent, the plurality of *torah* suggests Abraham's knowledge both of the text of the Mosaic scrolls and of some other source of teaching.

But notice the distinction between Vienna and Erfurt in the kind of extrascriptural content each finds concealed behind the biblical term. For Vienna, Abraham receives as revelation not only the commandments of the Torah, but also its principal topics, as well as the details of their enactment. It is not clear where these details are to be found, of course, although the terms "interpretations" and "specifications" imply that they are available in the text-interpretive tradition of the Sages transmitted in the contexts of the oral declamation and exposition of Scripture. The Erfurt text, however, supplies a far more explicit answer: the dual reference of *torot* implies Abraham's reception of two corpora of revealed knowledge: the text of the Sinaitic Torah and the body of scribal teaching which incorporates the "specifications" that enable the proper application of the text to covenant life. These too are *torah*; these too stem from the divine word.

The dual reading of MS Vienna and Erfurt represents more than an odd textual variant. Rather, each version takes a position in an important turning point in the conceptualization of the rabbinic tradition as such. MS Vienna's allusion to "specifications" intertextually alludes to the tradition recorded at Sifra, Behuqotai, par. 8:12, regarding the "applications, specifications, and interpretations" transmitted by God into Moses' hands at Sinai. Abraham, that is, knew what Moses would one day know, by a kind of prophetic precognition. The Erfurt version of the Tosefta, sharpening the implication of Vienna, argues that everything preserved in rabbinic legal memory—even the minutest contributions of the ancient scribes—is included among the "specifications" proferred to Moses and foreseen even before him by Abraham. Scribal traditions, isolated in the Mishnah from the main body of rabbinic tradition, have now penetrated that tradition and become a synonym for it. As the Babylonian Talmud would later have it in its own interpretive rendering of MS Erfurt's tradition: "All the same are the words of the Torah and the words of the scribes" (B. Yoma 28b).[38]

As far as the tradents of Mishnaic tradition are concerned, we have seen, the words of the scribes are a source of law secondary to and distinct from *halakhah*. But the Mishnaic current of tradition overlaps with and, indeed, is ultimately recast by a different perspective, now preserved in various forms in the Tosefta. In this view, words of the scribes are assimilated to halakhic tradition in both a jurisprudential and historical sense. On the one hand, the Toseftan tradents conceive scribal teaching as the Second Temple period equivalent of the *halakhah* embodied in the decisions and teachings of rabbinic Sages of the third century. The difference lies in terminology, not substance. Accordingly, on the other hand, the concept of *halakhah*, preserved in the Mishnah as a source of tradition quite distinct from scribal teachings, begins in the Tosefta and the midrashic literature to assimilate the latter to itself.

For the Galilean Amoraic heirs of the Tannaitic traditions, whose contribution to the concept of Torah in the Mouth will occupy us in chapter 7, it will become all but impossible to understand *halakhah* and words of the scribes as anything but distinct and equal components of the rabbinic legal system. Thus, Rabbi Yohanan, the late-third-century master, will be reported to have said that "words of the scribes overrule words of the Torah" (Y. Maaser Sheni 2:2, 53c) or that "words of the scribes are related to words of the Torah and as beloved as words of the Torah" (Y. Berakhot 1:7, 3b).[39] Words of the scribes will enjoy—with *halakhah, midrash, aggadah, talmud*, and other topics within the rabbinic curriculum—the status of the original, revealed companion to the Mosaic Torah bequeathed to Moses and Israel at Sinai.

Summary

Our study of the earliest results of rabbinic reflection on the origins, nature, and authority of halakhic tradition can now be briefly summarized. We observed in chapter 4 that a single, stable assumption—that rabbinic knowledge was transmitted orally in face-to-face tutoring—characterizes all Tannaitic sources from the Mishnah to the halakhic *midrash*im. The differences concern largely the degree to which distinct tradents of Tannaitic traditions took this fact of transmission to have ideological or jurisprudential significance. In this chapter we found that each compilation of Tannaitic tradition preserves a multiplicity of points of view. Yet at the same time, each displays certain characteristic tendencies which contextualize, and perhaps somewhat neutralize, materials preserving alternate perspectives.

The process of halakhic construction, for example, is represented in diverse and incommensurate ways. The Mishnah and the Tosefta are at one in preserving these diverse images. At times halakhic norms are legislated by the most sober of official deliberations, emerging from the most prestigious of national institutions; at others the *halakhah* is imposed by force through the crassest exercises of back-room politics in the lofts of private homes. In still others, a Sage can create a halakhic precedent simply through his own personal action without benefit of official action.

There is as well no unanimity regarding the antiquity of the tradition that serves as the foundation for the implementation of halakhic norms. Sinai, the source of the revelation of the Torah of Moses, is virtually ignored in the Mishnah and Tosefta as a foundation for the substance of the oral-performative halakhic tradition. The testimony of M. Avot, devoid of all interest in halakhic tradition, does not alter this picture. Rather, the tradition of legal reflection is consistently linked to individual founders of the late Second Temple period, predominantly Hillel, Shammai, and their disciples. But, as we have repeatedly noticed, midrashic compilations of traditions bearing the names of the very Sages who supply Mishnaic opinions consistently push every element of the rabbinic curriculum of learning—the *halakhah* included— back to the Sinaitic moment.

The related matter of the legal genealogy of halakhic tradition also presents itself in a variety of faces. Are halakhic norms derived by Sages exegetically from scriptural revelation as text-interpretive tradition, or do Sages legislate as they see fit in essential independence of exegetical legitimation? In the Mishnah and Tosefta the question is difficult to answer. Images of halakhic mountains hanging by thin threads of scriptural rules conjoin claims that all halakhic norms stem from the exegesis of scriptural commandments. Claims of locating the "essence" of halakhic tradition in scriptural exegesis are ignored by the acceptance of great bodies of binding norms that have no correlation with scriptural legislation. Yet, primarily in the midrashic compilations—precisely where the stakes for the authority of exegesis are highest— there is little doubt that everything legislated within the halakhic tradition can be collapsed back into relatively straightforward readings of the language of God recorded by Moses.

At best we have been able to discern a certain trajectory or motion of thought that tends to orchestrate the disparate points of view. There seems an unmistakable tendency in the Tosefta, and especially the halakhic midrashim, to bring halakhic oral-performative tradition of various sorts into ever closer proximity to a primordial Sinaitic revelation. We saw this most starkly just now in the post-Mishnaic destiny of the rather minor jurisprudential category of "words of the scribes." The least authoritative element in the hierarchy of Mishnaic jurisprudence was precisely that element selected in the Tosefta as the symbol of *halakhah* per se and its intimate association with Sinai.

In all this, it is surprising that the explicit reference to the dual revelation of a Written and Oral Torah plays such a minor role. Absent in M. Avot where we might most expect to find it, the theme emerges in only the faintest form and lies buried obscurely in but two passages of midrashic exegesis—not an auspicious beginning for an ideological conception that would, within a generation or two, come to dominate rabbinic discourse about the origins and authority of halakhic norms. But the fact remains: if the rabbinic movement had not survived the third century, had it reached the end of its literary life in the Tannaitic compilations, historians would have no reason to think that the notion of an Oral and Written Torah enjoyed any particular prominence among Sages, certainly no more than the equally scarce concept of *halakhah* delivered to Moses at Sinai, and far less than the richly represented view that halakhic tradition emerged in the recent and all-to-human deliberations of the recent generations of the disciples of Shammai, Hillel, and other Founders.

But the rabbinic literary tradition did not die. It was, to the contrary, delivered into hands that treasured it and mined it, digging ever more deeply into it, and finding ever more within it. Among the things these hands found—the hands of Palestinian Amoraim of the third and subsequent centuries—were clues that the *torah* of the Sages, equivalent after all to the words of the scribes, was indeed all delivered to Moses by God.

In chapter 7 I will trace some key moments in this discovery. I will also attempt to explain why, among other possible ways of conceptualizing the relation of rabbinic norms to scriptural revelation, the conception of Torah in the Mouth and Torah in Script ultimately seized the rabbinic imagination as did no other. But first we must confront one of the most perplexing puzzles of rabbinic literary history: the relation of the rabbinic oral-performative tradition itself to the surviving writings that claim to preserve it as Torah in the Mouth.

6

Composing the Tannaitic Oral-Literary Tradition

The Interpenetration of Oral and Written Composition

The third- and fourth-century editors of the Tannaitic compilations, we have seen, took for granted that the traditions they shaped into larger compositions had reached their circles by word of mouth. We noticed as well an emergent, but hardly universal, tendency to explain this perceived fact of life—the orally transmitted character of rabbinic teaching—in terms of a nascent theory of a primordial twofold revelation of *torah*. The written Scriptures, in this view, co-originated with an orally delivered body of exegesis and norms transmitted from Sinai in a chain of tradition culminating in the Sages.

It is important to realize, however, that within the Tannaitic corpus itself these claims about the oral origins and primordial transmission of the tradition refer only to discrete halakhic teachings (e.g., *halakhot* stemming from Moses on Sinai, as in M. Peah 2:6) or to isolated halakhic themes (e.g., *halakhot* of cleanness and uncleanness, as in M. Hagigah 1:8). We find no assertion, for example, that various compilations of Tannaitic teachings—such as the Mishnah—were themselves unwritten[1] or constituted some part of the primordial oral revelation.[2]

We are under no compulsion, therefore, from either logic or the testimony of the sources, to imagine that compilations such as the Mishnah were composed and edited solely through the mnemonically managed organization and manipulation of unwritten materials. Modern historians of the rabbinic literature, following precedents set by medieval scholars, have taken a number of positions on this question.[3] Some modern scholars argue for an entirely oral transmission of rabbinic literary tradition. On this view, rabbinic compilations such as the Mishnah were composed as oral performative literature and remained so until various constraints compelled rabbinic authorities to produce written transcriptions, more or less identical to the received medieval manuscripts.[4] Others hold that rabbinic compilations were, from the outset, produced as written texts, the oral-compositional tradition having effectively ended with the compilation of discrete traditions into larger compilations.[5]

This chapter attempts to carve out an intermediate position on this question.[6] My position respects the evidence, seen in the previous chapter, that rabbinic tradents transmitted discrete traditions largely through orally managed disciplines of memory. But it also presents grounds for suggesting that the mnemonically sophisticated formulations in the surviving rabbinic compilations have passed through the filter of scribal composition, particularly in the transition to documentary compilation. Thus, instead of insisting on the primacy of either oral or written compositional methods in the creation of rabbinic literature, we shall explore the model of interpenetration or interdependence of oral and written textual formations. That is, we shall present evidence that the earliest composition of rabbinic oral tradition, the Mishnah itself, reached its present form as its constituent traditions were shaped and revised in a continous circuit of oral performance and written recension—a circuit impossible to break artificially into an "oral substratum" and a "written recension" or vice versa. The goal of this chapter, then, is to increase appreciation of the peculiar ways in which the earliest surviving compilation of rabbinic literary tradition consistently fed and was fed by a fertile rabbinic oral-literary culture, even as the oral-performative character of the Mishnaic text is shaped by conventions particular to the skills of the scribe.

The notion of interpenetration, in my view, is crucial for any reflection upon the relation of the rabbinic writings to the oral-performative literary culture presumed to lie behind them. It is not helpful to conceive "orality" and "literacy" as mutually exclusive domains of rabbinic cultural transmission, serving essentially independent functions in the transmission of knowledge.[7] Indeed, the scriptural literacy of rabbinic Sages, and the foundations of Second Temple scribalism upon which rabbinic literary culture routinely drew, make it difficult to posit a rabbinic tradition of "pure" orally transmitted discourse prior to the Mishnah, uncontaminated by the intervention of writing. I claim that writerly modes of formulating language for sustained rhetorical presentation have shaped even extemporaneous learned discourses, just as such discourses have been reshaped by the constraints of written notation wherever they have been transcribed for further transmission. "Oral traditions," therefore, need not necessarily be ancient or independent of written transmission, nor need written material be recent or represent a "secondary" stage of a putatively primitive "oral" stage.[8]

The readings that follow treat the material inscribed in the Mishnah as the foundation of a scripted performance analogous in some ways to a dramatic or musical presentation.[9] The script or score is produced with the assumption that its meanings will be activated primarily in performance before an audience. Nevertheless, the performance is unalterably reflective of the prior labor of conception, compositional experimentation, and editing which produces a script or score. This labor, in my view, was to a significant degree scribal; that is, even to the degree that it rendered material memorized from oral-performative settings, the literary compilation involved tasks such as copying and revising texts transmitted in written form. The results of such editorial activity, such as the Mishnah itself, is neither the "original script" nor any of its performance versions. We have merely a text, the present versions of which have been preserved in writing for an unknown period prior to their earliest medieval manuscript versions. On this slender evidence I hope to build a model of oral-written penetration which can sustain empirical scrutiny and, perhaps, inspire further inquiry.

Our attention will focus first upon those aspects of Mishnaic tradition which, in view of the cross-cultural criterion of form, are most likely to have some relation to orally composed and preserved tradition—that is, narratives and lists.[10] It shall become clear, however, that it is impossible to determine whether such material emerged *first* out of "oral" or "written" composition, because the categories themselves, within the setting of rabbinic culture, are permeable. What can be shown, rather, is that these Mishnaic materials are complex weaves in which traits associated with "ideal types" of oral and written composition or transmission mutually shape each other.

These perspectives on oral tradition in the Mishnah are illustrated from four sample studies. The first is from M. Tamid, an idiosyncratic tractate in that it is mostly narrative rather than a compilation of legal discussion. It is of interest here because it shows the degree to which the rabbinic narrative tradition of the second century may have been hospitable to oral-poetic material. At the same time, I argue, the text as we have it has been handled throughout most of its composition and transmission in written form.

Two other textual examples, lists from Tractates Eruvin and Pesahim, are more conventionally Mishnaic in their concern for transmitting legal tradition. These lists constitute impressive testimony to the economy and sophistication of mnemonics in early rabbinic tradition. Indeed, a committed "oralist" might regard them as primary models of what orally composed and transmitted knowledge were in the second century. Yet, at the same time, in their present Mishnaic settings, these texts are now framed by compositional, exegetical, or redactional interventions which disclose the work of written composition. Putatively "oral" texts are separable from their settings only after laborious analysis, and even then they cannot be firmly represented as originating in unscripted, memorized oral composition and transmission.

The final study focuses on a fundamental problem in the study of oral-literary tradition: the relationship of fixed written texts to the diverse oral-performative versions out of which they emerge and in light of which their audiences hear and interpret them. In the study of early rabbinic literature, the only way to gain access to the performative tradition behind the surviving manuscript copies is through the study of textual parallels preserved in a variety of written compositional settings. In order to illustrate this issue in the rabbinic context, we shall explore the relationship between two parallel chapters of M. Parah and its Toseftan counterpart. After analysis, I will propose that the Mishnaic and Toseftan chapters are independent written recensions of an anterior oral-performative narrative regarding the purification rite associated with the red cow of Numbers 19.

In sum: I hope to show that the Mishnaic text, throughout the traceable course of its composition and transmission, was *seen* by its compilers and transmitters as well as heard. That is, the aural/oral traits inscribed in the text do not demonstrate an "oral origin" for the text. Rather, they reflect a literary milieu in which written composition was deeply shaped by oral-performative traditions, even as the performative tradition was shaped by scribal skills. On the basis of these results, it will be possible, in the final chapter, to assess the cultural meaning of the mature rabbinic conception of Torah in the Mouth as it took shape among the Galilean Amoraim of the third and fourth centuries.

Narrative and Song in Mishnah Tamid

Folkloric and anthropological studies suggest that the oral traditions of many cultures are most likely to be found in narrative and poetic traditions. Often transmitted as song, the rhythms and chants serve as a powerful aid to memory.[11] Taking as inspiration Rabbi Aqiva's advice to sing the oral tradition (T. Ahilut 16:8/T. Parah 4:7), our search for oral dimensions of Mishnaic composition should begin in those parts of the Mishnah that are preoccupied with extended narrative.

The typical conventions of Greco-Roman epic literature, however—character development, heroic struggle, resolutions of conflict—are entirely absent in Mishnaic narrative.[12] Neither does the Mishnah stand within any of the traditions of narrative construction preserved in the Hebrew Bible.[13] Rather, most of the Mishnah's extended narrative materials—quite brief by any comparative standard—tend to focus on spare descriptive accounts of the most important institutions in ancient Palestinian Jewish society: the Jerusalem Temple and the Sanhedrin. Some Mishnaic tractates, concerned with conduct of the Temple service or the courts, include sections of narrative which simply describe the appropriate proceedings.[14] In these tractates, the most common sort of Mishnaic tradition—reports of legal rulings and disputes in the names of Sages—are interlaced with descriptive accounts of the acts of priestly officiants, court officials, or the commoners affected by them. In a few other tractates there is little or no legal discussion at all; the tractates consist entirely of narration from beginning to end.[15]

Such narrative material is of great interest for the light it might shed on the question of rabbinic oral-literary culture. The following is a passage of the third chapter of Tractate Tamid (3:7 ff.), a narrative tractate from beginning to end, which describes the procedure for preparing and offering the morning and twilight daily sacrifices.

This citation begins as a designated priestly officiant is leading the lamb for the morning sacrifice to the place near the altar where it will be slaughtered:[16]

> *He came to the small northern door.*
> *Now, two small doors were in the Great Gate,*
> *One to the north and the other to the south.*
> *The southern one—no one entered it ever.*
>> and this is explained by Ezekiel:
>> "And the Lord spoke to me: This gate shall be locked, and no one should open it, nor shall he come in, for the Lord, the God of Israel, shall enter through it, and it shall be locked."
> *And he took the key and opened the small door,*
> *entered the cell,*
> *and from the cell to the sanctuary,*
> *until he reached the Great Gate.*
> *Upon reaching the Great Gate,*
> *he drew back the bolt and the locks,*
> *and opened it.*
> *The slaughterer would not slaughter*
> *until he heard the sound of the Great Gate opening.*

Even in Jericho,
they heard the sound
of the Great Gate opening.
Even in Jericho,
they heard the sound
of the tympanum.
Even in Jericho,
they heard the sound
of the wheel that Ben Qatin made for the basin.
Even in Jericho,
they heard the sound
of Gvini, the Crier.[17]
Even in Jericho,
they heard the sound
of the flute.
Even in Jericho,
they heard the sound
of the cymbals.
Even in Jericho,
they heard the sound
of the song.
Even in Jericho,
they heard the sound
of the shofar.

> And some say: also the sound of the High Priest, at the time he uttered the Name on Yom Kippurim.

Even in Jericho,
they smelled the fragrance
of the burning frankincense.

> Said Rabbi Eliezer b. Daglai:[18] Father had goats in the Mikhvar range,[19] and they would sneeze from the fragrance of the burning frankincense.

The one who won the removal of the ashes from the inner altar entered, and took the basket and placed it before himself. . . .

The narrative continues in this fashion to describe how the lamb is ultimately tied down, slaughtered, flayed, and offered. Of interest in this passage, however, are some textual peculiarities that I've highlighted through paragraphing and typography.

The italicized material represents the voice of the main narrator of the tractate. This voice, which dominates the tractate's composition from beginning to end, frames all other textual material within the tractate as interjections or asides. It is, in fact, similar to the distanced, descriptive voice of tractate Middot, a closely related tractate describing the dimensions of the Temple Mount. Indeed, both tractates begin with the same opening lines, each of which generates an independent narrative description. While Tamid describes Temple procedure, Middot describes the setting of that procedure.[20]

The narrative voice of Tamid does not locate itself in time, although rhetorically it presents itself as an eye-witness account of events as they took place. Nor is it possible to determine decisively whether this voice's narration stems from an oral-performative tradition or whether it represents a more writerly mode of composition.[21]

It is probable, however, that the Mishnah's rendering of the narrative reached its present form some time before the extant version of Tamid. I also believe that this form was that of written words on a scroll.

Note first of all that the italicized narrative is interspersed with two rather different types of expansions. These depart markedly from the narrative in literary style and are indicated in the translation by boldface and plain type. These represent interjections, as it were, from beyond the narrative voice and treat that voice as a textual entity in its own right. The plain-type supplements are typical of the Mishnah, for they ground in traditional lore some additional contribution to an established discussion.

The first of these plain-type supplements enhances the narrator's account of the priest's progress, summoning Scripture to explain why the priest enters the northern rather than the southern door. The final two address not the core narrative, but a second expansion of that narrative, a description of the impressive sensory power of the service in the Temple. This supplement is not in the narrator's voice either. Its lyrical rhythms and formulaic repetitions mark it as a poetic form clearly distinct from the prosaic narrative structure which constitutes its present setting. This poetic material is itself interrupted by the two final comments, already noted. Representing neither the narrator's voice nor that of the poet, they are the same voice that provided exegetical reference to Ezekiel.

Now let us reflect on what is before us. It is, I suppose, possible to insist that we have here a stenographic transcription of a text composed by an orator in public performance, as a strictly "oralist" model of rabbinic tradition would require. But is this really the soundest explanation? The variations of voice are easily explained in the language of textual description as successive supplementations of a text whose core enjoyed the stability made possible by either memorization or written preservation. That is, the primary narrative voice (in italics) is supplemented by a layer of poetic material (boldface); this new literary whole has then been subjected to a series of brief amplifications which, in the form of textual asides, supply information deemed relevant to the narrative as a whole. Simply put, a text has been edited and supplemented with other texts.

Is there anything here, then, that demands that we posit an originally oral composition at the heart of this text—that before us is a deposit in writing of material originating a purely oral compositional setting? One might very cautiously point to the Jericho material. Its balanced, repetitive phrases ("Even in Jericho they heard the sound/smelled the fragrance") may suggest that before us is a written rendering of a text composed in and for oral performance. It is a proud depiction of the greatness of the Temple service, so impressive as to have been experienced miles away in Jericho.[22] I am tempted to call it a popular song.[23] If its perfect verb-forms are not an editorial accommodation to the narrator's voice, it probably stems from the post-destruction era, a nostalgic reminiscence of the magnificence that has been lost.[24]

The independence of this "song" from its present setting is obvious, for the narrative it interrupts continues without any sign of the song's intervention. Moreover, the version of this song preserved in Y. Suk 5:3, 55b—which drops two of the "sounds" from our list—cites it independently of its present setting, introducing it as a list of "Six sounds which they heard in Jericho." Clearly, it was known as an independent unit and, as I've suggested, has now been inserted by an editor.[25] Relevant in a general way to the narrative, and even sharing a few key words, it now amplifies that narrative as a celebratory commentary.

Whether the song was known in written transcription or only in oral-performance prior to its use here is impossible to judge. The explication of the song's contents, however, suggest that its glossator surely worked with a written rendering. These comments are of a pattern that appears countless times in Mishnaic legal discussions. Material framed in this pattern usually provides alternative views on a passage transmitted by named or anonymous authorities. Why, then, have such prosaic amplifications become embedded in the song? The reason, I suggest, is that that song had long ceased to be sung as a song and had now found a new setting in the chants of learned tradition. Having been rendered in writing as part of a performance script, it now enjoyed three performative lives: the song as originally sung in social settings beyond the circles of Mishnaic learned tradition, the performative life of its recitation in the context of Mishnaic memorization and presentation, and the literary life of a manuscript which could receive notation and expansion in view of future performance. Perhaps "oral" in its origins, certainly "written" in its form of preservation, it would enjoy an ongoing oral-performative life precisely as a script, as part of what sages would memorize and recite as *matnytyn*, "our repeated tradition, our Mishnah."

List-Making in Mishnah Eruvin 10:10–14

While the search here for a "pure" orality in M. Tamid, uncontaminated by scribal interventions, has proved ambiguous, this need not be the end of the game. Anthropologists have also pointed out that oral culture is preserved in genres extending well beyond narratives and poetic constructions. A fundamental oral genre in many societies, both nonliterate and scribal, is the production of lists for preserving and organizing culturally significant information.[26] Lists and catalogues are also among the most common formulaic choices exercised in the editing of the Mishnah and the Tosefta.[27] To what degree, then, do such lists retain evidence of oral modes of composition?

For the most part, the Mishnah's lists consist of a superscription, announcing a topic, and a catalogue of appropriate items of information. In some cases, as in Mishnah Maaserot 1:5–8,[28] the lists are so integral to the redactional plan of the tractate that the very conception of the list appears to go hand in hand with the compilation of the tractate. In such cases it is clearly impossible to pursue a hypothetical oral history prior to when the transmitted list was deemed to cohere with some larger and more ambitious literary project.

But lists of this sort do not exhaust the Mishnah's repertoire. It is possible to find in the Mishnah evidence of materials that are quite imperfect by the usual literary standards of Mishnaic list-making; that is, they neither adhere to standard forms of lists nor play much of a role in the larger unfolding of a tractate's discourse on legal themes. Precisely here, therefore, we may have an opportunity to study the list as a source independent of its literary setting and to ask whether it preserves remnants of orally composed material.

M. Eruvin's list of distinctions between the rules of Sabbath rest in the Temple and the provinces is an appropriate example (10:10–14). Its redactional setting is a collection of miscellanies (9:1–10:15) which address themes already spelled out in detail elsewhere in Tractates Eruvin and Shabbat. Why these have not been worked into the appropriate portions of the existing tractates is difficult to say. A possible explanation, of course, is that they are later supplements to a compilation that was otherwise fairly complete as a recension of traditional material. But we cannot explore that possibility in this setting.[29]

In any event, this list follows a rather diffuse series of pericopae which focus on problems occasioned when persons or objects traverse on the Sabbath the demarcation between public and private domains (10:3–9). The last pericope in that series asserts that persons should not stand in one domain and, key in hand, unlock a door in the other. This statement sets the stage for our material, which takes up a related theme: acts that are deemed to constitute violations of the Sabbath rest when performed in the provinces but that do not constitute violations when performed in the Temple:[30]

1. *A doorbolt that has on its top a fastener—*
   Rabbi Elazar prohibits [its use, since it is not a tool]; but Rabbi Yose permits [its use, since it is a tool].
      Said Rabbi Elazar: A precedent—At a synagogue in Tiberias they treated it as permitted until Rabban Gamaliel and the Elders came and declared it prohibited to them.
      Rabbi Yose says: They treated it as prohibited [until] Rabban Gamaliel and the Elders came and declared it permitted to them!
2. *A doorbolt that is dragged [by a cord]—they lock with it in the Temple,*
   but not in the provinces.
   One resting [unattached]—here and there it is prohibited.
      Rabbi Yehudah says: The one that rests is permitted in the Temple, and the one that is dragged in the provinces.
3. *They re-attach a lower door-hinge—*
   in the Temple,
   but not in the provinces.
   And the upper—here and there it is prohibited.
      Rabbi Yehudah says: The upper in the Temple, and the lower in the provinces.[31]
4. *They re-bind a compress—*
   in the Temple;
   but not in the provinces.
   If [it is applied] afresh—here and there it is prohibited.
5. *They tie a harp-string—*
   in the Temple,
   but not in the provinces.
   If afresh—here and there it is prohibited.
6. *They cut off a wart—*
   in the Temple,
   but not in the provinces.
   But if he uses a tool—here and there it is prohibited.
7. *A priest who wounded his finger—*
   they wind a bandage around it in the Temple,
   but not in the provinces.
   If to absorb the blood—here and there it is prohibited.

8. *They sprinkle salt on the [altar] ramp so that they do not slip.*
9. *And [in the Temple] they fill from the Exposed Cistern*[32] *and from the Great Cistern with a rotation wheel on the Sabbath.*
10. *And [in the provinces they fill] from the Cold Spring on a Festival Day.*

This material violates the most general convention of Mishnaic list-making: it doesn't announce the subject of the list before listing the appropriate items. Second, the lack of superscription, which often provides a count of the items to follow, makes it difficult to know how many items are actually part of the list. In any event, I count ten items because these at least address a common legal theme. I have highlighted them with italics.

If there is in this list a primal tradition generated by oral composition and transmitted without writing, it probably lies in items 2–7 and their boldface qualifications. Here we have six items in wonderful formulaic balance. The mnemonic core is plotted in items 3–6:

> *They do X—in the Temple, but not in the provinces.*

The opening and closing items (2, 7) share the same apodosis with 3–6 (+ Temple/ –provinces) but modify the protasis into a casuistic form (An X—they do Y). The result is a highly manageable chiasmic sequence of A-B-B/B-B-A:

2. (A) *An X—they do Y, + Temple/ – provinces*
3. (B) *They do X— + Temple/ – provinces*
4. (B) *They do X— + Temple/ – provinces*
5. (B) *They do X— + Temple/ – provinces*
6. (B) *They do X— + Temple/ – provinces*
7. (A) *An X—they do Y, + Temple/ – provinces*

The boldface material is perfectly assimilated to this mnemonic core. Each supplement offers a contrary in the pattern:

> **if Y—here and there it is prohibited.**

Clearly this is a text shaped for memorization. The problem, of course, is that this obvious fact cannot lead us into any hypothetical moment of oral composition. Before us, at best, is a piece of writing structured by a mnemonic most hospitable to memorization and oral declamation.

Attention to the setting of the passage, furthermore, forces the conclusion that the text as a whole stands at a rather distant remove from any purely oral compositional setting. Italicized item 1 is a dispute, while 8–10 are declarative sentences. The former knows nothing in particular about the Temple/provinces distinction that concerns the rest of the list, while the latter assume the distinction but break the formulaic unity of 2–7. These must be regarded, therefore, as expansions of the primary list. It is difficult to say whether the purpose is to reach 10 items or simply to include other material deemed relevant.

All of these expansions employ formulary patterns equally suited to oral or written transmission. But during the time that items 2–7 may have circulated as an independent unit of learned tradition, it is most unlikely that any expansions would have departed from so elegant a pattern of formulation. Rather, additions should have been homogenized into the existing rhythmic pattern. The expansions in their present form, therefore, suggest the activity of an editor/compiler working with discrete sources who maintains their anterior stylistic integrity. It is possible that these sources are mediated orally and are shaped by slightly different patterns of formulation. But the editorial work of combining them seems more amenable to a scribal copyist/editor, untroubled by mnemonically managing an abundance of formulaic styles, than to a memorizer who seeks to assimilate new orally encountered material to the ingrained pattern established by older material firmly rooted in a prior oral-performative tradition.

The nature of the final contributions to the list certainly confirms this judgment. Comparable to what we have already observed in Tamid, we have a series of comments which assume the presence before the commentator of a completed text. He now supplies some useful but ultimately extrinsic bits of information in the names of acknowledged masters of tradition. The result is certainly still memorizable — but the composition of the whole implies the necessary use of written notation regardless of how the text may ultimately have reached its audience in peformance.[33]

The Complex Mnemonic of Mishnah Pesahim 2:5–6

Another probe into Mishnaic compositional phenomena will confirm the essential ambiguity of the evidence for an exclusively oral substrate to Mishnaic tradition. One important characteristic of oral tradition, highlighted especially by literary and anthropological research, is its complex mnemonic technology. Metrical conventions, syntactical rules, verbal homologies, and other techniques are all crucial to the composition and transmission of oral material.[34] This aspect of oral tradition surfaces in the Mishnah in a variety of settings. Here we consider the example of yet another list — indeed, a catalogue of four lists — which enumerates foods that satisfy certain requirements of the ritual meal consumed on the first evening of Passover.

The biblical text enjoins Israelites to sacrifice a lamb on the eve of Passover and to consume it roasted, with unleavened bread and bitter herbs (Ex. 12:8). The following is an account of the grain that might be used in the bread and the vegetables that might be served as the herb:[35]

> 1. *With these one fulfills his obligation on Pesah:*
>   —with wheat;
>   —with barley;
>   —with spelt;
>   —and with rye;
>   —and with oats.
> 2. *And they fulfill:*
>   —with doubtfully tithed produce;
>   —and with first tithe from which the heave-offering of the tithe is removed;
>   —and with second tithe or temple-dedications which are redeemed.
>   —and priests with dough-offering and with heave-offering.

But not:
—with untithed produce;
—and not with first tithe from which the heave-offering of the tithe has not been removed;
—and not with second tithe or temple-dedications which are not redeemed.
  Thank-offering loaves and the wafers of ascetics—if he made them for himself, he does not fulfill with them;

  if he made them to sell at market, he fulfills with them.

3. *And with these greens one fulfills his obligation on Pesah:*
—with lettuce;
—and with chicory;
—and with pepperwort;
—and with endive;
—and with bitter herb.
They fulfill with them whether fresh or dried, but not:
—with pickled;
—nor with stewed;
—nor with cooked.
  And they join together to constitute an olive's bulk.

4. *And they fulfill:*
—with their stalk;
—and with doubtfully tithed produce;
—and with first tithe from which the heave-offering of the tithe is removed;
—and from second tithe and Temple-dedications which are redeemed.

The italicized material identifies the organizing thematic superscriptions which structure the diverse lists. Boldface identifies the listed items. Material in plain type is formally and thematically secondary to the list. Let us turn to the lists themselves.

Lists 1 and 2 address the problem of grain that may be used to satisfy the obligation to eat unleavened bread at the seder. There are two issues: (1) the type of grains that yield bread and (2) the necessity to remove sanctified offerings from the grain prior to making and consuming the bread. Lists 1 and 2 are balanced by lists 3 and 4, which address a parallel question: which types of herbs may be used to satisfy the obligation to eat bitter herbs at the meal? Again two issues emerge: (3) identification of the types of greens and (4) the need to remove the appropriate offerings. The topical mnemonic structure is rather simple:

1 *types of grains*
2 *types of offerings*
      +
1 *types of greens*
2 *types of offerings*

This simple parallelism controls a more complex chiasmic structure within and between the two basic groups: Lists 3–4 are an inversion of lists 1–2. List 2, dealing with offerings from grain, is actually a balanced pair, divided into a positive ("they fulfull") and a negative ("but not") sublist. So too is list 3, which deals with types of greens. Lists 2 and 3, then, which constitute the transition from the topic of grain to that of greens, are mnemonically managed by the parallelism of their internal structure as lists of paired opposites. We can represent the mnemonic of the master list as follows:

1. (A) *They fulfill with* a (*grains*)
2. (B) *They fulfill with* b/*but not with* c (*tithes*)
   +
1. (B) *They fulfill with* d/*but not with* e (*greens*)
2. (A) *They fulfill with* f (*tithes*)

Now this is a remarkably powerful structure for transmitting the complex information of the list. In an ideal-typical oral setting one can imagine any number of migrations within the items of the list, while the superscriptions firmly control the basic contours of the informational package.[36]

Thus a strictly "oralist" analysis would isolate the series of superscriptions as the surviving oral elements behind Pesahim 2:5–6. The items under these rubrics would have probably varied from one setting to another in the oral-performative settings of transmission, since there is no fixed numerical mnemonic governing the items themselves. But, as before, the "oralist" analysis is made more complex by the literary framework of the text's preservation. That the present version of the list was known as a written source to the composers of Mishnah Pesahim seems confirmed by the material I have indented. These glosses, formally disjunctive and innocent of any concern for the mnemonic of the encompassing literary structure, are intruded episodically and without particular plan into the completed lists. As with the glosses earlier observed in the song of Mishnah Tamid, they testify to a transmissional setting in which scribes and copyists were quite free to add to texts on an ad hoc basis. Whether such additions arose first in the event of performance or only in the silence of a mind reflecting upon a mastered text is impossible to say. It is clear only that the intrusions have themselves in due course become part of the transmission and, thus, of the performance.[37]

M–T Parah and the Anterior Oral-Performative Tradition

Our final probe into the interpenetration of written texts and oral-performative tradition in the shaping of early rabbinic literature aims at contributing a new perspective on an abiding, and still unresolved, controversy regarding rabbinic literature. This is the literary relationship between the Mishnah and the Tosefta. The Tosefta's very name—"Supplement"—heralds its role as a supplementary collection of Tannaitic traditions to be studied as an accompaniment to the primary collection, the Mishnah. Few scholars since M. Zuckermandel have doubted that the Tosefta, containing the opinions of Sages of the mid-third century, reached its literary closure after the Mishnah.[38] Rather the issue concerns the relationship of discrete Toseftan units of tradition to their Mishnaic counterparts.

While much of the present Tosefta clearly seems to know and respond to materials redacted in the Mishnah, many Mishnaic passages seem to revise, abbreviate, or otherwise solve problems that are presented in the Toseftan text.[39] This phenomenon suggests that behind the written versions of the Mishnah and the Tosefta there stood an oral-performative tradition which the compilers of each textual collection drew upon in composing their own collections of Tannaitic halakhic tradition.[40]

That is to say, both the Mishnah and the Tosefta depend for their intelligibility as written texts upon an oral-performative tradition that supplied, through repeated performative versions, the interpretive context needed for the proper reception of the written version's meaning. This tradition included not only various versions of the texts now preserved in written redactions of the Mishnah and the Tosefta, but also amplifications of those versions that were part of the store of text-interpretive tradition taken for granted by the audience and the performers themselves.

Folk literature scholar John Miles Foley has developed the concept of textual "immanence" to account for the capacity of written texts that draw from oral-performative tradition to open beyond themselves to the orally mediated extratextual knowledge that sustains textual meaning. He has defined such "immanence" as:

> the set of metonymic, associative meanings institutionally delivered and received through a dedicated idiom or register either during or on the authority of traditional oral performance. The grammars or "words" at various levels—the formulaic phraseology, the typical narrative scenes, and the story-pattern as a whole—are understood as highly focused, densely encoded systems of integers that open onto implicit and ever-impinging worlds of signification.[41]

This chapter will offer one example of parallel texts in the Mishnah and the Tosefta that seems to exemplify the conception of immanence worked out through entirely different materials by Foley. The case will also show a number of ways in which the present relation between the Mishnaic and Toseftan materials need not be understood as cases of Toseftan expansion of a preexisting Mishnaic text. To the contrary, we will see passages in which the Mishnah seems to take for granted material already attested in the Tosefta. In others, moreover, both the Mishnah and Tosefta seem to know different versions of materials from an oral-performative tradition that preceded the redaction of both.

In order to develop the argument and provide a basis for observations, we need to make a detailed study of two parallel chapters of Mishnah and Tosefta. I have selected chapter 3 of M-T Parah. Like M. Tamid and other tractates rich in ritual narration, that chapter describes the conduct of a rite, discussing specifically the various procedures outlined in Numbers 19:1ff. for the slaughter and immolation of a red cow. The cow's carcass was to be burnt along with cedar wood, hyssop, and crimson wool. The resulting ash, when mixed with water, produced an agent capable of cleansing those contaminated from contact with a corpse. My comments will focus primarily on literary relationships and will elucidate specific content only enough to permit basic intelligibility.[42] For clarity, all texts that are substantially identical in the Mishnah and the Tosefta are in italics. Text in plain type is unique to either the Mishnah or the Tosefta, but not shared in both.[43]

Mishnah-Tosefta Parah, Chapter Three

M. Par. 3:1[44]

A. Seven days prior to the burning of the cow they separate the priest who burns the cow from his home to the chamber overlooking the Birah.[45] In the northeast it was, and the Stone House was it called.

B. And they sprinkle upon him all the seven days from all the purifications that were there.

C. Rabbi Yose says: They would sprinkle upon him only on the third and seventh days alone.

D. Rabbi Hananiah, the Prefect of the Priests, says: Upon the priest who burns the cow they sprinkle all seven days; but on [the priest] of the day of atonement they would sprinkle only on the third and seventh alone.

Comment: The Mishnah's account of the procedure for burning the red cow begins with precautions taken to ensure that the officiating priest is in a state of absolute cultic purity before performing his duties (A–B). The formulation recalls the opening statement of M. Yoma 1:1–2: "Seven days prior to the day of atonement they separate the High Priest from his home to the Palhedrin[46] chamber. . . . All seven days he flings the blood and offers the incense, and trims the wicks, and offers the head and shank." This intertextual connection at the level of narration will help us to interpret the Tosefta's opening pericope below. C and D interrupt the narrative voice. Rabbi Yose (C) differs with B on the procedure for purifying the priest from possible corpse contamination or contact with a mestruant. He insists that the biblical requirement for purifying unclean individuals through a sprinkling on the third and seventh day (Num. 19:12) should apply to the priest as well. B, supported by Rabbi Hananiah (D), insists on a more stringent measure.

T. Par. 3:1[47]

A. What is the difference between the priest who burns the cow and the priest of the day of atonement?

B. The priest of the day of atonement—his separation is for holiness, and his brother priests touch him; the priest who burns the cow—his separation is for purification, and his brother priests do not touch him, except for those who help him, since he sprinkles.

Comment: A–B stands beyond the narrative of M. Par. 3:1 and asks how it relates to a similar narrative initiated at M. Yoma 1:1–2 (cited in comment to M. Par. 3:1A–B above). If one were inclined to insist that materials in Toseftan tractates are generated by those in their corresponding Mishnaic tractates, one could argue that T. attempts to clarify the point of Rabbi Hananiah (M. Par. 3:1D), who introduces the distinction between the two priests.

But it is equally likely that A–B has in mind the two narrative strands represented by M. Par. 3:1 and M. Yoma 1:1–2. That is, the Tosefta responds not to Rabbi Hananiah of the Mishnah, but rather to a subtle problem arising when one compares narratives about priestly preparations for two crucial sacrifical rites. Whether the formulator of T. Par. 3:1 knew these narratives in their current Mishnaic form or in some other is impossible to say. They were certainly known, however, to the formulator of the halakhic midrash, Sifra to Leviticus (Tzav-Miluim, 37), who links the procedures for both the High Priest on the day of atonement and the priest who burns the cow to Lev. 8:34.

In any case, in the extant Tosefta, the question certainly must be read as a supplement to the Mishnah, as Neusner suggests,[48] but this need not have been its function as a preredaction tradition. Indeed, a far better example of such an exegetical

supplement to M. Par. 3:1 is offered in the opening Tannaitic tradition of B. Yoma
2a. Identical to M. Par. 3:1A–B, the Bavli's *baraita* continues: "And why was it called
the Stone House? For all functions within it were carried out with vessels of dung,
vessels of stone, or vessels of earth." Were our Toseftan chapter conceived as a comment on M. Parah, it could have begun more auspiciously with material much more
similar to that used (or shaped) by the Babylonian editor.

> *M. Par. 3:2*
>
> A. *Quarters there were in Jerusalem built upon stone, and beneath them was a hol-
> low space [insulating those above] from [contamination by] a submerged tomb.*
> B. *And they bring pregnant women to give birth there, and there they raise their
> sons.*
> C. *And they bring oxen, and upon them are doors, and the children sit upon them,*
> and cups of stone are in their hands.
> D. Upon reaching the Siloam, they dismounted and filled them, and remounted
> and sat upon them.
> E. Rabbi Yose says: From his place would he lower and fill.

Comment: A–D continue the Mishnaic narrative, describing precautions taken
to ensure that those who draw the water for the purification rite have never themselves been contaminated by corpse uncleanness. Rabbi Yose (E), responding to D,
breaks the narrative. Despite all precautions, dismounting from the oxen to draw water
might subject the children to a hidden contaminant,[49] so he has them remaining on
the oxen while drawing the water.

> *T. Par. 3:2–3*
>
> A. *Quarters there were in Jerusalem built upon stone, and beneath them was a hol-
> low space [insulating those above] from a submerged tomb.*
> B. *And they bring pregnant women to give birth there, and there they raise their sons*
> until they are seven or eight years old.[50]
> C. *And they bring oxen, and upon them are doors, and the children sit upon them.*
> D. Rabbi Yehudah says: Oxen whose bellies are broad, so that the children's feet
> should not protrude and become contaminated from a submerged tomb.
> E. And all[51] agree that the children require immersion [before they may sprinkle].
> F. [T. Par.3:3] They said before Rabbi Aqiva in the name of Rabbi Yishmael: Cups
> of stone were hung on the oxen's horns. When the oxen knelt to drink, the cups
> were filled.
> G. He said to them: Don't give the sectarians[52] a chance to challenge!

Comment: A–C shares the Mishnaic narrative but differs from that text in three
respects. The first is B's reference to the age of the children, which is unknown to
M. 3:2B. This does add a piece of information to the Mishnaic narrative, but we cannot
judge whether this is an exegetical amplification of the Mishnah on the part of the
Tosefta or an abbreviation of a minor detail in the Toseftan version on the part of the
redactor of the Mishnah.

The other two textual divergences stem from a difference of opinion on the part
of the Mishnaic and Toseftan compilers. C omits M. Par. 3:2C's specification that
the children on the oxen carry stone cups in their hands. In the Mishnah these are
used to draw the water from the Siloam as the children dismount (M. Par. 3:2D),
whereas the Tosefta omits this reference to dismounting entirely. Both of the Toseftan

deviations are explained by the fact that the Tosefta seems to share Rabbi Yose's (M. Par. 3:2E) concern that the children be protected from even the remotest possibility of contamination (D–E). The key point for the Tosefta is at F, which has the stone cups suspended from the oxen's horns. This requirement eliminates any need for the children to descend and also explains why they are not holding the cups in their hands. G records Aqiva's objection; presumably he would follow the procedure known from the Mishnah lest "sectarians" (more likely, Sadducees, as in M. 3:3G) ridicule the stringencies imposed by rabbinic tradition.

Has the Tosefta modified the narrative as it appears now in the M. Par. 3:2A–D, or does the Tosefta tell the story in light of its own conception (shared with the Mishnah's Rabbi Yose) of the hyper-purity of the rite? Or, perhaps, does the Mishnaic story retell the Tosefta's from the perspective of a less rigorous insistence on protection from contamination? There are no grounds here for choosing among these explanations. The Mishnah and the Tosefta tell the story differently—that is all that can be said. Behind each version of the narrative, I would suggest, stands an oral-performative narrative tradition upon which each preserved version draws in accord with its own perspective on the requirements of the rite.

> M. *Par.* 3:3
> A. They arrived at the Temple Mount and dismounted.
> B. The Temple Mount and the Courts—beneath them was a hollow space [insulating those above] from a submerged tomb.
> C. And at the entrance to the Court there was prepared a jar of purification ash.
> D. And they bring a male sheep and tie a rope between his horns, and tie a staff with a bushy end to the rope, and he throws it into the jar.
> E. And *he beats the male, and it recoils backward.*
> F. And *he takes [the spilled ash] and sanctifies it [in water]* so that it is visible on the surface of the water.
> G. Rabbi Yose says: Don't give the Sadducees[53] a chance to challenge! Rather, he takes it and sanctifies.

Comment: The Mishnah's narrative relates nothing about the journey from Siloam, where the narrative had last placed us, to the Temple Mount. In the new setting, interest shifts from preserving the purity of those gathering the water to the preservation of the ashes themselves from contamination (A–F). Rabbi Yose finds the precautions absurd (in contrast to his position on gathering the water [M. Par. 3:2E]). He prefers to abandon it lest rabbinic authority be undermined by Sadducean taunts. His language echoes that ascribed to Rabbi Aqiva at T. Par. 3:3G.

> T. *Par.*3:4–5
> A. They arrived at the Gate opening from the Women's Court to the Rampart.[54]
> B. And jars of stone were embedded in the stairs of the Women's Court, and their covers of stone were visible to the Rampart.
> C. And within them are the ashes of each and every cow that they had burned, as it is said: "And it shall be stored away for the congregation of Israel as waters of lustration for purification" (Num. 19:9)
> D. (T. Par. 3:5) *He beats the male and he recoils backward,* and the ash is spilled.
> E. *He takes [the spilled ash] and sanctifies it [in water]* and sprinkles from that which was spilled.

F. These procedures they did when they went up from Exile—the words of Rabbi Yehudah.

Rabbi Shimon says: Their ashes went down with them to Babylonia, and went [back] up [to the Land of Israel].

They said to him: But weren't they contaminated in a foreign land?

He replied to them: They did not declare foreign lands to be unclean until after they went up from Exile.

Comment: A–E has its own version of the Mishnah's depiction of the spilling of the ashes. First (A) the Tosefta takes up the story after the arrival at the Temple Mount itself (M. Par. 3:3A). Its scene opens at the Eastern Gate at which the spilling takes place (M. Par. 3:3C).[55] The Mishnah and the Tosefta also differ regarding the storage of the ashes. M. Par. 3:3C knows only of a single jar instead of B–C's rather more detailed description. Although it is possible to harmonize the two accounts by assuming that ashes were poured from many jars into one,[56] I prefer to preserve the integrity of each account as a separate depiction of the spilling. At D–E the Mishnaic and Toseftan accounts coincide, although there are interesting textual differences.

M. Par. 3:3D's account of the contraption tied to the horns of the male sheep is ignored in T. 3:4. The Toseftan redactor depends upon our knowledge of the Mishnaic account or of another including the same detail. D is identical to M. Par. 3:3E but adds the obvious point that as a result of the sheep's jerky motion, the ash is spilled from the jar. The point is so obvious that it is impossible to regard the Toseftan version as a clarification of some Mishnaic obscurity. Neither has the Mishnah abbreviated the Toseftan text. The two are simply variant formulations. The same is true of E and M. Par. 3:3F. Each includes an obvious clause absent from the other. I see no way of showing any priority of one version over the other. Read in tandem, however, they combine to make a perfectly intelligible proposition: "And he takes [the spilled ash] and sanctifies it [in water] so that it is visible on the surface of the water, and sprinkles from that which is spilled." It is likely that the Toseftan and Mishnaic versions both draw upon a fuller formulation such as that we have reconstructed.

F concludes with a debate concerning the possibility that the Second Temple procedures described above might have been more complex than those of the First Temple. The debate is as relevant to M. Par. 3:3 as it is to A–E and could have been formulated in response to either. In the context of the redacted Tosefta, of course, it responds to A–E and thus is a Toseftan comment upon a Toseftan tradition. Prior to the redaction of the Tosefta as a written text, however, it would surely have circulated as a supplement to the oral-performative narrative tradition that stands behind both the Mishnah and the Tosefta.

M. Par. 3:4

A. They would not prepare a purification offering in tandem with [the preparations for] a [prior] purification offering, nor a child in tandem with his fellow.

B. And the children needed to sprinkle [each other before sprinkling the priest]— the words of Rabbi Yose haGalili.

Rabbi Aqiva says: They needn't have sprinkled.

Comment: A does not advance the ongoing narration of the burning procedure but rather stands beyond the narration to make a general comment about it. I regard it as a legal opinion formulated so as to fit smoothly into the narrative flow. We will see a similar formulary style in the Toseftan materials at a number of points (T. Par. 3:9, 3:11–13). B is similar in style, although its dispute form clearly labels it as legal rather than a narrative tradition. The effect of A–B together is to interrupt the narrative flow. There are no Toseftan materials intersecting with M. Par. 3:4.

> M. Par. 3:5
>
> A. If they did not find [ashes] from seven [previous purification offerings], they would prepare from six, five, four, three, two, or one.
> B. Now who had prepared them?
>
>> The first Moshe prepared, and the second Ezra prepared, and there were five from Ezra onward—the words of Rabbi Meir.
>>
>> But Sages say: Seven from Ezra onward.
>>
>> And who had prepared them?
>>
>> Shimon the Righteous[57] and Yohanan the High Priest[58] prepared two each, Elyehoenai b. Haqof,[59] and Hanamel the Egyptian,[60] and Yishmael b. Phiabi[61] prepared one each.

Comment: As at M. Par. 3:4, the narrative is halted by materials (A) that raise a legal point in a style designed to blend with the larger narrative voice that structures the chapter. B now offers a dispute that serves as a commentary upon A.

> T. Par. 3:6
>
> A. Yishmael b. Phiabi [prepared] two—one [under the auspices of a person defined as] a same-day immerser,[62] and one [under the auspices of] a sun-setter.
> B. In regard to the same-day immerser, they would argue with him.
>
>> He said to them: Tithe may be eaten by a same-day immerser, but heave offering only by a sun-setter. Tithe, which is eaten by a same-day immerser—all the more so should they enhance its sanctity. . . . [63]
>>
>> They said to him: If we preserve them [i.e., the ashes prepared by sun-setters], we give a bad name to the former ones [who prepared the ashes as same-day immersers], for people will say: They were unclean.
>>
>> They decreed concerning it, and poured it out, and went and prepared another [under the auspices] of a same-day immerser.

Comment: The Toseftan context confers no intelligibility upon the passage unless we already know that it disputes M. Par. 3:5's claim that the High Priest, Yishmael b. Phiabi, had offered only one cow during his career. This is the first Toseftan passage of the chapter that unambiguously requires for its intelligibility a corresponding passage of M. Parah. Had this passage appeared as M. Par. 3:5C–D, we would have regarded it as an expansion of discourse like many others appearing in the Mishnah. Its acontextual setting in the redacted Toseftan chapter suggests that it was formed as a comment on M. Par. 3:5 but proved too lengthy for use in the sequence of spare commentary on the core narrative selected by the redactor. Accordingly, it was omitted at the time of the Mishnaic redaction. It is preserved by the Toseftan editor, who assumes that a teacher of the text will explicate the referent of the tradition for an audience of students. The overall effect is to confirm Rabbi Meir's Mishnaic view that Yishmael b. Phiabi offered only one *legitimate* cow.

> M. Par. 3:6
> A. *And they prepared a ramp from the Temple Mount to the Mount of Olives, arches upon arches, each arch overarching a solid mass [insulating those above] from a submerged tomb.*
> B. Upon it the priest who burns the cow, the cow, and all her attendants would proceed to the Mount of Olives.

Comment: The narrative voice resumes at A–B, describing the procession from the Eastern Gate (see M. Middot 1:3) and the precautions taken to prevent contamination from hidden sources of corpse matter as the cow's procession made its way from the Temple Mount to the site of the sacrificial rite and burning, on the Mount of Olives.

> T. Par. 3:7
> A. *They prepared a ramp from the Temple Mount to the Mount of Olives, arches upon arches, each arch overarching a solid mass [insulating those above] from a submerged tomb.*
> B. Rabbi Eliezer says: There was no ramp there, but pillars of marble were implanted there and boards of cedar on top of them, for the cow had no need to go out on a ramp.

Comment: A rejoins the narrative represented in the Mishnah. B interrupts, providing an utterly different picture of the structure supporting the procession. Rabbi Eliezer's scenario takes no precautions against contamination, reflecting the view that the cow itself cannot become unclean while alive.[64] The wooden slabs on top of the pillars simply serve as a covenient structure for the procession.[65]

It is possible that Rabbi Eliezer's opinion reflects an alternative narrative repressed by the Mishnah, rather than a legal tradition per se. That narrative would have replaced A (in both the Mishnah and the Tosefta) as follows: "Pillars of marble were implanted there and boards of cedar on top of them, upon which the priest who burns the cow, the cow, and all her attendants would proceed to the Mount of Olives."

> M. Par. 3:7
> A. If the cow did not want to go—they do not bring out a black one with her, lest they say: They slaughtered the black one; nor a red one, lest they say: They slaughtered two.
> B. Rabbi Yose says: Not for this reason; rather because of what is said: "And he shall bring her out" (Num. 19:3)—by herself.
> C. And the elders of Israel would precede [the cow] by foot to the Mount of Olives.
> D. And an immersion chamber was there.
> E. *And they would contaminate the priest who burns the cow, because of the Sadducees, so they could not say: It was prepared by a person [completely purified through] the setting sun.*

Comment: The narrative setting assumed at A is the processional up the ramp to the Mount of Olives, but A is not itself a narration. Rather, like M. Par. 3:4A, it is a legal opinion framed to fit smoothly into the narrative voice that structures the chapter. Rabbi Yose (B) agrees with the principle of A but rejects the reasoning that some might suspect the integrity of the rite. Rather he offers a biblical grounding. C–E takes us up to the site of the rite. D–E, in particular, focuses on the most controversial aspect of the rabbinic depiction of the rite: the contamination of the officiating priest so that he shall perform the slaughter and burning in a minor state of cultic impurity rather than in absolute purity.

> T. Par. 3:7–8
> A. *And they would contaminate the priest who burns the cow, because of the Sadducees, so they could not say: It was done by a person [completely purified through] the setting sun.*
> B. [T.Par. 3:8] An incident:
> C. A certain Sadducee[66] whose sun had set arrived to burn the cow.
>
> Now Rabban Yohanan b. Zakkai understood and went to lay his two hands upon him. He said to him: *Sir High Priest!* How suitable you are to be High Priest! *Descend and immerse once!*
>
> *He descended and immersed, and arose.* After he arose, [Rabban Yohanan b. Zakkai] tore his ear.
>
> He said to him: ben Zakkai—I'll deal with you when I have time! He replied to him: When you have time!
>
> Not three days passed until they placed him in his grave. His father came to Rabban Yohanan b. Zakkai and said to him: ben Zakkai! My son won't have time!

Comment: Sharing the Mishnaic narrative at A, the Tosefta interrupts with a second narrative in the form of a pronouncement story (B). The whole can be regarded as an explanation and illustration of the Mishnah[67] only if we insist that A is a citation of the Mishnaic text in its present form rather than a rendition of a narrative held in common by both the Mishnah and Tosefta and anterior to both versions. Without that assumption, what we have at B is an illustration of Rabban Yohanan b. Zakkai's exercise of Sages' traditions in the face of those priests who oppose them. Its exclusion from the Mishnaic account is explicable in light of the Mishnaic redactor's spare use of diverting glosses to supplement the core narrative. A second narrative would prove too disruptive. The looser redactional style pursued by the Tosefta permits greater freedom to introduce diverting material. For further comment on the italicized portion of B, see the comment to M. Par. 3:8 to follow.

> M. Par. 3:8
> A. They rested their hands upon him and say to him: *Sir High Priest! Immerse once! He descended and immersed, and arose* and dried himself.
> B. And wood was arranged there: cedar, and pine, and spruce, and smoothed fig branches. And they make it like a kind of tower, and open up spaces within it, and its facade faces west.

Comment: A describes the contamination of the priest through the laying on of hands and the command that initiates his purificatory immersion. B abruptly shifts the narrative to the description of the pyre built for the immolation of the cow.

The italicized material at A is shared with T. Par. 3:8C's account of Rabban Yohanan's intentional contamination of the priest. The Mishnah can hardly be said to have drawn upon this story for its own language; nor has T. Par. 3:8C drawn upon the Mishnah's language. Rather, both reflect an anterior tradition regarding the formula for addressing the High Priest (attested as well at M. Yoma 1:3) and the sequence of his immersion. Each textualization, that is, draws freely for its narrative purposes from the oral-performative traditions current in the communities of the textual tradents.

> M. Par. 3:9
> A. *They tied her with ropes of reeds and placed her upon the pyre, her head southward and her face westward.*
> B. The priest stands eastward and his face westward.
> C. *He slaughtered with his right [hand] and received the blood with his left.*
> D. *Rabbi Yehudah says: With his right did he receive it, and he places it in his left.*
> E. *And he sprinkles with his right.*
> F. He immersed [his finger] and sprinkled seven times toward the Holy of Holies, an immersion for each sprinkling.
> G. He finished sprinkling, wiping his hand on the body of the cow.
> H. He descended and kindled the fire with chips.
> I. Rabbi Aqiva says: with dried palm-branches.

Comment: The immersion of the officiating priest completed, the narrative now moves to the slaughter of the cow (A–C), the sprinkling of its blood toward the Sanctuary (E–F), and the beginning of the immolation (G). D and I interrupt the narrative flow with briefly worded alternative scenarios that blend smoothly with the diction of the narrative.

> T. Par. 3:9–10
> A. The place of her pit, and her pyre, and the immersion chamber were hollow [insulating those above] from a submerged tomb.
> B. *They tied her with ropes of reeds and placed her upon the pyre.*
> C. And some say: She went up on a machine.
>
>   But Rabbi Eliezer b. Yaaqov says: They make a ramp for her and she'd ascend.
> D. *Her head was southward and her face westward.*
> E. [T. Par. 3:10] How does he proceed?
> F. *He slaughters with his right [hand] and receives with his left, and sprinkles with his right finger.* And if he deviated, it is ruined.
> G. *Rabbi Yehudah says:* With his right did he slaughter it, and he places the knife before him or to the one standing by his side, and *receives with his right, and places it in his left,* and sprinkles with the right finger. And if he deviated, it is ruined.
> H. If it splashes from his hand when he is sprinkling—whether beyond her pit or beyond her pyre—it is ruined.
>
>   Rabbi Eliezer b. Yaaqov said: Beyond her pit, it is ruined; beyond her pyre, he shall bring it back. And if he brought it back it is viable.
> I. And if he brought the blood in his hand outside [the designated area] and then brought it back it is viable.

Comment: A adds a narrative detail absent in the Mishnaic parallel. The point, as at other junctures in the rite where there is a particular concern to protect the purity of the proceedings (M. Par. 3:2A/T. Par. 3:2A; M. Par. 3:3B; M. Par. 3:6A/T. Par. 3:7A), is to ensure that buried corpse-matter does not offer contamination. A is autonomous of the Mishnah, as Neusner says.[68] This is so only in the sense that it draws upon a narrative version of the rite that is shared with the Mishnah but upon which the redactors of each extant text draw selectively in light of their own priorities.

The Tosefta rejoins the Mishnaic narrative version at B and D, interrupted at C by the sort of intrusion of dissenting details characteristic of Tannaitic ritual narratives (e.g., the case of Mishnah Tamid discussed earlier).

E–G's account of the slaughter is of particular interest, for this is the only case in this chapter in which the Tosefta shares both the Mishnaic narrative (F) and an intrusionary disputing opinion (G). The whole is reformulated as well as the answer to a question (E). I do not regard this as a conscious improvement of a Mishnaic text already lying before the Toseftan redactor. Rather it is a legitimately independent formulation of material known to the Mishnah. That is, narrative material reaching both the Mishnaic and Toseftan editors already included within it Rabbi Yehudah's alternative rendering of the priest's actions.

H–I supplies important practical guidance about priestly procedures regarding the disposition of the blood that might disqualify the rite. The material is germane to both the Mishnah and the Tosefta but in its present setting must be read as a case of the Toseftan editor's commenting on materials with which he is textually engaged. That is, the writer is not commenting upon a completed Mishnaic text lying before him; rather he is continuing his own work at T. Par. 3:10E–G.

> M. Par. 3:10
> A. [When] she burst open, then he would stand outside her pit.
> B. He took cedar wood, hyssop, and scarlet wool. He said to them: Is this cedar wood? Is this cedar wood? Is this hyssop? Is this hyssop? Is this scarlet wool? Is this scarlet wool?—three times for each and every thing.
> C. And they replied to him: Yes! Yes!—three times for each and every thing.

Comment: The narrative of the burning continues at A–C. Once the cow's carcass splits open from the heat of the pyre, the priest ascends to the top of the pit in order to toss in the elements mandated at Num. 19:6. The point of the repetition and confirmation is to guarantee that the proper elements have been immolated.

> T. Par. 3:11–12
> A. [If] some of her skin, or her flesh, or her hair burst beyond her pit—
>
> he shall return it. And if he did not return it, it is ruined.
>
> Beyond her pyre—let him add wood to it and burn it where it is [as long as it remains within the pit].
> B. Rabbi Eliezer b. Yaakov says: An olive's bulk disqualifies [the procedure]; less than an olive's bulk does not disqualify it.
> C. [T. Par. 3:12] [If] some of her horn or hoof or excrement burst [beyond her pit], he needn't return it.
>
> For a flaw that does not disqualify her while alive cannot disqualify her in her immolation.
> D. And Rabbi Leazar b. Rabbi Shimon adds: Shall I throw? Shall I throw? Shall I throw? And they reply: Yes! Yes! Yes!—three times for each and every thing.

Comment: A–C, like T. Par. 3:6, is one of the few materials of this Toseftan chapter that require us to posit the corresponding Mishnaic passage (here, M. Par. 3:10A) as the occasion for their formulation. That is, A–C was formulated originally to circulate with M. Par. 3:10 as amplifying material. In light of the spare redactional program pursued by the Mishnaic redactor, already noted, they were omitted as extraneous and have found their way into the Tosefta. The conceptual issue, undeveloped in the Tosefta, is the degree to which—unlike sacrificial parts placed upon the Temple altar—the cow's remnants that leave the sacrificial space remain valid (cf. M. Zabim 9:1–6/T. Zabim 9:1–10).

The literary profile of D is a different matter. In its present form it surely responds to the scenario described at M. Par. 3:10B–C. But if we remove the attribution formula, what remains is the logical conclusion of the narrative describing the interchange between priest and witnesses. In my view, the Rabbi Leazar b. Rabbi Shimon dictum here preserves an element of the anterior narrative that stands behind both the Mishnah and the Tosefta.

> M. Par. 3:11
>
> A. He tied them together with the ends of the strip of wool and threw them into her immolation.
> B. [After] she was burned up, they beat her with staves, and sift her in sieves.
> C. Rabbi Yishmael says: With hammers of stone, and with sieves of stone was she prepared.
> D. A black piece that contains ash—they crush it; and one having none—they leave it.
> E. The bone, one way or the other, was crushed.
> F. *And they divide it into three parts: one is placed in the Rampart, and one is placed on the Mount of Olives, and one is divided among all the priestly squads.*

Comment: The narrator concludes his account with the immolation of the wood, herb, and wool (A), the reduction of the burned carcass to ash (B and D–E), and its disposition for future use (F). Rabbi Yishmael's intrusion at C points out that the process of crushing was undertaken with implements incapable of receiving or imparting uncleanness to the ashes. His words may retrieve for us an alternative narrative account ignored by the narrator of the Mishnaic account but deemed by the editor of this chapter as worthy of preservation as a minority opinion.

> T. Par. 3:12–14
>
> A. Whether he tore her by hand, whether he tore her with a knife, or whether she tore open of her own;
>
>   whether he threw [the bundle] into her body, whether he threw it into her immolation;
>
>   whether he threw the three items together, whether he threw them in one at a time—it is fit.
> B. If he put them in before the fire had burned most of it or after it had become ash—it is ruined.
> C. [T. Par. 3:13] If he took bone or a black piece and sanctified with it—he hasn't done anything at all.
> D. If there is upon it any amount of cinder from her body, he crushes it and sanctifies with it, and it is fit.

E. [T. Par. 3:14] *And they divide it into three parts: one is placed in the Rampart, and one is placed on the Mount of Olives, and one is divided among all the priestly squads.*

F. The one divided among all the priestly squads would Israel sprinkle from. The one placed on the Mount of Olives would the priests sanctify with. And the one placed on the Rampart they would preserve, as it is said: "And it shall be stored away for the congregation of Israel as waters of lustration for purification" (Num. 19:9).

Comment: At A–D the Tosefta supplies random points of clarification that are best understood as comments upon the extant version of M. Par. 3:11A–E. The Mishnaic narrative is resumed at E, and F supplies crucial material missing in the Mishnah. Had the Mishnaic editor known this material, I can't imagine why he would have omitted it. Therefore it is possible that F is an expansion of the extant Mishnah added as the chapter was under composition. At the same time, we cannot exclude the possibility that its origin in the Toseftan tradition stems from the anterior narrative of the rite of the red cow upon which both the Mishnaic and Toseftan redactions have drawn.

We may now summarize the results of this lengthy excursion into the intertextual connections of chapter 3 of Tractate Parah in its Mishnaic and Toseftan renditions. While the extant Tosefta can serve as a commentarial source for the elucidation of the extant Mishnaic text (as it has been used by virtually all medieval and modern interpreters of the Mishnah), the compositional units of the Mishnah and Tosefta exhibit more complex patterns of relationship. We have been forced repeatedly to distinguish, on the one hand, between the Mishnah and the Tosefta as redacted documents and, on the other, between the preexisting materials from which these documents have been compiled.

There are instances, for example, in which Toseftan materials are presupposed by the Mishnaic discourse. Thus M. Par. 3:3C assumes a change of scene from the Temple Mount to the Eastern Gate that is described explicitly at T. Par. 3:4A. Similarly, M. Par. 3:3F's description of the sanctification of the ash in the water is inextricably bound up with the description offered by T. Par. 3:4E. In many more instances, the Toseftan text is self-referential rather than directed toward the Mishnah in its present form. *It thus represents a literary structure parallel to but independent of the Mishnaic compilation.* Indeed, only a small part of the Toseftan chapter we have examined seems clearly to have been formulated with this Mishnah's text in clear view (e.g., T. Par. 3:6, T. Par. 3:11–12A–C, T. Par. 3:12–14A–D).

Our main conclusion, however, is particularly relevant to our attempt to situate the extant versions of the Mishnah and the Tosefta in relation to a hypothetical oral-performative tradition that preceded and was filtered through the written editions that have survived the Middle Ages. I have argued that Mishnaic and Toseftan narratives regarding the rite of the red cow draw selectively upon a preredactional narrative tradition that provides the foundation of their own narrative renditions. I have carefully isolated materials of each chapter that testify to such an anterior tradition. Divergence of the Toseftan narrative from its Mishnaic counterpart is not a result of Toseftan departure from the Mishnaic text in its redacted form; rather, *it is more likely*

to stem from a retrieval of a different performative version of a narrative tradition that
circulated in rabbinic communities prior to the redaction of either the Mishnah or the
Tosefta. The named authorities who comment on this narrative, in both the Mishnah
and Tosefta, are all figures of the mid to late second century. They thus provide evidence that the orally circulated version was known from some point after the destruction of the Temple (at which time alone it would have made sense to compose the
narrative at all) into the early second century.[69]

Summary

The results of these explorations of Mishnaic composition can now be summarized.
While the received texts of the Mishnah indeed reflect deep roots in a rabbinic culture of oral performance, that "orality" is thoroughly "literate" and, indeed, "literary." Thus the textual practices that produced the Mishnah included a crucial role
for writing in all aspects of the text's life—composition, editing, and transmission. It
is beyond the purview of this discussion to make pronouncements about the circumstances of pre-rabbinic traditions that may have entered rabbinic discourse, but it is
likely, despite the well-attested rabbinic perceptions of the basically oral character of
the tradition explored in previous chapters, that written versions of rabbinic teaching did exist at the earliest traceable origins of the tradition in the first century or
earlier.[70]

As a rendering of rabbinic tradition, therefore, the Mishnah is hardly a linear
culmination of early oral tradition now breaking into written textuality for the first
time. Rather, at any stage of Mishnaic tradition we can presently isolate, we are confronted with an "orality" which is at the same time a reflection and a creation of
writing. Surely, if the most compact and memorizable elements of Mishnaic tradition, such as those examined in this chapter, reveal the impact of the scribal pen, we
must conclude that the carefully orchestrated constructions represented by most
Mishnaic tractates likewise will have been deeply shaped by the written word as well—
a written word, however, closely in touch with aural requirements and oral rhythms
of diction. Similarly, our study of M-T Parah disclosed precisely how richly the written recording of narrative draws upon anterior contexts associated with performative
deliveries of the textual tradition in its living forms.

We must conclude, on the basis of the studies here, that, by the opening decades of the third century CE, *rabbinic disciples encountered as oral tradition the
performative embodiment of memorized rabbinic manuscript.* We shall likely never
learn precisely how closely the oral recitations conformed to various written versions,
but what is clear is that the continuous loop of manuscript and performance had no
"ground-zero" at which we can isolate at a distance of many centuries an oral text or
tradition as fundamental. On the one hand, memorized texts mastered in oral training and performance provided the substance of what might be inscribed for written
preservation. On the other, the literary techniques developed in the composition of
written documents came to shape the formation and performance of orally generated tradition. Within such a milieu, written texts enjoyed an essentially oral cultural life, subject to all the vagaries of oral transmission as they were memorized and

transmitted in face-to-face performance. Similarly, texts of oral exposition and inquiry were imprinted for transmission with the rich stylistic models developed within written tradition.

In the next chapter we will continue to explore this interpenetration of written and oral registers of literary discourse, but the focus will shift from the compilers of Tannaitic traditions into coherent compilations to the Galilean Amoraic communities whose work of preserving and transmitting compilations such as the Mishnah and the Tosefta yielded the Palestinian Talmud. There, finally, we will find the oral-performative setting in which the classic definitions of Torah in the Mouth received their inspiration.

7

Torah in the Mouth in Galilean Discipleship Communities

Written Texts and the Ideology of Orality

The compilation of Tannaitic tradition into coherent curricula of learning was recognized by the mid-third century as a kind of watershed in the history of rabbinic tradition. The self-consciousness, among the Palestinian and Babylonian heirs of the Tannaitic tradition, of standing at the far end of a yawning gulf of authority, is best exemplified in the way the heirs distinguished themselves from those who had bequeathed them the rich heritage of the Repeated Tradition.

The Aramaic term *tanna* (*tn'*) as a designation for those Sages who "repeated" the oral-performative traditions of rabbinic *torah* and framed them in such compilations as the Mishnah, is itself of mid-third-century coinage.[1] And those who coined it situated themselves in relation to Tannaitic tradition not as its repeaters, but rather as its expounders. Their task was not the creative one of articulating the Repeated Tradition; rather, it was to master and develop it, to expound rather than to legislate. Thus by the middle of the third century, we find references to specific masters of tradition who are designated *'amora'im*, from the Aramaic root *'mr* ("explain").[2]

Such Amoraim contributed to the Tannaitic tradition not only their interpretations of its laws, but also the interpretation of its significance as an oral-performative tradition. Indeed, in the Galilean centers of Amoraic learning in the third and fourth centuries, we detect an important debate about the implications of the vague references in the Tannaitic tradition to a *torah* transmitted solely by word of mouth. At the center of this controversy stood the paradox that the oral traditions of the Tannaim were known to exist not only in the memory but in written recensions.

The Galilean Amoraim included influential figures, such as Rabbi Yohanan b. Nappaha (d. 279), who seem to have held that, until recent times, nothing in the oral tradition inherited from the Tannaim had ever been written down.[3] Therefore, as a matter of principle, the Mishnah and other redacted curricula of Tannaitic traditions were themselves to be transmitted solely in the context of a memorized performance. Such written copies as may have existed were to be banned from use. This was only one view, however. We will also see that, in at least one fourth-century circle of disciples gathered around Rabbi Yonah, the ban against introducing written texts into the Sages' study circles seems to have been ignored. Thus even among masters who were themselves committed to the discipline of Torah in the Mouth, there was no univocal position on the propriety of preserving that Torah in written form.

This chapter probes this Galilean Amoraic preoccupation with the form of preserving Tannaitic tradition.[4] The terms of dispute are clear. Virtually all parties assumed that the recitation of study texts must be from memory in the context of an oral performance. At issue was whether written recensions of such study texts could be produced and consulted by students in the course of preparation. As we shall see, this apparently minor preoccupation with the appropriate media for transmitting rabbinic learning was bound up with a larger, more crucial issue that lurked behind it: the nature of the *torah* master as a religious authority and the sort of teaching relationships he should cultivate with his disciples. Thus Galilean Amoraic reflection upon the nature of Torah in the Mouth was not merely a disinterested, theoretical exercise in amplifying certain Tannaitic themes about the connection of the Tannaitic Sages' teaching to Sinai. It raised an ideological issue upon which rested the legitimacy of the entire Amoraic pedagogical system and, with it, the larger project of religious discipline promoted by these masters.

Perspectives on the oral nature of rabbinic tradition surface in a variety of Palestinian compilations that reached some sort of preliminary shaping between the fourth and sixth centuries. For our purposes, however, pride of place will be given to the Talmud Yerushalmi, which appears to have reached something like its extant form from about 375–400 CE.[5] As a collection of literary texts distinct from Mishnaic tractates but organized around their structure, the Yerushalmi represented a major innovation in fourth-century Galilean rabbinic literary culture.[6] By selecting the Mishnah text attributed to Rabbi Yehudah the Patriarch as its organizing set of textual cues, the Yerushalmi's compilers drew an analogy between this prestigious recension of Tannaitic tradition and that of the paradigmatic subject of commentary in Judaic culture, Scripture.[7] As the textual substratum of an extensive running commentary, the Mishnah was by definition *torah*, analogous to the Torah of Moses, encased like Moses' text of the Torah in a discursive web of text-intepretive tradition transmitted by Sages.

The Yerushalmi's discourses are dotted with literary representations of the Amoraic social and institutional settings in which Tannaitic textual traditions of diverse sorts were mastered, discussed, and transmitted. Such representations yield much information regarding the modes of study pursued among the Amoraic proponents of Oral Torah. They also provide us with abundant materials that can help to contextualize the Galilean Amoraic society of learning within the larger nonrabbinic cultural settings in which that learning thrived.

Such contextualization is, in fact, the primary contribution of this chapter. We shall explore ways in which the Amoraic controversy over the validity of written versions of learned tradition echoed themes that preoccupied other Gentile learned societies in late Roman and early Byzantine Galilee. We will attend first to ways in which the preparations for oral declamation in the third- to fifth-century rhetorical schools might illumine literary phenomena common in the Yerushalmi. One widespread preparatory exercise in such schools is particularly illuminating, for it was designed to produce disciplined oral variants of written sayings of famous teachers. If we bear in mind this model of oral transmission—in which a written source underlies a series of memorized variations—it will become possible to isolate within the Yerushalmi hints of a similar mnemonic method among the Galilean Sages.

The following discussion lends further support to the view that writing played more than an episodic role in the transmission of Tannaitic traditions within the circles of Amoraic tradents. The use of written sources in Amoraic learning, we shall see, is likely to have been far more widespread than was acknowledged among the Amoraim themselves; it had, in fact, a diverse impact on the presentation of textual material within the Yerushalmi. In illustrating this claim, I offer two studies of textual variation in the Yerushalmi—one within the genre of homiletics, and the other in the genre of halakhic recitation. These suggest that, in each genre, the nature of textual variation is consistent with the use of written texts as the basis of rhetorical discourses in which versions of the memorized texts are cited from memory.[8]

These textual studies will prepare us for the second major task of this chapter, which is to move the question of rabbinic oral and written tradition from the pedagogical to the ideological level of inquiry. Precisely as Amoraic teaching method continued to make use of written sources, Amoraic theorists of tradition grew increasingly insistent that the oral nature of the tradition as a whole not be exhausted by the orally delivered, mnemonically managed method of its daily performance before teachers and other students. Drawing upon and elaborating themes we have found already in place in Tannaitic midrashic compilations, they maintained that the *torah* received from Sages had been unwritten since its earliest disclosure at Sinai. To commit Tannaitic halakhic teachings to writing would be nearly equivalent to destroying them as *torah*. The primary architect of this viewpoint, Rabbi Yohanan of Tiberias, will figure prominently in the discussion, even as we trace the echoes of his position in later Palestinian compilations beyond the Yerushalmi.

This latter inquiry, like the pedagogical one that precedes it, benefits from a contextual approach. We will, therefore, draw parallels between—and distinctions among—the Amoraic communities of third- to fifth-century Galilee and other contemporary philosophical or religious communities grounded in close discipleship to explicators of venerated texts. The Amoraic dispute over the efficacy of writing, I claim, drew upon and contributed to a larger controversy that plagued diverse circles of religious discipleship in antiquity. At issue, for both the Galilean Amoraim and their contemporaries in philosophical schools or monastic circles, was the precise role of face-to-face encounters in the shaping of disciples. Where, after all, was the real text of instruction—in the written word or in the living presence of the teacher? The Galilean Amoraic embellishment of the Tannaitic perspectives on oral tradition were framed to answer this question decisively in favor of the teacher.

The Mnemonic Basis of Greco-Roman Declamation

Of particular importance for study of the oral and written foundations of rabbinic tradition is the educational setting in which its texts were mediated. While historians have for some time recognized the similarity of rabbinic educational methods and institutions to those of the surrounding Greco-Roman environment,[9] the relevance of the Greco-Roman material for interpreting the symbolic roles of writing and oral performance in rabbinic culture has yet to be fully explored. Some aspects of Greco-Roman rhetorical education in particular may help us to think about the role of oral and written texts in the education of rabbinic disciples.[10]

The rabbinic movement of Roman Galilee was not equivalent in all respects to a rhetorical or philosophical academy, yet an important body of recent scholarship shows that it bore important functional similarities to such schools.[11] Like the training offered by Sophists, rabbinic training bore a strong scholastic orientation, focused on guiding young men in the mastery of a literary tradition whose values they would personally embody. Like these men, rabbinic students were preparing in many cases for lives of public service in political, judicial, or ecclesiastical institutions. Finally, like the students of the rhetorical schools, many of those who studied in the rabbinic *bet midrash* would make their professional mark beyond it through skilled, effective public speech. As we shall soon note, such similarities extended beyond the institutional settings themselves; they are apparent as well in traits of literary style and substance.

In third- to fourth-century Galilee, non-Jewish political and social elites committed the advanced education of their male children to professional practitioners of the Greco-Roman rhetorical tradition. This tradition was available in two primary forms. The older of these, just beginning a long, slow decline from the heights of its second- and early third-century dominance of Greek and Latin literary culture, was the tradition of classical literary education fostered by the rhetoricians of the Second Sophistic.[12] The younger, beginning a path that would lead it to dominance in the fourth and fifth centuries, was the tradition of Christian preaching, teaching, and exegetical scholarship fostered by the Church's growing cadre of priest-intellectuals.[13]

Sophistic or Christian, rhetorical education was preparation for a life of public service. And such a life—as a lawyer, academic scholar, or other public official (in Christian circles, as a functionary in the Church hierarchy)—demanded skill in elegant, persuasive, oral address. What made an oral presentation elegant was its ability to cite or allude to well-known classical texts in the process of the speaker's development of his own thought. The orator's persuasive power was in part bound up with the weight of classical diction he could support without apparent effort; it was also dependent upon the apparently spontaneous organization of fresh ideas into well-known and easily recognizable patterns of presentation and argument. The psychological pressure of the rhetorical address was, in fact, the subject of some sardonic humor. As Philostratus notes in his Lives of the Sophists: "[The Sophist, Polemo,] . . . on seeing a gladiator dripping with sweat out of sheer terror of the life-and-death struggle before him, . . . remarked: 'You are in as great an agony as though you were going to declaim.'"[14] This rhetorical terror, it seems, proceeded from the insistence that something new be said within forms of speech venerated by centuries of literary tradition—and that it be said in such a way so as to appear to come from the top of one's head.

This illusion of effortless public performance was facilitated by an education that stressed the rote memorization and recitation of written texts of diverse kinds. Homeric texts or those of the great dramatists, for example, had to be summoned accurately and on cue in order for one to appropriately set off a particular turn of thought. Speeches of the Greek orators, such as Demosthenes, were memorized and performed as a prelude to the analyses of the structural principles that provided them their power. Moreover, teachers of rhetoric would commonly make available to students written copies of their own oral discourses for study. All of this training in memorizing the written word repaid itself in the characteristic posssession of the trained orator—the capacity to deliver, at length and with captivating effectiveness, a memorized composition without resorting to written mnemonic cues.[15]

Textbooks on rhetoric, produced between the first and sixth centuries in Greek and Latin, are useful sources for illustrating the relation of written and oral discourse in rhetorical training. These works, called by the generic title of *Progymnasmata*, amply illustrate the intertwined nature of written texts and oral discourse. In them we can see how memorized written literary sources nourished the education of orators, as well as the ways in which the mobilization of memorized written texts in oratory reconfigured those texts into fresh patterns.[16]

The illustrations in this chapter are drawn from the ways in which the authors of *Progymnasmata* instructed their readers in the nature and use of one of the most common literary forms of Greco-Roman tradition, the *chreia*. Written collections of *chreiae*, which circulated widely, constituted the basic store of wisdom and values that public speakers could assume they shared with their audiences. Not uncommonly, a single *chreia* might be ascribed to more than one authority, as the same text became naturalized in traditions with differing intellectual lineages. This malleability of transmission is part of the testimony that the circulation of a *chreia* in written form was only one aspect of its textual life. The *chreia* as a cultural possession was experienced in oral presentations of artistic speech.

As described by Theon of Alexandria, a first-century Sophist commonly considered to have composed the first rhetorical textbook, the *chreia* is "a concise statement or action which is attributed with aptness to some specified character or to something analogous to a character" (201, 17–20).[17] The main business of Theon's introduction is to flesh out this spare definition with the analysis of numerous examples. Among them is the following, ascribed here to Isocrates. Its evaluation of the relative importance of parents and teachers will figure in our discussion at a later point: "Isocrates the rhetor used to advise his students to honor their teachers before their parents, because the latter are the cause only of living, while teachers are the cause of living nobly" (207, 1–5).[18]

Much of Theon's discussion is concerned with typological analyses of various *chreia*-forms. These are distinguishable from each other by, for example, varying emphases on indirect discourse as opposed to direct discourse, privileging of action over discourse, the kinds of situations to which the hero of the *chreia* responds, and so forth. Of interest from the perspective of understanding the oral life of the written *chreia*, however, is Theon's careful exposition of various exercises by which orators may appropriate the text of the *chreia*, working it orally through a series of grammatical and rhetorical transformations. The foundational act of this performance is the mastering of the memorized text itself well enough to "report the assigned *chreia* very clearly in the same words or in others as well" (210, 8–10).[19] Upon this basis, the budding orator proceeds then to a series of revisions of the text.

The simplest of these is an exercise in restating the memorized text in terms of number. In the case of the following *chreia*, "Isocrates the rhetor used to say that gifted students are children of gods," Theon instructs:

> we inflect in this way: singular to singular, for example, "Isocrates the rhetor used to say that the gifted student is a child of gods." Dual to dual: "The two rhetors named Isocrates used to say that the two gifted students are two children of gods." Plural to plural: "The rhetors named Isocrates used to say that gifted students are children of gods." (210, 19–24)[20]

Such an exercise would not, of course, ever gain reflection in a public oration. It was purely preliminary, part of the discipline of rooting the text firmly in the mind by running it, so to speak, through its paces.

More complex inflections involved grammatical cases. These require the rewording of the *chreia*, usually transmitted in the nominative case, into other cases. Thus:

> In the genetive case we will inflect in this way. If it is a sayings-*chreia*, we will add to it "the statement is remembered" or "the saying is recalled of the one speaking." It is good style to add the former after the recitation of the whole *chreia*. For example: "Isocrates the rhetor's statement, when he said gifted students are children of gods, is remembered. (211, 5–11)[21]

Or, again:

> In the accusative case we will generally add to any *chreia* the words "they say," "it is said." For example, "They say (or it is said) that Diogenes the Cynic philosopher, on seeing a rich young man who was uneducated, said: 'This fellow is silver-plated filth.'" (203, 5–8)[22]

In both of these examples, the written text is worked through the memory by disciplined exercises in recasting its language. The product of this exercise is knowledge of the text as a multiform literary reality. The written version retains its form as transmitted, but it is malleable in light of the needs of the rhetorical situation. The text is at once its written version and the possiblities of its oral transformations.

Theon's discussion became foundational to the entire genre of *Progymnasmata* and was cited (explicitly or by allusion) and amplified by later Sophistic teachers. A particularly important example is that of the late second-century Sophist, Hermogenes of Tarsus. His discussion of the forms of the *chreia* and its inflections is much briefer than Theon's, but he introduces a subject of great relevance to the discussion of the interplay of oral and written texts. With marvelous theoretical rigor, he describes the manifold ways in which the public speaker may interweave *chreiae* into his discourse and adapt for his own purposes stories or epigrams widely known to his audience.

Hermogenes identifies this rhetorical practice as "elaboration" (*ergasia*) and defines it in terms of eight procedures: Praise (*enkomion*); Paraphrase (*paraphrasis*); Rationale (*aitia*); Statement from the Opposite (*kata to enantion*); Statement from Analogy (*ek paraboles*); Statement from Example (*ek paradeigmatos*); Statement from Authority (*ek kriseos*); Exhortations (*paraklesis*). These rhetorical procedures introduce the audience to the wisdom contained in it and unfold the implications and authority of it in a disciplined, easily followed manner.

Taking as his text the *chreia*, "Isocrates said that education's root is bitter, its fruit is sweet," Hermogenes illustrates these procedures as follows. The report of the *chreia* (step 2) is actually only a single element of a complex discourse to which it is structurally central:

(1) Praise: "Isocrates was wise," and you amplify the subject moderately.

(2) Then the *chreia*: "He said thus and so," and you are not to express it simply but rather by amplifying the presentation.

(3) Then the rationale: "For the most important affairs generally succeed because of toil, and once they have succeeded they bring pleasure."

(4) Then the statement from the opposite: "For ordinary affairs do not need toil, and they have an outcome that is entirely without pleasure; but serious affairs have the opposite outcome."

(5) Then the statement from analogy: "For just as it is the lot of farmers to reap their fruits after working with the land, so also is it for those working with words."

(6) Then the statement from example: "Demosthenes, after locking himself in a room and toiling long, later reaped his fruits: wreaths and public acclamations."

(7) It is also possible to argue from the statement by an authority. For example, Hesiod said: "In front of virtue gods have ordained sweat" . . . .

(8) At the end you are to add an exhortation to the effect that it is necessary to heed the one who has spoken or acted. (7, 16–8, 8).[23]

Hermogenes' method of elaboration supplements Theon's inflections as a further example of how rhetorical training was devoted to the oral transformation of written texts. In elaboration, the *chreia*'s text (step 2) serves as the springboard for a discourse that moves back and forth between the text itself and other cultural intertexts (steps 3–8), weaving the whole into a morally compelling rhetorical tapestry. Here, instead of the words of the text itself being changed (as in Theon), the *chreia*'s meaning is enriched by being woven into an expanded rhetorical fabric.

Discussions such as those of Theon and Hermogenes lend some nuance to our conception of the nature and purpose of textual memorization in Greco-Roman rhetorical culture. They show that memorization of a written text was compatible with, and indeed encouraged, the existence of the same text in a variety of orally presented versions. *The written record of a text was itself a version, whose literary purpose was fulfilled in the oral variations played upon it by the orator.* In other words, the variations of the text recorded in written versions of oral discourses are not everywhere and always the result of erroneous transmission or failures of memory. Rather, in many cases it appears that they are the intentional result of mastering a fixed written version for the purpose of communicating its meaning in diverse performative settings. At issue now is the degree to which the dialectical relation of written and oral textual versions cultivated by rhetorical deployment of *chreiae* can illumine textual phenomena familiar from the early rabbinic literature.

Performative Variation in Amoraic Homiletic Discourse

The foundational studies of such scholars as S. Lieberman, D. Daube, H. Fischel, and many others have shown that the rabbinic literature of Late Antiquity is heavily dependent upon literary forms current in the larger Greco-Roman literary environment.[24] The *chreia* is, perhaps, one of the most ubiquitous of such forms.[25] It is difficult to open a rabbinic compilation without stumbling immediately over statements of wisdom or law transmitted in the names of famous Sages, often placed in the context of a brief narrative.

In most cases it is impossible to document the intervention of written texts of such *chreiae* in the orally deployed versions now preserved in the manuscripts that have survived from the Middle Ages. There is, however, one famous *chreia* in which it is quite clear that both written and oral forms of transmission shaped the text during its long life in Jewish culture. Appearing in at least three rabbinic versions, it concerns the great first-century CE rabbinic Sages Hillel and Shammai.

I cite the version from Bavli Shabbat 31a (cf. Avot de-Rabbi Nathan A15, B29):

> It once happened that a certain Gentile approached Shammai and said: I shall become a Jew on condition that you teach me the entire Torah while I stand on one foot. Shammai beat him with a yardstick. The Gentile approached Hillel, who converted him, saying: *What is hateful to you don't do to your neighbor. That's the entire Torah. The rest is commentary. Go and study.*

The italicized punchline of Hillel's *chreia* migrated throughout the Jewish world of antiquity. Its first written testimony appeared as a literary apothegm in a Jewish novel from the Second Temple period, the Book of Tobit. The surviving Greek version is very close to that ascribed to Hillel (Tobit 4:15): "Do not do to anyone what you yourself would hate." In its best-known, positively framed variant—"Do unto others as you would have them do unto you. That is the Torah and the Prophets"—the comment pops up in the mouth of Jesus of Nazareth as an orally mediated teaching (Mat. 7:12/Luke 6:31).

It is an error to ask whether the historical Jesus borrowed this teaching from the historical Hillel, or whether either of these authorities had been a reader of Tobit. The point, rather, is that the apothegm floated around, as it were, in the ethers of Palestinian Jewish culture. It could be encountered by scribal professionals in written texts and pronounced orally in a diverse set of social situations as common wisdom. And, obviously, it could be assigned to anyone recognized as an important teacher of wisdom (including Rabbi Aqiva in Avot de-Rabbi Natan B26 [ed. Schechter, p. 27a]). Its oral life probably preceded its written recension in Tobit, and that oral life continued in a variety of contexts.[26]

The preceding example demonstrates that both written and oral media drew upon a common tradition in the transmission of a rather simple statement of gnomic wisdom.[27] But there is as yet no hint here of the distinctive trait of Greco-Roman rhetorical training—the disciplined memorization of a text in multiple versions. For an example of such practice in Amoraic Galilee we must turn to a more complicated literary form, the parable.[28] Let us examine an example from the Talmud Yerushalmi's tractate Berakhot (9:1, 13a). It shows how a well-known parable was mastered in a variety of versions, each textually distinct yet each sharing a common structure and point:[29]

    1. Rabbi Yudan [transmitted] in the name of Rabbi Yitzhak four versions:
        A. One of flesh and blood had a patron.
        B. They said to the patron: Your client has been arrested. He replied: I'll stand by him!

> They said to him, your client has been brought to court. He replied: I'll stand
> by him!

C. They said to him: Look, he's going to his crucifixion—what will become of
the client and where is his patron?

D. But the Blessed Holy One saved Moshe from the sword of Pharaoh, for so is
it written: "And He saved me from the sword of Pharaoh" (Ex. 18:4)! . . .[30]

2. Rabbi Yudan [transmitted] in the name of Rabbi Yitzhak another version:

A. One of flesh and blood had a patron.

B. They said to him: Your client has been arrested. He replied: I'll stand by him!

> They said to him: Your client has been brought to court. He replied: I'll stand
> by him!

C. They said to him: Your client has been thrown into the water—what will
become of the client and where is his patron?

D. But the Blessed Holy One saved Yonah from the belly of the fish, for it says
in Scripture: "And God spoke to the fish and he spit up Yonah" (Jon. 2:11).

3. Rabbi Yudan [transmitted] in the name of Rabbi Yitzhak another version:

A. One of flesh and blood had a patron.

B. They said to him: Your client has been arrested. He replied: I'll stand by
him!

> They said to him: Your client has been brought to court. He replied: I'll stand
> by him!

C. They said to him: Your client has been thrown into the fire—what will become of the client and where is his patron?

D. But the Blessed Holy One is not like this, for He saved Hananiah, Mishael,
and Azariah from the furnace of fire, for so is it written: "And Nebuchadnezar
replied, saying, Blessed is the God of Shadrakh, Mishakh, and Evednego"
(Dan. 3:28)!

4. Rabbi Yudan [transmitted] in the name of Rabbi Yitzhak another version:

A. One of flesh and blood had a patron.

B. So on and so forth until—[31]

C. Your patron has been thrown to the beasts.

D. But the Blessed Holy One saved Daniel from the den of lions, for so is it written: My God sent His angel who closed the mouth of the lions (Dan. 6:23)!

5. Rabbi Yudan stated in his own name:

A. One of flesh and blood has a patron.

B. When troubles overtake [the client], he does not immediately approach [his
patron]. Rather, he goes and stands at the gate of his patron and calls out to
the attendant or other member of the household. And the latter says to the
patron: So and So is waiting at the gate of your courtyard.

C. Maybe the patron will let him in; maybe he'll leave him there.

D. But the Blessed Holy One is not like this! When troubles overtake a person,
he shouldn't call either to Michael or to Gavriel. Rather let him call upon
Me and I shall respond immediately, for so is it written: "All who call upon
the name of the Lord shall be spared" (Joel 3:5)!

The parable of "the patron" richly evokes the Roman patronage system, of which
rabbinic culture stands as only one local variation.[32] But it is of interest to us in terms
of its mnemonic characteristics.

The set scene is the well-known judicial process of arrest, trial, and conviction. The orator and his audience both know that the patron can intercede on behalf of his client at the stage of arrest and trial (B), but that if conviction results, the patron is helpless (C). There is otherwise virtually nothing to remember, other than the repeated phrase "I'll stand by him" and the lament, "What will become of the client and where is his patron?" The helplessness of the patron at the moment of the test of his powers (C) sets up the contrast with the ultimate Patron and His client, Israel. The illustrative citation of an appropriate Scripture then concludes the parable with a demonstration of the orator's ability to link the parable and the Scripture into an illuminating relationship.

With these simple elements in mind, any decently prepared homilist could extemporize endlessly, from one performance setting to another, by varying the situations of threat to the client (B–C) and selecting appropriate verses for representing God's abiding patronage (D). Indeed, the copyist has abbreviated the fourth rendition, knowing full well that he could do so without interfering with the reader/performer's own rendition of the parable. Obviously, we should not search here for the "original" version of the "patron of flesh and blood" that inspired the others. Rather, each repetition constitutes its own authentic version. Even the one reported by Rabbi Yudan "in his own name," although it varies the content of texts 1–4, takes the basic elements of the parable for granted. At 5B the client calls upon the patron, while at 5C the patron's ineffectiveness is exposed. Finally, at 5D a scriptural text illustrates the incomparable power of the divine Patron.

Rhetorical pedagogy, we recall, would have presented the student with a written version of his parable. Was there, then, a written version of this parable before Rabbi Yudan that served as the starting point for a series of oral variations on its themes? The simplicity of this parable's structure would suggest no real need for a written version to serve as a mnemonic aid. But elsewhere in the Yerushalmi, in a passage discussing the utility of various *aides de memoire*, we are told in the name of Rabbi Yohanan that "It is a certainty that one who learns homiletics ['*gdh*] from a book will not quickly forget it" (Y. Berakhot 5:1, 9a).[33]

Since parables fall within the rabbinic genre of homiletics, perhaps we have in Rabbi Yohanan's dictum indirect evidence that at least some rabbinic parables circulated in written form, serving as the basis of orally performed renditions.[34] But we needn't push the evidence, which is at best indirect, grounded only upon the comparative case of the rhetorical schools. It is sufficient to observe that the Yerushalmi presents us with an example of rhetorical variation that is entirely commensurate with those practiced in contemporary rhetorical schools. In light of this contextualization of the rabbinic evidence in the larger setting of Greco-Roman rhetorical practice, the burden of proof seems to shift onto the shoulders of those arguing for an exclusively oral method of textual composition and transmission.

Performative Variation in Citations of Tannaitic *Halakhah*

An equally important, and far more widespread, example of disciplined textual transformation occurs routinely in the Yerushalmi's citations of Tannaitic texts. These are routinely transmitted in several versions in different literary settings. Among scholars committed to exclusively oral models for the transmission of rabbinic tradition, such variation has normally been interpreted as evidence for the fluidity of purely oral literature prior to its reduction to writing.[35] In light of the *Progymnasmata*, it is possible to explore the degree to which such variety may be as well explained by the hypothesis that Amoraic rhetorical education, including the intentional oral reconfiguration of written Tannaitic material, may lie behind diverse transmissional variations of such literary units.

Let us look at a repesentative case in which the Yerushalmi engages an array of Tannaitic variations of a single textual substrate. This example focuses upon a very brief unit of Tannaitic tradition in M. Yoma 4:6 and the exegetical contribution of Y. Yoma 4:6, 41d. The Mishnaic passage is part of a larger discussion, M. Yoma 4:4–6, that draws a series of distinctions between the daily Temple sacrificial procedures (Lev. 6:1 ff.) and those prescribed for Yom Kippur (Lev. 16:1 ff.).

The entirety of M. Yoma 4:4–6 is structured by a single mnemonic pattern: "on every day/but this day." The passage discussed below concerns a difference of opinion among mid-second-century Tannaim concerning the number of altar pyres lit for the liturgical needs of each day (M. Yoma 4:6):[36]

> On every day there were 4 pyres, but this day 5—words of Rabbi Meir.
>
> Rabbi Yose says: On each day 3, but this day 4.
>
> Rabbi Yehudah says: On each day 2, but this day 3.

To this the Yerushalmi now adds (Y. Yoma 4:6):[37]

> 1. What's the source behind Rabbi Meir?
>
>   —"And the fire on the altar shall burn on it and not go out" (Lev. 6:5)—this refers to the pyre for maintaining the fire.
>
>   —"and the priest shall burn upon it" (Lev. 6:5)—this refers to the pyre for consuming limbs and innards.
>
>   —"and he shall arrange the burnt offering on it" (Lev. 6:5)—this refers to the large pyre.
>
>   —"and he shall burn on it the fat of the whole offerings" (Lev. 6:5)—this refers to the incense pyre.
> 2. And Rabbi Yose does not count the pyre for consuming limbs and innards.
>
>   And Rabbi Yehudah does not count the pyre for maintaining the fire.
> 3. How does Rabbi Yehudah apply "a perpetual fire (Lev. 6:6)"?
>
>   The fire that I specified as "perpetual" shall only be on the outer altar. . . .[38]
> 4. And where do we know about the pyre for Yom Kippur?
>
>   Rabbi Yirmiyah in the name of Rabbi Pedat: "Coals of fire" (Lev. 16:12)—Why does Scripture specify "fire"?
>
>   For it is insignificant compared to the coals.

The Yerushalmi appears to supply a relatively straightforward exegesis of the Mishnah. Its basic interest is to define scriptural sources for Rabbi Meir's view (1, 4). Stichs 2–3 play a secondary role, with 2 explaining the deviating positions of

Rabbi Yose and Rabbi Yehudah, and 3 amplifying the minimalist view of Rabbi Yehudah in particular.

We shall see, however, that this simple exercise in Mishnaic exegesis is grounded in a complex set of intertextual references that link the Mishnaic text and the Yerushalmi to textual sources now preserved in the written redactions of other compilations. There are, in fact, three primary sources that must be considered in reconstructing the matrix of Y. Yoma's comment in a spectrum of oral and written literary tradition. Two sources are now found in extant Tannaitic compilations, the Tosefta and Sifra; a third is the foundation of the discussion of M. Yoma 4:6 in the Talmud Bavli. Here are the texts.

> *T. Kippurim* 2:11[39]
> On every day there were 2 pyres there, but this day 3.
>> 1 for the large pyre
>> and 1 for the second pyre
>> and 1 they added for the incense of the innermost chamber—
>> words of Rabbi Yehudah
> Rabbi Yose adds 1 for maintaining the fire.
>
> Rabbi Meir adds 1 for limbs and innards unconsumed from evening.

> *Sifra, Tzav per.* 2:11[40]
> Rabbi Yehudah says: 2 pyres on every day, and 3 on Yom Kippur.[41]
>
> Rabbi Yose says: 3 on every day, and 4 on Yom Kippur.
>> 1 for the large pyre
>> and 1 for the incense pyre
>> and 1 for maintaining the fire
>> and 1 they added for Yom Kippur
> Rabbi Meir says: 4 on every day, and 5 on Yom Kippur.
>> 1 for the large pyre
>> and 1 for the incense
>> and 1 for maintaining the fire
>> and 1 for limbs and innards unconsumed from evening
>> and 1 they added for Yom Kippur

> *B. Yoma* 45a[42]
> On every day there were 2 pyres, but this day 3
>> 1 for the large pyre
>> and 1 for the second pyre of incense
>> and 1 they added on that day—
>> words of Rabbi Yehudah
> Rabbi Yose says: On every day 3, but this day 4.
>> 1 for the large pyre
>> and 1 for the second pyre of incense
>> and 1 for maintaining the fire
>> and 1 they added on that day
> Rabbi Meir says: On every day 4, but this day 5.
>> 1 for the large pyre
>> and 1 for the second pyre of incense
>> and 1 for maintaining the fire
>> and 1 for limbs and innards unconsumed from evening
>> and 1 they added on that day

These texts bear complex relationships to each other as well as to M. Yoma. Let's summarize them briefly before reflecting on their connections to the Mishnah exegesis at Y. Yoma. We will then illumine these relationships in light of the model of oral permutations of a written text in the *Progymnasmata*.

M. Yoma differs from its parallel sources in two respects. The first concerns a mnemonic matter. M. lists its distinctions between daily liturgy and Yom Kippur in descending numerical order (Meir–4/5, Yose–3/4, Yehudah–3/2), while all the parallels reverse the mnemonic, moving in ascending numerical order from Yehudah through Meir. The second obvious difference is that all the parallel passages contain material absent from M. Yoma but crucial to grasping its implications—that is, only the parallels enumerate the precise sorts of pyres assumed by Meir, Yose, and Yehudah.

So the Tannaitic parallels together share traits that distinguish them collectively from the Mishnah. They also differ from each other, primarily in their economy of supplying the information missing from the Mishnah. T. Kippurim offers a complete list of pyres only for Yehudah's view and then specifies the further pyres Yose and Meir would add. Printed editions of Sifra and B. Yoma, for their part, are progressively more ample, the former supplying complete lists for Rabbis Yose and Meir, the latter supplying them for all three authorities; however, Codex Assemani's version of Sifra is virtually identical in this regard to the Bavli's text.

As renderings of Tannaitic tradition, all the pericopes are textually distinct from M. Yoma, but they fall into two basic groups. Bavli and Sifra, organized for mnemonic convenience, represent versions of a single textual tradition, while T. Kippurim, composed without mnemonic requirements in mind, represents an independent way of organizing the same information. The same mnemonic patterning in Sifra and B. Yoma indicates that both are closer than T. Kippurim to the mnemonically arranged textual tradition of M. Yoma. They merely reverse the order of M.'s mnemonic cues and fill in M.'s gaps, while T. Kippurim shows no attempt to follow the Mishnaic mnemonic at all.

Let us now reflect upon this complex set of literary relations with the help of the model offered by Greco-Roman rhetorical practice. In that setting, the disciplined transformation of memorized texts was a routine aspect of rhetorical training that prepared students to deploy texts in various versions in their spoken and written discourses. Moreover, the transformation of such texts involved not only expansive elaboration (as in Hermogenes) but also exercises in simple grammatical reconstructions of the core text (as in Theon). There are instructive analogies to such transformations in the Tannatic texts before us.

Surely it is not difficult to arrange M. Yoma, Sifra, and B. Yoma as a single pattern of transformations. All share an identical mnemonic (albeit in reverse order), and the latter two texts seem to expand M. Yet one must ask: is this expansion "exegetical" in the sense that it supplies information needed by a textual exegete to interpret the Mishnah? Or does it simply give textual expression to knowledge the Mishnaic tradent already assumed on the part of students? I suggest the latter. M. Yoma could hardly have conveyed much useful information at all unless its audience was already familiar with the kinds of pyres used in daily and festival liturgy.

The Mishnah is, in fact, formulated with such information in mind. In order to yield to the rigor of its overall mnemonic program (M. Yoma 4:4–6), M. 4:6 has simply omitted what its framers assumed could be taken for granted. Sifra and B. Yoma, from this perspective, are not "commentaries," supplying by exegetical ingenuity information wholly independent of the text they cite. Rather, they restore to the text the oral audience's implicit referential system. M. Yoma, then, is bound up with Sifra and B. Yoma in an oral-peformative hermeneutical circle that appears impossible to open from our own historical distance. On what grounds might we determine that the Mishnaic form is textually primary and the others secondary or, to the contrary, that the Mishnah formulates in its own way material already known in the forms preserved in Sifra and B. Yoma?

Here, it would seem, lies the one crucial difference between the example of the *Progymnasmata* and the Tannaitic examples. While the rhetoricians supply us with the written versions of the *chreiae* that serve as the basis of mnemono-technical exercises, there appears little hope in the rabbinic case of firmly determining which text — if any — is the "base" and which the "transformation." In this example, however, there may be a way out of the echo chamber of oral tradition. The key lies, perhaps, at T. Kippurim.

This Toseftan pericope contains all the information of its Tannaitic companions, identifying the various pyres and linking them to the appropriate Tannaim. Moreover, its listing of the sequence of Tannaim (Yehudah–Yose–Meir) conforms to that of Sifra and B. Yoma, in opposition to that of M. Yoma. Its fundamental deviation from all the other Tannaitic sources, as we have observed, lies in T.'s lack of a clearly recognizable mnemonic pattern for the effective recall and transmission of the information. How, then, does T. Kippurim fit into the textual complex of the mnemonically managed traditions with which it shares much content but little form?

The rhetorical model of the *Progymnasmata*, which prescribes the recycling of written texts into oral versions, suggests a way of imagining what is before us. T. Kippurim may indeed preserve a version of a written textual source standing behind the renderings of the Mishnah, Sifra, and the Bavli. The latter three, that is, may be read as rhetorically guided transformations of T. Kippurim, reshaping its written text for the oral-performative instructional setting in which Tannaitic traditions would be transmitted and analyzed. On this reading, M. Yoma, Sifra, and B. Yoma represent diverse oral-performative transformations of a foundational written text that happens now to be preserved in the version of T. Kippurim.

This reconstruction of the oral-written continuum, of course, suggests that M. Yoma 4:6 does not stand at the origins of the larger stream of tradition it itself exemplifies. Rather, M. *assumes* T.'s information on the nature of the pyres and the sources of the various opinions and organizes T. mnemonically for use in a larger literary setting in which the mnemonic "every day/this day" defines the formulation of the material. Sifra and B. Yoma, by contrast, preserve T.'s order of authorities and information on the pyres, but reorganize the information in light of the Mishnah's creation of a mnemonic pattern of paired numbers in sequential order.

This is the situation of tradition into which the composer of Y. Yoma 4:6 entered. His exegesis of the Mishnah is deeply intertwined with the Tannaitic materials we have just examined. Indeed, his own exegetical language echoes each of his sources so subtly that the literary critic has no grounds for isolating any single textual version as the primary source of the exegete's tradition. Nevertheless, the exegete's work is distinguishable from his tradition in a crucial respect: his main contribution to M., the elucidation of the scriptural foundation of the Tannaitic opinions, is fresh with his own enterprise. He comes to answer, in fact, the one question that the antecedent tradition has left unexplored—the scriptural foundations of the opinions.

Let me at this point stress the modesty of my claim about the role of written sources in the transmission of Tannaitic tradition. As is indicated in the introduction to this part of the discussion, reconstructive work with medieval manuscripts of the Yeruahalmi cannot offer definitive proof that writing was used in the construction and preservation of Tannaitic textual tradition. Neither, however, can it prove the absence of written sources in the literary milieu that ultimately yielded the written redactions in our hands. Our goal is simply to show that the existence of an exclusively oral Tannaitic literary tradition is neither likely in light of parallel Greco-Roman oral-educational settings, nor necessary in order to explain the presence of multiple versions of Tannaitic textual tradition.

The Suppression of Writing and the Ideology of Orality

We have established the likelihood that the use of written texts of rabbinic tradition was more widespread in discipleship training among Galilean Amoraic masters than the tradents of the Yerushalmi's textual traditions wished to acknowledge. Rabbinic disciples were not only exposed to written materials in the course of their training; the written versions could also serve as a textual standard for the correction of oral citations.

But, having acknowledged such uses of written texts, we nevertheless must accept the overwhelming representation of the Yerushalmi that resorting to such writings was ancillary to preparing for a learned performance in which written sources were accessed only through memory. This was the oral examination before a Sage, in which the disciple was expected to have extensive Tannaitic sources at his fingertips, available for accurate citation and rigorous exposition. The learning exchange, that is, constituted a social space that privileged orality as expressed in a give-and-take structured by a ritualized protocol of questions and answers.[43]

The Yerushalmi is rich in representations of analytic interchanges in which two or more colleagues, or teachers and students, are portrayed in dialogical analysis of shared orally reported texts.[44] These dialogues are presented, literarily, in spare formal terms. Commonly the introductory settings employ forms of the verb "sit," *ytb.* This yields such framing settings as the following: *rby X wrby Y hwwn ytbyn 'mryn* ("Rabbi X and Rabbi Y were in session, saying . . ."); or *rby X wrby Y hwwn ytbyn l'yyn b'wryyt'* ("Rabbi X and Rabbi Y were in session, laboring in *torah*"). With the introductory context established, the resulting interchange is normally framed with the simple verb "say," *'mr,* repeated as frequently as the discussion requires: "he said to him" (*'mr lyh*) . . . ; "he replied" (*'mr lyh*) . . . , and so on. Another verb commonly used to introduce a depiction of a learning session is "ask" (*š'l*), as in the passage we shall soon examine.

Commonly such dialogues include ample citation of Tannaitic material. These, of course, represent masters and disciples interpreting previously memorized texts. Almost universally, written texts of Tannaitic tradition play virtually no discernible role in such literary representations of study sessions, but this representation of the norm is belied by at least one clear discussion of a written halakhic source.

It is worth taking a look at how Y. Maaserot 2:4, 49d, cites the personal halakhic notebook (*pnqs*; *pinax*)[45] of the disciple Hilfai (early fourth century). It contained, among other things, versions of material now compiled in the Tosefta at T. Maaserot 2:3. For ease of comparison, the Tannaitic material is italicized:[46]

1. One who purchases dates that he intends to mash and dried figs that he intends to press—. . .

   Sages say: He makes a random snack of them and removes the offerings as produce that is certainly untithed.
2. R. Yose, R. Hela, R. Lazar in the name of Hilfai:
3. Said R. Yonah: We found this written in the notebook of Hilfai: *He makes a random snack of them and removes the offerings as produce that is doubtfully tithed.*
4. Now, here is a difficulty: for it is reasonable to assume that a person making a random snack of produce will eventually remove offerings as produce that is certainly untithed; but if he removes offerings as for doubtfully tithed produce, he should be forbidden from making a random snack.
5. R. Yose in the name of Hela: He makes a random snack of it on the grounds that it is incompletely processed, yet he removes the offerings as doubtfully tithed produce.
6. The reason is—since it is clear that entry into the home renders the produce forbidden for untithed use, even he will separate heave-offering as early as possible.

This passage offers a literary representation of an analytical exercise that would normally have been mounted in oral exposition of a Tannaitic source (1). But it differs from virtually all others in the Yerushalmi in two key respects. First, Hilfai's written version of that source (3) is cited as a serious challenge to the orally delivered version. Thus the citation of a written source is accepted for the purpose of textual criticism. More crucially, the source is subjected to an analytical interchange (4–6) that provides cogent grounds for accepting the version recorded in the notebook.

Here, then, is crucial evidence for the legitimate use of written materials to control the citation of a text in oral performance.[47] One can only guess, in light of the overall silence of the Yerushalmi on written Tannaitic sources, how many other alternative readings for Mishnaic or Toseftan materials had their basis in written versions of texts meant for oral delivery. But there is at least one other clear citation of a written halakhic tradition that may have important implications for this question.

Y. Kilaim 1:1, 27a, attributes to Rabbi Hillel b. Alas the habit of recording halakhic traditions on pinaxes and even walls, and it cites one of his texts. There, too, his text is introduced by the identical citational formula found in Y. Maaserot 2:4: *'škḥwn ktyb bpnqsy d-* . . . ("we found this written in the notes of X"). A key figure in the tradental chain of both texts is the leading mid-fourth-century Tiberian master Rabbi Yonah. This linkage of a specific transmissional formula with a key Tiberian master of that time suggests, first, that written rabbinic texts routinely circulated among important groups of masters. It also suggests that before us is at least one literary formula for citing such written materials. These two examples, therefore, may be the only survivors of a larger body of unpreserved Tiberian traditions that acknowledge citation from written sources.

The failure to preserve traditions citing written halakhic sources seems certainly due to the concerted attempts of at least one powerful circle of masters and disciples to suppress entirely the use of written texts in the training of disciples. The earliest reports of such suppression emerges, as we noted, in materials linked to the mid-third-century master Rabbi Yohanan, who is reported to have praised those who perused homiletical texts in efforts to memorize them (Y. Berakhot 5:1, 9a). On the matter of halakhic tradition, however, he is recorded in the Talmud Bavli as holding a very different view: "those who write down *halakhot* are like those who burn the Torah, and anyone who studies from such writings receives no reward!" (B. Temurah 14b)[48]

The Yerushalmi knows no comparable ruling ascribed to Rabbi Yohanan or any other Galilean master, but, as we shall see, there is ample evidence in the Yerushalmi that Rabbi Yohanan and his circle took the dimmest view of written texts of halakhic tradition. It is a view, moreover, entirely unprecedented in any extant Tannaitic compilation. Some of the Tannaitic authorities, we recall, had insisted upon the antiquity of rabbinic halakhic tradition stemming all the way from Sinai. Others had derived everything in the Oral Torah from scriptural exegesis. But within Rabbi Yohanan's circle a far bolder claim was formulated. Not only had halakhic tradition been, as a matter of fact, exclusively oral in its formulation and transmission; as a matter of principle, it could not be written down because its oral preservation and performance were the key to maintaining Israel's covenantal relationship with God. The oral-performative halakhic tradition stemming from Sinai was not merely the conceptual system in which scriptural norms were applied. It was superior in covenantal significance to the very Scriptures whose meaning it set out to define. As such it needed to be preserved in a form making it all but inaccessible to anyone but those privileged to share in the face-to-face learning community of rabbinic discipleship.

The richest source for this view is a well-known passage that appears, with variations, in no less than three tractates of the Talmud Yerushalmi. The opening unit of the discussion seems to have emerged in reflection upon M. Peah 2:6, in which Nahum the Liblarios ("copyist") presents, as a *"halakhah* to Moses on Sinai," a certain ruling regarding the leaving of corner-offerings in fields sown with two kinds of wheat. Accordingly, I cite the version preserved in Y. Peah 2:6, 17a:[49]

1. Said Rabbi Zeira in the name of Rabbi Yohanan: If a *halakhah* comes to your attention and you can't comprehend it, don't set it aside for another matter. For indeed, many *halakhot* were spoken to Moshe on Sinai, and all of them are embedded in the Repeated Tradition [*mšnh*].[50]
    2. Said Rabbi Avin: Quite so! [Take this ruling about] two kinds of wheat—had Nahum not come and explained [its origins] for us, would we have known?
3. Rabbi Zeira in the name of Rabbi Leazar [b. Pedat]: "Shall I write for him the greater portion of my Torah? [They would be like strangers!]" (Hos. 8:12). Now, indeed, is the majority of the Torah written down? Rather, matters derived from Scripture outnumber those derived from [what is taught by] the mouth [as *halakhah* to Moshe from Sinai].[51]

4. Really now! Rather, put it this way: Matters derived from [what is taught] by mouth are more precious than those derived from Scripture.[52]

5. Even so: "They would be like strangers!" (Hos. 8:12).

Said Rabbi Avin: Were I to write for you [i.e., Moshe] the greater portion of my Torah, wouldn't they [i.e., Israel] still be regarded as strangers?

[That is:] What distinguishes us from the Gentiles? These produce their books and those produce their books; these produce their records (*dyptr'*) and those produce their records![53]

6. Rabbi Haggai in the name of Rabbi Shmuel b. Nahman: Some things were spoken by mouth and others in script—yet we would not know which are more precious but for this which is written: "I have established a covenant with you and with Israel through these things taught orally (*'l py hdbrym h'lh*: Ex. 34:27)![54] This proves that those in the mouth are more precious![55]

7. Rabbi Yohanan and Rabbi Yudan b. Rabbi Shimon:

One said—if you preserve what is in the mouth and you preserve what is in script, I will establish My covenant with you. But if not, I will not establish My covenant with you.

The other said—if you preserve what is in the mouth and you fulfill what is in script, you will be rewarded. But if not, you will not be rewarded.

8. It is written: "And on them was written according to all the words which the Lord spoke to you on Sinai" (Dt. 9:10).

Rabbi Yehoshua b. Levi said:

Instead of "on them" we read "AND on them." Instead of "all" we read "ACCORDING to all." Instead of "words" we read "THE words." [These superfluous textual elements indicate that] Scripture, Repeated Tradition, Dialectics, and Homiletics—and even what a trained disciple (*tlmyd wtyq*)[56] will in the future expound before his Master—all were already spoken to Moshe on Sinai.

9. What's the proof? "Is there anything of which it can be said, See this is new?" (Qoh. 1:10) His companion will reply: "It has been since eternity!" (Qoh. 1:10)

The authorities mentioned in this passage lived from the first half of the third century (Rabbi Yehoshua b. Levi) through the first half of the fourth (Rabbi Haggai, Rabbi Avin). All but Rabbi Yehoshua b. Levi were younger contemporaries of Rabbi Yohanan (d. 279) or members of discipleship circles descended from his own. The editor shows no interest in a chronological arrangement of opinions and, as is common in the Yerushalmi, makes little effort to place the materials at his disposal into some sort of explicit sequence. The result is a series of discrete units of tradition (1–2, 3–5, 6–7, 8–9) pursuing no cumulative argument. But its several parts offer diverse expositions of how the Amoraic Sages surrounding Rabbi Yohanan understood the origins and significance of the *torah* they transmitted by mouth to their disciples.

Unit 1–2, responding to the Mishnaic comment, simply reinforces the well-attested Tannaitic notion that some *halakhot* entered the rabbinic tradition as early as Sinai. The point is merely to encourage the student to make every effort to grasp the inner details of the halakhic norms with which he is engaged, since one can never know which elements of the oral tradition may have Sinaitic origins.

An obscure verse in Hosea is thoroughly resignified at unit 3–5 in terms of the oral tradition, which is now claimed to constitute the major portion of the revelation at Sinai. At issue is the quantity of oral tradition derived directly from Moses in relation to the explicit Mosaic writings. In Rabbi Leazar's view (3), the rather small quantity of nonscriptural oral tradition originating with Moses is vastly exceeded by oral text-intepretive tradition stemming from the scriptural exegesis of later Sages.[57] Leazar's unnamed interlocutor (4) disputes this, offering the bold claim that the most precious element of the oral tradition is the portion, however small in quantity, that stands free of Scripture. The exegesis of the concluding stich of Hos. 8:12 explains why the oral tradition in general, and the Mosaic *halakhot* in particular, are so precious (5). In the game of religious one-upsmanship, each nation will produce its own historical genealogies to demonstrate its pedigree and accomplishments. In the oral-performative tradition, however, Israel has been given a gift that exempts it from this futile competition over literary tradition.

This thought is thoroughly explored at unit 6–7, in which the wordplay grounded in the language of Ex. 24:27 plays the crucial role. The covenantal status of Israel is linked firmly not to the Scriptures that record the covenant agreement, but rather to the oral-performative tradition of the Sages that determines the application of the Scripture. The corpus of halakhic tradition has now replaced the tablets of Sinai as the symbolic representation of Israel's possession of divine love. While the oral tradition is, therefore, more precious (6), both the written and oral revelations are necessary (7).

The foregoing sets the stage for the exposition of Rabbi Yehoshua b. Levi (8–9). Even though he is the earliest figure mentioned here, the tradition attributed to him stands as a kind of summary of the implications of what has gone before. Ignoring the more cautious perspectives of units 1–2 and 3–6, he offers the boldest claim about the nature of the oral tradition preserved among contemporary rabbinic Sages. Whatever insights dawn in the mind of a properly trained disciple are all an unfolding of the original oral disclosure to Moses. The most recent disciple, therefore, transmits in his mouth knowledge given by God to Moses at the very moment of the covenant's sealing. The guarantee of this is the disciple's own place in the line of tradition that extends, behind his own master, back to his master's master, and ultimately back to Moses himself.

This passage is like a stone thrown into the pool of Galilean Amoraic tradition, sending textual ripples out in a variety of directions, reaching ultimately the Amoraic circles of Babylonia.[58] But for the present it will be helpful to trace the impact of its arguments and language on other textual traditions that circulated in the Galilean environment. A theme of only marginal importance in the cited text— the oral tradition as a principle of distinction between Israel and the Gentiles (unit 5)—gradually moved into prominence as, under Byzantine rule, the Christianization of the Land of Israel proceeded apace. By the close of the sixth century, the unwritten character of rabbinic tradition figured as a standard theme in rabbinic polemics defending the authority of rabbinic teachings against Christian theological critics.

One text in particular carries within it loud echoes of the words just reviewed coming from the Galilean Amoraim in the circle of Rabbi Yohanan. It is preserved in a Palestinian homiletic collection of the late Byzantine period known as the Midrash of Rabbi Tanhuma (Ki Tissa 17):[59]

1. As for what Scripture says: "Shall I write for him the greater portion of my Torah?" (Hos. 8:12)—when the Blessed Holy One came to give the Torah, he spoke it to Moshe in a sequence: first the Scripture, then the Repeated Tradition (*hmšnh*), then Homiletics (*h'gdh*), and then Dialectics (*htlmwd*), for it is said: "And God spoke all these things" (Ex. 21:1). [Thus,] even what a trained disciple might ask from his Master the Blessed Holy One spoke to Moshe at that moment, for it is said: "And God spoke all these things."

2. When Moshe had mastered it all, the Blessed Holy One said to him: Go and teach it to My children!

   Said Moshe: Lord of the World, write it for Your children.

   He replied: I'd like to give it to them in script, but I know that one day the Nations of the World will subdue them and seek to take it from them, so that my sons will become like the other Nations. Rather: Let them have the Scriptures in writing. But the Repeated Tradition, Homiletics, and Dialectics shall remain in the mouth.

3. "And the Lord said to Moshe: write for Yourself" (Ex. 34:27)—this refers to Scripture.

   "But these are oral" (Ex. 34:27)—this refers to the Repeated Tradition and Dialectics, for these distinguish between Israel and the Nations of the World.

This smooth composition displays a number of intertextual connections to Y. Peah 2:6 and its Yerushalmi parallels. Note first, at unit 1, the assumption, shared with Y. Peah (unit 3–5), that Hos. 8:12 conceals a reference to the orally transmitted rabbinic tradition of learning. The tradent of the current passage, however, has now brought Rabbi Yehoshua b. Levi's statement about the seasoned disciple (Y. Peah, unit 8) into closer relationship to the Hosea passage. Tanhuma unit 2, for its part, picks up and enriches Y. Peah unit 5's note of competition between Israel and the Gentiles over the possession of written records. But now an entirely fresh issue has intruded into the discussion: at stake, it turns out, is the Gentile claim to possess the Scriptures of Israel. The point is driven home at unit 3, which restates in a fresh way the exegesis of Ex. 34:27 that figures so crucially in Y. Peah unit 6. Whereas the tradent of Y. Peah was concerned only to celebrate the covenantal preciousness of the oral tradition, Tanhuma's composer specifies that the covenantal significance is designed to exclude Gentiles from covenantal consideration.

Clearly, the "Nations of the World" who seek to appropriate Israel's precious heritage of Torah are not the pagan conquerors of Israel, but their Christian successors now ruling Byzantium. The passage counters Christian theological supercessionism, grounded in a hermeneutical appropriation of Jewish Scripture, with the bold claim that possession of Scripture alone is no sign of covenantal partnership with God. The midrashist claims that it is precisely the fact that part of the Torah is carried solely in the memory and the mouth, rather than in a book, that preserves the uniqueness of Israel. The incorporation of Torah into the body through memorization and enactment functions no less surely than that other mark on the body—circumcision—to distinguish Israel from those who would supplant it in God's favor.

The same Midrash of Rabbi Tanhuma (ed. Buber, vayera 6, 44b), and a roughly contemporary Palestinian collection known as Pesiqta Rabbati (ed. Friedmann, 14b), share a close parallel to this passage, glossing it in even stronger language. Since the

Pesiqta Rabbati passage is slightly more ample, we will use it as our text. Hear how the conversation between the Holy One and Moshe is reconstructed by Rabbi Yehudah bar Shalom into a dialogue between the Holy One and Byzantium:

> The Blessed Holy One foresaw that the Nations would translate the [Written] Torah and read it in Greek. And they would say: "They [i.e., the Jews] are not Israel!"[60] Said the Blessed Holy One to Moshe: "O Moshe! The Nations will say, 'We are Israel! We are the children of the Omnipresent!' And Israel, too, will say, 'We are the children of the Omnipresent!'"
> And the scales are in balance!

> Said the Blessed Holy Ones to the Nations: "What do you mean that you are my children? But I recognize only the one who holds my mystery in his hands. He alone is my son!"
> They said to Him: "What is this mystery?"
> He replied: "It is the Repeated Tradition!"

Here the crucial word, translated as mystery, is the Aramaic *mistoryn*, a borrowing from the Greek *mysterion*. As M. Bregman has recently demonstrated, this rabbinic appeal to the "mystery" of the Repeated Tradition is hardly a result of random chance.[61] It corresponds most directly to a precisely parallel usage of the term "mystery" in the work of the late-fourth-century Christian bishop Hilarius of Poitier. In his Latin commentary on the Septuagint's book of Psalms (Ps. 2:2–3), Hilarius puts forth the proposal that the guarantee of the Septuagintal text's validity lay in the fact that its translators possessed a hidden oral tradition, a *mysterium* of Mosiac origins, that was preserved in their translational work. As Hilarius' *mysterium* preserves the integrity of the Church's tradition of scriptural meaning, and thus its distinctive relation to God, so the Rabbi's *mistoryn*, its Repeated Tradition, serves as a firm basis legitimating Israel as God's sole covenantal partner.

In light of such passages, it would be easy to conclude that the rabbinic insistence on preserving the tradition of oral study was reactive—an attempt by a subdued political and social minority to preserve its cultural autonomy from a hegemonic Christian civilization that had stolen the Book symbolic of Judaic uniqueness.[62] We should not press this point too hard. After all, the privileging of the oral-performative tradition in rabbinic culture predates the rise of Christian political dominance by at least a century, if not more. Rabbinic literature, moreover, revealed little interest in Christianity until it became the state religion of the hated Roman Empire. Only at that point, with the historical rise of the persecuted Christian minority to political domination, would the question of Christianity's legitimacy become a pressing matter.[63]

I want to suggest, therefore, that the Galilean Sages' ideological commitment to the concept of an oral-performative rabbinic tradition that could not be transmitted in written form has its primary social significance much closer to the life of Amoraic society. While the concept of Torah in the Mouth is a useful polemical weapon in the Amoraic theological confrontation with Christianity, that confrontation is not the generative setting in which the unwritten nature of rabbinic tradition has its most compelling ideological force. Rather, the idea of Torah in the Mouth elaborated within Rabbi Yohanan's circle is best anchored in the need to explain and celebrate the distinctive social form of rabbinic community—the master–disciple relationship.

Let us, then, consider the details of that social setting and its impact on Amoraic conceptions of the oral-performative tradition.

Written Word and Oral Word in the Master–Disciple Relationship

It will be helpful, as usual, to first make a comparative detour, back to the already familiar Greco-Roman rhetorical school. We noted earlier, in a *chreia* attributed to Isocrates, that the bond of the rhetor and his student might be represented as displacing even that of parent and child. The point is a common one in rhetorical literature, appearing in numerous contexts.[64] This intimate bond of teacher and student was cemented through common devotion to a world of learning. Such bonds forged in study were not unique to rhetorical education in Antiquity, in which *paideia* commonly represented a path of personal cultivation in the venerable ways of tradition. It was common as well to a host of Greco-Roman instructional settings, *collegia*, in which the study of great works of the past served to solidify and shape students' embrace not only of ideas but of the patterns of life that embodied them. The international Greco-Roman philosophical schools were not bastions of unfettered intellectual curiosity. Rather, they placed a great premium on an emotional attachment to canonical ideas, akin in its way to conversion.[65]

Philosophical training involved, of course, intellectual mastery of the writings or orally transmitted teachings of philosophical founders.[66] But the primary goal of such study was not merely to master knowledge discursively. Rather, it was to be transformed by what one possessed. The privileged path to such transformation lay in emulating the living embodiment of that knowledge in the writings and deeds of one's teachers, and their teacher's teachers. In the person of the philosophical Sage, the instructional text came alive.

Pursuit of intimate discipleship in shaping a life of transformative piety played a crucial role as well in emerging Christian culture in the Roman Empire. Writings in — and well beyond — the Christian scriptural canon routinely represent disciple communities, grounded in the oral transmission of redemptive teachings, as the primitive form of the Church.[67] More important, the commitment to discipleship training in the formation both of Christian intellectual elites and ascetic communities became even stronger in the Byzantine milieu in which Galilean Sages shared living space — and intellectual traditions — with a growing body of Christian clerics and ascetic holy men.[68]

Judaic traditions of discipleship in Second Temple priestly, scribal, or prophetic settings surely preceded the engagement with these deeply Hellenized forms of discipleship.[69] Yet it is also clear that, by the turn of the Common Era, the social and intellectual forms of Judaic discipleship communities were deeply colored by centuries of immersion in the Greco-Roman social and cultural milieu.[70] This background of a culture-wide pursuit of life-transforming gnosis, bound up with an energetically embraced discipline of life, is the proper setting for appreciating the fundamental traits of rabbinic discipleship in all of its diverse manifestations.[71]

The early rabbinic literature, from the Mishnah on, is rich in depictions of learned fellowship as grounded in the personal relationship of disciples and Sages.

This relationship, at least in its ideal representations, supplanted and superseded even those of the patriarchal family. In a passage strikingly similar to Isocrates' advice to honor teachers above parents, the Mishnah teaches: "Where a disciple finds a lost object of his father's and of his master's, the return of his master's takes precedence, for his father brought him into This World, but his master, who has taught him wisdom, brings him into the Coming World" (M. Bava Metzia 2:11/T. Bava Metzia 2:30).[72]

The Yerushalmi, for its part, is no less preoccupied than its Tannaitic predecessors with representations of the life of discipleship. Among these are such common narrative settings as interchanges delivered while sitting before the Sage in instructional session, in the course of judicial deliberations, at meals, during a journey, while attending the Sage's personal needs, or at his deathbed.[73] A particularly illuminating text is preserved in its fullest form at Y. Sheqalim 2:7, although, as the notes to the following translation indicate, its component elements left their traces in numerous redactional settings throughout the Yerushalmi.

Stemming, significantly enough, from the circle of Rabbi Yohanan, the text offers a sharply etched portrait of the protocols of honor assumed by the Galilean Amoraic disciple circles. Crucial among these is the expectation that disciples transmit traditions in the names of those from whom they learned them. The disciple's mastery of the Master's words constituted a kind of transaction that not only benefited the disciple, it also provided the Sage with an invaluable gift. In this gift we may well find a fundamental clue to the privileging of the oral over the written text in Rabbi Yohanan's circle. Herewith, the text (Y. Sheqalim 2:7, 47a):[74]

1. Rabbi Yohanan was leaning upon Rabbi Hiyya b. Abba as he walked.[75] Now, Rabbi Eliezer saw them and hid from before them. Rabbi Yohanan noticed and said: These two things has this Babylonian done to me! First, he didn't offer greetings! Second, he hid!

   Said to him Rabbi Yaakov b. Idi: This is their custom—the younger doesn't greet the elder. They do this to fulfill the verse: "The youths saw me and hid, but the elders arose and stood" (Job 29:8).

2. [Rabbi Yaakov] asked [Rabbi Yohanan]: What's the rule? Is one permitted to pass before an idolatrous image? Said [Rabbi Yohanan]: Why give it any honor? Pass before it but don't look at it! Said [Rabbi Yaakov]: Then Rabbi Eliezer was proper in not passing before you![76]

3. [Rabbi Yohanan replied:] And yet another thing has this Babylonian done to me! He didn't repeat his traditions in my name! . . .[77]

   Rabbi Yaakov b. Idi came before him and said: "As God commanded his servant, Moshe, thus did Moshe command Yehoshua" (Josh. 11:15). Now, do you really think that every time Yehoshua sat and expounded he said: Thus spoke Moshe!? Rather, he sat and expounded and everyone understood that this was the *torah* of Moshe. So in your case—Eliezer sits and expounds, and everyone knows it's your *torah*![78]

   Rabbi Yohanan said to the other disciples: How come the rest of you can't appease me like our colleague, ben Idi?

4. Now, why was Rabbi Yohanan so concerned that traditions be recited in his name?

5. Indeed, David already prayed for this, as it is said: "May I abide in Your Tent eternally, may I take refuge in the shelter of Your wings, selah!" (Ps. 61:5). Now,

could David have imagined that he'd live forever? Rather, this is what David said before the Blessed Holy One: Lord of the World! May I merit that my words be recited in the synagogues and study circles!

6. Shimon b Nezira in the name of Rabbi Yitzhak said:

When a [deceased] Sage's traditions are recited in this world his lips move simultaneously in the grave, as it is said: "[Your palate is like fine wine,] moving the lips of those who sleep" (Song 7:10).[79]

Like a mass of heated grapes that drips as a person presses a finger upon them, so too are the lips of the righteous [Sages who have departed] — when one recites a word of *halakhah* from the mouths of the righteous, their lips move with him in their graves.

7. What kind of pleasure does [the deceased] receive?

Said bar Nezira:

Like someone drinking honeyed wine.

Said Rabbi Yitzhak:

Like someone drinking aged wine. Even though he drank it [long ago], the taste remains in his mouth.

8. Gidol[80] said: One who recites a tradition in the name of its transmitter should imagine him standing before him, as it is said: "Man walks about as a mere shadow *['k bṣlm ythlk 'yš]* [. . . amassing and not knowing who will gather in]" (Ps. 39:7)[81]

9. It is written: "Many a person does he call his friend" — this refers to most people; "but a trustworthy person, who can find?" (Prov. 20:6) — this refers to Rabbi Zeira.

For Rabbi Zeira said: We needn't pay attention to the traditions of Rav Sheshet,[82] since he is blind [and cannot reliably verify from whom he heard his traditions: so *Qorban HaEdah*].

10. Said Rabbi Zeira to Rabbi Assi: Does the Master know bar Petaya in whose name you recite traditions? He replied: Rabbi Yohanan [who knows bar Petaya] recited them in his name!

Said Rabbi Zeira to Rabbi Assi:[83] Does the Master know Rav in whose name you recite traditions? He replied: Rabbi Adda bar Ahavah recited them in his name!

Let us move sequentially through the discourse established by this loose chain of texts. The brief narrative about the indignity suffered by Rabbi Yohanan and the means of his appeasement (unit 1–3) offers a rich representation of the tacit assumptions of the Galilean community regarding the protocols of honoring the master. The unfortunate Babylonian immigrant Rabbi Eliezer offends his mster inadvertently by practicng a form of deference to authority that, in Palestine, signifies contempt (1). In his defense, a second disciple, Rabbi Yaakov b. Idi, offers two arguments. The first provides, as it were, a sociological explanation of Rabbi Eliezer's faux pas (1). The second effort — rhetorically more clever, but equally unsuccessful — draws out the master on an apparently unconnected halakhic issue that, in a surprising way, clarifies the propriety of Rabbi Eliezer's motives (2). The implicit suggestion is that, on his own halakhic principles, Rabbi Yohanan should forgive the snub to his honor.

It turns out, however, that Rabbi Eliezer's unintended slight is only the pretext for Rabbi Yohanan's anger. Rabbi Yohanan finally discloses the underlying source of his resentment—the offending disciple consistently fails to acknowledge the master as the source of his own *torah* traditions (3). Leaping again to the defense, Rabbi Yaakov finally adduces a compelling precedent from Joshua's reporting of Moses' teachings. Rabbi Yohanan sees the point and congratulates his disciple on his interpersonal skills.

Let us focus now on the motive of Rabbi Yohanan's resentment. The narrative on its own suggests that his displeasure is grounded in some proprietary desire to receive credit for his own teachings. He wants his disciples to acknowledge him as the immediate source of their *torah*. But this is not how the contributor of units 4 and 5–7 understands the story. At stake for Rabbi Yohanan is not authorial prestige, but a certain immortality as his traditions of *torah* live after him in continued association with his name. The Psalmist, David, serves as the biblical archetype of one whose words bring him immortality as they are recited by worshippers after his death (5). A second, more pertinent, example of immortality (6–7) is now associated not with the prophetic writings of David, but with the unwritten traditions of the Sages.

The halakhic teachings of departed Sages confer upon them a kind of immortality. The words of *torah*, in the mouth of the disciple, are not merely transmissions of information. They are, rather, bonds that link master and disciple—in this world during the master's life, and even after the master departs for the world to come. The disciple in this world keeps his master's teachings in his mouth so that even the master's earthly remains can, in a minor way, be restored to physical life through the sweet refreshment of his own teaching. As his disciples transmit his traditions, the dead master enjoys a kind of postmortem participation in the revivifying life of learning. The life of the study circle, at the center of which stands the Sage, is extended to him after his death by the very students to whom he gave the eternal life of *torah*.

The statement of Gidol (unit 8) is entirely independent of the foregoing and seems at first a mere afterthought. But, from the perspective of understanding the bonds linking master and disciple, it is perhaps the most telling. Why does one summon up the image of the teacher while reciting his teachings? The prooftext from Ps. 39:7 at first seems to offer no help at all. Indeed, Palestinian Amoraic tradition had already generated, in association with Gen. 39:11, the notion that Joseph derived the power to resist the allure of Potiphar's wife by imagining the face of Jacob, his father.[84] That verse, or some other involving, for example, Moses and Joshua, would surely have been more to the point in the present context. In any event, it is difficult to construct a more far-fetched correlation of a rabbinic norm with its scriptural warrant.

The apparent absurdity of the prooftext, however, dissolves when we reconstruct the sense that Gidol assumes his rabbinic audience will supply to the Hebrew text of Psalms. As elsewhere in midrashic exegesis, much depends upon the sounds of words and the intertextual reverberations they create in the ears of the scripturally literate. The present exegesis depends upon two radical resignifications of scriptural meaning grounded in aural experience of the text. The first concerns the term *ṣlm* ("shadow"), and the second focuses on the term *ythlk* ("walk about").

The Hebrew *ṣlm* surely signifies insubstantiality in the setting of Psalms 39:7. But the midrashist is reading it intertextually with an eye and ear attuned to the far more familiar sense the term bears in Genesis, where it refers to the divine image in which humanity is created (Gen. 1:26–27). With *ṣlm* heard through the intertextual filter of the creation of humanity, the term *ythlk* is then opened up to other meanings that emerge in the Genesis account of human origins. There figures such as Noah (Gen.6:9) and Enoch (Gen. 5:24) "walk with God." To conclude: simply in terms of inner-scriptural intertexts, Ps. 39:7 is being read here to state that "In the image of God shall a person conduct himself."

But there is yet another aural-associative dimension to this scriptural quotation. In a rabbinic setting, *ythlk* reverberates with perhaps the most ideologically rich usage of the verbal root *hlk*—namely, the term for rabbinic tradition, *halakhah*. The assonance of *ythlk* and *hlkh* in a rabbinic setting conveys a message regarding the disciple's own effort to "conduct himself" in accord with the tradition of *halakhah* learned from the Sage.[85] Once we resignify the quotation from Psalms by hearing it with rabbinic ears, its relevance as a prooftext for Gidol's observation could not be more direct. The disciple imagines his teacher while reciting his teachings because, as Scripture proves: "only through the image [*ṣlm*] [of God disclosed through the being of the master] shall a person transform himself into an embodiment of halakhic norms [*ythlk 'yš*]."

In Gidol's midrash, then, we find a powerful claim about the role of the master's personal teaching in the spiritual formation and transformation of his disciples. The discipline of textual memorization and behavioral transformation that defined the life of the disciple is grounded in the living presence of the master. It is a presence that dominates not only in the moment of instruction, but even at a distance, as it is internalized and associated with the memorized traditions so firmly lodged through oral performance. Just as the disciple's recitation of the master's traditions revive the latter even after his death, it is the presence of the master, preserved in the memory of the disciple, that empowers the latter to revive his mentor. Disciple and master constitute a mutually redemptive relationship through the medium of orally performed tradition.

This insistence upon the indispensable presence of the master as the security of the disciple's learning finds a final reinforcement in unit 9–10. Here the point is most direct. Rabbi Zeira is troubled, at 9, by the fact that the blind Rav Sheshet may have misassigned traditions learned from one master to another, since he hadn't the mnemonic advantage of linking the heard words to the visage of the teacher. A solution to his problem is provided at 10. Even if one hasn't learned directly from a master, it is possible to rely on the testimony of disciples who had done so. Thus the chain of tradition that revives the master and transforms the life of the disciple is not threatened by gaps in direct face-to-face reception and transmission. The crucial nourishment of Torah in the Mouth sustains and transforms as long as memories are disciplined to preserve the proper associations of teachers and their teachings.

Summary

Galilean masters of this period claimed access to revealed knowledge that could be learned only in discipleship. They made this claim, to be sure, in an idiom of their own, but the claim itself marked the Sages' position within a larger Greco-Roman conversation. At stake were the relative merits of knowledge gleaned from books as opposed to knowledge gained from the embodiment of books in the form of a living teacher.[86]

To be sure, the Amoraim inherited from Tannaitic tradition a rich body of thought regarding the oral nature of rabbinic tradition, including the terminological germ of the conception of Torah in the Mouth as a primordial complement to the Torah in Script. But they contributed more than some refinements and amplifi-cations of the connections between Sinai and rabbinic traditions. Their crucial and distinctive contribution was to link the idea of Torah in the Mouth firmly to the pedagogical reality of discipleship training. They elevated to a new level the primacy of the Sage as mediator of a transforming body of knowledge in which his own pres-ence was the principal mode of mediation.[87] Thus his own acts and teachings were apprehended in a dual aspect—as impartings of unbroken traditions stemming back into the past, and as disclosures of how that tradition might attain authoritative ex-pression in the present. Since such a body of knowledge was perpetually in process, one could master it only by placing oneself directly in its path—by attending the Sage in whose life the tradition was embodied.[88]

In basic structure, then, the Galilean Amoraic model of oral-performative tradi-tion recapitulated—and drew to their ultimate conclusions—the pedagogical assump-tions of nonrabbinic, Greco-Roman predecessors and contemporaries. The trans-formative power of the Sage's teachings depended upon more than his personal charisma. It could become effective only to the degree that it carried forward an unbroken line of transmission within a privileged community of traditional learn-ing. Those who might read the texts of rabbinic teaching in isolation from the dis-cipleship experience had neither the complete text nor any *torah*, for properly trans-formative knowledge could not be gained by discursive understanding of any text on its own—not even that of the Torah inscribed in Scripture. Rather, it was won exis-tentially by living a life open to dialogue with the Sage, in whom *torah* was present as a mode of his embodied existence. For *torah* to be present, the Sage must be present as its unmediated source and embodiment in word and deed.

The Galilean masters' insistence upon the exclusively oral nature of their text-in-terpretive and oral-performative traditions, therefore, is thoroughly intelligible on the basis of the internal needs of their own discipleship circles. That is, the jurisprudential utility of the distinction between scriptural and scribal-rabbinic legal traditions, and its power in polemically defending the hermeneutical foundations of rabbinic halakhic norms, were rhetorically grounded in a more fundamental concern to explain and celebrate the radical change of life demanded by discipleship to the Sage.

It explained, first of all, how the discipleship community's attachment to the Sage offered a way of life distinct from (and more authentic than) other forms of Jewish community from which disciples had been drawn. The answer was that the covenantal imperative inscribed in the Scriptures, which was bequeathed to all Israel, could be embodied only by a life emulating the Sage's way. Thus the arduous service of the Sage received its fundamental theological legitimation. More important, perhaps, it was necessary to privilege the living presence of the Sage as a source of transforma-tive instruction over against any written versions of his teaching that, by virtue of being permanently inscribed, could be freed from the hermeneutical authority of his own presence or that of disciples, who might further extend his teaching by virtue of their embodied extension of his presence. The efforts to suppress the use of written texts in the transmission of rabbinic *torah* are, therefore, eloquent expressions of the de-sire to preserve the living Sage's transformative teaching presence as the crucial ele-ment in Amoraic *paideia*. Torah came from the mouth, even if that mouth sounded out the silent syllables first inscribed in texts.

Epilogue

This study opened with reflection upon a talmudic text, and reflection upon one text after another has been its substance. It might as well, then, close with a text. This one, drawn from the Talmud Yerushalmi, is about wine, wealth, and *torah*; their effects upon a person's outward demeanor are deemed, in rabbinic culture, too similar for complete comfort.

Thus we are told (Y. Pesahim 10:1, 37c):[1]

A. Rabbi Yehudah b. Rabbi Ilai drank four cups of wine on the Eve of Passover and had to bandage his head [for over six months] until the Festival of Sukkot.

A certain Roman Lady saw him with his face aglow and said to him: Codger! Codger! One of three do I find in thee—either a drunk, a usurer, or a pig farmer!

He replied: May Madam's breath fail her! Yet none of these be found in me! Rather, my studies inspire me, as it is written: "A man's wisdom sets his face aglow!" (Ecc. 8:1)

B. Rabbi Abbahu came to Tiberias. Rabbi Yohanan's disciples saw him with his face aglow.

They said before Rabbi Yohanan: Rabbi Abbahu has found a treasure!

He replied: How so? They replied: His face is aglow! He replied: Perhaps he has heard some new *torah*?

When he came before him, [Rabbi Yohanan] said: Have you heard some new *torah*? He replied: An ancient addition to the Repeated Tradition have I heard!

[Rabbi Yohanan] applied this Scripture to him: "A man's wisdom sets his face aglow!"

The Galilean masters who transmitted these stories shared, with anyone who had enjoyed or aspired to either, knowledge of the intoxicating potential of wine and wealth. But the intoxication of *torah* was something they believed only they could possess and understand. The Roman Lady, therefore, was completely wrong in her diagnosis of Rabbi Yehudah's glowing face, as we might expect; but even the disciples of Rabbi Yohanan, who surely should have known better, mistook Rabbi Abbahu's beaming countenance as evidence that he had found yet another source to add to his already considerable material wealth.

Baruch Bokser, a recent student of this text whose life was cut short far too early, has found a number of persistent apologetic themes of rabbinic culture submerged in these stories.[2] Roman observers of the Sages might suppose, for example, that their *joie de vivre* stemmed from wealth they had extorted from Jews under their guardianship (A). Even disciples might take the Sage's beaming face as a symptom of delight in some worldly good fortune (B). In fact, the perceptions of both hostile and friendly observers are wrong: the joy of the Sage in this world stems from the very thing that connects him to the other world—his *torah*.

Bokser's reading has much to recommend it. Let me build upon it one further structure of interpretation. This text, first of all, is not merely about *torah*—it is in particular about Torah in the Mouth, as the interchange between Rabbi Yohanan and Rabbi Abbahu makes clear. Rabbi Abbahu's intoxication stems from a new word of Repeated Tradition—a *tosefta*—that (in ways the narrator conceals from us) he has managed to hear. Because he has absorbed it into his memory through repetition, it now affects him physiologically, transforming his face. Outsiders, noting the symptom, misinterpret its cause. The outward sign of the presence of Torah in the Mouth is similar to the sign produced by other stimulants—the glowing face—but the reality behind the sign is another thing entirely. Neither wealth nor wine has transformed the face of the Master—it is his *torah* at work within him.

The master's glowing face, then, is an ambiguous sign that both reveals and conceals the presence of *torah*, depending upon who is interpreting it. Appearing as a sign of satisfied appetite to those who are dominated by appetite, *torah* is concealed in the sign of the glowing face. But to those who know the intoxication of having Torah in the Mouth, the glowing face recalls the other glowing countenance of Moses, whose face beamed light after his descent from Sinai.

Let me now stretch the final text well beyond its original frame of reference. For I find within its meditation upon visual representation and the concealment of *torah* some pointer toward what I have tried to understand throughout this study: the rabbinic Sages' insistence upon the memorization and oral transmission of rabbinic *torah*. I am intrigued by the point that a single symptom—in this case, the glowing face of the master—discloses one meaning to those outside the range of rabbinic fellowship and quite another to those wholly within it. I am wondering if something like this willingness to embrace the ambiguity of the merely visible can help us get a final hold on the oxymoron so central to the classical rabbinic discipline of Torah in the Mouth: that its texts were no less readable in material representations than those of the Torah in Script, but they enjoyed their fullest being as *torah* only when memorized, internalized, and performed.

The very *writtenness* of the texts of Torah in the Mouth was the ambiguous sign that enabled them to conceal what the Midrash Tanhuma terms a "mystery" that might be shared only within the closed circles of discipleship to the Sage. For, as anyone who has entered rabbinic literary culture from beyond the circle of those raised in its traditions will attest, the written texts of Torah in the Mouth—even those that have benefitted from fine printings in scientific editions—are composed of simple words that add up to incomprehensible thoughts. The words are there on the page for anyone with a dictionary to decipher. But their meaning—simply with regard to

their subject matter, and more crucially with regard to their claim to constitute *torah* —
is somewhere else entirely.

That "somewhere else," of course, is within the circle of the master. Without
him, the written words of Torah in the Mouth may be decipherable as language, but
they remain unintelligible as teaching. They lie there inert before the eyes, endlessly
repeating themselves as scanned, disclosing nothing more than their syllables. Only
the master can give them life as he repeats and explains them, drawing out invisible
connections and unintuited contextualizations, linking them back toward tradition
already known and forward to horizons of interpretation scarcely discerned.

Thus, in a comment on the imperative to "make for yourself a master" (M. Avot
1:6), Avot de-Rabbi Natan A8 [ed. Schechter, p. 18a–b] supplies the following
elaboration:

> How so? This teaches that he should make for himself a single Master and study
> with him Scripture and *mishnah*, *midrash*, *halakhah*, and *aggadah*. In this way an
> insight neglected in the study of Scripture will reappear in the study of *mishnah*,
> an insight neglected in the study of *mishnah* will reappear in the study of *midrash*,
> an insight neglected in the study of *midrash* will reappear in the study of *halakhah*,
> and an insight neglected in the study of *halakhah* will reappear in the study of
> *aggadah*. So he remains in one place and is filled with goodness and blessing!

The master is a fountain whose *torah* overflows from one vessel of tradition into another, eventually reaching the cup of the disciple. It is that fountain of language that
the disciple drinks and absorbs into his body. To switch metaphors, only the master
can guide the disciple along the path that promises, at its end, to reproduce in the disciple what the master has experienced: the blending of memorized, fully mastered *torah*,
into one's personal subjectivity; the self-overcoming that transforms a person of flesh
and blood into a servant of the Creator and an echo of His revelation.

The written texts of Torah in the Mouth, that is to say, are not *torah* at all as long
as they remain merely written on inscribed material surfaces; the real inscription of
Torah in the Mouth must be in memory, as memory is shaped by the sounds of the
teacher's own rendition and, as the Amora Gidol insisted, by recalling the beaming
face of the master as he taught. This, I take it, is the simple meaning behind the insistence of Rabbi Yohanan and his school that Torah in the Mouth could not be
learned from written texts. It is not that there were no such texts; rather, the texts
themselves, precisely in their written form, were not *torah* and should not be con-
fused with such. The challenge of Rabbi Yohanan's circle was precisely to those who
might have grasped the written text of rabbinic *torah* and thought thereby, without
the transformative experience of serving the master, that they too had acquired *torah*.

I have argued elsewhere, in one of the preliminary studies that led to this volume, that the written texts of the Mishnah and other compilations of Torah in the
Mouth were distinguished, in the Sages' imagination, from two other sorts of writings.[3] One class of writings, the holy Scriptures, were *torah* by virtue of their being
records of revelation preserved in writing. They were *torah* simply as physical objects prepared in accordance with halakhic specifications, even if no one should read
them. A second class of writings, what moderns would call "literature," could never

be *torah*, since they came solely from the musings of human tradition. Within this category of texts fell not only the writings of the Greco-Roman literary tradition, but also much of the quasi-scriptural literature recorded by Jewish scribes of the Second Temple period.

But the writings of Torah in the Mouth fell between these two classes of text. As written, they were not *torah*. Accordingly no traditions regarding the rules for producing the physical scrolls of such texts had been transmitted. As material objects, they were equivalent to "literature." Nevertheless, the fact that the words of these texts stemmed from Sinai enabled them also to serve as signs that pointed beyond themselves to *torah*. When performed from memory, in the setting of the discipleship circle before the Master, these writings were retrieved from the derivative status of the sign and became the very thing toward which they pointed.

Reconstituted as *torah* in performance, they infused the being of the person who gave them voice, brought beams of intoxication to the face, and reproduced the moment at which Moses himself received his chapter of Repeated Tradition from the Omnipotent and taught it, as he had heard it, to Aaron, and from him to all Israel:

> Moshe was sanctified in the cloud and received the Torah at Sinai. . . . Said Rabbi Natan: Why was Moshe detained for six days until the Word came to rest upon him? So that his innards would become emptied of all food and drink prior to his sanctification, so he could become like the ministering angels. (Avot de-Rabbi Natan A1 [ed. Schechter, p. 1])

In the study circle of the master, the beams streaming from Moses' sanctified form illuminated the face of the disciple as well. The glow would even accompany one into the world to come. There, where neither wealth nor wine might follow, one's *torah* alone would bring one into the community of the transformed, the community of angels.

Appendix

The following text, based upon the literary analyses offered on pp. 111–123, represents a reconstruction of the hypothetical oral-performative narration of the burning of the cow as it is attested by the fragmentary materials of the Mishnah and Tosefta. Text in plain type corresponds to material found solely in the Mishnah. Italicized text is shared virtually identically in the Mishnah and the Tosefta, and boldtype corresponds to material preserved solely in the Tosefta. All text-critical and exegetical notes, present in my earlier literary analyses, have been omitted for purposes of clarity.

(M. Par. 3:1) Seven days prior to the burning of the cow they separate the priest who burns the cow from his home to the chamber overlooking the Birah. In the northeast it was, and the Stone House was it called.

And they sprinkle upon him all the seven days from all the purifications that were there.

(M. Par. 3:2/T. Par. 3:2) *Quarters there were in Jerusalem built upon stone, and beneath them was a hollow space [insulating those above] from [contamination by] a submerged tomb.*

And they bring pregnant women to give birth there, and there they raise their sons **until they are seven or eight years.**

And they bring oxen, and upon them are doors, and the children sit upon them, and cups of stone are in their hands.

Upon reaching the Siloam, they dismounted and filled them, and remounted and sat upon them.

(M. Par. 3:3) They arrived at the Temple Mount and dismounted.

The Temple Mount and the Courts—beneath them was a hollow space [insulating those above] from a submerged tomb.

(T. Par. 3:4) **They arrived at the Gate opening from the Women's Court to the Rampart.**

(M. Par. 3:3) At the entrance to the Court there was prepared a jar of purification ash.

(T. Par. 3:4) And jars of stone were embedded in the stairs of the Women's Court, and their covers of stone were visible to the Rampart.

And within them are the ashes of each and every cow that they had burned, as it is said: "And it shall be stored away for the congregation of Israel, as waters of lustration, for purification" (Num.19:9).

(M. Par. 3:3/T. Par. 3:5) And they bring a male sheep and tie a rope between his horns, and tie a staff with a bushy end to the rope, and he throws it into the jar, and *beats the male, and he recoils backward.*

And he takes [the spilled ash] and sanctifies it [in water] so that it is visible on the surface of the water, **and sprinkles from that which is spilled.**

(M. Par. 3:4) They would not prepare a purification offering in tandem with [the preparations for] a [prior] purification offering, nor a child in tandem with his fellow.

(M. Par. 3:5)If they did not find [ashes] from seven [previous purification offerings], they would prepare from six, five, four, three, two, or one.

(M. Par. 3:6/T. Par. 3:7) *And they prepared a ramp from the Temple Mount to the Mount of Olives, arches upon arches, each arch overarching a solid mass [insulating those above] from a submerged tomb.* Upon it the priest who burns the cow, the cow, and all her attendants would proceed to the Mount of Olives.

(M. Par. 3:7) If the cow did not want to go—they do not bring out a black one with her, lest they say: They slaughtered the black one; nor a red one, lest they say: they slaughtered two.

And the elders of Israel would precede [her] by foot to the Mount of Olives.

And an immersion chamber was there.

And they would contaminate the priest who burns the cow, because of the Sadducees, so they would not say: It was done by a person [completely purified through] the setting sun.

(M. Par. 3:8) They rested their hands upon him and say to him: *Sir High Priest! Immerse once!*

He descended and immersed, and arose and dried himself.

And wood was arranged there: cedar, and pine, and spruce, and smoothed fig branches.

And they make it like a kind of tower, and open up spaces within it, and its facade faces west.

(T. Par. 3:9) The place of her pit, and her pyre, and the immersion chamber were hollow [insulating those above] from a submerged tomb.

(M. Par. 3:9/T. Par. 3:9) *They tied her with ropes of reeds and placed her upon the pyre, her head southward and her face westward.*

The priest stands eastward and his face westward.

(T. Par. 3:10) **How does he proceed?** *He slaughters with his right [hand] and receives with his left, and sprinkles with his right* **finger**.

He immersed [his finger] and sprinkled seven times toward the Holy of Holies, an immersion for each sprinkling.

If it splashes from his hand when he is sprinkling—whether beyond her pit or beyond her pyre—it is ruined.

He finished sprinkling, wiping his hand on the body of the cow.

He descended and kindled the fire with chips.

(M. Par. 3:10) [When] she burst open, then he would stand outside her pit.

(T. Par. 3:11) [If] some of her skin, or her flesh, or her hair burst beyond her pit—he shall return it. And if he did not return it, it is ruined.

Beyond her pyre—let him add wood to it and burn it where it is.

(T. Par. 3:12) [If] some of her horn or hoof or excrement burst [beyond her pit], he needn't return it, for a flaw that does not disqualify her while alive cannot disqualify her in her immolation.

(M. Par. 3:10) He took cedar wood, hyssop, and scarlet wool. He said to them: Is this cedar wood? Is this cedar wood? Is this hyssop? Is this hyssop? Is this scarlet wool? Is this scarlet wool—three times for each and every thing.

And they replied to him: Yes! Yes!—three times for each and every thing.

(T. Par. 3:12) **Shall I throw? Shall I throw? Shall I throw? And they reply: Yes! Yes! Yes!—three times for each and every thing.**

(M. Par. 3:11) He tied them together with the ends of the strip of wool and threw them into her immolation.

(T. Par. 3:12) **Whether he tore her by hand, whether he tore her with a knife, or whether she tore open of her own; whether he threw [the bundle] into her body, whether he threw it into her immolation; whether he threw the three items together, whether he threw them in one at a time—it is fit.**

If he put them in before the fire had burned most of it or after it had become ash—it is ruined.

(M. Par. 3:11) [After] she was burned up, they beat her with staves, and sift her in sieves.

A black piece that contains ash—they crush it; and one having none—they leave it.

The bone, one way or the other, was crushed.

(T. Par. 3:13) **If he took bone or a black piece and sanctified with it—he hasn't done anything at all. If there is upon it any amount of cinder from her body, he crushes it and sanctifies it, and it is fit.**

(M. Par. 3:11/T. Par.3:14) *And they divide it into three parts: one is placed in the Rampart, and one is placed on the Mount of Olives, and one is divided among all the priestly squads.*

The one divided among all the priestly squads would Israel sprinkle from. The one placed on the Mount of Olives would the priests sanctify with. And the one placed in the Rampart they would preserve, as it is said: "And it shall be stored away for the purification of Israel, as waters of lustration, for purification" (Num. 19:9).

Notes

Introduction

1. This text has been commented on extensively by historians of rabbinic tradition. Those that have most shaped my own reading include B. Gerhardsson, *Memory and Manuscript*, pp. 134–135; J. Neusner, "Oral Torah and Oral Tradition," pp. 61–62; and P. Schäfer, *Studien zur Geschichte und Theologie*, pp. 186–188. Neusner's most recent discussion of the text may be consulted in J. Neusner, *What, Exactly, Did the rabbinic Sages Mean by "The Oral Torah"?* pp. 174–178. I differ from Neusner primarily in my skepticism that the *mishnah* referred to in this text denotes the redacted compilation ascribed to Rabbi Yehudah the Patriarch.

2. See A. Kohut, *Aruch Completum*, s.v. *mšnh*.

3. See the pioneering discussion of W. Bacher, *Traditionen und Tradenten*, pp. 22–24, and the important philological observations of Y. Blidstein, "The Foundations of the Concept Torah in the Mouth" (Heb.), pp. 496–498. For the English reader, the best place to begin is G. Stemberger, *Introduction to Talmud and Midrash*, pp. 31–44.

4. There is a growing consensus that the Babylonian Talmud in particular circulated in diverse oral recensions until around the tenth century. The occasion for producing written recensions seems to have been the need to extend the authority of Geonic institutions beyond the Middle East and North Africa into Europe. For an up-to-date review of this discussion, see R. Brody, *The Geonim of Babylonia*, pp. 155–170.

For a recent discussion of the relative lack of scribal forms of technical literacy among Babylonian masters as a causal factor contributing to the preservation of the Babylonian Talmud as an oral text, see Y. Elman, "Orality and the Redaction of the Babylonian Talmud," (forthcoming). Elman's work is one very good reason that I have omitted discussion of the Babylonian Amoraim from this study. He has opened up so many new questions about the distinctions between Palestinian and Babylonian literary cultures that it would be hazardous to generalize about the Babylonian context without a good deal of further work and reflection within the scholarly community.

As for the written preservation of Palestinian rabbinic writings, this has been pushed back to as early as the sixth or seventh century on the basis of material evidence. See Y. Zussman, "The Inscription in the Synagogue at Rehob," pp. 146–151, for a discussion of the earliest known fragment of rabbinic literature (textually quite close to the Palestinian Talmud), and M. Bregman, "An Early Fragment of Avot de-Rabbi Nathan in a Scroll" (Heb.), pp. 201–222.

5. F. Bäuml, "Medieval Texts and Two Theories of Oral-Formulaic Composition," pp. 42–43.

6. In the meantime, readers might consult J. Neusner, *What, Exactly, Did the rabbinic Sages Mean by "The Oral Torah"?* pp. 208–221. Neusner's comparative discussions of the Palestinian and Babylonian contributions to the conceptualization of Oral Torah suggest to him that the Bavli's formulations constitute a "final statement" in relationship to which the Palestinian is only "intermediate." I am more inclined, on the basis of Neusner's own discussion, to the view that the Babylonians provide footnotes to the basic ideological positions of their Palestinian colleagues. But I leave it to readers to make their own judgments.

7. Let me acknowledge a few intellectual debts at this point. I have learned much about the interconnections of oral and written tradition in late antiquity from the excellent introduction to the problem by D. Aune, "Prolegomena to the Study of Oral Tradition in the Hellenistic World," pp. 59–105. Students of early Christianity have been particularly influential in shaping my own perspective on the rabbinic material. These include B. Gerhardsson, *Memory and Manuscript*; W. Kelber, *The Oral and the Written Gospel*; H. Gamble, *Books and Readers in the Early Church*; J. Dewey, ed., *Orality and Textuality in Early Christian Literature*; P. J. Achtemeier, "Omne Verbum Sonat," pp. 3–27; P. J. J. Botha, "Greco-Roman Literacy as Setting for New Testament Writings," pp. 195–213; and V. Robbins, "Writing as a Rhetorical Act in Plutarch and the Gospels," pp. 142–168.

8. O. Anderson, "Oral Tradition," p. 30. See his comments, pp. 43–53, on the particular problems posed by the commission of oral tradition to writing.

9. Useful discussions of the economy of oral and written tradition in societies having both media are available in J. Goody, *The Logic of Writing*, pp. 1–44, and W. Ong, *Orality and Literacy*, pp. 78–116.

10. Let one citation stand for a hundred: R. Bauman, *Story, Performance, Event*.

11. Here I try to make my own what I learned from the chapter on "Continuities of Reception" in J. Foley, *The Singer of Tales in Performance*, pp. 136–180. I am reasonably certain that the last thing that Foley was thinking about as he wrote was the scribal tradition in early Judaism.

12. These three aspects condense for my own purposes the eleven "parameters of oral tradition" enumerated by O. Anderson in "Oral Tradition," pp. 32–37.

13. For a representative bibliography and sober discussion of the issues regarding the nature and antiquity of an exclusively oral-literary tradition in Rabbinic Judaism, see G. Stemberger, *Introduction to Talmud and Midrash*, pp. 31–44. Stemberger omits a provocative discussion of the semiotics of orality and writing in rabbinic culture by Faur, *Golden Doves with Silver Dots*, pp. 84–113.

The most exhaustive treatment of rabbinic oral tradition is the first half of B. Gerhardsson's *Memory and Manuscript*. Gerhardsson's enormously useful work is marred by his tendency to allow the rabbinic literature to serve as a source for describing the oral-literary tradition of Second Temple Pharisaism. Thus, for example, he argues:

> It seems entirely improbable that transmission before Aqiba [i.e., late first to early second century CE] can have taken place following entirely different principles from those later observed, though there may have been certain differences. *The balance of probability is that the basic material in the oral Torah was transmitted and learned in a fixed form as early as during the last century of the Temple; this material was arranged in blocks, grouped on midrashic and mishnaic principles.* (p. 111; brackets and italics added)

For other examples of Gerhardsson's confidence that the basic model of rabbinic oral tradition typified Pharisaic tradition as well, see pp. 21–25, 29–30, 58–59, 76–77, 158.

Neusner's work has been the clearest in distinguishing the textual substance of oral-literary tradition from the question of the ideological formations that constitute its legitimation. This distinction has permitted him to make the important point that Jewish "oral tradition" and rabbinic "Oral Torah" need not stand for one and the same literary complex. See his classic statement in J. Neusner, "Oral Tradition and Oral Torah," pp. 59–75. In his foreword to the recent reprint of Gerhardsson, Neusner repents of his earlier criticisms of Gerhardsson (pp. xxv–xxxii). For my part, I have always found them convincing and still do.

14. In rabbinic literature, the earliest authorities represented as mentioning the term Torah in the Mouth are Hillel and Shammai, both of whom lived at the turn of the Common Era. The term appears in one story that survives in parallel versions in the later strata of rabbinic literary tradition (B. Shabbat 31a/Avot de-Rabbi Nathan A15, B29). In chapter 5, we shall find reason to doubt the historical reliability of this ascription.

15. On the folktale, see A. Olrik, "Epic Laws of Folk Narrative," in A. Dundes, *The Study of Folklore*, pp. 131–141, and V. Propp, *Morphology of the Folktale*.

16. See, for example, R. Finnegan, "What Is Oral Literature Anyway?" pp. 127–166. Of particular interest in the present context is the study of "folk law," which has produced a rich historical and ethnographic literature without yielding much in the way of general principles for the form and structure of unwritten legal traditions. See A. D. Renteln and A. Dundes, eds., *Folk Law*, vol. 1, pp. 1–4.

17. A. B. Lord, *The Singer of Tales*, is the crucial statement of the rootedness of oral-literary tradition (particularly epic poetry) in the setting of performance; cf. R. Bauman, "Verbal Art as Performance," pp. 291–311. Lord's most influential interpreter, J. Foley, provides wide-ranging theoretical reflection on the performative nature of oral-traditional texts in *The Singer of Tales in Performance*. See his introductory comments, pp. 1–28.

18. For the Vedic instance, see F. Staal, *Rules Without Meaning*, pp. 37–46, 157–163, 369–385. For the ancient Hellenistic world, see D. E. Aune, "Prolegomena to the Study of Oral Tradition in the Hellenistic World," pp. 83–90.

1. Social Settings of Literary and Scribal Orality

1. Discussing the finds, at the Wadi Murabba'at caves, of such documents as bills of sale for land and goods, marriage contracts, and the like, J. Milik observes, "Judean triglossia, already quite pronounced during the Herodian period, maintained itself up until the War of Ben Kosba" (P. Benoit et al., *Discoveries in the Judean Desert*, 2, p. 69).

2. A thorough description of Palestinian coinage and the various languages attested on their inscriptions is available in Y. Meshorer, *Ancient Jewish Coinage*. See in particular his discussion of the political dimension of coinage, pp. 81–90.

3. See the survey essays on the extant literature outside the canon of the Hebrew Bible in M. E. Stone, ed., *Jewish Writings of the Second Temple Period*.

Additionally, biblical scholars are increasingly aware that the canonizing processes yielding the Hebrew Bible by the end of the first century CE included extensive reshaping of literary materials that survived from the monarchic period of Judean history prior to 587 BCE. That is, much of the present Hebrew Bible not merely is a literary tradition preserved by Second Temple scribal circles, but is indeed a tradition created largely by them. See P. R. Davies, *Scribes and Schools*, and M. Haran, *The Scriptural Collection*.

4. The intersection of sectarian social identity and polemical literary activity has been examined most recently by A. Baumgarten, *The Flourishing of Jewish Sects in the Maccabean Era*, pp. 114–136.

5. Greek translations of the Torah and other Hebrew texts circulated in Alexandrian circles from the third century BCE, forming the basis of the Septuagint and other Greek ren-

derings. The presence in two of the Qumran caves of Greek translations of parts of Exodus, Leviticus, Numbers, and Deuteronomy indicates that there was an audience for a Greek Torah in Palestine as well. For the texts from Cave 7, see M. Baillet et al., eds., *Discoveries in the Judean Desert*, 3, pp. 142–143. Writings from Cave 4 are published in P. Skehan et al., eds., *Discoveries in the Judean Desert*, 9, pp. 161–197.

The translation of the Torah and other important works into Aramaic, the native language of Palestinian Jewry through much of this period, is commonly believed to have been widespread, although rabbinic sources suggest that such translations were not normally written down. See S. Fraade, "Rabbinic Views on the Practice of Targum, and Multilingualism in the Jewish Galilee of the Third–Sixth Centuries," pp. 253–286. The Qumran caves yield a small fragment of an Aramaic translation of Leviticus (J. Milik, ed., *Discoveries in the Judean Desert*, 6, pp. 86–89) and a large part of an Aramaic translation of Job (M. Sokoloff, *The Targum to Job from Qumran Cave XI*), in addition to the Genesis Apocryphon, an expansive rendition in Aramaic of portions of Genesis (J. Fitzmyer, *The Genesis Apocryphon of Qumran Cave I*).

For brief descriptions of the Greek and Aramaic biblical translations from Qumran and for further bibliography, see L. Schiffman, *Reclaiming the Dead Sea Scrolls*, pp. 212–215.

6. A very effective summary of the vast scholarship on the impact of the printing press on the nature of reading is offered by W. Graham, in *Beyond the Written Word*, pp. 9–29.

7. For a useful categorization of various levels and styles of literacy in ancient Israel, see S. Niditch, *Oral World and Written Word*, pp. 39–59. Compare the observations of Harris in the note following.

In a study of Palestinian Jewish literacy in the first centuries CE, M. Bar-Ilan, who uses as his standard of literacy the ability to read from the Torah scroll in a public ceremony, suggests the following ("Illiteracy in the Land of Israel in the First Centuries CE," pp. 46–61):

> Even if we assume that in cities . . . the literacy rate was double and even triple in comparison with the towns, still the figures of literacy are around 2–15%. With the assumption that the rural population was around 70% (with 0% literacy), 20% of urban population (with 1–5% literacy),and 10% of highly urban population (with 2–15% literacy), the total population literacy is still very low. Thus, it is no exaggeration to say that the total literacy rate in the Land of Israel at that time . . . was probably less than 3%.

In the same study, he estimates the literacy rate during Hasmonean times at 1.5%. In a concluding footnote (n. 29), Bar-Ilan offers a final observation that the 3% figure might be raised as high as 20% of adult males in urban centers "if we ignore women . . . , take into consideration children above the age of seven only, forget the far-away farmers, and regard literacy of the non-educated people (e.g., one who cannot read the Torah but reads a *bulla*, that is: pragmatic literacy)."

8. The definition of "literacy" is itself a vexed question for the historian of antiquity. My own discussion is grounded in the distinction offered by W. V. Harris between "scribal literacy" and "craftsman's literacy" in his influential book, *Ancient Literacy*, pp. 7–8:

> By the former term I mean the sort of literacy which predominated in ancient Near Eastern cultures and the Minoan and Mycenaean worlds, literacy restricted to a specialized social group which used it for such purposes as maintaining palace records. . . . By craftsman's literacy I mean . . . the condition in which the majority, or a near-majority, of skilled craftsmen are literate, while women and unskilled labourers and peasants are mainly not.

In these terms, literacy of any kind in the ancient Mediterranean world was normally restricted to less than 10 percent of the male population, even in urban settings, while the creative literacy of the scribe was rare.

9. The history of reading as a cultural practice—as opposed to the history of the book as a cultural object—is a relatively recent discipline that has become crucial to understanding distinctions between the construction of knowledge in cultures of the manuscript and cultures of print. See W. Ong, *Orality and Literacy*, pp. 117–138; M. Carruthers, *The Book of Memory*, pp. 156–188; M. Calinescu, "Orality and Literacy," pp. 175–190; and R. Chartier, *Forms and Meanings*, pp. 15–18.

10. See M. Goodman, "Texts, Scribes and Power in Roman Judaea," pp. 99–108, and S. Niditch, *Oral World and Written Word*, pp. 83–88. From a cross-cultural perspective, see J. Goody, *The Logic of Writing and the Organization of Society*, pp. 1–44.

11. The nature—and very existence—of libraries in Second Temple Judaism has recently engendered some controversy. The earliest clear literary reference to a library (*bibliothekon*) in Jerusalem comes from 2 Macc. 2:13–15, a historical review written in the mid-second century BCE in order to legitimize the new Hasmonean regime of High Priestly rule. Ascribing the original collection to Nehemiah, the text goes on to praise Judas Maccabeus for collecting and storing "all the books that had been scattered as a result of our recent conflict." The Hasmoneans thus are credited with preserving the ancient Judean cultural heritage.

This text, and scarce references in Josephus (e.g., Antiquities 3:38, 4:302–304, 5:61) and early rabbinic literature (e.g., M. Moed Qatan 3:4) to "writings" (*grammaton, graphe*), a "book" (*biblos*), or a "scroll" (*sefer*) housed in the Temple, have until recently satisfied most historians that the Temple indeed contained some sort of library (e.g., R. T. Beckwith, "Formation of the Hebrew Bible," pp. 40–45). Nevertheless, as H. Gamble, *Books and Readers in the Early Church*, p. 196, points out, the best that can be said is that there is "a strong presumption of the existence of a library and archives in the Jerusalem temple, though [the sources do] not provide any clear idea of what the library was like." The recent discussions of Davies, *Scribes and Schools*, pp. 85–87, and S. Niditch, *Oral World and Written Word*, pp. 61–69, are equally reticent about the nature of the Temple library.

In the domain of Qumran studies it has long been common to speak of the "Qumran library." A vocal supporter of the hypothesis that Qumran Cave 4 actually housed a sectarian community library is L. Schiffman, *Reclaiming the Dead Sea Scrolls*, pp. 54–57. It is important, however, to keep in mind the caveat of Y. Shavit ("The 'Qumran Library' in the Light of the Attitude Towards Books and Libraries in the Second Temple Period," pp. 306–307): ". . . there can be no doubt that Jews in the Second Temple period wrote many books. . . . But the sources mention only isolated names out of a wide corpus, and we have no evidence at all that there were collections of books, and even less, that there were public libraries, such as existed in Hellenistic centers of learning."

12. My distinction between libraries and archives draws upon P. R. Davies, *Scribes and Schools*, pp. 17–19.

13. Thus, for example, the Isaiah scroll found in Qumran Cave 1 (1QIs^a) is estimated to have originally been about 24 feet long (M. Burrows, ed. *The Dead Sea Scrolls of St. Mark's Monastery*, vol. 1, p. xiv). The longest recovered scroll, the Temple Scroll (11QTemple), is about 28½ feet in length.

For aspects of the physical nature of papyrus, leather, and other materials as repositories of writing, see M. Haran, "Book-Scrolls at the Beginning of the Second Temple Period: The Transition from Papyrus to Skins," pp. 111–122; M. Bar-Ilan, "Scribes and Books in the Late Second Commonwealth and the Rabbinic Period," pp. 24–28; idem, articles "Papyrus," and "Parchment" in E. Meyers, ed., *The New Oxford Encyclopedia of Archeology in the Near*

East, vol. 4, pp. 146–148; H. Gamble, *Books and Readers in the Early Church*, pp. 43–48; and S. Niditch, *Oral World and Written Word*, pp. 71–77.

14. Observations about the difficulties of working with scrolls may be consulted in S. Niditch, *Oral World and Written Word*, pp. 113–114, and R. Chartier, *Forms and Meanings*, pp. 18–20. H. Gamble, *Books and Readers in the Early Church*, pp. 55–57, cautions against overestimating the inconvenience of the scroll in expaining the ultimate victory of the codex in Christian culture. The fullest description of the use of books in a variety of Greco-Roman settings—including those of diverse Second Temple Jewish communities—is the recent Yale University dissertation of H. G. Snyder, *Teachers, Texts, and Students: Textual Performance and Patterns of Authority in Greco-Roman Schools* (Ann Arbor: University of Michigan, 1998). For his observations on the success of the codex in early Christianity, see pp. 326–328.

15. M. Martin, *The Scribal Character of the Dead Sea Scrolls*, vol. 1, pp. 6–7.

16. The oral-performative, ritualized nature of reading throughout the ancient world has been generally recognized among classicists for some time (e.g., J. Balogh, "*Voces Paginarum*," pp. 83–109, 202–240). The impact of this model of ancient reading has had an important impact on the study of early Christianity (e.g., P. Achtemeier, "*Omne Verbum Sonat*," pp. 3–27) and on the study of the Hebrew Bible (e.g., Niditch, *Oral World and Written Word*). It has recently made headway as well among students of Second Temple Judaism (e.g., S. Talmon, "Oral Tradition and Written Transmission," pp. 122–158). For a synthetic, comparative treatment of Jewish and non-Jewish oral-performative textual practices, see H. G. Snyder, *Teachers, Texts, and Students*.

17. Such a figure seems clearly to stand behind the terms '*yš dwrš btwrh* ("a man who expounds the Torah," 1QS 6:6) and *dwrš htwrh* ("expounder of the Torah," CD 7:18, 4QFlor 1:11) that appear in some of the Qumran scrolls. We will discuss such ritualized Qumranian expositions of the book in the next chapter.

18. This is, of course, the fundamental postulate of all form-criticism of the Hebrew Bible. See, for example, R. Rendtorff, *The Old Testament*, pp. 77–128, and the representative essays in R. C. Culley, ed., *Oral Tradition and Old Testament Studies*. While the insights and methods of form-criticism have been employed with great success in adjacent literatures, such as early Christian and rabbinic writings, there seems to be no comprehensive form-critical attention devoted to the Second Temple literature, other than the extensive interest in the genre of Apocalyptic.

19. Crucial observations on the various relationships between works in manuscript and their oral-performative background are offered by F. Bäuml, "Medieval Texts and the Two Theories of Oral-Formulaic Composition," pp. 31–49.

20. M. Parry's demonstration of this proposition with regard to Homeric verse transformed the study of the Western classics, with repercussions throughout the humanities. See M. Parry, *The Making of Homeric Verse*; J. M. Foley, *The Theory of Oral Composition*, pp. 19–35; and idem, *The Singer of Tales in Performance*, pp. 60–98. The insights of Foley and others were largely unexplored in the context of Second Temple studies until the recent work of S. Niditch.

21. The Qumran scrolls, in which multiple copies of specific works are preserved, have been crucial in demonstrating the flexible boundaries of even the most authoritative books. For a discussion of the diverse character of the biblical texts, see E. Tov, *Textual Criticism of the Hebrew Bible*, pp. 100–117.

22. Thus see E. Tov, "Scribal Practices Reflected in Texts From the Judaean Desert," p. 424:

> When copying from an existing text, most ancient scribes incorporated their thoughts on that text into the new version which they produced. Thus they added,

omitted, and altered elements; all of these changes became part of the newly created text, in which the new features were not easily recognizable since they were
not marked in a special way. . . . In the newly created text scribes and readers inserted sundry changes, which are recognizable because the limitations of the ancient materials and the rigid form of the manuscript did not allow them to hide
the intervention.

Cf. the comments of M. Fishbane, *Biblical Interpretation in Ancient Israel*, pp. 86–87, who
draws a "continuum between purely scribal-redactional procedures on the one hand, and
authorial-compositional ones on the other." This phenomenon is common across a variety
of scribal cultures. See, for example, A. N. Doane, "The Ethnography of Scribal Writing
and Anglo-Saxon Poetry," pp. 420–439.

23. See S. Talmon, "Oral Tradition and Written Transmission," pp. 148–151.

24. See F. M. Cross, "The Evolution of a Theory of Local Texts," pp. 306–320, and the
qualifications of E. Tov, *Textual Criticism of the Hebrew Bible*, pp. 185–187.

25. For introductory descriptions of some of the most striking examples, see
L. Schiffman, *Rediscovering the Dead Sea Scrolls*, pp. 169–180, and bibliographical comments, pp. 430–431.

26. The textual antecedents to the Masoretic text are extensively described in E. Tov,
Textual Criticism of the Hebrew Bible, pp. 22–79.

27. M. Fishbane, "From Scribalism to Rabbinism," in idem, *The Garments of Torah*,
p. 65, speaks of an "axial transformation" in early Judaism bound up with the emergence of
a distinction between the authorized, fixed sacred text and its exegetical amplification. I share
his view, pointing out only that this transition is part of a larger reorientation within Judaism
toward the oral and written word.

One must also add that this "transformation" did not occur in a matter of decades.
B. Albrektson, in "Reflections on the Emergence of a Standard Text of the Hebrew Bible,"
p. 63, points out most persuasively that the biblical text that became normative in rabbinic
circles "is not the result of a thorough-going recension, it is based on manuscripts which
happened to be preserved after the downfall [of Judea], and its dominating position is not
based on text-critical grounds. . . ."

28. On the range of functions assigned to scribes, see M. Fishbane, *Biblical Interpretation in Ancient Israel*, pp. 27–40; J. Blenkinsopp, "The Sage, the Scribe, and Scribalism,"
pp. 307–315; and E. Tov, "The Scribes of the Texts Found in the Judean Desert," pp. 131–
135. The most recent comprehensive discussion of the various terms and their significations
in the various sources relevant to Second Temple Judaism is that of C. Schams, *Jewish Scribes
in the Second-Temple Period*, pp. 36–273. The present study is concerned fundamentally with
the culture surrounding those "scribes" particularly involved in the composition and transmission of historical and legal literary tradition.

29. The question of the degree to which High Priests shared political power with other
governing bodies (e.g., the *gerousia* or *sunedrion/sanhedrin*) is currently under debate. The
traditional view, that such bodies exercised significant (or even decisive) power from the
Persian period on, is defended in E. Schürer, *The History of the Jewish People in the Age of
Jesus Christ*, vol. 2, pp. 200–226. For a stimulating critical review of the sources, see
D. Goodblatt, *The Monarchic Principle*, pp. 57–130, who concludes: "[W]hat is missing [in
the sources] is clear evidence for a regular and institutionalized coming together of . . . a
council. A conciliar institution cannot be excluded, given the limitations of the available
evidence. But I think conciliar supremacy can be excluded. . . . Instead what the ancient
sources clearly indicate is a regime of priestly monarchy in which the high priest is at the
apex of Judean self-government" (p. 130).

30. See, for example, M. Bar-Ilan, "Scribes and Books in the Late Second Common-wealth and Rabbinic Period," pp. 21–38. Bar-Ilan's account of scribalism (esp. pp. 21–23) is dependent almost entirely upon later rabbinic sources, which he then reads back into the Second Temple setting. For more cautious estimates of what can be known about the social profile of Palestinian scribes in our period, see P. R. Davies, *Scribes and Schools*, pp. 74–83; E. Tov, "The Scribes of the Texts Found in the Judean Desert," pp. 131–135; and most re-cently, the excellent survey of scholarship in C. Schams, *Jewish Scribes in the Second-Temple Period*, pp. 11–35.

31. The translation is that of P. Skehan and A. Di Lella, *The Wisdom of Ben Sira*, p. 573. The Hebrew of MS. B reads: *byt mdršy* ("my house of learning"). Skehan and Di Lella, ar-guing that this portion of the text is a Hebrew retroversion from the Syriac translation (*byt 'wlpn'*), restore the original as *byt mwsr* ("house of discipline/instruction"). See Di Lella's comment on pp. 403–404. This translation also accords well with the Greek rendering, *en oiko paideias* ("house of instruction").

32. Psalm 119 is frequently cited as a key early Second Temple text that testifies to a distinctive scribal piety linked to detailed mastery of texts of sacred instruction. See M. Fishbane, "From Scribalism to Rabbinism" pp. 66–67, and J. Levenson, "The Sources of Torah." C. Schams, *Jewish Scribes in the Second-Temple Period*, pp. 99–106, 278–287, is skeptical regarding the degree to which the writings of Yeshua b. Sira can serve more gen-eral depictions of the values embodied in the scribal literati.

33. So M. Haran, *The Scriptural Collection*, pp. 60–61.

34. In contrast to relatively little information about the intellectual formation of scribes, there is more archeological evidence about training in the art of writing. For the Second Temple period, the Judean desert finds contain some parchments and ostraca used for practicing the alphabet as well as crudely inscribed documents that appear to have been used as training samples. For discussion and bibliography, see E. Tov, "The Scribes of the Texts Found in the Judean Desert," pp. 139–141. C. Schams's discussion of inscriptional and papyrological evidence focuses upon the titles and functions assumed by scribes rather than upon the evidence of their training (*Jewish Scribes in the Second-Temple Period*, pp. 209–216, 234–238).

35. In his pioneering study of the training and techniques of the scribes responsible for the six scrolls recovered from Qumran Cave 1, M. Martin concluded that "if a scribal school existed there, it had neither an imposed and accepted style of presentation nor normative rules of orthography nor official and fixed methods of textual indication" (*The Scribal Char-acter of the Dead Sea Scrolls*, vol. 2, p. 710). The question of a discrete, sectarian scribal school accounting for some or many of the Qumran scrolls has been debated for decades. A recent conclusion by a master of scribal practices bears taking seriously: "The different texts indeed belong to different scribal centers or scribal schools, although the nature of these schools is a matter of some speculation (E. Tov, "Scribal Practices Reflected in the Paleo-Hebrew Texts from the Judean Desert," p. 273).

36. Well-studied examples of the legal genres either transmitted within or produced by the Tzadokite community include the controversial "Halakhic Letter," 4QMMT, CD 15:1–16:20 + 9:1–14:22, and 1QS 6:8–7:25. On the general character of Qumranian legal tradi-tion see the classic study of L. Schiffman, *The Halakhah at Qumran*. For an assessment of the impact of the recently published "Halakhic Letter" (4QMMT) on the understanding of sectarian law, see the essays gathered in J. Kampen and M. Bernstein, eds., *Reading 4QMMT*.

Another anti-Hasmonean composition, the Book of Jubilees, almost certainly circulated prior to the formation of the community that seems to stand behind the Tzadokite texts. Its legal traditions — particularly regarding the computation of the Temple ritual calendar — were preserved and amplified by the scribes who transmitted distinctively Tzadokite views. See S. Talmon, "The Calendar of the Covenanters of the Judean Desert," pp. 147–185.

37. The various Second Temple works composed within the apocalyptic genre fall into this category, in which the Enochic literature and the Testaments of the Twelve Patriarchs provide well-studied examples. For a general introduction to this genre in its Second Temple setting, see J. J. Collins, *The Apocalyptic Imagination*.

38. The most famous example of "revisionist history," designed to deligitimate the reigning Hasmonean claim to fulfill divine intentions in Jerusalem is the "admonition" of the Damascus Document (CD 1:1–8:21 + 19:1–20:34). A survey of scholarly attempts to decode this cryptic survey of *Heilsgeshichte* is available in P. R. Davies, *The Damascus Covenant*, pp. 3–47.

39. Well-studied examples include the Thanksgiving (*Hodayot*) texts found in Qumran Caves 1 and 4 and the Songs of the Sabbath Sacrifice found in Caves 4 and 11. See B. P. Kittel, *The Hymns of Qumran*; B. Nitzan, *Qumran Prayer and Religious Poetry*, pp. 173–355; and S. Segert, "Observations on the Poetic Structures of the Songs of the Sabbath Sacrifice," pp. 215–224.

40. The case of Yeshua b. Eliezer b. Sira is instructive. If he was not from a priestly family himself, he was certainly very comfortable in priestly circles. See S. Olyan, "Ben Sira's Relationship to the Priesthood," pp. 261–286; J. G. Gammie, "The Sage in Sirach," pp. 364–365; and B. G. Wright III, "'Fear the Lord and Honor the Priest,'" pp. 192–196.

With regard to other scribes, such as those who composed and copied the texts found among the Dead Sea Scrolls that speak of a community of the "Sons of Tzadok," it seems fair as well to assume some sort of priestly origins. Even if the community behind such documents might not have been composed exclusively of genealogically verified priestly families, it certainly preserved legal traditions consistent with those ascribed elsewhere to Jerusalemite priestly tradition, and it entertained hopes of regaining control of the Temple administration.

41. Proponents of the existence of an influential lay-scribal community throughout the last centuries of the Second Temple period include, among many others, G. F. Moore, *Judaism in the First Centuries of the Christian Era*, vol. 1, pp. 308–309; E. J. Bickerman, *From Ezra to the Last of the Maccabees*, pp. 67–71; B. Gerhardsson, *Memory and Manuscript*, pp. 56–66; M. Hengel, *Judaism and Hellenism*, pp. 78–83; and E. Schürer, *The History of the Jewish People in the Age of Jesus Christ*, vol. 2, pp. 322–323. The most recent scholar to propose the existence of a relatively extensive urbanized literary elite producing a literature reflective of distinctly nonpriestly perspectives is J. Berquist, *Judaism in Persia's Shadow*, pp. 161–176.

P. Davies, *Scribes and Schools*, pp. 82–83, and A. Baumgarten, *The Flourishing of Jewish Sects in the Maccabean Era*, pp. 117–123, acknowledge a broadening of scribal education beyond priestly circles but confine this to a narrow, wealthy elite. Recent challenges to the earlier consensus include R. Gray, *Prophetic Figures in Late Second Temple Jewish Palestine*, pp. 53–58, and A. J. Saldarini, *Pharisees, Scribes, and Sadducees in Palestinian Society*, pp. 273–276.

C. Schams, *Jewish Scribes in the Second-Temple Period*, pp. 287–296, finds scribal skills distributed rather broadly beyond priestly circles toward the end of our period, but partly because of the broadening use of scribal titles in the period to designate a wide variety of skilled professionals beyond the composers and transmitters of literary works.

My own position on this question has been shaped by S. Fraade's unpublished paper on the topic, "'They Shall Teach Your Statutes to Jacob': Priests, Scribes, and Sages in Second Temple Times." I thank him for sharing it with me.

42. During the Hasmonean and Herodian periods Judea and the Galilee were dotted with Hellenistic *poleis*, but this urbanization affected few Jews, who remained largely in villages or small towns. The urbanization of Palestinian Jewry, beyond the central city of Jerusalem, is for the most part a phenomenon of the second and third centuries CE, and it occurs not in war-devastated Judea, but in the Galilee. For the nature of Jewish urban administration in general,

see E. Schürer, *The History of the Jewish People in the Age of Jesus Christ*, vol. 2, pp. 184–198, which offers the opinon that "one town alone in Judaea proper, namely Jerusalem, may have enjoyed the rank of *polis* in the strict Graeco-Roman sense" (p. 188). The dominance of Jerusalem in the social life of Second Temple Galilee, and the rise of the Galilean towns Sepphoris and Tiberias as centers of Judaic cultural life in the post-bar Kosiva period are conveniently described in Horsely, *Galilee*, pp. 111–185. For the connection between the development of Hasmonean Jerusalem as an urban cultural center and the rise of literacy in its environs, see A. Baumgarten, *The Flourishing of Jewish Sects in the Maccabean Era*, pp. 143–146.

43. The earliest inscriptional evidence, the Theodotus inscription from first-century CE Jerusalem, specifies the synagogue as a place for "reciting the Torah (*nomos*) and studying the commandments" among other functions, such as hospitality. First-century literary evidence of the role of textual study in the synagogue setting includes testimonies from Josephus (e.g., Antiquities 16.2.4, Apion 2:17) and the Gospels (Mark 1:21, 6:2; Luke 4:16–22), all of which suggest a ritualized public reading of the text accompanied by brief explanation. For further discussion of these and other sources, see L. Levine, "The Second Temple Synagogue," esp. pp. 15–19.

44. See D. Goodblatt, "Sources for the Origins of Organized Jewish Education in the Land of Israel," pp. 83–103. The contrasting view, positing on the basis of primarily rabbinic texts a widespread educational system, is represented in E. Schürer, *The Jewish People in the Age of Jesus Christ*, vol 2, pp. 417–422.

45. A. Baumgarten, *The Flourishing of Jewish Sects in the Maccabean Era*, pp. 114–136, detects suggestive connections between the extension of literacy beyond professional scribal circles, beginning with the second century BCE, and the creation of conditions leading to sectarian ideologies.

46. M. Smith, *Palestinian Parties and Politics*, pp. 15–16, refers to the Hebrew Bible as "a cult collection" designed "to tell the worshipers of Yahweh what they should do and to persuade them that they had better do it." Smith was anticipated in this judgment about the cultic relevance of the canon by the often overlooked study of G. Östborn, *Cult and Canon*. Östborn attempts to offer a comprehensive explanation of how each of the canonical books served the larger purposes of cultic representation of divine power and activity.

47. Books posing persistent problems for speculation about the ideological coherence of the ultimate Hebrew canon include Ruth, Esther, Job, Qoheleth, and Song of Songs, all of which are in the canon of Ketuvim and all of which have little cultic interest. Solutions to these problems tend to focus on particular models of the scribal groups said to stand behind the development of the canonical tradition. See discussions in M. Smith, *Palestinian Parties and Politics*, pp. 148–192; J. Sanders, *Torah and Canon*, pp. 110–116; J. Blenskinsopp, *Prophecy and Canon*, pp. 124–138; and the following note.

48. A useful general discussion is that of R. T. Beckwith in "Formation of the Hebrew Bible," pp. 39–86. For recent attempts at reconstructing the process of canon formation that yielded the Hebrew Scriptures, see M. Haran, *The Scriptural Collection*, esp. pp. 23–140; and P. R. Davies, *Scribes and Schools*, pp. 89–151.

49. Cf. T. Levi 8:16–17, in which the descendants of Levi inherit the roles of "high priests, and judges, and scribes." I follow the translation of H. C. Kee, "Testaments of the Twelve Patriarchs," in J. Charlesworth, *The Old Testament Pseudepigrapha*, vol. 1, pp. 792–793. Kee's translation is based upon the Greek text of the Bodleian library, edited by R. Charles.

50. I follow the translation of O. Wintermute, "Jubilees," p. 137, who translates the Ethopic text edited by R. Charles. See A. Baumgarten, *The Flourishing of Jewish Sects in the Maccabean Era*, pp. 117–118, for discussion of these sources.

51. The fullest recent discussion of the theoretical issues in the study of literary pseudonymity in antiquity is that of D. Meade, *Pseudonymity and Canon*, pp. 1–16. M. Fishbane,

Biblical Interpretation in Ancient Israel, pp. 257–266, has focused on the particular role of pseudonymity in exegetically extending the authority of the scriptural text to cover the voice of the exegete. See also the recent study of B. M. Levinson, *Deuteronomy and the Hermeneutics of Legal Innovation,* pp. 144–157.

52. Yeshua b. Eliezer b. Sira is the only Second Temple period scribe whose name survives on a literary work of his own creation (see Sira 50:27 and discussions in E. Schürer, *The History of the Jewish People in the Age of Jesus Christ,* vol. 3.1, p. 201, and P. Skehan and A. Di Lella, *The Wisdom of Ben Sira,* pp. 556–558). Characteristically, however, his book concludes with an elaborate literary homage to Israel's ancestors (Sira 44:1–50:24), among whom he numbers such characteristic scribal types as "Sages with their literary discourse, or framers of prophecies and pointed maxims; composers of melodious psalms, or authors with lyric themes" (Sira 44:4–5).

53. Thus, in summarizing his findings regarding the rhetorical meaning of pseudonymity in Second Temple literature, D. Meade writes: "Therefore, we can conclude that in the prophetic, wisdom, and apocalyptic traditions, literary attribution [to a pseudonymous ancestor] is primarily an assertion of authoritative tradition, not literary origins" (*Pseudonymity and Canon,* p. 105).

54. I quote from M. Knibb, *The Ethiopic Book of Enoch,* vol. 2, p. 187.

55. See D. Suter, *Tradition and Composition in the Parables of Enoch,* pp. 125–156, and D. Meade, *Pseudonymity and Canon,* pp. 91–101, for discussions of the composite character of 1 Enoch in particular and the manner of its being knitted into a coherent "tradition." Suter is particularly sensitive to the presence of oral-literary tradition in the parables per se and their reconstruction in the final written literary work. I am not aware of other students of the Second Temple visionary tradition who have pursued this line of thought.

56. Wintermute, p. 53.

57. The first line of each testament announces that it is "a copy of the testament" of the appropriate patriarch.

58. B. Metzger, trans., "The Fourth Book of Ezra," pp. 554–555. The translation is based upon the Latin text published by R. Bensly.

59. Cited from F. H. Colson, trans., *Philo 6,* p. 467. The story of the inspired origins of the Greek version of the Torah first appears in Aristeas 301–311, from which it makes its way to Philo and Josephus, Antiquities 12:11–18. A rabbinic parody appears at B. Megillah 9a.

60. The number conforms to the assumptions of other first-century authors and the eventual rabbinic canon, suggesting that by the early second century there had emerged a generally acknowledged sense of the range of the scriptural collection. S. Leiman (*The Canonization of the Hebrew Scripture,* pp. 30–34) regards the 4 Ezra evidence as warranting a canonical collection even prior to the first century CE.

61. A. Klijn, trans., "2 (Syriac Apocalypse of) Baruch," pp. 637–638, following the Syriac text of Bibliotheca Ambrosiana.

2. *Performative Reading and Text Interpretation at Qumran*

1. Werner Kelber, "Jesus and Tradition," p. 159.

2. A. Baumgarten, *The Flourishing of Jewish Sects in the Maccabean Era.* See the important predecessor, M. Smith, "The Dead Sea Sect in Relation to Ancient Judaism," pp. 347–360.

3. M. Fishbane, *Biblical Interpretation in Ancient Israel.*

4. See, for example, D. J. Harrington, "Palestinian Adaptations of Biblical Narratives and Prophecies," pp. 239–257, and D. Dimant, "Use and Interpretation of Mikra in the Apocrypha and Pseudepigrapha," pp. 379–419.

5. As an outsider to Qumran scholarship, I hesitate to take a firm stand on the question of the identity of the sectarian community assumed to have been headquarterd at the Qumran site. In this study I follow the view that some sort of self-conscious dissident community, bearing a priestly (i.e., Tzadokite) ideology of its origins and legitimacy, did live a more or less uninterrupted existence at Qumran for most of the Hasmonean period and on through the rebellion of 66 CE. It seems to have referred to itself as the "Yahad" (Community). For the purposes of the present discussion, at any rate, it is immaterial whether the group was Essene, an Essene splinter group, a representative of Enochic Judaism, or a group with Sadducean origins. What matters is that it was thoroughly at home in scribal culture.

A convenient collection of all the ancient external sources on the Essenes, with original texts and English translation, has been offered by G. Vermes and M. Goodman, eds., in *The Essenes According to the Classical Sources.* For a balanced account of the debate concerning the so-called "Essene Hypothesis" from one of its supporters, see J. VanderKam, *The Dead Sea Scrolls Today,* pp. 71–98. The basic claims of the "Essene Hypothesis" are: (1) the Qumran site was a central headquarters of a larger Essene movement with settlements throughout Palestine, and (2) the movement originated sometime after 152 BCE among a group rejecting the consolidation of the Hasmonean High Priesthood under Jonathan. For a fair-minded critique, see A. Baumgarten, *The Flourishing of Jewish Sects in the Maccabean Era,* pp. 42–80.

6. Most notable among these are N. Golb, *Who Wrote the Dead Sea Scrolls?* esp. 3–41, and, more moderately, M. Wise et al., *The Dead Sea Scrolls,* pp. 20–24.

7. The most important is that ancient authors such as Pliny, Philo, and Josephus represent the Essenes as a monastic community, while the evidence of many of the scrolls and of the Qumran cemetary suggest at least some presence of women and children within the community. Among those scholars who reject the dominant "Essene hypothesis," there has emerged little consensus regarding the origins or identity of the group. A careful survey of diverse opinions with extensive bibliographical guidance is offered in F. Martinez, "The Origins of the Essene Movement and of the Qumran Sect," pp. 77–96. J. Baumgarten, *The Flourishing of Jewish Sects in the Maccabean Era,* pp. 81–113, offers a useful account of how the similarities among many Second Temple sectarian communities makes it hazardous to offer a firm identification of the Qumran group on the basis of available evidence.

8. The two partial manuscript copies of the Damascus Covenant were discovered by Solomon Schechter in the storage room of a Cairo Synagogue in 1896 and labeled Text A and Text B. Schechter dated the copies to the tenth and twelfth centuries, but the provenance of the original texts was the subject of much speculation until parallels and additional texts in the identical style showed up in the manuscripts discovered in Qumran Caves 4–6 from 1948. In what follows, citations from the Cairo manuscripts are identified by the abbreviation CD, while citations from Qumranic parallels are indicated by cave location and fragment number (e.g., 4Q267). All translations are my own, rendered in consultation with full range of available English translations. The translations are based upon the Hebrew edition of J. Baumgarten and D. Schwartz, "The Damascus Dcoument."

9. This text was among the original compositions discovered in Cave 1. Its opening line refers to a *spr srk hyḥd* that underlies the early—inexact—scholarly designation as "Manual of Discipline." Contemporary scholarship more commonly refers to the text as the Rule of the Community or the Communal Rule. There are at least ten partial copies of this text, most of them found in Cave 4 (4Q255–264). A full study of all these copies is now available in S. Metso, *The Textual Development of the Qumran Community Rule.* My translations, made in consultation with many others, are based upon the Hebrew text edited by J. Charlesworth, "The Rule of the Community."

10. The so-called *pesher* commentaries decode specific passages from some prophetic books (including Psalms) in reference to events in the historical memory of the community.

Of particular importance in identifying the *pesher* commentaries with the Tzadokites are the *pesharim* to the books of Habakkuk (1QpHab), Nahum (4QpNah [4Q169]), and Psalms (1QpPs [1Q16], 4QpPs^b [4Q173, fr. 5]). I have used the Hebrew edition, with English translations and extensive commentaries, of M. Horgan, *Pesharim*.

11. In light of the omission of references to the *bny ṣdwq* in some recently published fragments of 1QS from Cave 4, A. Baumgarten ("The Zadokite Priests at Qumran," pp. 137–156) has argued persuasively that the claim of Tzadokite origins emerged sometime after the origins of the group in an attempt to limit charismatic authority. The issue remains up for debate, and its resolution needn't affect the results of the present study.

12. J. Baumgarten, "The Unwritten Law in the Pre-Rabbinic Period," pp. 7–29.

13. S. Fraade, "Interpretive Authority in the Studying Community at Qumran," pp. 46–69, and idem, "Looking for Legal Midrash at Qumran," pp. 59–79.

14. L. Schiffman, *The Halakhah at Qumran*, pp. 22–76, and idem, *Sectarian Law in the Dead Sea Scrolls*, pp. 1–21.

15. S. Talmon, "Oral Tradition and Written Transmission," pp. 121–158.

16. Indeed, M. Heer, "Continuity of Tradition in the Transmission of the Torah," pp. 52–55, makes the important point that the Yahad's historical memory, which posited a centuries-long ceasura in the transmission of Torah until the rise of the Righteous Teacher, legitimates the group's claim that its own teachings constitute a renewal of revelation.

17. "The ten" is apparently a reference to the ten members of the Community Council mentioned in 1QS 6:3–4. See below. The parallel at 4Q263 breaks off precisely at this point and does permit clarification of the reference. The close parallel at CD 13:2 has: "and in a place of ten" (*wbmqwm 'śrh*).

18. J. Charlesworth, "The Rule of the Community," p. 27, proposes emending the text as follows: *'l ḥlypwt 'yš lr'hw*: "each man relieving another," i.e., in a study rotation. The precise rendering does not materially affect the present discussion.

19. The parallel at 4Q267 resumes at just this point and thus offers no comparative testimony to the wording of the medieval text.

20. This interpretation is followed in the translations of G. Vermes, *The Dead Sea Scrolls in English*, p. 77; F. Martinez, *The Dead Sea Scrolls Translated*, p. 9; and M. Wise et al., *The Dead Sea Scrolls*, p. 134. P. Wernberg-Møller, *The Manual of Discipline*, p. 30, and J. Charlesworth, "The Rule of the Community," p. 27, ignore the problem by failing to represent the *vav* in translation.

21. This path is followed by A. Leaney, *The Rule of Qumran and Its Meaning*, p. 185.

22. The evidence from the scribe's own practice in copying out the present text is inconclusive. He has introduced no vacat into his text to indicate a separation of the two rulings. But this is not uncommon in 1QS in general, where gaps of a few letters normally separate literary units of several sentences only. The lack of a gap between two topically related rulings here, therefore, offers us no real indication how the scribe viewed their relationship.

23. There is a vacat of two or three letters at this point. Since this is the copy of a medieval scribe, I am hesitant to view it as a clue to the understanding of the relationship between the two rulings at Qumran.

24. G. Vermes, *The Dead Sea Scrolls in English*, p. 111, and J. Baumgarten and D. Schwartz, "The Damascus Document," p. 53, render "but." F. Martinez, *The Dead Sea Scrolls Translated*, p. 43, renders "and," while M. Wise et al., *The Dead Sea Scrolls*, p. 70, fails to render the *vav*.

25. For a concise discussion of the options in identifying this work, see S. Fraade, "The Book of Hagu," in *Encyclopedia of the Dead Sea Scrolls* (2000). I thank Professor Fraade for sharing a prepublication typescript with me.

Most scholars have derived *hgy/w* from the root *hgh*, "to meditate or reflect." Thus the term would have as its canonical intertexts such passages as Josh. 1:8 and Ps. 1:2, in which the Torah is an object of meditation "day and night." As for the identity of the book, at least two possibilities stand before us. One frequent suggestion is that the term *spr hgy*—the "book of meditation"—is an honorific term for the Torah. In this case, our passage describes a straightforward study of the Torah's content (e.g., L. Schiffman, *Reclaiming the Dead Sea Scrolls*, p. 123, S. Fraade, "The Book of Hagu"). A problem with this interpretation is that CD in particular frequently uses the term *htwrh* ("the Torah") in a variety of constructions, such as *spr htwrh* ("the book of the Torah": CD 5:2), *'l py htwrh* ("according to the Torah": CD 20:28), and so forth. Why should it now resort to an epithet? Moreover, in the reconstructed text of CD 14:7–8, the "book of Hagi" appears in apposition to "all the rulings of the Torah," suggesting a distinction between the two. The other possibility, suggested by M. Goshen-Gottstein, "'Sefer Hagu'—The End of a Puzzle," *Vetus Testamentum* 8 (1958), p. 288, is that "the Sefer Hahege contained basic commandments and customs of the sect." This view has been followed most recently by J. Baumgarten and D. Schwartz in their translation ("The Damascus Document," p. 45).

26. See L. Schiffman, *The Halakhah at Qumran*, pp. 54–60.

27. The establishment of a minimum of ten as a communal quorum clearly anticipates rabbinic practice, in which a minimum of ten men is necessary for the performance of certain public rituals (e.g., M. Megillah 4::3). The principle, enunciated in the Babylonian Talmud, is that "any activity invoking holiness shall take place among no less than ten" (B. Megillah 23b; cf. Y. Megillah 4:4, 75a–b). The point is linked exegetically to Lev. 22:32 and Num. 14:27. None of the Qumran texts appears to offer an exegetical warrant for the institution of the communal quorum of ten.

28. The division of the night into three units has its echoes in early rabbinic sources as well (e.g., M. Berakhot 1:1/T. Berakhot 1:1 [ed. Lieberman]). This supports the majority of interpreters who argue that the requirement is to spend the latter third of each night in study. See P.Wernberg-Møller, *The Manual of Discipline*, p. 104, and A. Leaney, *The Rule of Qumran and Its Meaning*, p. 185.

29. The conception here is clearly related to the explicit indication in 1QpHab 7:1–8 that the Righteous Teacher's inspired interpretations of prophetic words disclosed meanings hidden to the prophetic authors themselves. Yet neither CD nor 1QS gives any indication that the Teacher is to be equated with the "expounder of the Torah." In fact, the Teacher is mentioned only as an expositor of prophetic visions, decoding them in light of the Yahad's historical experience. For an account of the role of the Teacher, and the relation of his oral teaching to written traditions circulated in his name, see S. Byrskog, *Jesus the Only Teacher*, pp. 165–170.

30. See especially L. Schiffman, *The Halakhah at Qumran*, pp. 22–32.

31. This phrase is absent in two Cave 4 fragments (4Q256, fr.5, and 4Q258, fr.1, col.1), both of which locate the reception of definitive revelation in "the council of the men of the Community" (*'ṣt 'nšy hyḥd*) rather than in the sons of Tzadok. Metso, *The Textual Development of the Qumran Community Rule*, p. 106, considers these fragments to represent earlier versions of the text preserved in 1QS. The implications of this tradition-historical observation for reconstructing the history of the community behind 1QS have been discussed by A. Baumgarten in "The Zadokite Priests at Qumran."

32. I follow the rendering of J. Charlesworth, "Rule of the Community," p. 37. Compare G. Vermes, *The Dead Sea Scrolls in English*, p. 81, and F. Martinez, *The Dead Sea Scrolls Translated*, p. 13: "age to age," and M. Wise et al., *The Dead Sea Scrolls*, p. 34: "time and again."

33. S. Fraade, "Interpretive Authority in the Studying Community at Qumran," pp. 63–64.

34. See, for example, A. Leaney, *The Rule of Qumran and Its Meaning*, pp. 224–225.

35. Compare the following renderings of the italicized text: "the right offerings of lips as a proper sweetness" (P. Wernberg-Møller, *The Manual of Discipline*, p. 35); "and the offering of the lips according to precept is like a sweet-savoured offering" (A. Leaney, *The Rule of Qumran and Its Meaning*, p. 210); "And prayer rightly offered shall be as an acceptable fragrance" (G. Vermes, *Dead Sea Scrolls in English*, p. 82); "the offering of the lips in compliance with the decree will be like the pleasant aroma of justice" (F. Martinez, *The Dead Sea Scrolls Translated*, p. 13); "and prayer, becoming—as it were—justice itself, a sweet savor of righteousness" (M. Wise et al., *The Dead Sea Scrolls*, p. 139); "The proper offerings of the lips for judgment [is as] a righteous sweetness" (J. Charlesworth, "The Rule of the Community," p. 39).

36. L. Schiffman, *The Halakhah at Qumran*, pp. 42–49.

37. So Fraade, "Looking for Legal Midrash at Qumran," p. 77: "Whereas the earlier revelation was *nglh*, revealed to *all* of Israel, the more recent revelation was *nstr*, hidden from unworthy Israel as a whole and made known to the covenantal returnees *alone*" (original italics).

38. This has been Schiffman's consistent view. See L. Schiffman, *The Halakhah at Qumran*, pp. 75–76.

39. See Fraade, "Looking for Legal Midrash at Qumran," p. 76.

40. Cf. Baumgarten, "The Unwritten Law in the Pre-Rabbinic Period," pp. 9–11, and S. Fraade, "Interpretive Authority in the Studying Community of Qumran," pp. 65–69.

41. The discovery of Cave 4 fragments of both CD and 1QS has made it possible to study the recension history of both documents. J. Baumgarten summarizes some key implications for the history of CD's laws and their relationship to those of 1QS in "The Laws of the Damascus Document in Current Research," pp. 51–57. A comprehensive study of the recension history of 1QS is provided by S. Metso, *The Textual Development of the Qumran Community Rule*, pp. 107–149.

42. See Golb, *Who Wrote the Dead Sea Scrolls?* pp. 151–171.

43. S. Byrskog, *Jesus the Only Teacher*, p. 170. See also the detailed discussion of the entire range of textual material used in the Yahad offered now in Snyder, *Teachers, Texts, and Students*, pp. 223–263.

44. See H. Snyder, *Teachers, Texts and Students*, pp. 360–377, for an acute analysis of the oral-performative dimensions of this *pesher*. On the traits of the genre in general, he concludes: "Close inspection of the format and paleography of the pesher manuscripts shows that some of them, at least, were performed in a public setting. The scribe of the Habakkuk pesher, for example, has deliberately formatted the document for purposes of public reading, and added certain cues that would have been of use to readers performing the text" (p. 234).

3. The Media of Pharisaic Text-Interpretive Tradition

1. E. Schürer, *The History of the Jewish People in the Age of Jesus Christ*, vol. II, pp. 389–390.

2. The most useful collection of ancient sources in translation on the Pharisees remains that of J. Bowker, *Jesus and the Pharisees*. An excellent survey and discussion of the sources is that of A. Saldarini, "Pharisees," *The Anchor Bible Dictionary*, vol. 5, pp. 289–303.

Among the influential proponents of the view that the Pharisees originated the rabbinic conceptions of an exclusively oral text-interpretive tradition stemming from Sinai are E. Rivkin, *A Hidden Revolution*, passim; B. Gerhardsson, *Memory and Manuscript*, pp. 21–32, and M. Hengel, *Judaism and Hellenism*, vol. 1, pp. 173–175. A similar perspective has been recently asserted by P. Alexander, "Orality in Pharisaic-rabbinic Judaism," p. 161. He offers a masterful account of orality in classical rabbinic culture based entirely upon rabbinic sources but simply takes for granted that his discussion applies to Pharisaism.

The matter is, in any event, bound up with a larger historiographic dispute regarding the overall relationship of classical rabbinism to pre-70 Pharisaism. The above scholars insist upon a close connection of pre-70 Pharisaism and post-70 rabbinism and thus feel confident in reading as "Pharisaic" ideas attested in rabbinic texts of later centuries. The most recent, comprehensive review of modern research on the Pharisees in German and English scholarship is that of R. Deines, *Die Pharisäer*. While recognizing some of the difficulties in using rabbinic sources to construct an understanding of the Pharisees, Deines tends toward more confidence than recent English language scholarship would warrant (see pp. 534–555).

Scholars suggesting more tenuous connection between rabbinism and the Pharisees include M. Smith, "Palestinian Judaism in the First Century," pp. 67–81; J. Neusner, *From Politics to Piety*, pp. 81–141; E. P. Sanders, *Jewish Law from Jesus to the Mishnah*, pp. 97–254; and G. Stemberger, *Jewish Contemporaries of Jesus*, pp. 38–66. The heatedness of the debate may be appreciated if one consults M. Hengel's and R. Deines' joint review of the work of E. Sanders appearing in *The Journal of Theological Studies* 46 (1995), pp. 1–70.

3. I discuss the difficult cases of Paul and Josephus below. Most scholars of this generation recognize that our knowledge of Second Temple Judaism is much too fragmentary to allow certainty in identifying the origins of anonymous or pseudepigraphical writings.

This stands in marked contrast to the situation in 1913 upon the publication of R. Charles, ed., *The Apocrypha and Pseudepigrapha of the Old Testament*, which is still routinely consulted. The contributors to that classic enumerated no less than eleven works as clearly Pharisaic in authorship or bearing Pharisaic affinities. The latter category included such works as 3 Maccabees (described as "Hasidic"), 1 Baruch ("from the school of Yohanan b. Zakkai"), Susanna ("from the school of Shimon b. Shetah"), and 4 Ezra ("Rabbinic-Apocalyptic").

Works firmly identified as "Pharisaic" included 2 Maccabees (J. Moffat, vol. 1, p. 129); Judith (A. E. Cowley, vol. 1, p. 245); Jubilees (R. H. Charles, vol. 2, p. 1); Testaments of the Twelve (Charles, vol. 2, p. 282); Assumption of Moses (Charles, vol. 2, p. 407); 2 Baruch (Charles, vol. 2, p. 470); and Psalms of Solomon (G. B. Gray, vol. 2, p. 630).

In his introduction to his edition of "the Zadokite Fragment" (now referred to by Dead Sea Scroll specialists as CD), Charles identified the work as anti-Pharisaic (vol. 2, p. 785). But a Pharisaic origin for that work was claimed in the next decade by L. Ginzberg in *An Unknown Jewish Sect*, p. 267.

4. The main texts are 1QHodayot 2:15, 2:32; 4QpIs^c, fr. 23, 2:10; 4QpNah fr. 3–4, 1:2, 2:2–4, 3:3–7; 4Q177, fr. 9, 1–4; and CD 1:18–21. See the excellent survey of the sources offered by A. Baumgarten, "Seekers After Smooth Things," in *Encyclopedia of the Dead Sea Scrolls* (2000). I thank Professor Baumgarten for sharing his prepublication typescript of the entry.

5. For recent discussions of Josephus' use of this source, see D. Schwartz, "Josephus and Nicolaus on the Pharisees," pp. 157–171; D. Goodblatt, "The Place of the Pharisees in First Century Judaism," pp. 12–30; D. Williams, "Josephus or Nicolaus on the Pharisees?" pp. 43–58; S. Mason, *Flavius Josephus on the Pharisees*, pp. 37–39; and S. Schwartz, *Josephus and Judaean Politics*, pp. 119–123.

6. The common interpretation of this passage, that it testifies to Josephus' participation in the Pharisaic community, has recently been called into serious question by S. Mason, *Flavius Josephus on the Pharisees*, pp. 342–356.

7. An up-to-date survey of the various appraisals of the historical value of Josephus as a source on the Pharisees is available in S. Mason, *Flavius Josephus on the Pharisees*, pp. 1–53.

8. There is at present no universally accepted account of precisely how the diverse intellectual communities of pre-70 Palestine coalesced by the late second century into the rabbinic community led by Rabbi Yehudah, the Patriarch. Important perspectives on the crucial period from 70 until the end of the first century are offered by J. Neusner, "The Formation of Rabbinic Judaism," pp. 3–42; S. Cohen, "The Significance of Yavneh," pp. 27–53; and S. Schwartz, *Josephus and Judaean Politics*, pp. 200–208.

9. The discussion later bears out the observation of S. Cohen, "Significance of Yavneh," pp. 39–40.

10. Cf. 4Q177 (4Q Catena^a) fr. 9, 1:4, where the group is referred to as an *'dh*, "party."

11. The Jerusalem milieu is corroborated in 4QpIsa^c, fr. 23, 2:10–11. See discussion of this passage later.

12. For further help in decoding the historical references in 4QpNah, see M. Horgan, *Pesharim*, pp. 160–161, 172–174.

13. G. Martinez, *Dead Sea Scrolls Translated*, p. 210.

14. The view seems to have appeared first in M. Burrows, *The Dead Sea Scrolls*, p. 250, and received support from S. Hoenig, "Dorshe Halakot in Pesher Nahum," pp. 119–138. See most recently L. Schiffman, "Pharisees and Sadducees in Pesher Nahum," p. 276. N. Bronznik, "On the Interpretation of the Epithet 'Dorshei Halaqot,'" pp. 653–657, proposes that the *hlqwt* in question are general interpretive traditions grounded in Scripture rather than halakhic rulings per se.

15. A similarly overhasty attempt to read a Qumranian phrase in light of later attested rabbinic usage has governed interpretation of the term *tlmwd šqrm* ("their deceptive teaching") in 4QpNah, fr. 3–4:8. Since the context clearly refers to another code word for the Pharisees, "the Deceivers of Ephraim," some have argued that this reference to *talmud* implies an orally transmitted tradition of learning similar to that of rabbinic Judaism. See B. Wacholder, "A Qumran Attack on the Oral Exegesis?" pp. 575–578. While this is the earliest appearance of the noun *talmud* in the sense of "teaching," there is no inner-textual warrant for assuming a semantic equivalent to the formal terminology later attested in rabbinic literature. For bibliography and discussion, see M. Horgan, *Pesharim*, p. 184.

16. The same phenomenon, of a reference to the Expounders of Smooth Things raised in a verse contiguous with a scriptural reference to *hlqwt*, occurs in 4Q177, fr. 9:4–5. Ps. 12:3–4 denounces the "lips of *hlqwt*" that God will cut off. Although comment on this passage has not survived, 4Q177 offers the following comment in the apparent context of Pss. 12 and 13: ["the]y are the party (*'dt*) of the Expounders of [Smooth Things who] . . . in their zeal and in their animosity . . ." I translate this fragment as it appears in Allegro, *Discoveries*, vol. 5, p. 70. The translations of Martinez (p. 210) and Wise et al. (p. 236) suggest a fuller text, but I have not been able to determine its source.

17. For discussion of the *pesher* genre, see M. Horgan, *Pesharim*, pp. 229–259.

18. All translations follow the Revised Standard Version of the New Testament.

19. P. Tomson, *Paul and the Jewish Law*, offers a perceptive and learned study of the rich resonances of Pauline thought with legal traditions attested in Jewish sources from the Qumran corpus through that of later rabbinic Judaism. But he is overconfident that all legal traditions in Paul's thought that cannot be ascribed to Saducean or Qumranian sources "should be seen as being in touch with what we may consider to be the polymorphous tradition carried on by the Pharisaic Sages" (p. 26).

20. Compare the similar formulation placed in Paul's mouth by the Lukan composer: "educated according to the strict manner of the law of our fathers" (*kata akribeian tou patroou nomou*: Acts 22:3).

21. A standard account of Q as a literary source is that of J. Kloppenborg, *The Formation of Q*. My enumeration of Q follows the text presented in J. Kloppenborg et al., *Q Thomas*

Reader, pp. 53–54. See also S. Mason and T. Robinson, eds., *An Early Christian Reader,* pp. 113–142.

22. For discussion of the passage, see J. Kloppenborg, *The Formation of Q,* pp. 139–142, and A. Jacobson, *The First Gospel,* pp. 172–181..

23. The Gospel of John, probably from the 90s, represents a rather independent refraction of the gospel traditions. It supplies images of Pharisees that supplement those found in the synoptic Gospels but contains nothing that will alter the synoptics' representation of Pharisaic tradition in particular. Accordingly, I omit discussion of Johannine materials in this survey.

24. Such parenthetical material is common in the redactional level of Mark. See E. Trocme, *The Formation of the Gospel According to Mark,* pp. 198–199, n. 1, and E. Pryke, *Redactional Style in the Markan Gospel,* pp. 49–50.

25. A. Baumgarten, "The Pharisaic Paradosis," pp. 66–67.

26. Neusner dates these materials to the pre-70 period in J. Neusner, *Judaism,* pp. 53–54.

27. Ritual hand-washing in preparation for prayer is attested as "the custom of all Jews" as early as the second century BCE (Aristeas, 305–306), and rinsing of the hands and body for purposes of purification was certainly an element of Qumranian piety (Schiffman, *Halakhah at Qumran,* p. 102). The exegetical question of whether *kai pantes oi ioudaioi* should be rendered to include the Pharisees among other Jews in this practice, or whether to single out the Pharisees in particular, is discussed in R. Bratcher and E. Nida, *A Translator's Handbook on the Gospel of Mark,* p. 221.

28. For a provocative interpretation of the ethical meaning of hand-washing in Pharisaism, see J. Poirier, "Why Did the Pharisees Wash Their Hands?", pp. 219–233.

29. See, e.g., M. Nedarim 2:1–2 and T. Nedarim 1:5. Cf. S. Lachs, *A Rabbinic Commentary on the New Testament,* pp. 246–247, and literature cited there.

30. See Josephus, Apion 1:167, who comments that the term korban "will be found in no other nation except the Jews, and, translated from the Hebrew, it means something like 'God's gift.'" In the earliest rabbinic literature the term *qwnm* (*qonam*) is the routine verbal utterance for embracing a vow to prohibit an object for one's pleasure. M. Nedarim 1:2–4 understands this as euphemism for *qrbn*; that is, the person utters the vow by referring obliquely to the Temple sacra (M. Nedarim 2:2). A rich discussion of the rabbinic terminology for vows and oaths in the context of Greco-Roman culture is offered in S. Lieberman, *Greek in Jewish Palestine,* pp. 115–141.

31. The refrain that Jesus teaches with authority is stressed throughout the Gospels. It is interesting, in this connection, that Luke 4:16–30's portrayal of Jesus' textual-interpretive practice in the synagogue at Nazareth declines to name Pharisees as among the outraged congregants. Cf. Mark 1:21–28, which has Jesus in the Capernaum synagogue besting scribes rather than Pharisees.

A useful exploration of early Christian representations of Jesus' charismatic authority in contrast to rabbinic patterns is that of Hengel, *The Charismatic Leader and His Followers,* pp. 38–83. Hengel's confidence that rabbinic patterns are by definition also Pharisaic flaws his discussion. By contrast, Byrskog, *Jesus the Only Teacher,* pp. 199–236, shows that Jesus' uniqueness as a teacher is understood within the Matthean community in ways that intersect with rabbinic models of discipleship to a Sage.

32. Studies of ways in which developing rabbinic tradition deals with memories of charismatic figures in its own lineage are offered by W. Green, "Palestinian Holy Men: Charismatic Leadership and rabbinic Tradition," pp. 619–647, and B. Bokser, "Wonder-Working and the rabbinic Tradition: The Case of Hanina ben Dosa," pp. 42–92.

33. The main Josephan references are War 1:107–114, 571; 2:162–166; Antiquities 13:171–173, 288–298, 400–432; 17:41–45; 18:12–15; Life 10–12, 189–198.

34. The most helpful meditation on the value of Josephan and Christian accounts of Pharisaic legal expertise (*akribeia*) in identifying the origins of the term "Pharisees" is offered by A. Baumgarten, "The Name of the Pharisees," pp. 411–428.

35. The rabbinic parallel to this narrative at B. Qiddushin 66a will occupy us below as well.

36. All translations of this passage follow that of Mason, *Flavius Josephus on the Pharisees*, pp. 216–217.

37. Important recent discussions include J. Baumgarten, "The Unwritten Law in the Pre-rabbinic Period," pp. 12–14; E. Rivkin, *A Hidden Revolution*, pp. 36–43; and M. Hengel and R. Deines, "E. P. Sanders' 'Common Judaism,' Jesus and the Pharisees," pp. 29–32.

38. See J. Neusner, "Oral Torah and Oral Tradition," p. 70. 70, E. P. Sanders, *Jewish Law from Jesus to the Mishnah*, pp. 99–100.

39. Mason, *Flavius Josephus on the Pharisees*, pp. 230–239.

40. Mason, *Flavius Josephus on the Pharisees*, p. 243.

41. For text, see Qimron and Strugnell, *Discoveries*, vol. 10, p. 63. Qimron argues that the author of the letter is most likely the Righteous Teacher and that his addressee is the Hasmonean dynast symbolized as the Wicked Priest (pp. 114–121). Strugnell, in the same volume (pp. 204–206), is hesitant to identify the principals. D. Schwartz, "MMT, Josephus, and the Pharisees," identifies the author as "a Qumran spokesman early in the Hasmonean period" (p. 79) and the addressee as Pharisees in temporary coalition with the Hasmonean High Priesthood (pp. 79–80).

42. The identification as "the Elder" (*hzqn*) is episodic (e.g., M. Rosh Hashannah 2:5, M. Orlah 2:12) and is intended to distinguish him from his grandson, of the same name, who appears to have succeeded Rabban Yohanan b. Zakkai as the guiding force of the Yavnean Academy in the 80s of the first century CE. On the problems of distinguishing the traditions about the two figures, see J. Neusner, *Rabbinic Traditions About the Pharisees Before 70*, vol. 1, pp. 341–342. The major study of the traditions of the Yavnean Rabban Gamaliel is that of S. Kanter, *Rabban Gamaliel II: The Legal Traditions*.

43. See the survey of the Gamaliel traditions in J. Neusner, *Rabbinic Traditions About the Pharisees Before 70*, vol. 1, pp. 342–376. Neusner concludes that "Gamaliel was both a Temple-council member, as Acts alleges, and a leader within the Pharisaic sect, as the rabbinic traditions hold" (p. 376). In fact, it is the tradition of Acts, rather than that of the Rabbis, which explicitly names Gamaliel as a Pharisee. Nevertheless, his Pharisaic connection seems certain.

44. In rabbinic tradition, Rabban Shimon b. Gamaliel occupies a shadowy place, for no legal prescriptions are transmitted directly in his name. Many materials transmitted in the name of Rabban Shimon b. Gamaliel presuppose a post-70 setting, and therefore refer to his grandson of the same name, who flourished in the early third of the second century CE. See J. Neusner, *Rabbinic Traditions About the Pharisees Before 70*, vol. 1, pp. 377–388, for a study of the narrative traditions.

45. J. Neusner, *Rabbinic Traditions About the Pharisees Before 70*, vol. 1, p. 159.

46. E. Rivkin, *A Hidden Revolution*, p. 131, points out that only texts in which *prwšym* and *ṣdwqym* are juxtaposed provide the most secure foundations for historical reconstructions of the Pharisees. He also points out that a number of rabbinic references to *prwšym* refer not to Pharisees, but rather to various practitioners of pietistic disciplines that received more or less unfavorable rabbinic comment (pp. 162–173). G. Stemberger, *Jewish Contemporaries of Jesus*, pp. 40–45, focuses in particular on M. Hagigah 2:7, M. Sotah 3:4, T. Sotah 15:11–12, T. Shabbat 1:15, Y. Sotah 5:7, 20a (Y. Berakhot 9:7, 14b), and B. Sotah 22a.

47. See, for example: T. Rosh Hashannah 1:15, M. Pesahim 5:8, M. Yoma 1:5/T. Yoma 1:8, T. Niddah 5:3. For the occasional use of "scribes" (*swprym*), see chapter 4.

48. E. Rivkin, *A Hidden Revolution*, pp. 137–139, enumerates M. Makkot 1:6, T. Yoma 1:8, and B. Niddah 33b as other examples. In fact none of these supports his claim. In M. Makkot 1:6 and T. Kippurim 1:8 it is "Sages"—not "Pharisees"—who come into conflict with Sadducees or Boethusians. The term *prwšym* does not appear in the texts. Rivkin's equation of Sages with Pharisees thus assumes what he wants to prove.

The Tannaitic passage cited at B. Niddah 33b, for its part, states that the wives of Sadducees "live in fear of the Pharisees and [w] show their menstrual blood to the Sages." In this passage the Pharisees and Sages are enumerated as distinct, not identical, groups. Moreover, in the parallel at T. Niddah 5:3, the term *ḥkm* is used exclusively, with no mention of *prwšym*. Even if we grant Rivkin's reading of this passage, it suggests only that a very late Babylonian version of T. Niddah 5:3 has begun to equate Pharisees and Sages. B. Qiddushin 66a exemplifies this same process, as we shall see.

49. See E. Rivkin, *A Hidden Revolution*, pp. 142–145.

50. J. Neusner, *Rabbinic Traditions About the Pharisees Before 70*, vol. 1, pp. 173–176 notes and analyzes the numerous discrepancies between the two versions. In the talmudic account, the king is Alexander Jannaeus, known as Yannai the King. The Sadducee, Jonathan, of Josephus' version, is here identified merely as "a scoffer, with an evil and rebellious heart, and Elazar b. Poerah was his name." So the Talmud differs from Josephus both on the chronology of the event that resulted in royal persecution of Pharisees and on the role of a Sadducee as an instigator. It also differs on the name and loyalty of the person who points out the king's tainted lineage. The Talmud's Yehudah b. Gederah, apparently a Sage, replaces Josephus' "evil-natured guest, Elazar" (Antiquities 13:290) as the Pharisaic figure, while Josephus' Elazar has been assimilated to the Talmud's Elazar b. Poerah.

51. For further discussion, see the recent article of A. Baumgarten, "Rabbinic Literature as a Source for the History of Jewish Sectarianism in the Second Temple Period," pp. 36–52.

52. For discussion of the place of this passage in the larger tradition of Shimon b. Shetah, see J. Neusner, *Rabbinic Traditions About the Pharisees Before 70*, vol. 1, pp. 108–109.

53. All other references to Yannai the King occur in the Babylonian Talmud: e.g., B. Sotah 22b (which alludes to Josephus' report that Alexander Jannaeus urged Alexandra Salome to curry Pharisaic favor after his death), B. Sotah 47a (which knows of Yannai's murder of the Sages), and B. Bava Batra 133b, without earlier parallel. For discussion of the latter two passages, see J. Neusner, *Rabbinic Traditions About the Pharisees Before 70*, vol. 1, pp. 83–86, 73–76.

54. In addition to the materials of M. Yadayim 4:6–7, Pharisees are explicitly identified in M. Yadayim 4:8, T. Yadayim 2:20, M. Hagigah 2:7, and T. Hagigah 3:35. These and more debatable references to Pharisees in the Mishnah and the Tosefta are discussed in G. Stemberger, *Jewish Contemporaries of Jesus*, pp. 45–64.

55. I omit here the continuation of the passage at M. Yadayim 4:8. The latter shares the same formulaic complaint against Pharisees, but the disputant is identified in the best manuscripts as a "Galilean heretic" (*myn*) rather than a *ṣdwqy*.

56. The Sadducean point here is an ironic one: sacred books render the hands unclean, while books of pagan mythology do not.

Rabbinic tradition holds that sacred texts convey uncleanness to the hands (e.g., M. Kelim 15:6; M. Yadayim 3:4–5, 4:5; T. Yadayim 2:10–14, 19 [ed. Zuckermandel, pp. 683–684]). The explanation, according to later talmudic tradition (B. Shabbat 14a), is that this is a precaution against storing biblical scrolls with priestly offerings, lest rodents attracted to the food damage the scrolls. If the scrolls are regarded as conveyers of contamination to the hands, they can then contaminate priestly offerings as well. On the sources and their explanation, see S. Leiman, *The Canonization of Hebrew Scripture*, pp. 102–120.

57. As earlier, the point is ironic. The bones of an unclean creature convey no impurity, while the bones of a saintly High Priest render those touching them unclean from corpse contamination. The Sadducees here would not dispute the uncleanness of the High Priests bones but would dispute the incapacity of an unclean animal's bones to convey uncleanness. Lev. 11:24 points out that carcasses of beasts convey uncleanness to those touching them. M. Tohorot 1:4/M. Hullin 9:1 indeed adds that while the flesh of dead beasts conveys uncleanness, the bones do not contribute the requisite quantity of flesh deemed capable of transmitting this contamination. On the uncleanness of the human corpse, including its bones and extruding fluids, see Num. 19:16 and M. Ohalot 2:1–3.

58. That is, if clean liquid is poured into an unclean vessel, the vessel contaminates the liquid within it and also causes the uncleanness to climb up the spout of water to contaminate the contents of the pure vessel. The Mishnaic source reflecting this view is M. Tohorot 8:9 (cf. Makhshirin 5:9).

59. Since the source of the water comes from the ground, the water cannot contract uncleanness from any corpse matter it contacts in the graveyard (cf. M. Miqvaot 1:4). The Sadducees presumably agree with this on the basis of Lev. 11:36. The point is then ironic: if the Sadducees do not believe that contamination downstream within the graveyard moves upstream to contaminate the source, why do they hold precisely this in connection with a spout? The examples are hardly analogous, however, as traditional commentaries point out (e.g., Tiferet Yisrael, ad loc.). Nevertheless, for the rhetorical purposes of the present context the point serves.

60. See M. Bava Qamma 8:4.

61. On the basis of this observation, M. Yadayim 4:8, which has the Pharisees besting their interlocuters, seems to have been appended to 4:6–7 at the penultimate stage of its reworking for the purpose of concluding Tractate Yadayim.

62. E. Qimron and J. Strugnell, *Discoveries*, vol. 10, pp. 48, 53 (text) and 155–156, 161–162 (commentary). See pp. 131–177 for a comprehensive discussion of the various conceptual parallels of legal positions staked out in 4QMMT and in rabbinic texts. The pioneering study, which has not been outdated by the publication of Qimron and Strugnell, is that of Y. Zussman, "Research in the History of the Halakhah and the Scrolls of the Judean Desert" (Heb.), pp. 11–76 (an English summary of which appears in Qimron and Strugnell, pp. 179–200). The tendency to link the legal positions of 4QMMT's addressee to those of the Pharisaic and later rabbinic traditions, with particular reference to the question of the spout of liquid, is effectively challenged by Y. Elman, "Some Remarks on 4QMMT," pp. 99–128.

63. See, for example, S. Lieberman, "The Discipline in the So-Called Dead Sea Manual of Discipline," p. 202. Lieberman's trenchant critique of efforts to link the Association to the Yahad is grounded in an unargued assumption that the Association is a Pharisaic group. Cf. C. Rabin, *Qumran Studies*, who argues, to the contrary, that "the Qumran community . . . represents the old haburah [Association] more faithfully than does the 'rabbinic' community of the Tannaitic period, because the latter had made extensive concessions in halakhic matters in order to enable non-Pharisees to share in its life" (p. viii). Thus, in contrast to Lieberman, Rabin finds Pharisaic origins for both the Yahad and the Association. In order to make this view workable, Rabin argues for a no-longer-tenable first-century CE dating for the Damascus Document.

64. The most important discussion of the literary relationship of M. and T. Demai is that of R. Sarason, *A Study of Tractate Demai*, pp. 69–107. Following Neusner's paradigm of the Tosefta as a commentary on the Mishnah, Sarason views T. Demai 2:2–3:9 as an extensive expansion of the Mishnah's slim notice. For reasons I will elaborate in chapter 6 of this study, the relationship of any given Mishnaic passage to its Toseftan parallel is likely to be more complex. This is one of those passages. In my view, M. Demai 2:2–3 is a brief allusion

to the fuller Toseftan passage that circulated as a unit of tradition prior to the redaction of the extant tractates of the Mishnah and the Tosefta (a possibility entertained by Sarason as well, pp. 77, 79). In any event, the question of the M.–T. relationship does not affect our discussion of the relation of the Associates to the Pharisees, since mention of Pharisees is conspicuously absent in both sources.

65. According to S. Lieberman, *Tosefta Ki-fshuta*, vol. 1, p. 209, the differences refer to different stages of entry into the Association: "the Mishnah refers to the practices of the Associates after they have already accepted the rules of the Association, but the Tosefta specifies the conditions that a disciple of the Sages or an undisciplined Jew must accept prior to entry into the Association."

66. This is the reading of MS Erfurt and the first edition. MS Vienna has "for" (*l*). Lieberman, *Tosefta Ki-fshuta*, vol. 1, p. 216 prefers the reading of MS Erfurt.

67. C. Rabin, *Qumran Studies*, pp. 1–21. Most of the Sages who comment upon the Mishnaic and Toseftan rulings come from the mid-second century, post-bar Kosiva generation. This fact suggests that the formulation of the foundational material is somewhat removed from the pre-70 milieu. If so, the terminology need no longer accurately represent putative first-century usage.

68. In many contexts, the phrase *tlmyd ḥkm* is equivalent to "Sage." Here, since it stands in apposition to the term *ḥkm* in ruling 2, the intention is to distinguish between an apprentice and a fully qualified Sage. See next note.

69. B. Bekhorot 30b: *zqn* ("Elder"). This variant confirms that the use of *tlmyd ḥkm* in ruling 1 is intended to refer to a disciple.

70. So MS Vienna. Abba Shaul's comment is lacking in MS Erfurt and the Toseftan parallel at Y. Demai 2:3, 22d, but attested at B. Bekhorot 30b.

71. In this judgment, I agree with E. Rivkin, *A Hidden Revolution*, p. 174, although I admit to finding more ambiguity in the matter than he does.

72. See the summaries of pre-70 traditions incorporated into later Mishnaic tractates in J. Neusner, *Judaism*, pp. 45–75.

73. See the convenient collection in R. Herford, *Christianity in Talmud and Midrash*, pp. 35–96. Herford notes some sixteen passages in the Talmud Bavli that contain clear or veiled references to Jesus and only one umistakable reference in the Yerushalmi (Y. Taanit 2:1, 65b).

74. Whether this was conceived as the cultivation of priestly levels of purity among nonpriests remains a controversial matter. See the dispute between E. P. Sanders, *Jewish Law From Jesus to the Mishnah*, pp. 130–254, and J. Neusner, *Judaic Law from Jesus to the Mishnah*, pp. 205–230, 247–273.

75. A useful comparative study of Qumranian and rabbinic purity laws is offered by H. Harrington in *The Impurity Systems of Qumran and the Rabbis*. See in particular her comments on the Sanders–Neusner debate regarding the nature of Pharisaic purity concerns, pp. 267–281.

4. Tannaitic Tradition as an Object of Rabbinic Reflection

1. Useful discussions of the social history of Palestinian Jewry in the second and early third centuries are M. Goodman, *State and Society in Roman Galilee*, pp. 27–89; R. Horsley, *Galilee*, pp. 111–282; J. Sanders, *Schismatics, Sectarians, Dissidents, Deviants*, pp. 40–151; and H. Lapin, *Early Rabbinic Civil Law and the Social History of Roman Galilee*, pp. 119–235. See also the several important essays in W. Horbury et al., *The Cambridge History of Judaism, volume 3*. This work appeared too recently to make an impact on my study.

2. See S. Fraade, *From Tradition to Commentary*, pp. 73–74, and especially the sources cited on p. 232, n. 202.

3. For the early history of the term, see H. Lapin, "Rabbi," in D. Freedman, *The Anchor Bible Dictionary*, vol. 5, pp. 600–602. On the shape of the nascent rabbinic movement in second- and early third-century Galilee, see M. Goodman, *State and Society in Roman Galilee*, pp. 93–171; R. Horsley, *Galilee*, pp. 94–103; S. Fraade, *From Tradition to Commentary*, pp. 69–121; and S. Cohen, "The Place of the Rabbi in Jewish Society of the Second Century," in L. Levine, ed., *The Galilee in Late Antiquity*, pp. 157–173.

4. C. Hezser, *The Social Structure of the Rabbinic Movement*, pp. 1–42, offers a fine survey of the scholarship.

5. See the rabbinic sources woven into the account of Jewish scribal practice offered by M. Bar-Ilan in "Scribes and Books in the Late Second Commonwealth and the Rabbinic Period," pp. 21–37.

6. This is reflected in a number of ways. First, rabbinic historical memory represents Second Temple Sadducees as subjected in their cultic practice to the Sages' authority (e.g., T. Kippurim 1:8, T. Parah 3:8). For a thorough survey of sources and their interpretation, see G. Alon, *Jews, Judaism, and the Classical World*, pp. 48–88.

Second, prerogatives assigned in Scripture to priests in the evaluation of states of uncleanness are appropriated by Sages in rabbinic *halakhah* (e.g., M. Negaim 3:1, Sifra, Negaim, per. 1:8–9 [Lev. 13:2]). Priests are thus transformed from their scriptural status as interpreters of the Torah in their own right to executors of Sages' will. The issue is explored in further depth in J. Neusner, *A History of the Mishnaic Law of Purities*, vol. 8, pp. 139–145, 254–256.

Related to this point, the inherited status of holiness enjoyed by the priesthood is made secondary to the acquired status of holiness conferred by study of *torah* under the direction of Sages (e.g., M. Horayot 3:8). On this matter, see M. Jaffee, *Horayot*, pp. 24–28.

Finally, with the single exception of Shimon the Righteous, all First and Second Temple priests are omitted from the chain of authoritative *torah* tradition (M. Avot 1:1ff). On the implications, see M. Heer, "Continuity of Tradition in the Transmission of Torah," pp. 43–56.

C. Hezser discusses the post-70 relationship between the emerging rabbinic movement and the priestly caste in *The Social Structure of the rabbinic Movement*, pp. 480–489.

7. For example, a first-century figure, Nahum the Lavlar (Greek: *liblarios*, a copier of documents), figures at M. Peah 2:6 in the transmission of a halakhic tradition of Mosaic origins. The second-century Sage, Rabbi Meir, is remembered as having been a skilled scribe (*ḥkm wswpr*: B. Gittin 67a, Avot de-Rabbi Nathan, A18) who could copy out the entire text of the Esther scroll from memory (T. Megillah 2:5). In general, however, scribes as literary professionals (in contrast to notaries or clerks) are not normally portrayed as insiders to the rabbinic community. See B. Gerhardsson, *Memory and Manuscript*, 45–51, and C. Schams, *Jewish Scribes in the Second-Temple Period*, pp. 288–289.

8. The only explicit case in the Mishnah and Tosefta is at M. Kelim 13:7/M. Tevul Yom 4:6, paralleled in T. Kelim, Bava Metzia 3:14/T. Tevul Yom 2:14. A second example appears at Sifre Num. 5:18, pis. 8. A final possible example is from the late appendix to M. Avot (6:9): "I come from a great city of Sages and scribes." Terms such as "judicial scribes" (*swpry hdyynym*: e.g., M. Sanhedrin 4:3, T. Sandhedrin 9:1) refer to court clerks rather than Sages per se. J. Weingreen ("Oral Torah and Written Records," pp. 56–59) has argued, unpersuasively in my view, that the records of such scribes formed an important written substratum of the traditions that ultimately came to be known in rabbinic Judaism as the Oral Torah.

9. Neusner's most recent contribution to the discussion (J. Neusner, *What Exactly Did the Sages Mean by "The Oral Torah"?* pp. 211–213), seems to place the idea in the post-Mishnaic period that produced the halakhic midrashim, the Palestinian Talmud, and the great Palestinian midrashic compilations. P. Schäfer, "Das Dogma von der Mündlichen Torah," pp. 196–197, finds the thematic origins of the idea in "early Tannaitic times," al-

though it is only in Amoraic times that he finds "the dogma of linking the entire oral Torah back to Moses." See also D. Kraemer, "On the Reliability of the Attributions in the Babylonian Talmud," pp. 185–190; he argues for the primacy of the circle of the mid-third-century Sage, Rabbi Yohanan bar Nappaha. The concluding chapter of this volume will confirm and amplify arguments for a mid-third-century setting.

10. For the term *tn'* and variants as designations for tradents of Mishnaic and other early traditions, see W. Bacher, *Terminologie*, vol. 2, p. 241, and M. Sokoloff, A *Dictionary of Jewish Palestinian Aramaic*, p. 386, s.v., *tnwy*. See also B. Gerhardsson, *Memory and Manuscript*, pp. 93ff. I will discuss the corresponding term, *'mwr'* (Amora), and its variants in chapter 7.

11. Y. Epstein, *Introduction to the Text of the Mishnah*, pp. 673–726, has shown that the extant texts of the Mishnah stemming from medieval manuscripts cannot be regarded as identical to the textual traditions that circulated from the early third century under the authority of Rabbi Yehudah the Patriarch. Nevertheless, these texts must serve. For a fruitful new approach to the gradual emergence of the Mishnaic text in the discipleship circles of the third century, see the dissertation of E. Alexander, *Study Practices that Made the Mishnah*. Citations of the Mishnah in this book are translated by the author from the edition of C. Albeck unless otherwise noted.

12. Scholarly positions on the dating of this crucial compilation of Tannaitic tradition have ranged from the mid-third century through the eighth. For a fine survey of the options, with a creative distinction between a mid-third-century written redaction circulating in Palestine and an oral redaction circulating primarily in Babylonia at a much later date, see Y. Elman, *Authority and Tradition*, pp. 1–46. On the specific question of the oral transmission of the Tosefta, see Y. Elman, "Orality and the Transmission of Tosefta Pisha in Talmudic Tradition," in H. Fox and T. Meacham, *Introducing Tosefta*, pp. 123–180.

Citations of the Tosefta in this book are translated by the author. The edition used for the Orders of Agriculture, Festivals, Women, and the Bavot is that of S. Lieberman. Other citations are drawn from the edition of K. Rengstorf, where available, and from that of M. Zuckermandel.

13. Critical opinion regarding the dates for the compilation and circulation of these diverse collections is conveniently surveyed in G. Stemberger, *Introduction to Talmud and Midrash*, pp. 248–276. Author's translations are from the following editions: Mekhilta of Rabbi Ishmael, ed. Horovitz and Rabin; Sifra to Leviticus, ed. Weiss; Sifre to Numbers, ed. Horovitz; Sifre to Deuteronomy, ed. Finkelstein.

14. My own discussion rehearses much that can be found in B. Gerhardsson, *Memory and Manuscript*, pp. 19–32, although I am less confident than Gerhardsson that the distinction between *qr'* and *šnh* has much relevance in the Second Temple period.

15. This assumption is confirmed by the ruling of M. Sotah 7:7 that part of the Temple scriptural reading for Yom Kippur be read by the High Priest *'l ph* ("from memory") rather than from a written copy. This is understood as an exception permissible only for the sake of the congregation, which might be disturbed by the interruption of rolling the scroll of the Torah from the first reading of the day, Lev. 23:26–32, to the second reading, Num. 29:7–11. See also T. Megillah 2:5, which specifies that "one who recites [the Esther Scroll] from memory has not satisfied his obligation." For the semantic range of the root *qr'* and the noun *mqr'* in the rabbinic literature, see Bacher, *Terminologie*, vol. 1, pp. 174–176; vol. 2, pp. 193–196.

16. There are some exceptions in which a recitation of Scripture is incorporated into the term for oral recitation from memory. See, e.g., Avot de-Rabbi Nathan, A18, in which, responding to Rabbi Tarfon's request to "repeat for me" (*šnh ly*), a disciple is said to have "brought Scripture, repeated tradition, exegetical tradition, legal tradition, and homiletic tradition." On *šnh* in general, see W. Bacher, *Terminologie*, vol. 1, pp. 193–195; vol. 2, pp. 225–

226. A helpful discussion of the use of the stem *šm'* in early rabbinic halakhic tradition to denote the medium of transmitted knowledge is that of Goldin, "On the Account of the Banning of R. Eliezer b. Hyrcanus," pp. 285–288.

17. The gap between this representation of matters and the suggestive evidence of the texts themselves that writing was employed in their composition at some level will concern us in chapter 7. For the moment we will simply accept the Tannaitic testimony as it is presented.

18. For similar usage of *mšnh* in the construct state, see M. Avot 3:7–8: "one who interrupts his recitation (*mšntw*)"; "one who forgets a single point of his recitation (*mšntw*). Cf. Y. Moed Qatan 3:7, 83b: "whoever neglects his affairs in preference for his recitation (*mšntw*)." On this point S. Lieberman, *Hellenism in Jewish Palestine*, pp. 88–96, assumes that the term *mšnh* in its construct state refers to coherent corpora of traditions transmitted orally among early Tannaim, e.g., in the circle of Rabbi Aqiva. This usage, in fact, is attested only in relation to Masters of the third century (e.g., Y. Maaserot 3:7, 50d, which speaks of "the Mishnah of" (*mšntw šl*) Rabbi Hiyya, Rabbi Hoshaya, and bar Qappara). See Y. Epstein, *Introduction to the Text of the Mishnah*, pp. 25–74.

19. The distinction between *mishnah* as a designation of a circumscribed logion and Mishnah as the designation of a redacted literary work is not always obvious. It is preserved as well in both Talmuds, in which the Aramaic term *mtnyt'* ("repeated teaching") commonly refers to any reputedly Tannaitic teaching, while *mtnytyn* ("our repeated tradition") refers to the formal learning curriculum of the community embodied in the Mishnah of Rabbi Yehudah. See Bacher, *Terminologie*, vol. 1, p. 194; Y. Epstein, *Introduction to the Text of the Mishnah*, pp. 813–814; and C. Albeck, *Introduction to the Mishnah.*, pp. 1–2.

20. See Y. Epstein, *Introduction to the Text of the Mishnah*, pp. 25–163.

21. For discussion of the sixth chapter of M. Avot, see M. Lerner, "The Tractate Avot," pp. 273–275.

22. I quote from Schechter, ed., p. 28b. See chapter 5, n. 3, for bibliography regarding the position of Avot d'Rabbi Natan in emerging rabbinic tradition.

23. Bracketed material does not appear in the text. The context of the story, which describes a man who strove for a high level of piety, requires this qualification.

24. In versions of this passage cited in Y. Berakhot 3:4, 6c and B. Berakhot 22a, the females are excluded so as to avoid the obvious implication that women are permitted to read the Torah in public. See D. Boyarin, *Carnal Israel*, pp. 180–181.

25. The claim is usually based upon an enigmatic passage in M. Eduyot 1:3 (B. Gerhardsson, *Memory and Manuscript*, p. 131; D. Zlotnick, *Iron Pillar Mishnah*, p. 40; J. Faur, *Golden Doves with Silver Dots*, pp. 89–90). In dispute with Shammai over the quantity of drawn water that nullifies the purifying power of an immersion pool, Hillel employs the antiquated measurement of a *hin* in place of the term *qav*, preferred elsewhere in rabbbinic usage. The Mishnah's glossator explains Hillel's terminological choice as follows: "for a person is obliged to report [a tradition] in the expression used by his Master [*blšwn rbw*]."

It is significant that T. Eduyyot 1:3, which offers a parallel to M. Eduyyot 1:3's dispute, has both Hillel and Shammai employing the term *hin* and offers no further comment. In Mishnaic context, therefore, the explanation simply justifies Hillel's preservation of an antiquated term; it makes no claim about the verbatim memorization of entire utterances. The citation of this gloss at B. Berakhot 47a suggests that, among later Babylonians, the point was indeed extended beyond terminological precision even to grammatical forms. But this still does not amount to a requirement for verbatim transmission of all utterances.

Another passage quoted as Tannaitic tradition in B. Sukkah 28a in the name of the first-century Rabbi Eliezer b. Hyrcanus is also often cited in support of the existence of an institutionalized mandate of verbatim memorization (e.g., D. Zlotnick, *Iron Pillar Mishnah*, p. 65).

The passage reads: "You [Sages] implore me to report a matter [*dbr*] I haven't heard from my Masters. [But,] in my entire life no one has ever preceded me to the House of Study, nor have I dozed off in the House of Study . . . , nor have I left anyone remaining in the House of Study, nor have I uttered a word of idle conversation, nor have I ever reported a matter [*dbr*] I did not hear from my Masters." Eliezer's point, as the context makes clear, is that he refuses to offer a ruling on a topic unless he has heard a tradition from his teachers.

In any event, the wide range of textual variation characteristic of the transmission of specific teachings in rabbinic literature—in both halakhic and aggadic genres—testifies to the fact that rabbinic tradents valued what Latin rhetoricians termed *memoria ad res* above *memoria ad verbum* (see M. Carruthers, *The Book of Memory*, pp. 86–89). For recent perspectives on the significance and reliability of the attributions of teachings to specific autorities, see J. Neusner, "Evaluating the Attributions," pp. 93–111; S. Stern, "Attribution and Authorship," pp. 28–51; idem, "The Concept of Authorship," pp. 183–185; D. Kraemer, "On the Reliability of Attributions," pp. 175–190; R. Brody, "Geonic Literature and the Text of the Talmud (Heb.)," pp. 257–259, 282; R. Kalmin, *Sages, Stories, Authors, and Editors*, pp. 127–140; and C. Hezser, *The Social Structure of the rabbinic Movement*, pp. 334–335.

26. See T. Parah 11:8 (ed. Rengstorf): "The authorities do not dispute the substance of the halakhah, but rather the formulation" (*hlšwn*). The most exhaustive catalogue of the forms and formulaic patterns employed in the Mishnah and Tosefta in particular is that of J. Neusner, A *History of the Mishnaic Law of Purities*, vol. XXI, pp. 164–246.

27. A similar testimony to the recasting of a tradition on the basis of rational considerations, drawn from Mekhilta of Rabbi Shimon b. Yohai, Pisha (Ex. 13:5), serves as D. Nelson's route into the oral-performative world of rabbinic midrashic literature. See his recent dissertation, *Textuality and Talmud Torah*, pp. 1–2.

28. Cf. T. Parah 4:7 (ed. Rengstorf). Later Babylonian traditions are clear that students memorized their Mishnaic materials with the mnemonic aid of cantillation: B. Sanhedrin 99b, B. Megillah 32a. Helpful discussions of the role of chanting and song in the memorization of Tannaitic traditions may be consulted in B. Gerhardsson, *Memory and Manuscript*, pp. 163–168; B. Bayer, "Oral Law in the 'Oral Law,'" pp. 1148–150; and D. Zlotnick, *The Iron Pillar Mishnah*, pp. 54–60. An ethnomusicological study of the oral performance of the Mishnah based upon medieval manuscript traditions of Aleppo has been offered in F. Alvarez-Pereyre, *La Transmission Orale de la Mishnah*.

29. My discussion here revises and amplifies arguments I first set forth in M. Jaffee, "Halakhah in Early rabbinic Judaism," pp. 113–132. I wish to thank the publisher, Walter de Gruyter, for permission to use this material.

30. There are only two appearances in the Mishnah. M. Sheqalim 6:1 reports that the families of Rabban Gamaliel I and Rabbi Hananiah, Prefect of the Priests, had a "*masoret* from their fathers" that the original Ark was hidden at a certain spot in the Temple. The second appearance (M. Avot 3:13), "the *masoret* [some versions: *mesorah*] is a fence for the Torah," refers narrowly to the traditions by which the text of the Torah was preserved and its words pronounced. The two examples in the Tosefta (Bekhorot 1:12 and Arakhin 5:16) follow the usage of M. Sheqalim. See Bacher, *Terminologie*, vol. 1, p. 108, and 2, p. 115.

31. The one example in the Mishnah and the Tosefta is that of M. Taanit 2:1, which introduces a citation of Joel 2:13 with the phrase, "and in the *qabbalah* it says," thus indicating that *qabbalah* designates the tradition of the Prophets. See Bacher, *Terminologie*, vol. 1, pp. 105–106.

32. On the semantic range of this term, see Bacher, *Terminologie*, vol. 1, pp. 42–43, and 2, pp. 53–56. Etymological discussions may be consulted in Lieberman, *Hellenism*, 83, n. 3; Safrai, *Literature of the Sages*, 121–122; and most recently, Abusch, "Alaktu and Halakhah,"

pp. 15–42. While Abusch's etymological case is very provocative, my own study of the actual usage of *halakhah* in early rabbinic sources shows that, where it does bear the connotation of revealed law, it does so only in the post-Mishnaic sources which have already begun to reflect upon the term in light of theological and jurisprudential concerns.

33. T. Gittin 4:6 offers a ruling that assumes the position staked out in the Mishnah by Rabbi Yose, but it betrays no special knowledge of the dispute between the latter and Rabbi Haninah.

34. For a richer exposition of the metaphorical character of Mishnaic thought on tents than I can offer here, see the discussion in J. Neusner, *History of the Mishnaic Law of Purities*, vol. V, pp. 174–184.

35. I translate the version of MS. Parma De Rossi 138, supported by a number of early witnesses. Albeck's text must be rendered "and decides in accordance with it" instead of "it may rely on it."

36. See references to the "earlier teaching" (*mšnh r'šwnh*), which is then superseded by a more recent ruling, e.g., M. Ketubot 5:3, Gittin 5:6. Relevant here as well are the numerous instances of the formulary: "In early days they would say, . . . but they reconsidered and said, . . ." and its variants, e.g., M. Nedarim 11:12, Gittin 6:5, and M. Sheqalim 7:5. The body of tradition identified as "scribal teachings" (*dbry swprym*) also falls into this category. See the discussion in chapter 5.

37. While *halakhah* may frequently bear the value of the Latin *lex* (legal precept or rule), it is difficult in any context to see it as equivalent to *ius* (principle of justice expressed through rules). But it is precisely the latter sense that informs the various aspects of rabbinic legislation discussed in the present paragraph. Pospisil's anthropological definition of law helps illumine the early rabbinic evidence (*Anthropology of Law*, pp. 37):

> . . . law (*ius*) manifests itself in the form of a decision passed by a legal authority (council, chief, headman, judge, and the like), by which a dispute is solved, or a party is advised before any legally relevant behavior takes place, or by which approval is given to a previous solution of a dispute made by the participants before the dispute was brought to the attention of the authority.

Insofar as halakhic concerns are applied in the resolution of disputes and in matters of social control, they overlap with *ius*. But they range widely beyond these issues as well, and to that extent they pass beyond the phenomenology of law.

38. Scattered Tannaitic references to the jurisdictional range of the High Court are conveniently assembled and compared with nonrabbinic testimonies in E. Schürer, *History of the Jews*, vol. 2, pp. 218–223. More recently, D. Goodblatt, *The Monarchic Principle*, pp. 103–130, has called into doubt the very existence of a Second Temple High Court or Sanhedrin of the kind described in rabbinic literature. That historical issue does not affect this study, since the concern here is precisely with rabbinic perceptions of the past.

39. On the early development of rabbinic conceptions of legislation, see M. Jaffee, "The Taqqanah in Rabbinic Literature," pp. 204–225.

40. The reference is not entirely clear. For possible identifications, see K. Rengstorf, *Die Tosefta*, vol. 6:2, p. 83, n. 34 and S. Klein, *The Book of Jewish Settlement* (Heb.), vol. 1, pp. 122–123.

41. The Mishnah-Tosefta relationship will be discussed in detail in chapter 6, where a full set of bibliographical references will be provided.

42. The Mishnah's picture of *halakhah* in judicial process bears striking similarities to what the historian of Roman jurisprudence F. Schulz (*History of Roman Legal Science*, pp. 16–17) has described as the pre-Hellenistic responsa on sacerdotal law within the courts of the archaic Roman pontifices:

When the question among the priests was whether a contemplated sacral act was admissible and, if so, in what form, the opinion would be in the nature of advice on action to be taken. . . . But the priests might also be prayed to pronounce on the legality of an act already performed; in this case the answer would be in the nature of a judicial pronouncement, though not of a judicial sentence in the legal sense.

If one substitutes the Sages' court for that of the Roman priests, the procedures and results correspond to the Mishnah's own assumptions. The rabbinic court passes judgment upon a question of ritual, the *halakhah*, but its judgment, while it may yield *halakhah*, need not be conceived as a law.

43. The four examples I have found (T. Berakhot 4:15, Berakhot 5:2, Pasha 10:12, Yom Tov 2:12) depict meals presided over by Rabban Gamaliel II or his son, Rabban Shimon b. Gamaliel, and are thus set at the beginning and end of the Yavnean Academy.

44. I find three such reports: T. Berakhot 1:4, Demai 5:24, and Hagigah 3:33. All involve figures central in the post-70 decades at Yavneh, e.g., Rabban Gamaliel, Rabbi Aqiva, Rabbi Tarfon, Rabbi Ishmael, and Rabbi Eleazar b. Azariah.

45. The relevant materials, all involving either the pre-70 Sanhedrin or early Yavnean contexts, are T. Megillah 3:5, Sanhedrin 7:7, 7:10, Yevamot 14:5, Sotah 7:10, Parah 5:10, and Zabim 1:5.

46. The reports include two concerning Hillel's controversies with unnamed opponents in the Temple courtyard (T. Pasha 4:13–14) and with the House of Shammai (T. Hagigah 2:11). The third involves early Ushan figures, Rabbi Eleazar, Rabbi Meir, and R. Yehudah b. Betyra (T. Nazir 5:1).

47. Those set in Second Temple times are T. Hagigah 2:9/Sanhedrin 7:1 and Sanhedrin 6:6; for the Yavnean period: T. Taaniyot 2:5, Bava Qamma 6:5, Hullin 3:10, Miqvaot 4:6, and Parah 7:4; at Usha: T. Miqvaot 4:7, Niddah 7:1.

48. I cite from the version in T. Hagigah 2:9, in the edition of Lieberman, vol. 2, pp. 383–384. The text is substantially identical to that of T. Sanhedrin 7:1, as found in Zuckermandel, ed., p. 425.

49. The word *hlkh* appears in the T. Sanhedrin passage and in MS Erfurt of T. Hagigah 2:9.

50. MS Erfurt and T. Sanhedrin 7:1 read: *š'ylh*, "question."

51. The phrase "and two Torahs emerged" appears only in MS. Vienna of T. Hagigah 2:9.

52. This formulation of the problem is deeply indebted to the observation of R. Goldenberg, "The Problem of Originality in Talmudic Thought," p. 25: "The early Rabbis' ambivalence toward innovation in the transmission of Torah was part of a more pervasive ambivalence toward their own inventiveness."

53. Cf. T. Yadayim 2:16 (ed. Zuckermandel, p. 683), which includes "the Pairs [*hzwgwt*] and the Prophets" in the chain of tradition linking Rabban Yohanan b. Zakkai's teaching to that of Moses.

54. On the Mosaic court and its relation to rabbinic courts, see M. Rosh Hashannah 2:9.

55. See the comments of S. Safrai in *Literature of the Sages*, pp. 182–183, on the work of other scholars. He nevertheless also tends to submerge the concept of Mosaic *halakhah* within an encompassing context of Oral Torah: "In sum, we may state that *halakhot* which are called '*halakha* to Moses from Sinai' . . . are a part of the Oral Tora which goes hand in hand with the Written Tora; and the latter is seen as given through Moses in his time and thus for the generations" (p. 185).

Safrai is certainly correct regarding the later rabbinic conception, as discussions in, e.g., P. Peah 2:6, 17a and B. Men. 29b show. Indeed, in the Talmuds the term "a *halakhah* of Moses from Sinai" is used rather indiscriminately as a tool of jurisprudence. Thus, for example, rulings that, in the Mishnah itself, are revised by the formula "they really said . . ." are taken to be Mosaic *halakhot* (e.g, B. Berakhot 20b; cf. Y. Shabbat 1:4, 3b).

For further discussion of this complex problem, see the foundational studies of: S. Kaatz, *Die Mündliche Lehre und ihr Dogma*, vol. 1, pp. 4–15, and vol. 2, pp. 44–59; W. Bacher, *Tradition und Tradenten*, pp. 33–46; P. Schäfer, "Das Dogma von der Mündlichen Torah im Rabbinischen Judentum," pp. 153–197, and the recent treatment in J. Neusner, *What, Exactly, Did the rabbinic Sages Mean by "Oral Torah"?* pp. 1–2, 6–11.

56. The Mishnah and Tosefta are virtually identical at units 1–2. Unit 3, which supplies the judgment over the Shammaite victory, appears only in the Tosefta and parallels cited at Y. Shabbat 1:4, 3c and B. Shabbat 17a. See the textual discussion in S. Lieberman, *Tosefta Ki-fshuta*, vol. 3, pp. 13–15.

57. In the same passage Abba Shaul argues that the practice is in fact a clear biblical commandment (Lev.23:39). See the comment of J. Neusner, *What, Exactly, Did the rabbinic Sages Mean by "The Oral Torah"?* p. 18.

5. The Ideological Construction of Torah in the Mouth

1. Of the numerous literary, rhetorical, and traditio-historical studies of this material, the following are particularly helpful: E. Bickerman, "La chaine de la tradition Pharisienne," pp. 153–165; M. Heer, "Continuity of Tradition in the Transmission of Torah," pp. 43–56; J. Neusner, *The Mishnah*, pp. 206–214; idem, *What, Exactly, Did the Rabbinic Sages Mean By, "The Oral Torah"?* pp. 27–31; M. Lerner, "The Tractate Avot," pp. 263–276; and A. Saldarini, *Scholastic Rabbinism*, pp. 9–23. See also the brief but penetrating comments of S. Fraade, *From Tradition to Commentary*, pp. 69–72, and M. Swartz, *Scholastic Magic*, pp. 175–178. H. Strack and G. Stemberger, in *Introduction to Talmud and Midrash*, pp. 120–121, provide an excellent introductory bibliography. This has unfortunately been omitted in the second edition under Stemberger's name.

2. There remains no consensus regarding the precise point at which Avot came to be routinely circulated within the larger mishnaic corpus, or why it was included among the other tractates in the order of Damages. See G. Stemberger, *Introduction to Talmud and Midrash*, pp. 122–123.

3. The ascription of this post-mishnaic compilation to a Tanna of the late second century has long puzzled scholars. For a survey of scholarly opinion regarding the relation of Avot de-Rabbi Nathan to the Mishnah, the relations of its two versions to each other, and other questions, see M. Lerner, "The External Tractates," pp. 370–378. S. Schechter's standard edition of the two versions of Avot de-Rabbi Natan (published in 1887) has recently been reissued with an introduction by M. Kister. These summarize his more extensive text- and tradition-critical study, M. Kister, *Studies in Avot de-Rabbi Nathan*.

4. See, for example, E. Rivkin, *A Hidden Revolution*, p. 129, and D. Zlotnick, *Iron Pillar Mishnah*, p. 145. Compare the more nuanced view of D. Rozental, "Oral Torah and Torah from Sinai," pp. 455–460, who accepts the antiquity of the term but recognizes that its implications were not fully worked out until the post-mishnaic period. Unlike Avot, Avot de-Rabbi Natan is familiar with the terminology of Written and Oral Torah. See version A15 and version B29 (ed. Schechter, p. 61), paralleled by B. Shabbat 31a. It is all the more puzzling, therefore, that Avot de-Rabbi Natan A1 makes no mention of the Oral Torah in its opening gloss of M. Avot's chain of tradition: "Moses was sanctified in the cloud and received Torah from Sinai" (ed. Schechter, p. 1).

5. S. Fraade, *From Tradition to Commentary*, p. 71.

6. The quotation is from J. Levenson, "The Sources of Torah," p. 570.

7. Compare J. Neusner, *What, Exactly, Did the Rabbinic Sages Mean By "The Oral Torah"?* pp. 3–4.

8. This is the commonly attested reading. Cf. the proposed emendation of B. Hagigah 11b: *hn whn* ("these and those"). The Bavli's revision is born of discomfort with the Mishnah's acceptance of certain bodies of *halakhah* as more "essential" than others, but there is little reticence on this point in Tannaitic materials. See, e.g., T. Shabbat 2:10, in which Rabban Shimon b. Gamaliel points out that "the *halakhot* of Temple Dedications, purification offerings, and tithes are the essence of the Torah [yet] are transmitted to undisciplined Jews." In M. Avot 3:18 the honorific status of "essence of the *halakhot*" is applied to the obscure and difficult topics of bird offerings and the calculation of the onset of menstrual impurity. For further discussion of these and other sources, see S. Lieberman, *Tosefta Kifshutah*, vol. III, p. 470.

9. This pronouncement will indeed trouble later compilers of the Talmuds (Y. Hagigah 1:8, 76c–d, B. Hagigah 10a; cf. B. Nazir 62a). Both Talmuds begin their discussions of M. Hagigah 1:8 by quoting an identical Tannaitic tradition, in the names of Rabbi Eliezer and Rabbi Yehoshua, to the effect that the Sages' capacity to release vows has at least some scriptural support. Indeed, the Yerushalmi selects M. Hagigah 1:8 as one of the three occasions on which it cites the tradition of Rabbi Yehoshua b. Levi, that whatever a seasoned disciple will in the future recite before his master was already disclosed to Moses on Sinai. The entire context of this passage will be discussed in chapter 7.

10. See Weiss-Halivni, *Sources and Traditions*, vol. 2, pp. 590–593.

11. In later rabbinic tradition, however, it is argued that the *halakhot* are the essence of *torah* whether or not they are scripturally grounded. See B. Hagigah 11b and the comment of Rashi ad loc. Cf. the discussion of M. Gruber, "Oral Torah", pp. 115–116.

12. For other Mishnaic examples that equate rabbinic teaching with *torah*, see M. Peah 1:1, Sotah 3:4, and Sanhedrin 11:2. While Avot is clearly the richest expression of the inclusionary usage of *torah*, Neusner has tended to overstate its singularity in this regard. See J. Neusner, *Torah*, pp. 31–56. Cf. Gruber, "Oral Torah", p. 116, n. 19.

13. Minor textual variants at unit 4 in particular do not affect our interpretation. See the textual apparatus supplied by Lieberman, *Tosefta*, vol. 2, pp. 139 and 379.

14. I omit at this point a later and irrelevant interpolation in the name of Rabbi Yehoshua regarding the origins of the first thongs. It appears in both parallels of this passage and so has strong textual attestation, but its point here is obscure. See S. Lieberman, *Tosefta Ki-fshuta*, vol. 3, p. 469.

15. The concern with grounding specific halakhic prescriptions in scriptural precedent seems to preoccupy tradents of Toseftan materials more than the Mishnah's compilers. Thus R. Tarfon is portrayed in astonished admiration for R. Aqiva: "I heard [the *halakhah*] but could not interpret it, while your exegesis turns out [independently] to conform to the *halakhah!*" (T. Zevahim 1:8). Similarly, R. Aqiva of R. Eliezer: "Three hundred *halakhot* would R. Eliezer derive [from this verse]" (T. Sanhedrin 11:5).

16. An excellent overview of the problem is offered by S. Fraade, "Literary Composition and Oral Performance in Early Midrashim."

17. I do not suppose, incidentally, that these texts accurately represent the original exegetical reasoning by which Mishnaic or Toseftan norms were first generated from scriptural study. This view, proposed in its classic form by J. Lauterbach (*Rabbinic Essays*, pp. 163–256) is no longer tenable. Rather, I am more inclined to Neusner's view that these texts function to legitimate halakhic norms by demonstrating their scriptural genealogy.

For the range of thought on this issue, the following are representative: E. Z. Melammed, *The Relationship of the Halakhic Midrashim to the Mishnah and Tosefta*; J. Neusner, *Midrash in Context*, pp. 21–52; D. Weiss-Halivni, *Midrash, Mishnah, and Gemara*, pp. 18–65; S. Fraade, *From Tradition to Commentary*, pp. 25–68; D. Boyarin, *Intertextuality and the Reading of Midrash*, pp. 22–38.

R. Reichman, *Mishnah und Sifra*, has now reopened the possibility that the extant Mishnah knows and reframes material now found in Sifra to Leviticus. See, most recently, the concluding chapter of D. Nelson, *Textuality and Talmud Torah*, pp. 173–218, on the role of Mishnaic and Toseftan materials in Mekhilta de-Rabbi Shimon b. Yohai.

18. The only genuine Toseftan example, as far as I can determine, is T. Sotah 7:20–21 (in the versions of both the Erfurt and Vienna manuscripts reproduced by Lieberman, *Tosefta*, vol. 4, pp. 199–200).

19. Variants do not appreciably change the point. See the edition of Horovitz-Rabin, p. 157, nn. 7–8, and that of Lauterbach, vol. 2, p. 96.

20. The theme is particularly rich in Sifre to Deuteronomy. See Sifre to Deuteronomy 32:10, par. 313 (Finkelstein, p. 355):

> "He caused him to understand"—the Ten Utterances. This teaches that when the Word proceeded from the mouth of the Blessed Holy One, Israel would see it and become enlightened by it, and know how much *midrash* was contained within it, and how much *halakhah* was contained within it, and how many logical deductions were contained within it, and how many exegetical inferences were contained within it.

Compare also Sifre to Deuteronomy 11:22, par. 48 (Finkelstein, p. 113):

> "For not by bread alone shall a person live" (Dt. 8:3)—this refers to *midrash*.

> "but rather, by all that comes from the mouth of YHWH"—these are the *halakhot* and *aggadot*.

21. See p. 408, n. 12, to his edition of Sifre Deuteronomy.

22. It is entirely possible that he was inspired by an exegesis of the sort attested in Sifra Behuqotai to Lev. 26:46. See the discussion below.

23. J. Neusner, *Rabbinic Traditions About the Pharisees Before 70*, vol. 1, p. 343, assigns this story to Rabban Gamaliel I (early first century CE) without explanation, and S. Kanter, *Gamaliel II*, omits it, also without explanation, from his discussion of the Yavnean Gamaliel's traditions. There are two grounds for assigning the story a Yavnean setting. First, a parallel is told with Rabban Yohanan b. Zakkai as the rabbinic hero (Midrash Tannaim, ed. Hoffman, p. 215), suggesting a Yavnean milieu for the narrative. Second, Sifre Dt. 344 knows of a second case in which Rome sends two officials "to Rabban Gamaliel of Usha" to study "*mishnah, midrash, halakhot*, and *aggadot*." I cannot explain the puzzling mention of Usha in connection with Rabban Gamaliel. But the narrator clearly has Rabban Gamaliel II in mind. Moreover, the subject of the tale—Gentiles who approach a Sage in order to learn Torah—is similar to that of the Sifra passage.

P. Schäfer, "Das Dogma von der Mündlichen Torah," pp. 181–183, argues on the basis of these passages and others involving Hillel and Shammai (e.g., B. Shab. 31a, Avot de-Rabbi Nathan, A15/B29) that the conception of two Torahs emerged in the social setting of controversies with non-Jews in the Yavnean period.

24. The term appears in the following Tannaitic compilations:

Mishnah: Orlah 3:9; Yevamot 2:4, 9:3; Sanhedrin 11:3; Parah 11:5–6; Tohorot 4:7 + 11; Yadayim 3:2.

Tosefta: Taaniyot 2:6; Yevamot 2:4, 3:1 (/M. Yevamot 2:4); Qiddushin 5:21; Eduyyot 1:1 + 5; Kelim Bava Batra 7:7; Parah 11:5; Niddah 9:14; Miqvaot 5:4; Tevul Yom 1:10.

Sifra: Shemini per. 2:11; Shemini par. 8:5; Zabim par. 2:13; Emor par. 10:11 (/M. Orlah 3:9); Behar per. 4:5.

Sifre Numbers: Behaalotekha 73, 75.

Sifre Deuteronomy: Re'eh 115, Shofetim 154.

For discussion of the general problem of the "words of the Scribes," see S. Safrai, *The Literature of the Sages*, pp. 148–153; E. Urbach, *The Halakhah*, pp. 102–105; and E. P. Sanders, *Jewish Law from Jesus to the Mishnah*, pp. 115–117. My own discussion here is drawn from an earlier article, M. Jaffee, "Halakhah as Primordial Tradition," pp. 99–107. I wish to thank the original publisher, New York University Press, for permission to use this material.

25. Compare on this point the comments of E. Urbach, *The Halakhah*, pp. 102–103.

26. The Hebrew, *'rlh* literally refers to the foreskin. In rabbinic usage the term is extended metaphorically to tree-fruit prior to its fourth year of bearing. The metaphor is grounded in Lev. 19:23: "You shall regard its foreskin, its fruit, as uncircumcized [*w'rltm 'rltw 't pryw*]."

27. The exegetical grounds are supplied at Sifra, Emor, par. 10:11, which itself depends upon a formulation attested at M. Qiddushin 1:9. This is an excellent example of what later talmudic jurisprudence terms a ruling bearing the authority of the Torah (*d'oraita*). In talmudic contexts, the term encompasses both explicit scriptural proscriptions and those exegetically derived from those proscriptions. For discussion, see J. Roth, *The Halakhic Process*, pp. 13–48, and M. Gruber, "The Meaning of *'orait'a* in the Babylonian Talmud," pp. 25–33.

28. Y. Orlah 63b and B. Qiddushin 38b–39a record a dispute over this issue between the mid-third-century Amoraim, Samuel and Rabbi Yohanan. The former holds that *halakhah* in this context refers simply to local custom (*hilkhot hamedinah*: cf M Baba Metzia 7:8), while the latter maintains that the reference is to Mosaic *halakhah* received at Sinai. Neither party expresses an opinion on the import of *divrei soferim*, yet the ensuing analysis in Qiddushin 39a (bottom) makes it clear that, for the editors of this discussion at least, the "scribes" are merely Sages who enacted an edict against diverse kinds in the diaspora (*bhwṣ l'rṣ nmy gzrw bhw rbnn*). As I hope my own discussion makes clear, this editorial understanding must be seen as already reflecting the process by which various sources of tradition have come to be homogenized into a monolithic *halakhah* stemming from the distant past yet incorporating within it mechanisms of innovation reserved for the Sages.

29. Cf. Mekhilta de-Rabbi Ishmael, Mishpatim, par. 2: The Torah said [of the servant who prefers servitude to freedom (Ex. 21:6)]: "And his master shall pierce his ear with an awl"; but the *halakhah* said [he does so] with any tool.

The Palestinian Talmud intensifies the point by having the *halakhah* "supersede" the Torah (*'wqpt*: Y. Qiddushin 59d). Cf. B. Sotah 16a ("uproot," *'wqrt*).

30. One oft-cited exception, upon examination, turns out to be no exception at all. M. Sanhedrin 11:3 states, "The words of the scribes bear greater sanction than the words of the Torah." In the context of the passage, the point is that, as far as the teaching of the law is concerned, misrepresentation of scribal teaching is more serious than a misrepresentation of scriptural law, for scriptural law is publicly known while scribal teaching remains the professional, therefore private, possession of the scribes. It is in this light that I interpret the other early passage, this from T. Taaniyot 2:6/T. Yevamot 2:4, which holds that scribal teachings should be more strictly enforced than scriptural rules. The reason is that they are less known and bear lesser intrinsic authority. In general, my position accords with that of E. Sanders, *Jewish Law from Jesus to the Mishnah*, pp. 115–117. For a diametrically opposed interpretation of this matter, which identifies scribal teachings with Sages' halakhic traditions, see S. Safrai, *The Literature of the Sages*, p. 151.

31. The scriptural ruling deems food unclean if, after it has been dampened with water, it comes into contact with a primary source of uncleanness, such as a dead animal

(Lev. 11:35). The scribal tradition adds to this rule a more attenuated degree of uncleanness befalling food that has come into contact with the unclean food (M. Zabim 5:12). Such food is intended here.

32. In contrast to Lev.11:34, which knows only that water can be a conveyer of uncleanness, scribal tradition includes other liquids: dew, wine, oil, blood, milk, and bee honey (M. Makhshirin 6:7). Sifra to Leviticus, Shemini, per. 11:6–7, provides the exegetical inferences behind the ruling. See also B. Niddah 7b, s.v. *wrbnn hw' dgzrw gzrh*.

33. B. Shabbat 14a, commenting on M. Zabim 5:12, explains this form of uncleanness as a precaution instituted to discourage laxity with regard to proper ritual immersions for purification.

34. On this identification and others, see the classical commentaries to M. Tohorot 4:11 ad loc.

35. The theme seems to be as old as the Book of Jubilees, in which Abraham is depicted as celebrating the Festivals of Sukkot (Jubilees 16:20–31) and Shavuot (Jubilees 22:1–9). See also his blessing for Jacob (Jubilees 23:16) in which he implores his son to avoid eating with Gentiles.

Closer to the rabbinic period, the first century Jewish exegete, Philo wrote that Abraham performed the commandments "not taught by written words, but unwritten nature gave him the zeal to follow where wholesome and untainted impulse led him" (On Abraham 275, pp. 133–135).

S. Sandmel, *Philo's Place in Judaism*, pp. 30–95, surveys the image of the founding patriarch of Judaism in the Palestinian and diaspora literature of the Second Temple period. On pp. 354–356 he notes the similarity in the Philonic and later Toseftan appreciation of Abraham's pre-Sinaitic piety. See also the extensive note of L. Ginzberg, *The Legends of the Jews*, vol. 5, p. 259.

36. I cite the text of ed., Lieberman, vol. 3, p. 299.

37. I cite the text of ed., Zuckermandel, p. 344.

38. The printed text reads: "all the same are the Torah in Script and Torah in the Mouth." I cite the manuscript versions recommended by R. Rabbinowicz, *Diqduqei Soferim*, ad loc., n. 90. In an important article, M. Gruber points out that the version of the printed text is a medieval revision grounded in Rashi's commentary on Gen. 26:5 (M. Gruber, "Rashi's Torah Commentary," pp. 225–228).

39. There is, overall, a tendency in the Talmud Yerushalmi to identify the Sages with the ancient scribes. This identification then permits scribal teaching and halakhic tradition to appear identical. Thus Y. Eruvin 5:1, 22c, offers a discussion of the seven names of the Temple's Eastern Gate. One of these names, the New Gate, is explained as follows: "For there the Scribes declared innovations in the *halakhah*." Here scribes are assimilated to the role of Sages in developing and extending halakhic norms. Cf. Y. Sheqalim 5:1, 48c, with regard to Ezra, who is portrayed as uniting within himself the traditions of both scribes and Sages: "just as he counted the words of the Torah, so too did he count the words of the Sages."

6. Composing the Tannaitic Oral-Literary Tradition

1. Indeed, S. Lieberman (*Hellenism in Jewish Palestine*, pp. 86–88, 207–208) long ago acknowledged the use of written *aides de memoire* in rabbinic circles, although he insisted that official publication of such texts as the Mishnah were exclusively oral. He was, however, vague on the question of composition. The rare depictions of the Tannaim editing traditions are also unclear with regard to the methods of compiling those traditions into larger collections. See the descriptions of Rabbi Aqiva's activities in T. Zabim 1:5 and Avot de-Rabbi Nathan A18, and the discussions of S. Lieberman, *Hellenism in Jewish Palestine*, pp. 91–93;

J. Faur, *Golden Doves with Silver Dots*, pp. 84–89 and 98–99; and D. Zlotnick, *Iron Pillar Mishnah*, pp. 31–32. For criticism of Lieberman's account in particular, see M. Jaffee, "How Much Orality in Oral Torah?" pp. 68–69.

More recently, cogent arguments have been offered for the early existence of written recensions of the Tosefta (Y. Elman, *Authority and Tradition*, pp. 275–281) and Sifra to Leviticus (S. Naeh, "Structure and Divisions of the Midrash Torat Kohanim").

2. M. Gruber, "The Mishnah as Oral Torah," pp. 112–122, has shown that the Mishnah itself includes no claim that it constitutes a redacted text of the original Oral Torah. The dual meaning of the Hebrew term, *mšnh*—as "repeated tradition" in general or as a particular compilation of such tradition, e.g., the Mishnah—can at times lead to confusion in this regard. For example, the idea that "many *halakhot* were given to Moses on Sinai and all are embedded in *mšnh*" (Y. Peah 2:6, 17a and parallels; see chapter 7) refers to "repeated tradition" in the generic sense. So too B. Eruvin 54b's well-known answer to the question, "How was *mšnh* arranged?" See chapter 7 for extensive discussion of Y. Peah 2:6. In both cases the referent of *mšnh* is the halakhic tradition in general out of which specific compilations emerge, rather than the redacted Mishnah in particular.

3. The fundamental medieval source on the media for transmitting the earliest rabbinic literature is the responsum of the tenth-century Geonic authority Rabbi Sherira b. Hanina. He supplied the first coherent history of rabbinic literary tradition. The text has survived in two recensions, usually identifed as the "French version" and the "Spanish version." See the edition of B. Lewin, *Iggeret Rav Sherira Gaon*. M. Schlütter, *Auf welche Weise wurde die Mishna geschrieben?* pp. 5–21, has criticized this picture of the text's recensional history and redefined the manuscript traditions as the "B-recension," based upon MS Berlin (Lewin's "French recension"), and the "Y-recension," based upon the 1566 publication of the text in Sefer HaYuhasin.

The two versions of Rav Sherira's letter differ significantly on the question of the role of writing in rabbinic tradition. The B-recension tends to favor a purely oral model of the transmission of the Mishnah and the Talmud until nearly post-talmudic times, whereas the Y-recension tends to claim early written versions (e.g., Lewin's text, pp. 21–23, and Schlütter's translation, pp. 80–81). The B-recension, circulating more widely in Ashkenazic European culture, influenced Ashkenazic scholarship to propose an exclusively oral process of literary redaction (e.g., Rashi, B. Bava Metsia 86a, s.v., *swp hwr'h*; B. Shabbat 13b, s.v., *mgylt t'nyt*); correspondingly, Sephardic scholars were most influenced by the Y-recension and proved more amenable to imagining writing as a medium for the composition and transmission of texts of Oral Torah (e.g., Maimonides' "Introduction" to his Mishneh Torah).

For further discussion of Rav Sherira's conception of the form of editing and transmitting the Mishnah and other rabbinic texts, see M. Schlütter, "Was the Mishnah Written?" pp. 213–218.

4. Influential works arguing for an essentially oral composition and transmission of the Mishnah include B. Gerhardsson, *Memory and Manuscript*, pp. 79–84, and D. Zlotnick, *Iron Pillar Mishnah*, pp. 72–106.

5. The role of writing in the preservation of early rabbinic tradition, however, has been recognized since the beginnings of the modern study of rabbinic literature, as in the work of Z. Frankel, *The Methods of the Mishnah*, pp. 228–231. Further refinements of this position can be found throughout the twentieth century in the work of J. Kaplan, *The Redaction of the Babylonian Talmud*, pp. 261–280; L. Finkelstein, "The Transmission of Early rabbinic Tradition," pp. 224*–244*; C. Albeck, *Introduction to the Mishnah*, pp. 111–115; Y. Epstein, *Introduction to the Text of the Mishnah*, pp. 692–706; J. Weingreen, "Oral Torah and Written Records," pp. 76–96; S. Safrai, "Oral Tora," pp. 72–75.

From the present perspective, there are two key flaws in all of these works. The first is their viewing the passage from oral tradition to written text in evolutionary terms, such that an oral tradition "reduced to writing" ceases to shape the written text's history of transmission and interpretation. The second is their assumption concerning the essential reliability of the written text as a neutral medium for preserving the tradition in unchanged form.

Jacob Neusner's many studies of the Mishnah and other rabbinic texts offers strong criticisms of the second of these assumptions, but he waffles on the nature of the Mishnah's composition and transmission. While usually accepting S. Lieberman's model of the oral composition and promulgation of the Mishnah (e.g., *Oral Tradition in Judaism*, p. 74), Neusner often represents writing as crucial to the process of Mishnaic composition (e.g., *Introduction to rabbinic Literature*, p. 24). I have commented more extensively on Neusner's conception of oral tradition in M. Jaffee, "Oral Tradition in the Writings of rabbinic Oral Torah" (2000).

6. The chapter revises and significantly amplifies an earlier article, "Writing and rabbinic Oral Tradition: On Mishnaic Narrative, Lists and Mnemonics," *Journal of Jewish Thought and Philosophy* 4 (1994), pp. 123–146.

7. Contemporary theory in the study of orality and literacy has moved substantially beyond the positing of an exclusively oral register of poetic composition that is lost as soon as written text versions enter the stream of tradition. Instructive general discussions of the mutual impact of written and oral tradition may be consulted in R. H. Finnegan, *Literacy and Orality*, and J. Goody, *The Interface Between the Written and the Oral*. For more particular case studies, see, for example, the interactive models worked out by F. Bäuml, "Medieval Texts and the Two Theories of Oral-Formulaic Composition," pp. 31–49; J. M. Foley, "Word-Power, Performance and Tradition," pp. 275–301; and, most recently, M. Calinescu, "Orality in Literacy," pp. 175–190.

For discussions of the relevance of interactive oral-literary theoretical perspectives for the study of rabbinic literary tradition, see A. Shinan, "Aggadic Literature Between Oral Recitation and Written Tradition," pp. 44–60; S. Fraade, *From Tradition to Commentary*, pp. 18–20 and 188–89; and M. Jaffee, "A Rabbinic Ontology of the Written and Spoken Word," pp. 533–540.

8. The brilliant detective work of L. Finkelstein in distinguishing written from oral tradition in Mekhilta materials is marred, from the present point of view, precisely by the assumption that the oral "catchwords" embedded in various versions of a midrashic discourse ascribed to Rabbi Eleazar of Modin "were fixed before they were reduced to writing" ("The Transmission of Early Rabbinic Tradition," p. 116).

9. I draw this analogy from Calinescu, "Orality and Literacy," pp. 183–184.

10. The twentieth-century study of oral tradition was founded in the study of epic narratives and folklore, and these continue to be an important area of research. See, for example, J. M. Foley, *Traditional Oral Epic*. List-making, often regarded by students of the ancient Middle East as a quintessentially scribal (i.e., literate) phenomenon, is nevertheless very common in nonliterate tribal cultures (J. Vansina, *Oral Tradition*, pp. 151–154) as well as in literate cultures that privilege exclusively oral preservation of sacred tradition, such as that which produced the Vedic ritual and grammatical lists (F. Staal, *Rules Without Meaning*, pp. 369–385).

11. See A. Lord, *The Singer of Tales*.

12. See, for example, C. M. Bowra, *Heroic Poetry*, especially chapter 5, "The Mechanics of Narrative."

13. See R. Alter, *The Art of Biblical Narrative*, and M. Sternberg, *The Poetics of Biblical Narrative*.

14. For cult-centered narratives see, for example, M. Bikkurim 3:2–6, M. Sheqalim 5:1–7:7, M. Yoma 1:1–9:5, M. Taanit 2:1–7, M. Sotah 1:4–4:7, M. Parah 3:1–11, and M. Negaim 14:1–13. For court-centered narratives, see M. Rosh Hashannah 2:1–3:1; M. Sanhedrin 3:6–7, 4:3–6:6, and 11:2.

15. In addition to M. Tamid and M. Middot, which form a linked pair, see M. Yoma 1:1–9:5. Modern scholarship has tended to see the idiosyncratic nature of these tractates as evidence that they were completed in the first century, prior to the emergence of stylistic traits characteristic of the Mishnah as a whole. See, for example, C. Albeck, *Introduction to the Mishnah*, pp. 85–87, and E. Z. Melamed, *Introductory Comments on the Talmudic Literature*, pp. 58–63. Neusner, to the contrary, shows that the narrative materials can all be explained in light of a second-century setting among the tradents responsible for the creation of other Mishnaic literary forms. See J. Neusner, *A History of the Mishnaic Law of Holy Things, Part Six*, pp. 196–210.

On the connections between Yoma and Tamid in particular, see A. Goldberg, "The Tosefta to Tractate Tamid," pp. 18–42. While the proposition that Yoma contains parts of a "lost Tosefta" to Tamid is impossible to test, Goldberg's observations about the relationships of the narrative materials in the tractates remain illuminating. Cf. Y. Epstein, *Introduction to Tannaitic Literature*, pp. 28–29.

16. Albeck's text includes two refrains ("sound of the song/sound of the shofar") omitted from the citation of this passage appearing in Y. Sukkah 5:3, 55b. The Mishnah version presented in B. Tamid 30b contains textual variations and repetitions but otherwise differs little from Albeck. See M. Schachter, *The Babylonian and Palestinian Mishnah Textually Compared*, pp. 317–318, and Albeck, *Six Orders of the Mishnah*, vol. 5, p. 426–427.

17. Later traditions extol the carrying power of Gvini's voice, reporting that King Agrippas was able to hear it from a great distance (B. Yoma 20b: three Persian miles; Y. Sheqalim 5:2, 48d: eight Persian miles; the version of Y. Sheqalim published in the Babylonian Talmud 14a: five Persian miles).

18. R. Eliezer b. Daglai (var.: Elazar b. Dalgai [Y. Sukkah 5:3] or Yose b. Dulgai [B. Yoma 39b]) appears, according to Albeck (*Six Orders of the Mishnah*, vol. 5, p. 427), in no other rabbinic sources. In light of his obscurity, it is difficult to propose a date for this figure. J. Neusner, observing that other glosses in Tamid (3:2: Rabbi Matya b. Shmuel; 5:2: Rabbi Eliezer b. Yaaqov; 7:2: Rabbi Yehudah) bear the names of second-century figures, assigns our authority to the same period (*The Mishnaic Law of Holy Things, Part 6*, pp. 196–197).

19. That is, well beyond the boundary of Jericho. B-Z Segal, *Mishnaic Geography*, pp. 86–87, locates the Mikhvar range in the hill country east of the Dead Sea midway between Moav and Amon, in contemporary Jordan. Rabbinic sources know the area as a site for the pyres that signaled the New Moon (T. Rosh Hashannah 1:17).

20. L. Ginzberg, who regards Tamid as the oldest Mishnaic tractate to survive in its original form, follows Y. Yoma 2:3, 39d/B. Yoma 14b in attributing its authorship to Rabbi Shimon of Mitzpeh, an obscure first-century figure (L. Ginzberg, "The Mishnah Tamid," pp. 284–293). Epstein, *Introduction to Tannaitic Literature*, pp. 29–31, also regards Tamid and Middot as early and related compilations. The views of Ginzberg and Epstein regarding the dating of these tractates and their authorship are vigorously challenged by Neusner, who links their themes to issues of interest exclusively to mid to late second-century authorities (*History of the Mishnaic Order of Holy Things, Part Six*, pp. 203–208).

21. The lack of a Toseftan tractate Tamid makes it impossible to engage in the reconstructive activity I attempt further on in this chapter for the narrative of M-T Parah, chapter 3.

22. The road distance between contemporary Jerusalem and Jericho is about 36 km or 22 miles. The distance is 10 Persian miles in rabbinic computation: B. Yoma 20b/39b.

23. A. Goldberg ("The Mishnah," p. 215) has noted the "poetic" quality of certain Mishnaic passages, such as M. Tamid 7:3 and M. Bikkurim 3:3, without specifying the specific context of such poetic activity.

24. The uniqueness of the stylistic traits of this song within the rabbinic corpus suggests that before us are the preserved remains of a popular tradition which was appropriated by rabbinic participants in the larger Palestinian Jewish culture. I have not, however, found any parallels in non-rabbinic Jewish literature of the period which confirm memories of spectacular sounds or aromas.

To the contrary, the Letter of Aristeas, 92–95, stresses the profound *silence* of the Temple service. Similarly, the description in 3 Maccabees 1:9–10 of Potelemy IV Philopater's entry into the Temple praises its "immaculate and dignified appearance" and "orderliness." The theme of extreme dignity and orderliness is carried through in Josephus, Apion 2:104–108. Nonrabbinic reports of wonders associated with the Temple are spare, e.g., rainfall that occurred only during respites in construction (Josephus, Antiquities, 15:425) or a magnificent fountain of water proceeding from the Temple whose sound "fills the deep channel of the stream as it exits" (Philo the Epic Poet, as cited in Eusebius, *Praeparatio Evangelica* 9.37.1–3; but cf. Ezek. 47:5).

25. Cf. Avot de-Rabbi Nathan, B39, which appends the song to M. Avot 5:5's list of ten miracles associated with the Temple service. Indeed, both L. Ginzberg, "The Mishnah Tamid," p. 40, and Y. Epstein, *Introduction to the Tannaitic Literature*, p. 30, regard the inclusion of this material as an interpolation postdating the completion of the Mishnah as a whole. Their reasoning is grounded in two assumptions: (1) that Tamid was completed by the late first century and (2) that the third-century Amoraic discussants of B. Yoma 39b overlook this material because they do not know it. Neusner's discussions make a first-century setting for the tractate's completion unlikely, and the citation of the passage in Y. Sukkah demonstrates that the material was certainly available to third-century authorities.

26. See J. Goody, *Domestication of the Savage Mind*, pp. 74–111, and J. Z. Smith, "Sacred Persistence," pp. 44–52. An important critique of Goody's overstatements regarding the impact of literacy upon list-making may be consulted in J. Halverson, "Goody and the Implosion of the Literacy Thesis," pp. 307–308.

27. See J. Neusner, *A History of the Mishnaic Law of Purities*, vol. 21, pp. 191–196; he counts 70 lists in the Order of Purities alone.

28. My first publication provided a detailed analysis of this list: M. Jaffee, "Deciphering Mishnaic Lists: A Form-Analytical Approach," pp. 19–34. Unfortunately, at the time of writing that article I was as yet unsensitized to the oral-compositional issues that occupy the discussion here.

29. For comments on the overall structure of M. Eruvin, see J. Neusner, *A History of the Mishnaic Law of Appointed Times, Part Two*, pp. 3–14. I confess to finding less order in the latter part of this tractate than does Neusner. For an attempt to identify its underlying sources, see Y. Epstein, *Introduction to the Tannaitic Literature*, pp. 300–303.

30. Albeck's text is substantially identical to the Mishnah texts of B. Eruvin 101b–104a and Y. Eruvin 25d–26a. But see the following note. T. Eruvin 8:15 and 18–20 (ed. Lieberman) record versions or expansions of items 2, 3, 5, and 6 respectively. T. preserves no version of the list as a whole and ignores M.'s mnemonic patterns. Indeed, on the basis of T.'s materials, one would never suspect that its comments presupposed a formal list such as that found in the Mishnah.

31. Rabbi Yehudah's gloss is missing from the Mishnah version of the Palestinian Talmud, T. Eruvin 8:18, and some early editions of the Babylonian Talmud. See Schachter, *The Babylonian and Palestinian Mishnah Textually Compared*, p. 64.

32, I follow Epstein's rendering of *hgwlh* (*Introduction to Tannaitic Literature*, p. 322).

33. On the basis of the authorities mentioned in the dispute at item 1, Neusner assigns the composition of the whole to the Ushan center of rabbinic learning. See J. Neusner, *A History of the Mishnaic Law of Appointed Times, Part Six*, p. 102.

34. For a historical survey of the development of the study of oral literature and its mnemonic techniques, see J. M. Foley, *The Theory of Oral Composition*. For examples of analytical studies of mnemonic formulae, see the collection of essays gathered in B. Stolz and S. Shannon, eds., *Oral Literature and the Formula*.

The works of J. Neusner remain fundamental for understanding rabbinic mnemonics, for they are the first to classify in a rigorous way the formulaic patterns that underlie Mishnaic diction in particular. See, for example, J. Neusner, *The Oral Tradition in Judaism*, pp. 61–98. A contrasting view of the nature of Mishnaic mnemonics, which ignores formal matters in preference to a focus on rhetoric and repetition, may be consulted in Faur, *Golden Doves with Silver Dots*, and Zlotnick, *The Iron Pillar Mishnah*, pp. 72–106. Since neither Faur nor Zlotnick confronts the massive data collected by Neusner, it is difficult to evaluate their assumptions that the processes they uncover necessarily lie in orally transmitted material.

35. The Mishnah versions at B. Pesahim 35a, 39a and Y. Pesahim 28b are substantially identical with that of Albeck.

36. For examples of some other items that may just as well have fit into these lists' categories, see T. Pasha 2:17–21. The items in M.'s list 1 circulate as a unit for use in new settings at M. Hallah 1:1 and M. Menahot 10:7. Those of list 2 and 4 appear as well at M. Eruvin 3:2.

37. In view of the very basic nature of its concerns, Neusner dates this list as a whole to the Yavnean period (ca. 80–130 CE). This dating is plausible for the origins of the essential mnemonic structure we have identified. Insofar as the intrusions into the list reveal interests that occupy tractate Pesahim as a whole, however, it is likely that the present form dates from the late second century at the earliest, when the tractate received its current literary outlines. Cf. Neusner, *A History of the Mishnaic Law of Appointed Times, Part Six*, pp. 108–109.

38. See the surveys of scholarly opinion in Stemberger, *Introduction to Talmud and Midrash*, pp. 152–156; Goldberg, "The Tosefta," pp. 293–295, and most recently, R. Zeidman, "An Introduction to the Genesis and Nature of Tosefta," pp. 73–75.

39. Neusner's Mishnah commentaries note many instances in which Mishnaic material appears to be embedded in more expansive Toseftan compositions. But he interprets virtually all of these as cases of Toseftan "commentary" on the Mishnah. Recent work on the formation of the Tannaitic tradition, shaped in large measure by awareness of the oral-performative nature of the tradition, has been more flexible in its view of the relationships between discrete passages of the Mishnah and Tosefta. See, for example, S. Friedman, "An Ancient Tosefta (1)," pp. 151–189; idem, "An Ancient Tosefta (2)," pp. 277–288; idem, "The Primacy of Tosefta to Mishnah in Synoptic Parallels," pp. 99–121; A. Houtman, *Mishnah and Tosefta*, pp. 226–228; and E. Alexander, *Study Practices that Made the Mishnah*, pp. 27–39.

The Toseftan studies of A. Goldberg, summarized in "The Tosefta," pp. 285–289, anticipated the more recent development, although Goldberg's theory of diverse Mishnaic and Toseftan "layers" that migrate between the redacted versions of the Mishnah and the Tosefta, is more complex than necessary to describe these relationships. R. Zeidman's recent use of the metaphor "contrapuntal" to describe the Mishnah–Tosefta relation is remarkably apt (R. Zeidman, "An Introduction to the Genesis and Nature of Tosefta," p. 85).

40. The case is made with great persuasive power by E. Alexander in *Study Practices that Made the Mishnah*, with particular reference to tractate Shavuot of the Mishnah and the Tosefta. She concludes: "I am not inclined to say that the Tosefta knew the Mishnah as a text. I believe the Tosephta reproduces long fragments of Mishnaic materials because it

participated in the same oral performative culture that the Mishnah did" (p. 38). The recent Hebrew Union College dissertation of D. Nelson, *Textuality and Talmud Torah*, pp. 120–172, has employed a similar model of oral-performative tradition for understanding the relationships between the Mekhilta de-Rabbi Yishmael and the Mekhilta de-Rabbi Shimon b. Yohai.

The most authoritative statement upon the relation of extant Toseftan materials to oral-performative antecedents is offered now by Y. Elman, "Orality and the Transmission of Tosefta Pisha in Talmudic Literature," pp. 123–180.

41. J. Foley, *The Singer of Tales in Performance*, p. 7.

42. For a far richer account of the presuppositions of the law, I refer the reader to the translation and commentary of Jacob Neusner, upon the foundations of which the present study is built. See J. Neusner, *A History of the Mishnaic Law of Purities*, vol. 9, pp. 44–62, and his summary of Mishnah–Tosefta relationships in vol. 10, p. 81–82. There he describes virtually the entire third chapter of the Tosefta, with the exception of T. Par. 3:1, as a Toseftan commentary on the Mishnah.

43. The appendix to this volume offers a reconstruction of a hypothetical oral-peformative narrative that might have served as a source for the written versions before us.

44. I translate the text of Albeck, *Six Orders of the Mishnah*, vol. 6, pp. 261–266.

45. I leave this term untranslated, as its reference is already under dispute in the mid-third century. According to Rabbi Shimon b. Laqish, it refers to the entire Temple compound, while Rabbi Yohanan claims that it denotes a certain tower within it (Y. Pesahim 7:8, 35a and B. Yoma 2a).

46. Some texts read *prhdryn* ("Parhedrin"). Lieberman (*Tosefta Ki-fshutah*, vol. 4, p. 717) sees here a reference to the Greek *prohedroi*, a gathering place for city officials. In any event, the reference—like that to the Birah—is already unclear to second-century Tannaitic Sages such as Rabbi Yehudah (T. Kippurim 1:1), and confusion continues into the third century (Y. Yoma 1:1, 38c, B. Yoma 8b–9a).

47. I translate the Toseftan text edited by K. Rengstorf, *Die Tosefta*, vol. 6:2, pp. 190–194.

48. J. Neusner, *History of the Mishnaic Law of Purities*, vol. 9, p. 49.

49. This point is made clear in B. Sukkah 21a's slightly expanded citation of M. Par. 3:2. See also Tosefot ad loc., s.v. *yrdw*.

50. MS Vienna: *bny šmwnh 'srh šnh* ("eighteen years old"). I follow the emendation of S. Lieberman, *Tosefet Rishonim*, vol. 3, p. 215, who argues that a scribe misread the letters *zayin* and *ḥet* ("seven," "eight"") as *yod-ḥet* ("eighteen"). Lieberman's emendation was already suggested by the traditional Tosefta commentators, David Pardo (*Hasdei David*, vol. 2, p. 111) and Elijah of Vilna (*Biur haGR"A*, ad loc).

51. According to Tosefot, B. Sukkah 21a, s.v. *whtynwqwt*, the reference is to the disputants, Rabbi Yose haGalili and Rabbi Aqiva, at M. Par. 3:4B.

52. MS Vienna: *mynym. Biur haGra*, following Tosefot (B. Sukkah 21a, s.v. *yrdw*), emends to *ṣdwqym*, "Sadducees." The emendation seems preferable in light of the Second Temple milieu evoked by the narrative. Moreover, rabbinic memory is clear that Sages required the rite to be conducted by a priest who had been purified by immersion on that day (e.g., Sifre Numbers 129 [ed. Horowitz, p. 166, l. 9–10]). This is interpreted as a measure to counter Sadducean arguments that the rite was valid only if performed by a person whose immersion had been followed by the setting of the sun.

On the other hand, most manuscripts of M. Par. 3:3G read *mynym* where the received text has *ṣdwqym*. This suggests that the reading "Sadducees" is a result of censorship. Finally, Neusner's analysis of the various legal strata of M-T Parah should be taken into account:

[I]t is exceedingly difficult to demonstrate that the theory of making the priest unclean just prior to his immersion and then his act of slaughter is known at Yavneh, and the rest of the Yavnean rulings on this subject . . . are clear that the highest degree . . . of cleanness is to be required. Since it is at the time of Nathan that we have explicit reference to the *tevul yom* and clear evidence that the rite is supposed to be carried out not in accord with Temple rules of cleanness . . . , I am inclined to suspect the matter has been anachronistically assigned to Yavneans, primarily through stories. . . . But it was in fact an issue in Ushan or still later times. (J. Neusner, A *History of the Mishnaic Law of Purities*, vol. 10, pp. 151–152)

Neusner here seems to ignore M. Par. 3:7E/T. Par. 3:7–8A, in which all textual witnesses concur in assigning to the Sadducees the view that the cow must be burned by a priest who has completed the entire purification process, including the setting of the sun. In light of this I am inclined to prefer the reading "Sadducees" where there is an uncertainty in the textual tradition. See note 53.

   53. J. Neusner, A *History of the Mishnaic Law of Purities*, vol. 9, p. 51, lists no less than eight manuscripts and early editions that read *mynym*, "sectarians." Rengstorf (*Die Tosefta*, vol. 6.2, p. 26, n. 24) prefers to emend the Mishnah in light of this evidence.

   54. We saw earlier that T. Sanhedrin 7:1/T. Hagigah 2:9 recalled the Rampart as one of two sites in Jerusalem selected for convening courts of three. According to M. Tamid 2:3, the Rampart was a walkway 10 cubits in width that circumscribed the Temple compound itself and, with its appended partition, divided the compound from the surrounding plaza of the Temple Mount. The gate in question was the Eastern Gate, leading into the Women's Court at the eastern extreme of the compound.

   55. See Yom Tov Lipmann Heller, *Tosefot Yom Tov*, M. Par. 3:3, s.v. *wbpth h'zrh*.

   56. See *Hasdei David*, vol. 2, p. 111.

   57. Most likely the Shimon b. Yohanan mentioned in Sira 50:1. He served as High Priest from 219 to 196 BCE (see P. Skehan and D. DiLella, *Wisdom of Ben Sira*, p. 550) and figures prominently in rabbinic memory (see J. Neusner, *rabbinic Traditions About the Pharisees*, vol. 1, pp. 24–59).

   58. Probably the Hasmonean John Hyrcanus, who served as king and High Priest from 134 to 104 BCE. See J. Neusner, *Rabbinic Traditions About the Pharisees*, vol. 1, pp. 160–176.

   59. Probably Elionaeus b. Cantheras, appointed by Agrippa I, ca. 44 CE. See E. Schürer, *History of the Jewish People in the Age of Jesus Christ*, vol. 2, p. 231, n. 14.

   60. Probably Ananel, appointed by Herod, 37–36 BCE. See E. Schürer, *History of the Jewish People in the Age of Jesus Christ*, vol. 2, p. 229, n. 5.

   61. Appointed by Agrippa II, ca. 59–61 CE. See E. Schürer, A *History of the Jewish People in the Age of Jesus Christ*, vol. 2, p. 231. For discussion of the chronological disjunctions of this list of High Priests, see Y. Epstein, *Introduction to the Tannaitic Literature*, p. 45.

   62. *tbwl ywm*. This category of uncleanness is derived from scriptural sources, such as Lev. 22:4–7, which describes the stringencies associated with priestly purity:

If one touches anything made unclean by a corpse, or if a man has an emission of semen, or if a man touches any swarming thing by which he is made unclean or any human being by whom he is made unclean . . . the person who touches such shall be unclean until evening and shall not eat of the sacred donations unless he has washed his body in water. As soon as the sun sets, he shall be clean; and afterward he may eat of the sacred donations, for they are his food.

M-T Tevul Yom explores issues arising from the capacity of the same-day immerser to contaminate food in the highest state of holiness. M-T Parah, at least in their final forms, assume that the priest who burns the cow must be in the status of the same-day immerser. The Sadducees, on the contrary, are recalled as having insisted that the priest be in the fully purified status of "the sun-setter" (*m'wrby šmš*: M. Par. 3:7E/T. Par. 3:7–8A). See n. 52.

63. I abbreviate the text insofar as its details are complex and will distract attention from the primary purpose here.

64. See O. Bertinora's commentary in standard Mishnah editions, M. Par. 3:6, s.v. *wkl mṣ'dyh* and *Biur haGRA* ad loc.

65. So *Biur haGRA* ad loc. and *Hasdei David*, vol. 2, p. 114.

66. MS Vienna: *ṣdwqy 'ḥd*. The first edition of T. and *Hasdei David* read: *'ḥd*, "one whose sun had set." It is hard to explain why the reference to the Sadducee would have been omitted. Therefore it is probably the more secure reading, despite being preserved only in late witnesses.

67. So J. Neusner, *A History of the Mishnaic Law of Purities*, vol. 9, p. 57.

68. J. Neusner, *A History of the Mishnaic Law of Purities*, vol. 9, p. 59.

69. Here I am in essential agreement with the dating of this narrative suggested by J. Neusner, *A History of the Mishnaic Law of Purities*, vol. 10, pp. 149–153.

70. An undisputable example of a written document that enters rabbinic tradition as an authoritative source of "oral" law is Megillat Taanit, the "Fasting Scroll." The Aramaic core of the text is cited at M. Taanit 2:8 as a written document ("Whatever is written in Megillat Taanit . . ."; cf. T. Taaniyot 2:4). At the same time, T. Taaniyot 2:6 assumes that certain fast days mentioned in Megillat Taanit are "words of the scribes which require enforcement." This clearly implies that Megillat Taanit is viewed as standing within the line of rabbinic tradition. Amoraic authorities as well quote the work with the formula, "Our rabbis taught," reserved for texts which Sages assigned as part of the curriculum of oral learning (e.g., B. Taanit 17b). An exhaustive list of rabbinic citations of Megillat Taanit may be consulted in H. Lichtenstein's edition of the work.

7. *Torah in the Mouth in Galilean Discipleship Communities*

1. See our discussion of the range of this term in chapter 4.

2. According to M. Sokoloff, *A Dictionary of Jewish Palestinian Aramaic*, s.v. *'mwr*, p. 62, the term Amora (*'mwr'*) seems to be rooted in the setting of oral study, in which a designated speaker would repeat loudly what the teacher had taught in a lower voice. Thus a common formula for citing the teaching of a master of the third or fourth centuries is: "Rabbi X directed Y, his Expounder, to declare before the community: Z" (see entries in M. Kosovsky, *Concordance to the Talmud Yerushalmi*, vol. 1, pp. 950–951). The term then was extended to acts of expounding the Repeated Tradition ascribed to Tannaitic authorities. In this context, the Mishnaic interpretations of two or more authorities are commonly transmitted formulaically as follows: "There are two Amoraim, Rabbi A and Rabbi B. One explains X; the other explains Y" (see Kosovsky's concordance, vol. 1, p. 951).

3. J. Faur, in *Golden Doves with Silver Dots*, pp. 100–108, offers a thoughtfully nuanced argument that there was no ban upon the actual writing of halakhic compilations, but only against formally transmitting halakhic traditions from such sources. His discussion depends upon a subtle distinction between a "written" and an "oral" text in which the terms apply not to the material form of the text, but rather to the extent that the text is subjected to the application of hermeneutical rules appropriate to Scripture. In this view, the term "written" when applied to a text:

> expresses a legal status. To begin with, it involves an element of intentionality: whether or not a text was consigned for writing. Once a formal pronouncement was made,

with the purpose of being legally registered, the text acquires the status of being "written," regardless of whether the document was actually written. . . . Conversely, a certain class of statements which the law considers as "not to be consigned for writing" will retain the status of "oral" although an actual document was registered to this effect. The distinction of "written" and "oral" Law follows similar lines. (p. 107)

In any event, we shall soon see that at least some Galilean Amoraim had no scruples against correcting orally transmitted traditions in light of written versions.

4. In what follows I revise and expand observations first published in M. Jaffee, "The Oral-Cultural Context of the Talmud Yerushalmi," pp. 27–61. I wish to thank the original publisher, Mohr Siebeck, for permission to use this material.

5 See G. Stemberger, *Introduction to Talmud and Midrash*, pp. 171–176. Compare H-J Becker, *Die Grossen Rabbinischen Sammelwerke Palästinas*, pp. 149–156.

6. Here I disagree with scholars, such as J. Neusner and A. Goldberg, who characterize the Tosefta as the "Mishnah's first commentary," in terms of which the Yerushalmi and the Bavli are modeled (J. Neusner, *The Tosefta: An Introduction* [Atlanta: Scholars, 1992], p. xvii; A. Goldberg, "The Tosefta," p. 283). As I argued in chapter 6, this position confuses the redacted form of the Tosefta, which certainly supplements the Mishnah, with the constituent materials of which the Tosefta is formed. The Tosefta's literary tradition shares similar patterns of formulation and diction as that of the Mishnah, despite its rather more chaotic organization. The Yerushalmi, by contrast, is constructed of materials that self-consciously distinguish themselves from all Tannaitic literary tradition, including the Mishnah's. Approaching the Mishnaic text from a rhetorical position beyond Tannaitic discourse, the Yerushalmi displays a consciousness of the Mishnah as a cogent source, a literary "voice" distinct from its own. Such a consciousness is rarely evident in the Tosefta. For incisive discussion of the distinctions between the Toseftan appropriation of Mishnaic materials and those in the two Talmuds, see E. Alexander, *Study Practices that Made the Mishnah*, pp. 27–61.

7. On the significance of scriptural midrash as a model for constructing a literary companion to the Mishnah, see J. Neusner, *Midrash in Context: Exegesis in Formative Judaism* (Philadelphia: Fortress, 1983), pp. 53–110, and B. Bokser, *Post-Mishnaic Judaism*, pp. 461–484. For a fine study of the history of Amoraic traditions prior to the period at which they were formulated as companions to either Scripture or the Mishnah, see the recent comparative study of the Yerushalmi and the midrash Genesis Rabbah offered by H-J Becker, *Die Grossen Rabbinischen Sammelwerke Palästinas*. See especially pp. 101–104, 132–133, 146–147.

8. A similar method of reconstructing rabbinic transmissional and editorial methods from the analogous, and rather more fully documented, activities of Greco-Roman literary scholars has recently been employed to great effect by C. Hezser, "The Codification of Legal Knowledge in Late Antiquity," pp. 581–641. Her specific focus is to compare the literary activities of the codifiers of Roman legal codes with those of the compilers of the Yerushalmi.

9. See the excellent collection of essays on this topic gathered by H. Fischel, *Essays in Greco-Roman and Related Talmudic Literature*, and Fischel's "Prolegomenon," which includes a comprehensive bibliography, pp. xiii–lxxvi. Useful observations may also be found in S. Lieberman, *Hellenism in Jewish Palestine*, pp. 20–114: B. Gerhardsson, *Memory and Manuscript*, pp. 59–66; A. Wasserstein, "Greek Language and Philosophy in the Early rabbinic Academies," pp. 221–231.

10. Introductions to aspects of rhetorical education in the Greco-Roman world may be consulted in H. Marrou, *A History of Education in Antiquity*, pp. 194–226, 284–298, and S. F. Bonner, *Education in Ancient Rome*, pp. 65–96, 250–287. For a broader overview of the entire range of educational institutions and relationships in Greco-Roman culture, see L. C. A. Alexander, "Schools, Hellenistic," pp. 1005–1011.

11. The most comprehensive discussion of all aspects of the rabbinic movement in third-to fifth-century Galilee within the comparative perspective of the Roman social and cultural setting is that of C. Hezser, *The Social Structure of the rabbinic Movement.* The earlier study of L. Levine, *The Rabbinic Class of Roman Palestine,* can still be consulted with profit.

Specific institutional comparisons between the rabbinic *bet midrash* and other Greco-Roman educational settings are complicated by the difficulty in distinguishing the Amoraic Galilean institution from Palestinian predecessors or later Babylonian transformations. See, for example, M. Schwabe, "On the Jewish and Greco-Roman Schools", pp. 112–123; B. Gerhardsson, *Memory and Manuscript,* pp. 123–130; A. I. Baumgarten, "The Politics of Reconciliation," pp. 213–225; P. Alexander, "Quid Athenis et Hierosolymis?" pp. 101–123. An important methodological model is the essay of S. J. D. Cohen, "Patriarchs and Scholarchs," pp. 57–85.

12. For general discussion, see: G. Bowersock, *Greek Sophists in the Roman Empire;* G. Anderson, *The Second Sophistic: A Cultural Phenomenon in the Roman Empire;* G. A. Kennedy, *A New History of Classical Rhetoric,* pp. 201–256.

13. An instructive cultural portrait of this group, with particular attention to the role of rhetorical education in its larger political and religious aspirations, is provided by P. Brown, *Power and Persuasion in Late Antiquity,* especially pp. 35–70.

14. Cited from the translation of Wright, *Lives of the Sophists,* 541, pp. 129–131.

15. Even where texts were composed in writing prior to performance, the performance had to appear extemporaneous. See T. Olbricht, "Delivery and Memory," pp. 159–167.

16. My discussion of the *Progymnasmata* depends entirely upon the collection of translated texts and comments compiled in R. F. Hock and E. N. O'Neil, eds., *The Chreia in Ancient Rhetoric.* See their introduction to the genre, pp. 3–58. See also G. A. Kennedy, *A New History of Classical Rhetoric,* pp. 202–217. An important model for applying the material of the *Progymnasmata* to the interpretation of early Christian rhetoric in particular is that of V. Robbins, "Progymnasmatic Rhetorical Composition and Pre-Gospel Traditions," pp. 111–147.

17. Hock and O'Neil, *The Chreia,* p. 83.

18. Hock and O'Neil, *The Chreia,* p. 91.

19. Hock and O'Neil, *The Chreia,* p. 95

20. Hock and O'Neil, *The Chreia,* p. 95

21. Hock and O'Neil, *The Chreia,* p. 97.

22. Hock and O'Neil, *The Chreia,* p. 85.

23. Hock and O'Neil, *The Chreia,* p. 177.

24. See, for example, S. Lieberman, *Hellenism in Jewish Palestine,* pp. 28–82; D. Daube, "Alexandrian Methods of Interpretation and the Rabbis," pp. 165–182; idem, "Texts and Interpretation in Roman and Jewish Law," pp. 240–255; idem, "Rabbinic Methods of Interpretation and Hellenistic Rhetoric," *Hebrew Union College Annual* 12 (1949), pp. 239–264; H. Fischel, "Story and History: Observations on Greco-Roman Rhetoric and Pharisaism," pp. 443–472; idem, "Studies in Cynicism and the Ancient Near East: The Transformation of a Chria," pp. 372–411; idem, *Rabbinic Literature and Greco-Roman Philosophy.*

More recent exemplary studies include: R. Birchman, "Rabbinic Syllogistic," pp. 81–98; B. Visotzky, *Fathers of the World,* pp. 28–40; P. Alexander, "Quid Athenis et Hierosolymis?" (n. 15); A. Avery-Peck, "Rhetorical Argumentation in Early Rabbinic Pronouncement Stories," pp. 49–69; and C. Hezser, "Die Verwendung der Hellenistichen Gattung Chrie," pp. 371–439.

25. A. Avery-Peck, "Early Rabbinic Pronouncement Stories," p. 67, offers a catalogue of Tannaitic *chreiae* conforming to the patterns outlined here by Hermogenes. Avery-Peck's concern is to demonstrate rabbinic use of rhetorical patterns known also to the Second So-

phistic; my own interest, to the contrary, concerns the light that Sophistic usage of written texts, as demonstrated in the oral deployment of memorized *chreiae*, sheds on the mnemonic practices of the Amoraim.

26. Indeed, this particular apothegm had a long life outside of Judaic circles as well. See R. Collins, "The Golden Rule," pp. 1070–1071.

27. For excellent studies of the relation between written and oral sources in the rabbinic preservation of the folklore of Second Temple Judaism, see E. Yassif, "Traces of Folk-Traditions of the Second Temple Period in Rabbinic Literature," pp. 212–233, and P. van der Horst, "Two Notes on Hellenistic Lore in Early Rabbinic Literature," pp. 252–262.

28. The most thorough study of the rabbinic parable (*mashal*) is that of D. Stern, *Parables in Midrash*. He does not discuss the parable sequence of Y. Berakhot 9:1 in his book, but in a personal communication of May 25, 1999, Stern points out that this series falls into the subgenre of the "antithetical mashal" in which a powerful figure representative of the Roman social and political order is contrasted dismissively with the majestic God of Israel. See Stern, p. 23 and p. 94 for a description and examples from other Palestinian Tannaitic and Amoraic literature.

29. For the text, see P. Schäfer and H-J Becker, eds., *Synopse zum Talmud Yerushalmi*, vol. I/1–2, pp. 223–226.

30. In extant texts of the Yerushalmi, this first version is supplemented by thematically related, but formally disconnected materal, which interrupts the sequence of Rabbi Yudan's discourse. I omit this material and pick up the text when it returns to the second of Rabbi Yudan's four versions.

31. This scribal elision appears in all extant manuscripts of the Yerushalmi, as well as the Leiden and Amsterdam editions.

32. For a thorough analysis of patronage in the shaping of the rabbinic movement's relationship to its own disciples and to the Palestinian Patriarchate, see C. Hezser, *The Social Structure of the rabbinic Movement*, pp. 329–449.

33. Cf. B. Temurah 14b: "Rabbi Yohanan and Resh Laqish were perusing a book of *aggadah* on the Sabbath and expounded as follows: 'It is time to act for the Lord; they have abandoned your Torah' (Ps. 119:126)—better that [one letter of] your Torah be uprooted, but let it not be forgotten [entirely] in Israel."

In contrast, Rabbi Yehoshua b. Levi, a predecessor of Rabbi Yohanan, is recalled as a firm opponent of using written aggadic texts (Y. Shabbat 16:1, 15c): "As for *aggadah*—whoever writes it down has no portion [in the Coming World]; whoever expounds [the written copy] will roast [in Gehinnom]; and whoever hears it will receive no reward. . . . As for me, in all my days I never looked in a book of *aggadah* except for once, when I looked and forgot."

34. Compare D. Stern, *Parables in Midrash*, p. 36, on the problem of the oral or written composition of parables in general: "Many of the *meshalim* . . . may therefore be literary creations in the literal sense, composed by editors for readers—who may, however, have included among their ranks *darshanim* who then used the *meshalim* in sermons of their own, delivering them orally to live audiences."

35. See, for example, L. Finkelstein, "Studies in the Tannaitic Midrashim" and "The Transmission of the Early Rabbinic Traditions," both now collected in L. Finkelstein, *Sifra on Leviticus*, vol. V, pp. 151*–190*, pp. 224*–244*; S. Safrai, "Oral Tora," in S. Safrai, ed., *The Literature of the Sages*, pp. 52–72; and D. Zlotnick, *Iron Pillar Mishnah*, pp. 51–71.

B. Gerhardsson, in the first part of *Memory and Manuscript*, has produced the most important study of rabbinic literary tradition grounded in the assumption that writing played at best a minor role in recording the tradition. Gerhardsson's model is a subtle one, in which orally formulated texts in fixed forms served as the foundation of more fluid secondary textual forms, corresponding roughly to "Mishnah" and "Gemara" (see pp. 79–84, 94–98, and

171–181). While Gerhardsson acknowledges that some rabbinic material was written, he follows Lieberman (*Hellenism in Jewish Palestine*, pp. 83–99) in discounting the possibility that writing played more than an episodic role at best in preserving Tannaitic literary tradition.

36. Cited from C. Albeck, ed., *Six Orders of the Mishnah*, vol. 2, p. 235.

37. Cited from ed. Krotoschin, checked against Ms. Leiden.

38. Here and at stich 5 I have deleted material that does not affect the present discussion.

39. Cited from S. Lieberman, ed., *The Tosefta*, vol. 2, p. 236.

40. Cited from *Sifra de-ve Rav*, p. 32a, compared with Codex Assemani 66, p. 134.

41. At this point Codex Assemani 66 enumerates the specific pyres as in the remainder of the text.

42. R. Rabbinowicz, *Sefer Diqduqei Soferim*, Vol. 1, pp. 24–25, records no significant textual variants of this passage in the manuscript tradition of the Bavli.

43. It is likely, as S. Fraade argues in "Literary Composition and Oral Performance in Early Midrashim," that this model applies as well to at least those later Tannaitic circles responsible for the shaping of the Tannaitic midrashic compilations. The Amoraic material, however, seems to me to offer the richer and more easily accessible materials.

44. For discussion of these formulaic terms, see W. Bacher, "Zur Geschichte der Schulen Palästina's im 3. und 4. Jahrhundert. Die Genossen," pp. 345–346; M. Gewirtsmann, "The Concept, Yetiv, and Its Meaning", pp. 9–20; and C. Hezser, *The Social Structure of the Rabbinic Movement*, pp. 337–339. The most exhaustive study concerns the formulaic use of these terms in the Bavli: D. Goodblatt, *Rabbinic Instruction in Sassanian Babylonia*, pp. 199–259.

45. Such personal records of halakhic material are attested among Tannaitic authorities at T. Shabbat 1:13, in which the Yavnean Sage, Rabbi Ishmael b. Elisha, is depicted as writing in his *pinax* an annotation on a halakhic topic. For discussion of the various uses of the *pinax* in rabbinic culture, see Lieberman, *Hellenism*, pp. 203–208.

46. The citation is from MS. Leiden, compared against textual witnesses gathered in P. Schaefer and H.-J. Becker, *Synopse* I/6–11, pp. 176–177. At stich 2 delete *dbry*. At stichs 3 and 5 correct *wdyy > dm'y*. See also S. Lieberman, *Tosefta Ki-fshuta, Part II*, pp. 678–679.

47. Lieberman, *Hellenism in Jewish Palestine*, p. 87, and Faur, *Golden Doves with Silver Dots*, p. 100, seem entirely to miss the significance of this passage as testimony to the legitimacy of introducing a written source into the oral performative tradition.

48. A. Rozental, "Oral Torah and Torah From Sinai, p. 465, offers the suggestive possibility—based upon the absence of the term *aggadah* in a tradition of Rabbi Yohanan's at B. Meg. 19b—that, in Rabbi Yohanan's view, *aggadic* tradition was not considered part of the Oral Torah. Thus only halakhic tradition fell under his proscription against preservation in writing. We will return to this problem later.

The context of this ruling, constructed by the anonymous editor of the *sugya*, is shocked that Rav Dimi would consider discussing a disputed halakhic issue via correspondence with the Babylonian master, Rav Yosef (B. Temurah 14a–b). Indeed, the use of mail in soliciting halakhic information was hardly rare (cf. Y. Gittin 5:3, 46d //B. Ketubot 68a–69b, where halakhic questions are intruded "between the lines" of personal correspondence). The editor of the passage here in B. Temurah has preserved the evidence of the practice of writing down such materials, even as he criticizes it. Here, as in the cases of Y. Maaserot 2:4 and Y. Kilaim 1:1, it is clear that the prohibition against writing is mounted against the widespread practice of recording *halakhot* in written form for various purposes.

Rabbi Yohanan's formulation of his prohibition is an intertextual allusion to T. Berakhot 13:4: "Those who write down blessings are like those who burn the Torah." There the prohibition against writing down blessings is explained as a precaution, lest prayer texts be found in a burning building, from which they may not be spared on the Sabbath. Rabbi Yohanan's appropriation of the epithet "those who burn the Torah" recalls the Toseftan text but radically reorients its original intention and subject matter.

49. Cited from Schäfer, *Synopse*, I/1–2, pp. 300–302. See parallels in Y. Megillah 4:1, 74d, Y. Hagigah 1:8, 76d, and B. Gittin 60a. For discussion, see P. Schäfer, "Das 'Dogma' von der Mündlichen Torah," pp 166–179, and J. Neusner, *What, Exactly, Did the rabbinic Sages Mean by "The Oral Torah"?* pp. 40–46.

50. Scholars of various persuasions, such as M. Gruber ("The Mishnah as Oral Torah," p. 116), D. Zlotnick (*Iron Pillar Mishnah*, p. 146), and J. Neusner (*What, Exactly, Did the rabbinic Sages Mean by "The Oral Torah"?* p. 41) assume that this is a reference to Rabbi Yehudah the Patriarch's redaction of Repeated Tradition, known as the Mishnah per se. My translation seeks to preserve the ambiguity suggested by the well-attested cases in the Yerushalmi in which nouns formed of the roots *šnh* and *tny* clearly refer to Tannaitic traditions whether or not they are found in the compilation ascribed to Rabbi Yehudah the Patriarch. For an example of the term *mšnh* in the nontitular sense, see Y. Ketubot 5:4, 29d, s.v. *mtnytn l' kmšnh r'šwnh*. Cf. A. Kohut, *Aruch Completum*, v. 5, p 279, s.v. *mšnh*. With regard to *mtnyt'* and *mtnytyn* in the Yerushalmi, see M. Sokoloff, *A Dictionary of Palestinian Aramaic*, pp. 337–338, s.v. *mtny*.

51. The parenthetical material is based upon the comments of *Pnei Moshe*, ad loc.

52. I delete here a brief interjection that is not germane to the thrust of the passage.

53. On the interpretation of the term *dyptr'*, in the context of this passage, see S. Lieberman, *Hellenism in Jewish Palestine*, pp. 205–208.

54. Literally, "in accord with these things." I translate following the comments of M. Margoliot, *Pnei Moshe*. Cf. Rashi, B. Gittin 60b, s.v. *ky 'l py*.

55. At Y. Berakhot 1:7, 3b Rabbi Yohanan is ascribed a similar sentiment, except that he substitutes the term *dbry swprym* ("words of the Scribes") for "things in the mouth." This is another example of the phenomenon described in chapter 5, of scribal teachings being assimilated to Sinaitic revelation.

56. The term *wtyq* appears in numerous settings in rabbinic literature and has recently received a thorough philological examination by D. Golinkin in "*wtyqyn*, *wtyq*, and *tlmyd wtyq* in the Book of Ben Sira and the Talmudic Literature." See pp. 55–58 in particular.

57. Recall M. Hagigah 1:8's distinction between halakhic topics that "are like mountains hanging by a hair" and those that "have something upon which to rely." Rabbi Leazar's distinction is broadly parallel, which explains why a version of this passage is redacted at Y. Hagigah specifically for circulation with M. Hagigah 1:8.

58. Note the way the Yerushalmi material is reframed for use in B. Gittin 60b and B. Temurah 14b.

59. Citation is from Midrash Tanhuma, Buber, ed., pp. 58b–59a, with a close parallel at Shemot Rabbah, par. 47:1. See the comments of S. Buber, p. 58b, n. 120, on the relation of the passage in the Buber edition to the printed Midrash Tanhuma. For a presentation of the various parallels and a discussion of their details, see P. Schäfer, "Das 'Dogma' von der Mündlichen Torah," pp. 167ff.

60. Tanhuma: "We too are Israel!"

61. M. Bregman, "Mishnah as Mystery" (Hebrew), *E. E. Urbach Memorial Volume* (forthcoming). I am grateful to Professor Bregman for making his essay available to me prior to its publication.

62. P. Schäfer, in "Das 'Dogma' von der Mündlichen Torah," pp. 196–197, has argued that, in general, the conception of Torah in the Mouth emerges in controversy with pagans but reaches "the highpoint of its development" in controversy with Christianity.

63. See J. Neusner, *Judaism and Christianity in the Age of Constantine*.

64. Philostratus, for example, describes relations between a second-century Sophist, Favorinus, and his student as follows: "[Favorinus] was very intimate with Herodes the Sophist who regarded him as his teacher and father, and wrote to him: 'When shall I see you, and when shall I lick the honey from your lips?' Accordingly at his death he bequeathed to Herodes all the books that he had collected, his house in Rome, and [his slave] Autolecythus" (Lives, 490, p. 25). Here the disciple, like a son, inherits the teacher's worldly possessions.

65. On the theme of philosophical conversion, see A. D. Nock, Conversion, pp. 164–186; R. L. Wilken, "Collegia, Philosophical Schools, and Theology," pp. 268–291; M. Hengel, *The Charismatic Leader and His Followers*, pp. 27–33; I. Hadot, "The Spiritual Guide," pp. 436–359; and P. Hadot, "Forms of Life and Forms of Discourse in Ancient Philosophy," pp. 483–505.

66. See D. Aune, "Prolegomena to the Study of Oral Tradition in the Hellenistic World," pp. 87–90, and R. Valantasis, *Spiritual Guides of the Third Century*, pp. 35–61.

67. For a comprehensive study of the role of discipleship in shaping the nature of the Jesus-sayings traditions in particular, see S. Byrskog, *Jesus the Only Teacher*, pp. 199–402.

68. There is an increasing appreciation of the manifold intersections of patristic and rabbinic theological and exegetical tradition. See J. R. Baskin, "Rabbinic-Patristic Exegetical Contexts in Late Antiquity," pp. 53–80. Recent studies of the rabbinic-patristic discussion over scriptural interpretation in particular include B. Visotzky, *Fathers of the World*, and M. Hirshman, *A Rivalry of Genius*.

69. For useful essays that place ancient Israelite discipleship communities in helpful Mediterranean and Mesopotamian cultural context, see J. Gammie and L. Perdue, eds., *The Sage in Israel and the Ancient Near East*.

70. The penchant, therefore, of Josephus and Philo for describing Jewish communal associations in terms of philosophical discipleship need not be entirely beside the mark. The point has been made quite sharply by S. Mason in "Philosophia as a Group-Designation in Graeco-Roman Society, Judaism, and Early Christianity."

Important comparative discussions of discipleship patterns in early Judaism from the perspective of the transmission of teaching traditions may be consulted in Hengel, *The Charismatic Leader and His Followers*, pp. 16–60, and S. Byrskog, *Jesus the Only Teacher*, pp. 35–196. See also the illuminating discussion of Greco-Roman philosophical discipleship in L. C. A. Alexander, "Schools, Hellenistic," pp. 1007–1009.

71. The most comprehensive collection of source-material on the master–disciple relationship in rabbinic circles is, unfortunately, marred by an ahistorical tendency to posit a single pattern of discipleship throughout the Tannaitic and Amoraic communities. See M. Averbach, *Jewish Education in the Mishnaic and Talmudic Period*, pp. 93–212.

72. For Isocrates' remarks, see p. 130. The Mishnah's placing of the fruits of wisdom in an eschatological framework is, perhaps, a reflex of its rabbinic milieau. The Toseftan textual witnesses seem troubled by the appearance of *hokhmah* (wisdom) where *torah* is to be expected, but they nevertheless attest the Mishnah's choice. Cf. the Toseftan version cited at B. Bava Metzia 33a and the comments of S. Lieberman, *Tosefta Ki-fshutah. Part 9*, p. 168.

73. See C. Hezser, *The Social Structure of the Rabbinic Movement*, pp. 332–352, and L. Levine, *The Rabbinic Class*, pp. 59–69.

74. This entire section is introduced into the margin of MS Leiden by a hand other than that of the original scribe. It appears in virtually identical form in all printed editions of Y. Sheqalim. See Y. Zussman, "The Study Tradition and Textual Tradition of the Talmud Yerushalmi," p. 48.

75. *hwh msmyk w'zyl 'l*: following the emendation of *Qorban HaEdah*, ad loc.

76. Compare the way in which Rabbi Yohanan's opinion is deployed in the briefer narrative setting of Y. Avodah Zarah 3:13, 43b.

77. I omit here a brief narrative in which Rabbi Ammi and Rabbi Assi attempt to appease Rabbi Yohanan by pointing to the negative example of two Sages who, in the midst of a halakhic disagreement, tear a Torah scroll in the synagogue. This negative example fails to appease Rabbi Yohanan, setting the stage for the continuation of the text.

78. The parallel at Y. Berakhot 2:1, 4b/Y. Moed Qatan 3:7, 83c, has a similar example drawn from among the disciples of Rabbi Aqiva that makes the same point.

79. The linkage of this verse to *torah* study in general, and to reviving dead Sages in particular, is a commonplace. See Y. Berakhot 2:1, 4b/Y. Moed Qatan 3:7, 83b. In B. Sanhedrin 90b and B. Bekhorot 31b, unlike in the Yerushalmi, the exegesis is ascribed to Rabbi Yohanan.

80. The version of Y. Sheqalim transmitted in the Babylonian Talmud incorrectly has "Rav Gidol." See Y. Epstein, "Some Details of the Yerushalmi," p. 42.

81. I follow the translation of the Jewish Publication Society. For the midrashic meaning, see later discussion. This exegesis appears as well at Y. Shabbat 1:2, 3a, and Y. Qiddushin 1:7, 61a.

82. I render the text of Y. Sheqalim in accordance with the parallel at Y. Shab. 1:2, 3a. This is followed in the Bavli's version of Y. Sheqalim and is preferable to the garbled text of MS Leiden. Cf. S. Lieberman, *Hayerushalmi Kiphshuto*, pp. 21–22.

83. The parallel to unit 9–10 at Y. Shabbat 1:2, 3a, identifies Rabbi Zeira's interlocutor as Rabbi Ba b. Zavda.

84. See Bereshit Rabbah, 87:11 (ed. Theodor-Albeck, vol. 3, p. 1073). The notion is transmitted in Rabbi Yohanan's name at B. Sotah 36b.

85. I wish I could claim originality for this observation, but while preparing the manuscript of this book for the publisher, I discovered that it was first noticed by S. Lieberman in *Hayerushalmi Kiphshuto*, p. 21.

86. See, for example, R. Valantasis, *Spiritual Guides of the Third Century*, pp. 35–61 and 147–155, and L. C. A. Alexander, "The Living Voice," pp. 221–247.

87. For discussion of how the representation of the orality of tradition enhances the figure of the Sage and the value of discipleship, see S. Fraade, *From Tradition to Commentary*, pp. 13–23, 69–121.

88. Service to the Sage, which provided the opportunity to observe firsthand his embodiment of Torah, is portrayed in Tannaitic texts as a *sine qua non* for the preservation of tradition in its pristine form. Lapses in service, correspondingly, are portrayed as the cause of dispute and social fragmentation.

The classic source is T. Hag. 2:9/Sot. 9:9: "With the increase of disciples of Hillel and Shammai who served insufficiently [*šl' šmšw kl srkn*], disputes increased in Israel, and two Torahs resulted" (ed. Lieberman, vol. 2, p. 384). Note that this most explicit Tannaitic reference to "two Torahs" has nothing to do with the Torah in Script and the Torah in the Mouth! Rather, it refers to discord among halakhic schools of thought.

The versions transmitted in Y. San. 1:4, 19c, and Y. Hag. 1:2, 75d, differ from each other and from T., in minor ways, but each shares a common amplification of the Toseftan version: "who served *their masters* [*rbyhn*] insufficiently." Thus the Yerushalmi's appropriation of the Tannaitic passage renders explicit what is already implicit in its source—the primacy of the master.

For textual discussion see S. Lieberman, *Tosefta Ki-fshutah: Part 5*, pp. 1298–1299. Broader discussion of the role of emulation and personal service to the Sage in the shaping of rabbinic disciples may be found in M. Averbach, *Jewish Education in the Period of the Mishnah and Talmud*, pp. 94–99.

8. Epilogue

1. I translate ed. Krotoschin, checked against MS Leiden.

2. See B. Bokser, *Yerushalmi Pesahim*, p. 485. His rather different rendering of the passage may be consulted on pp. 481–482.

3. M. Jaffee, "A Rabbinic Ontology of the Written and Spoken Word," pp. 540–542.

Bibliography

Editions and Translations of Primary Sources.

Aland, K., et al., eds., *The Greek New Testament.* 3rd ed. (Stuttgart: United Bible Societies, 1983).

Albeck, C., ed., *Six Orders of the Mishnah*, vol. 1–6 (Jerusalem & Tel Aviv: Mosad Bialik & Dvir, 1973).

Allegro, J., ed., *Discoveries in the Judaean Desert of Jordan. V. Qumran Cave 4. I* (4Q158–4Q186) (Oxford: Clarendon Press, 1968).

Baillet, M., et al., eds., *Discoveries in the Judean Desert, 3: Les 'Petites Grottes' de Qumran* (Oxford: Clarendon Press, 1962).

Baumgarten, J., and D. Schwartz, eds. and trans., "The Damascus Document," in J. Charlesworth, ed., *The Dead Sea Scrolls, 2: Damascus Document, War Scroll, and Related Documents* (Tübingen & Louisville: J. C. B. Mohr [Paul Siebeck] & Westminster John Knox Press, 1995), 4–57.

Buber, S., ed., *Midrash Tanhuma*, vols. 1–2 (repr. Israel, n.d.).

Burrows, M., ed., *The Dead Sea Scrolls of St. Mark's Monastery, Vol. 1: The Isaiah Manuscript and the Habakkuk Commentary* (New Haven, CT: American Schools of Oriental Research, 1950).

Charles, R., ed. *The Apocrypha and Pseudepigrapha of the Old Testament*, vols. 1–2 (Oxford: Clarendon Press, 1913).

Charlesworth, J., ed., *The Old Testament Pseudepigrapha*, vols. 1–2 (Garden City, NY: Doubleday, 1983).

———, ed. and trans., "The Rule of the Community," in idem, *The Dead Sea Scrolls, 1: Rule of the Community and Related Documents* (Tübingen & Louisville: J. C. B. Mohr [Paul Siebeck] & Westminster John Knox, 1994), 1–51.

Colson, F., trans., *Philo VI* (Cambridge, MA & London: Harvard University Press & William Heinemann, 1935).

Finkelstein, L., ed., *Sifra on Leviticus According to the Vatican Manuscript Assemani 66 with Variants from Other Manuscripts*, vols. 1–5 (New York: Jewish Theological Seminary of America, 1989–1991).

Fitzmyer, J., *The Genesis Apocryphon of Qumran Cave I: A Comentary.* 2nd ed. (Rome: Biblical Institute Press, 1971).

Friedmann (Ish Shalom), M., ed., *Pesiqta Rabbati* (Repr. Tel Aviv, 1963).

Horgan, M., *Pesharim: Qumran Interpretations of Biblical Books* (Washington, DC: Catholic Biblical Association of America, 1979).

Horovitz, H., ed., *Siphre d'be Rab: Siphre ad Numeros adjecto Siphre Zutta, Cum Variis Lectionibus et Adnotationibus* (repr. Jerusalem: Wahrmann, 1966).

Horovitz, H. and I. Rabin, eds., *Mechilta D'Rabbi Ismael, Cum Variis Lectionibus et adnotationibus* (repr. Jerusalem: Wahrmann, 1970).

Klijn, A. trans., "2 (Syriac Apocalypse of) Baruch," in J. Charlesworth, *The Old Testament Pseudepigrapha*, vol. 1, 615–152.

Knibb, M. A., *The Ethiopic Book of Enoch: A New Edition in Light of the Aramaic Dead Sea Fragments*, vols. 1–2 (Oxford: Clarendon Press, 1978).

Lauterbach, J., ed., *Mekilta de-Rabbi Ishmael. A Critical Edition on the Basis of the Manuscripts and Early Editions with an English Translation, Introduction and Notes*, vols. 1–3 (repr. Philadelphia: Jewish Publication Society, 1976).

Leaney, A., *The Rule of Qumran and Its Meaning: Introduction, Translation and Commentary* (Philadelphia: Westminster, 1966).

Lichtenstein, H., ed., "Die Fastenrolle: Eine Untersuchung zur Jüdisch-Hellenistischen Geschichte," *Hebrew Union College Annual* 8–9 (1931–1932), 331–351.

Lieberman, S., ed., *The Tosefta According to Codex Vienna, with Variants from Codex Erfurt, Genizah MSS. and Editio Princeps (Venice 1521)*, vols. 1–5 (New York: Jewish Theological Seminary of America, 1955–1988).

Marcus, R., trans., *Josephus. Jewish Antiquities. Books XII–XIV* (Cambridge, MA & London: Harvard University Press & William Heinemann, 1933).

Martinez, F., *The Dead Sea Scrolls Translated: The Qumran Texts in English*. 2nd ed. (Leiden: E. J. Brill; Grand Rapids: Eerdman's, 1996).

Metzger, B., trans., "The Fourth Book of Ezra," in J. Charlesworth, *The Old Testament Pseudepigrapha*, vol. 1, 517–559.

Milik, J., ed., *Discoveries in the Judean Desert, 6: Qumran Cave 4, II: I. Archeologie II. Targums (4Q128–4Q157)* (Oxford: Clarendon Press, 1987).

Pardo, D., *Sefer Hasdei David*, 2 vols. (repr. Jerusalem, 1970).

Qimron, E., and J. Strugnell, eds., *Discoveries in the Judean Desert, 10. Qumran Cave 4.V: Miqṣat Ma'ase haTorah* (Oxford: Clarendon, 1994).

Rabbinowicz, R., ed., *Sefer Diqduqei Soferim*, vols. 1–2 (repr. New York: M.P. Press, 1976).

Rengstorf, K., ed., *Die Tosefta: Übersetzung und Erklärung. Seder VI: Tohorot, 2: Para-Mikwaot* (trans. G. Lisowsky and E. Schereschewsky) (Stuttgard: W. Kohlhammer, 1965).

Schachter, M., ed., *The Babylonian and Palestinian Mishnah Textually Compared* (Heb.) (Jerusalem: Mosad HaRav Kuk, 1959).

Schäfer, P., and H.-J. Becker, eds., *Synopse zum Talmud Yerushalmi. Band I/1–2. Ordnung Zera'im: Berakhot und Pe'a* (Tübingen: J. C. B. Mohr [Paul Siebeck], 1991).

———, eds., *Synopse zum Talmud Yerushalmi. Band I/6–11. Ordnung Zerai'im: Terumot, Ma'aserot, Ma'aser Sheni, Halla, 'Orla und Bikkurim* (Tübingen: J. C. B. Mohr [Paul Siebeck], 1992).

Schechter, S., ed., *Aboth de Rabbi Nathan* (repr. New York: Feldheim, 1967).

Schlütter, M., ed. and trans., *Auf Welche Weise Wurde die Mishnah Geschrieben? Das Antwortschreiben des Rav Sherira Gaon* (Tübingen: J. C. B. Mohr [Paul Siebeck], 1993).

Sifra de-ve Rav: Torat Kohanim, with Commentaries of Ravad and Rabbi Shimshon of Sens (Jerusalem: Sifra, 1969).

Sifra or Torah Kohanim According to Codex Assemani 66, with a Hebrew Introduction by L. Finkelstein (New York: Jewish Theological Seminary of America, 1956).

Skehan, P., *The Wisdom of Ben Sira. A New Translation with Notes. Introduction and Commentary by A. A. Di Lella* (New York: Doubleday, 1987).

Skehan, P., et al., eds., *Discoveries in the Judean Desert, 9: Qumran Cave 4, IV: Palaeo-Hebrew and Greek Biblical Manuscripts* (Oxford: Clarendon Press, 1992).

Sokoloff, M., ed., *The Targum to Job from Qumran Cave XI* (Ramat Gan: Bar Ilan University Press, 1974).

Talmud Bavli, Codex Munich 95, vols. 1–3 (Jerusalem: Sefer, 1971).

Talmud Bavli, Vilna ed. with commentaries (repr. Jerusalem, 1975).

Talmud Yerushalmi, MS Leiden, Cod. Scal. 3, with an Introduction by S. Lieberman, vols. 1–2 (Jerusalem: Kedem, 1971).

Talmud Yerushalmi, Krotoschin ed. with brief commentary (repr. Jerusalem: Shiloh, 1969).

Talmud Yerushalmi, Vilna ed. with commentaries (repr. Israel, n.d.).

Thackeray, H. St.J., trans., *Josephus. The Jewish War. Books I–III, Books IV–VI* (Cambridge, MA & London: Harvard University Press & William Heinemann, 1927–1928).

——, trans., *Josephus. The Life. Against Apion I* (Cambridge, MA & London: Harvard University Press & William Heinemann, 1946).

Theodor, J., and C. Albeck, eds., *Midrash Bereshit Rabba. Critical Edition with Notes and Commentary*, vols. 1–3 (Jerusalem: Wahrmann, 1965).

Vermes, G., ed. and trans., *The Dead Sea Scrolls in English.* 4th ed. (London & New York: Penguin, 1995).

Vermes, G., and M. Goodman, eds., *The Essenes According to the Classical Sources* (Sheffield: JSOT Press, 1989).

Wernberg-Møller, P., *The Manual of Discipline. Translated and Annotated with an Introduction* (Leiden: E. J. Brill, 1957).

Wintermute, O., trans., "Jubilees," in J. Charlesworth, *The Old Testament Pseudepigrapha*, vol. 2, 35–142.

Wise, M., et al., eds. and trans., *The Dead Sea Scrolls: A New Translation* (San Francisco: Harper Collins, 1996).

Wright, W., trans., *Philostratus and Eunapius. Lives of the Sophists* (London & Cambridge, MA: Harvard University, 1921).

Zuckermandel, ed., *Tosephta, Based on the Erfurt and Vienna Codices. Revised with a Supplement by S. Lieberman* (repr. Jerusalem: Wahrmann, 1970).

Secondary Literature.

Abusch, T., "Alaktu and Halakhah: Oracular Decision, Divine Revelation," *Harvard Theological Review* 80 (1987), 15–42.

Achtemeier, P. J., "*Omne Verbum Sonat*: The New Testament and the Oral Environment of Late Western Antiquity," in *Journal of Biblical Literature* 109 (1990), 3–27.

Albeck, C., *Introduction to the Mishnah* (Heb.) (Jerusalem and Tel Aviv: Bialik and Dvir, 1964).

Albrektson, B., "Reflections on the Emergence of a Standard Text of the Hebrew Bible," *Supplements to Vetus Testamentum XXIX. Congress Volume* (Göttingen, 1977), 49–65.

Alexander, E., *Study Practices that Made the Mishnah: The Evolution of a Tradition of Exegesis* (Yale University Dissertation, 1998).

Alexander, L. C. A., "The Living Voice: Scepticism Towards the Written Word in Early Christian and in Graeco-Roman Texts," in D. Clines et al., eds., *The Bible in Three Dimensions: Essays in Celebration of Forty Years of Biblical Studies in the University of Sheffield* (Sheffield: JSOT Press, 1990), 221–247.

——, "Schools, Hellenistic," in D. Freedman, *The Anchor Bible Dictionary*, vol. 5, 1005–1011.

Alexander, P., "Orality in Pharisaic-Rabbinic Judaism at the Turn of the Eras," in H. Wansbrough, *Jesus and the Oral Gospel Tradition*, 159–184.

——, "*Quid Athenis et Hierosolymis?* Rabbinic Midrash and Hermeneutics in the Graeco-Roman World," in P. Davies and R. White, eds., *A Tribute to Geza Vermes: Essays on Jewish and Christian Literature and History* (Sheffield: JSOT Press, 1990), 101–123.

Alon, G., *Jews, Judaism, and the Classical World* (Jerusalem: Magnes Press, 1977).

Alter, R., *The Art of Biblical Narrative* (New York: Basic Books, 1981).

Alverez-Pereyre, A., *La Transmission Orale de la Mishnah: Une Methode d'Analyse Appliquee a la Tradition d'Alep* (Paris: Editions Peeters, 1990).

Anderson, G., *The Second Sophistic: A Cultural Phenomenon in the Roman Empire* (New York: Routledge, 1993).

Anderson, O., "Oral Tradition," in H. Wansbrough, *Jesus and the Oral Gospel Tradition*, 17–57.

Aune, D., "Prolegomena to the Study of Oral Tradition in the Hellenistic World," in H. Wansbrough, *Jesus and the Oral Gospel Tradition*, 59–105.

Averbach, M., *Jewish Education in the Mishnaic and Talmudic Period* (Heb.) (Jerusalem: Reuven Maas; Baltimore: Hebrew College, 1983).

Avery-Peck, A., "Rhetorical Argumentation in Early Rabbinic Pronouncement Stories," in V. Robbins, ed., *Semeia 64: The Rhetoric of Pronouncement* (Atlanta: Scholars Press, 1994), 49–69.

Bacher, W., "Zur Geschichte der Schulen Palästinas im 3. und 4. Jahrhundert. Die Genossen," *Monatschrift für die Geschichte und Wissenschaft des Judentums* 43 (1899), 345–346.

——, *Die Exegetische Terminologie der Jüdischen Traditionsliteratur.* vols. 1–2 (repr. Hildesheim: Georg Olms, 1965).

——, *Tradition und Tradenten in den Schulen Palästinas und Babyloniens* (repr. Berlin: de Gruyter, 1965).

Bakker, E., "Activation and Preservation: The Interdependence of Text and Performance in Oral Tradition, " *Oral Tradition* 8 (1993), 5–20.

Balogh, J., "*Voces Paginarum*: Beiträge zur Geschichte des lauten Lesens und Schreibens," *Philologus* 82 (1926–1927), 83–109, 202–240.

Bar-Ilan, M., "Scribes and Books in the Late Second Commonwealth and the Rabbinic Period," in M. Mulder, *Mikra*, 21–37.

——, "Illiteracy in the Land of Israel in the First Centuries CE," in S. Fishbane et al., eds., *Essays in the Social Scientific Study of Judaism and Jewish Society*, vol. 2 (New York: KTAV, 1992), 46–61.

——, "Papyrus," in E. Meyers, *The Oxford Encyclopedia of Archeology in the Near East*, vol. 4, 246–247.

——, "Parchment," in E. Meyers, *The Oxford Encyclopedia of Archeology in the Near East*, vol. 4, 247–248.

Baskin, J., "Rabbinic-Patristic Exegetical Contacts in Late Antiquity: A Bibliographical Reappraisal, in W. Green, ed., *Approaches to Ancient Judaism*, vol. 5 (Atlanta: Scholars Press, 1985), 53–80.

Bauman, R., "Verbal Art as Performance," *American Anthropologist* 77 (1975), 291–311.

——, *Story, Performance, and Event: Contextual Studies of Oral Narrative* (Cambridge: Cambridge University Press, 1986).

Bauman R., and J. Sherzer, eds., *Explorations in the Ethnography of Speaking*, 2nd ed. (Cambridge: Cambridge University Press, 1989).

Baumgarten, A., "The Politics of Reconciliation: The Education of R. Judah the Prince," in E. P. Sanders, ed., *Jewish and Christian Self-Definition: Volume Two. Aspects of Judaism in the Greco-Roman Period* (Philadelphia: Fortress Press, 1981), 213–225.

———, "The Name of the Pharisees," *Journal of Biblical Literature* 102 (1983), 411–428.

———, "The Pharisaic Paradosis," *Harvard Theological Review* 80 (1987), 63–77.

———, "Rabbinic Literature as a Source for the History of Jewish Sectarianism in the Second Temple Period," *Dead Sea Discoveries* 2 (1995), 36–52.

———, *The Flourishing of Jewish Sects in the Maccabean Era: An Interpretation* (Leiden: E. J. Brill, 1997).

———, "The Zadokite Priests at Qumran: A Reconsideration," *Dead Sea Discoveries* 4 (1997), 137–156.

———, "Seekers After Smooth Things," in *Encyclopedia of the Dead Sea Scrolls* (2000).

Baumgarten, J., "The Unwritten Law in the Pre-Rabbinic Period," *Journal for the Study of Judaism* 3 (1972), 7–29.

———, "Form Criticism and the Oral Law," *Journal for the Study of Judaism* 4 (1974), 34–40.

———, *Studies in Qumran Law* (Leiden: E. J. Brill, 1977).

———, "The Laws of the Damascus Document in Current Research, " in M. Broshi, ed., *The Damascus Document Reconsidered* (Jerusalem: Israel Exploration Society, 1992), 51–62.

Bäuml, F., "Medieval Texts and the Two Theories of Oral-Formulaic Composition: A Proposal for a Third Theory," *New Literary History* 16 (1984–1985), 31–49.

Bayer, Bathja, "Oral Law in the 'Oral Law'": The Early Mishnah and Its Cantillation," in J. Cohen, ed., *Proceedings of the World Congress in Jewish Music: Jerusalem, 1978* (Tel Aviv: Institute for the Translation of Hebrew Literature, 1982), 148–159.

Becker, H.-J., *Die Grossen Rabbinischen Sammelwerke Palästinas: zur Literarischen Genese von Talmud Yerushalmi und Midrash Bereshit Rabba* (Tübingen: Mohr Siebeck, 1999).

Beckwith, R., "Formation of the Hebrew Bible," in M. Mulder, *Mikra*, 39–86.

Bennison, G. "Repetition in Oral Literature," *Journal of American Folklore* 84 (1971), 289–303.

Benoit, P., et al., eds., *Discoveries in the Judean Desert, 2: Les Grottes des Murabba'at. Texte* (Oxford: Clarendon Press, 1961).

Berquist, J. L., *Judaism in Persia's Shadow: A Social and Historical Approach* (Minneapolis: Fortress Press, 1995).

Bickerman, E., "La Chaine de la Tradition Pharisienne," *Revue Biblique* 59 (1951), 153–165.

———, *From Ezra to the Last of the Maccabees: The Foundations of Postbiblical Judaism* (New York: Schocken, 1962).

Birchman, R., "Rabbinic Syllogistic: The Case of Mishnah-Tosefta Tohorot," in W. Green, ed., *Approaches to Ancient Judaism*, vol. 5 (Atlanta: Scholars Press, 1985), 81–98.

Blenkinsopp, J., *Prophecy and Canon: A Contribution to the Study of Jewish Origins* (Notre Dame & London: University of Notre Dame Press, 1977).

———, "The Sage, The Scribe, and Scribalism," in J. Gammie and L. Perdue, *The Sage in Israel and the Ancient Near East*, 307–315.

Blidstein, Y., "On the Foundations of the Concept Torah in the Mouth" (Heb.), *Tarbiz* 42 (1973), 496–498.

Bokser, B., *Post-Mishnaic Judaism in Transition: Samuel on Berakhot and the Beginnings of Gemara* (Chico, CA: Scholars Press, 1980).

———, "Wonder-Working and the Rabbinic Tradition: The Case of Hanina ben Dosa," *Journal for the Study of Judaism* 16 (1985), 42–92.

———, trans., completed and ed. by L. Schiffman, *The Talmud of the Land of Israel: A Preliminary Translation and Explanation*, vol. 13 (Chicago & London: University of Chicago Press, 1994).

Bonner, S., *Education in Ancient Rome* (London: Methuen, 1977).

Botha, Pieter J. J., "Mute Manuscripts: Analyzing a Neglected Aspect of Ancient Communication," *Theologica Evangelica* 23 (1990), 35–47.

——, "Orality-Literacy Studies: Exploring the Interaction Between Culture and Communication Technology," *Communicatio* 17 (1991), 2–15.

——, "Greco-Roman Literacy as Setting for NT Writings," *Neot* 26 (1992), 195–215.

——, "Letter Writing and Oral Communication in Antiquity," *Scriptura* 42 (1992), 17–34.

——, "The Verbal Art of Pauline Letters: Rhetoric, Performance, and Presence," in S. Porter and T. Olbricht, eds., *Rhetoric and the New Testament* (Sheffield: Sheffield Academic, 1993), 409–428.

Bowersock, G., *Greek Sophists in the Roman Empire* (Oxford: Clarendon Press, 1969).

Bowman, A. K., and G. Woolf, eds., *Literacy and Power in the Ancient World* (Cambridge: Cambridge University Press, 1994).

Bowra, C., *Heroic Poetry* (New York: St. Martin's Press, 1966).

Boyarin, D., *Intertextuality and the Reading of Midrash* (Bloomington & Indianapolis: Indiana University Press, 1990).

——, *Carnal Israel: Reading Sex in Talmudic Culture* (Berkeley: University of California Press, 1993).

Bratcher, R., and E. Nida, *A Translator's Handbook on the Gospel of Mark* (Leiden: E. J. Brill, 1961).

Bregman, M., "An Early Fragment of Avot D'Rabbi Nathan in a Scroll" (Heb.), *Tarbiz* 52 (1983), 201–222.

——, "Mishnah as Mystery" (Heb.), in *E. E. Urbach Memorial Volume* (forthcoming).

R. Brody, "Geonic Literature and the Text of the Talmud" (Heb.), in Y. Zussman and D. Rozental, eds., *Talmudic Studies*, vol. 1 (Jerusalem: Magnes Press, 1990), 237–303.

Bronznik, N., "On the Interpretation of the Epithet 'Dorshei Halaqot'" (Heb.), *Tarbiz* 60 (1991), 653–657.

Brown, P., *Power and Persuasion in Late Antiquity: Towards a Christian Empire* (Madison: University of Wisconsin, 1992).

Burrows, M., *The Dead Sea Scrolls* (New York: Viking, 1955).

Byrskog, S., *Jesus the Only Teacher: Didactic Authority and Transmission in Ancient Israel, Ancient Judaism and the Matthean Community* (Stockholm: Almqvist & Wiksell International, 1994).

Calinescu, M., "Orality and Literacy: Some Historical Paradoxes of Reading," *Yale Journal of Criticism* 6 (1993), 175–190.

Carruthers, M., *The Book of Memory: A Study of Memory in Medieval Culture* (Cambridge: Cambridge University Press, 1990).

Chartier, R., *Forms and Meanings: Texts, Performances, and Audiences from Codex to Computer* (Philadelphia: University of Pennsylvania Press, 1995).

Cobin, M., "An Oral Interpreter's Index to Quintillian," *Quarterly Journal of Speech* 44 (1958), 61–66.

Cohen, S., "Patriarchs and Scholarchs," *Proceedings of the American Academy of Jewish Research* 48 (1981), 57–85.

——, "The Significance of Yavneh: Pharisees, Rabbis, and the End of Jewish Sectarianism," *Hebrew Union College Annual* 55 (1984), 27–53.

——, "The Place of the Rabbi in Jewish Society in the Second Century," in L. Levine, ed., *The Galilee in Late Antiquity*, 157–173.

Collins, J. J., *The Apocalyptic Imagination* (New York: Crossroad, 1984).

Collins, R., "The Golden Rule," in D. Freedman, *The Anchor Bible Dictionary*, vol. 2, 1070–1071.

Cross, F. M., "The Evolution of a Theory of Local Texts," in F. M. Cross and S. Talmon, eds., *Qumran and the History of the Biblical Text* (Cambridge, MA & London: Harvard University Press, 1975), 306–320.

Culley, R. C., ed., *Semeia 5. Oral Tradition and Old Testament Studies* (Missoula, MT: Scholars Press, 1976).

Daube, D., "Rabbinic Methods of Interpretation and Hellenistic Rhetoric," *Hebrew Union College Annual* 12 (1949), 239–264.

———, "Alexandrian Methods of Interpretation and the Rabbis," repr. in H. Fischel, *Essays*, 165–182.

———, "Texts and Interpretation in Roman and Jewish Law," repr. in H. Fischel, *Essays*, 240–255.

Davies, P., *The Damascus Covenant: An Interpretation of the "Damascus Document"* (Sheffield: University of Sheffield Press, 1983).

———, *Scribes and Schools: The Canonization of the Hebrew Scriptures* (Louisville, KY: Westminster John Knox Press, 1998).

Dewey, J., ed., *Semeia 65: Orality and Textuality in Early Christian Literature* (Atlanta: Scholars Press, 1995).

Dimant, D., "Use and Interpretation of Mikra in the Apocrypha and Pseudepigrapha," in M. Mulder, *Mikra*, 379–419.

Doane, A. N., "The Ethnography of Scribal Writing and Anglo-Saxon Poetry: The Scribe as Performer," *Oral Tradition* 9 (1994), 420–439.

Elman, Y., *Authority and Tradition: Toseftan Baraitot in Talmudic Babylonia* (Hoboken, NJ: KTAV, 1994).

———, "Some Remarks on 4QMMT and the Rabbinic Tradition: or, When Is a Parallel Not a Parallel?" in J. Kampen and M. Bernstein, *Reading 4QMMT*, 99–128.

———, "Orality and the Transmission of Tosefta Pisha in Talmudic Literature," in H. Fox and T. Meacham, *Introducing Tosefta*, 123–180.

———, "Orality and the Redaction of the Babylonian Talmud," *Oral Tradition* 14 (1999).

Epstein, Y., "Some Details of the Yerushalmi" (Heb.), *Tarbiz* 6 (1934), 38–55.

———, *Introduction to Tannaitic Literature: Mishnah, Tosephta and Halakhic Midrashim* (Heb.) (Jerusalem & Tel Aviv: Magnes and Dvir, 1957).

———, *Introduction to the Text of the Mishnah* (Heb.). 2nd ed. (Jerusalem & Tel Aviv: Magnes Press and Dvir, 1964).

Faur, J., *Golden Doves with Silver Dots: Semiotics and Textuality in Rabbinic Tradition* (Bloomington: Indiana University Press, 1986).

Finkelstein, L., "Studies in the Tannaitic Midrashim," in idem, *Sifra on Leviticus*, vol. 5, 151*–190*.

———, "The Transmission of the Early Rabbinic Traditions," in idem, *Sifra on Leviticus*, vol. 5, 224*–244*.

Finnegan, R., "What Is Oral Literature Anyway? Comments in the Light of Some African and Other Examples," in B. Stolz and R. Shannon, eds., *Oral Literature and the Formula* (Ann Arbor: University of Michigan, 1976), 127–166.

———, *Literacy and Orality: Studies in the Technology of Communication* (Oxford: Blackwell, 1988).

Fischel, H., "Studies in Cynicism and the Ancient Near East: The Transformation of a Chria," in J. Neusner, ed., *Religions in Antiquity: Essays in Memory of Erwin Ramsdell Goodenough* (Leiden: E. J. Brill, 1968), 372–411.

———, *Rabbinic Literature and Greco-Roman Philosophy* (Leiden: E. J. Brill, 1973).

——, ed., *Essays in Greco-Roman and Related Talmudic Literature* (New York: KTAV, 1977).

——, "Story and History: Observations on Greco-Roman Rhetoric and Pharisaism," in idem, *Essays*, 443–472.

Fishbane, M., *Biblical Interpretation in Ancient Israel* (Oxford: Clarendon Press, 1985).

——, "From Scribalism to Rabbinism: Perspectives on the Emergence of Classical Judaism," in idem, *Garments of Torah: Essays in Biblical Hermeneutics* (Bloomington & Indianapolis: Indiana University Press, 1989).

Flint, P., and J. VanderKam, eds., *The Dead Sea Scrolls After Fifty Years: A Comprehensive Assessment*, vols. 1–2 (Leiden: E. J. Brill, 1998).

Flusser, D., "Pharisees, Sadducees, and Essenes in the Nahum Pesher" (Heb.), in *Gedaliah Alon Memorial Volume* (Tel Aviv, 1960), pp. 133–168.

Foley, J. M., *The Theory of Oral Composition* (Bloomington: Indiana University Press, 1988).

——, *Orality and Literacy: Modern Critical Methods* (Hamden, CT: Archon, 1988).

——, *Traditional Oral Epic: The Odyssey, Beowulf and the Serbo-Croatian Return Song* (Berkeley: University of California Press, 1990).

——, "Word-Power, Performance and Tradition," *Journal of American Folklore* 105 (1992), 275–301.

——, *The Singer of Tales in Performance* (Bloomington & Indianapolis: Indiana University Press, 1995).

Fox, H., and T. Meacham, eds., *Introducing Tosefta: Textual, Intratextual and Intertextual Studies* (Hoboken, NJ: KTAV, 1999).

Fraade, S., *From Tradition to Commentary: Torah and Its Interpretation in the Midrash Sifre to Deuteronomy* (Albany: State University of New York Press, 1991).

——, "The Early Rabbinic Sage," in J. Gammie and L. Perdue, *The Sage in Israel and the Ancient Near East*, 417–436.

— — — , "Rabbinic Views on the Practice of Targum, and Multilingualism in the Jewish Galilee in the Third–Sixth Centuries," in L. Levine, *The Galilee in Late Antiquity*, 253–286.

——, "Interpretive Authority in the Studying Community at Qumran," *Journal of Jewish Studies* 44 (1993), 46–69.

——, "Looking for Legal Midrash at Qumran, in M. Stone and E Chazon, eds., *Biblical Perspectives: Early Use and Interpretation of the Bible in Light of the Dead Sea Scrolls* (Leiden: E. J. Brill, 1998), 59–79.

——, "Literary Composition and Oral Performance in Early Midrashim," *Oral Tradition* 14 (1999).

Frankel, Z., *The Methods of the Mishnah* (Heb.) (repr. Tel Aviv: Sinai, n.d.).

Freedman, D., ed., *The Anchor Bible Dictionary*, vols. 1–6 (New York: Doubleday, 1992).

Friedman, S., "An Ancient Tosefta: On the Relationship of Parallels in the Mishnah and Tosefta (1)—Shabbat 16:1" (Heb.), *Tarbiz* 62 (1993), 314–338.

——, "An Ancient Tosefta: On the Relationship of Parallels in the Mishnah and Tosfeta (2)—The Story of Rabban Gamaliel and the Elders" (Heb.), *Bar Ilan Annual* 26–27 (1995), 277–288.

——, "The Primacy of Tosefta to Mishnah in Synoptic Parallels," in H. Fox and T. Meacham, *Introducing Tosefta*, 99–121.

Gamble, H., *Books and Readers in the Early Church: A History of Early Christian Texts* (New Haven: Yale University Press, 1995).

Gammie, J., "The Sage in Sirach," in J. Gammie and L. Perdue, *The Sage in Israel and the Ancient Near East*, 355–372.

Gammie, J., and L. Perdue, eds., *The Sage in Israel and the Ancient Near East* (Winona Lake, IN: Eisenbraun's, 1990).

Gerhardsson, B., *Memory and Manuscript: Oral Tradition and Written Transmission in Rabbinic Judaism and Early Christianity with Tradition and Transmission in Early Christianity*, Foreword by Jacob Neusner (repr. Grand Rapids, MI: Eerdman's Publishing, 1998).

Gewirtsmann, M., "The Concept, Yetiv, and Its Meaning" (Heb.), *Sinai* 65 (1969), 9–20.

Ginzberg, L., *The Legends of the Jews* (Philadelphia: Jewish Publication Society, 1910).

——, "The Mishnah Tamid," *Journal of Jewish Lore and Philosophy* 1 (1919), 284–293.

Golb, N., *Who Wrote the Dead Sea Scrolls? The Search for the Secret of Qumran* (New York: Scribner, 1995).

Goldberg, A., "The Tosefta to Tractate Tamid," in E. Melammed, ed., *Festschrift in Memory of Benjamin DeVries* (Heb.) (Jerusalem: Tel Aviv University, 1969), 18–42.

——, "The Mishna—A Study Book of Halakha," in S. Safrai, *The Literature of the Sages*, 211–251.

——, "The Tosefta—Companion to the Mishna," in S. Safrai, *The Literature of the Sages*, 283–302.

Goldenberg, R., "The Problem of Originality in Talmudic Thought," in J. Neusner et al., eds., *From Ancient Israel to Modern Judaism: Intellect in Quest of Understanding. Essays in Honor of Marvin Fox*, vol. 2 (Atlanta: Scholars Press, 1989), 19–27.

Goldin, Judah, "On the Account of the Banning of R. Eliezer b. Hyrcanus," in B. Eichler and J. Tigay, eds., *Studies in Midrash and Related Literature* (Philadelphia: Jewish Publication Society, 1984), 283–297.

Golinkin, D., "The Meaning of the Concepts *wtyqyn*, *wtyq*, and *tlmyd wtyq* in the Book of Ben Sira and the Talmudic Literature" (Heb.), *Sidra* 13 (1997), 47–60.

Goodblatt, D., *Rabbinic Instruction in Sassanian Babylonia* (Leiden: E. J. Brill, 1975).

——, "Sources for the Origins of Organized Jewish Education in the Land of Israel" (Heb.), in B. Oded, ed., *Studies in the History of the Jewish People and the Land of Israel* (Haifa: University of Haifa, 1980), 83–103.

——, "The Place of the Pharisees in First Century Judaism: The State of the Debate," *Journal for the Study of Judaism* 20 (1989), 12–30.

——, *The Monarchic Principle: Studies in Jewish Self-Government in Antiquity* (Tübingen: J. C. B. Mohr [Paul Siebeck], 1994).

Goodman, M., *State and Society in Roman Galilee, A.D. 132–212* (Totowa, NJ: Rowman & Allenheld, 1983).

——, "Texts, Scribes, and Power in Roman Judaea," in A. Bowman and G. Woolf, *Literacy and Power in the Ancient World*, 99–108.

Goody, J., *The Domestication of the Savage Mind* (Cambridge: Cambridge University Press, 1977).

——, *The Logic of Writing and the Organization of Society* (Cambridge: Cambridge University Press, 1986).

——, *The Interface Between the Written and the Oral* (Cambridge: Cambridge University Press, 1987).

Goshen-Gottstein, M., "'Sefer Hagu'—the End of a Puzzle," *Vetus Testamentum* 8 (1958), 286–288.

Graham, W., *Beyond the Written Word: Oral Aspects of Scripture in the History of Religion* (Cambridge: Cambridge University Press, 1987).

Gray, R., *Prophetic Figures in Late Second Temple Jewish Palestine* (New York & Oxford: Oxford University Press, 1993).

Green, W., "Palestinian Holy Men: Charismatic Leadership and Rabbinic Tradition," in W. Haase, ed., *Aufstieg und Niedergang der Römischen Welt*, II, 19.2 (Berlin: Walter de Gruyter, 1979), 619–647.

Gruber, M., "The Meaning of *'orait'a* in the Babylonian Talmud," *Hebrew Studies* 22 (1981), 25–33.

——, "The Mishnah as Oral Torah: A Reconsideration," *Journal for the Study of Judaism* 15 (1984), 112–122.

——, "Rashi's Torah Commentary as a Source of Corruption in Talmudic Aggadah" (Heb.), *Sinai* 106 (1990), 225–228.

Hadot, I., "The Spiritual Guide," in A. H. Armstrong, ed., *Classical Mediterranean Spirituality: Egyptian, Greek, Roman* (New York: Crossroad, 1986).

Hadot, P., "Forms of Life and Forms of Discoursse in Ancient Philosophy," *Critical Inquiry* 16 (1990), 483–505.

Halverson, J., "Goody and the Implosion of the Literacy Thesis," *Man* n.s. 27 (1992), 301–317.

Haran, M., "Book-Scrolls at the Beginning of the Second Temple Period: The Transition from Papyrus to Skins," *Hebrew Union College Annual* 54 (1983), 111–122.

——, "On the Diffusion of Literacy and Schools in Ancient Israel," in J. Emerton, ed., *Congress Volume. Jerusalem 1986. Vetus Testamentum Supplement* 40 (Leiden: E. J. Brill, 1988), 81–95.

——, *The Scriptural Collection: Processes of Formation Until the End of the Second Temple Period and Transformations Until the Middle Ages* (Heb.) (Jerusalem: Mosad Bialik and Magnes Press of the Hebrew University, 1996).

Harrington, D. J., "Palestinian Adaptations of Biblical Narratives and Prophecies," in R. Kraft and G. Nickelsburg, eds., *Early Judaism and Its Modern Interpreters*, 239–247.

Harrington, H., *The Impurity Systems of Qumran and the Rabbis: Biblical Foundations* (Atlanta: Scholars Press, 1993).

Harris, W. V., *Ancient Literacy* (Cambridge, MA & London: Harvard University Press, 1989).

Heer, M. D., "Continuity of Tradition in the Transmission of Torah" (Heb.), *Zion* 44 (1979/1980), 43–56.

Hengel, M., *Judaism and Hellenism: Studies in Their Encounter in Palestine During the Early Hellenistic Period*, vols. 1–2 (Philadelphia: Fortress Press, 1974).

——, *The Charismatic Leader and His Followers* (Edinburgh: T&T Clark, 1981).

Hengel, M., and R. Deines, "E.P. Sanders' 'Common Judaism,' Jesus and the Pharisees: A Review Essay," *Journal of Theological Studies* 46 (1995), 1–70.

Herford, R., *Christianity in Talmud and Midrash* (repr. New York: KTAV, 1975).

Hezser, C., "Die Verwendung der Hellenistischen Gattung Chrie im frühen Christentum und Judentum," *Journal for the Study of Judaism* 27 (1996), 371–439.

——, *The Social Structure of the Rabbinic Movement in Roman Palestine* (Tübingen: Mohr Siebeck, 1997).

——, "The Codification of Legal Knowledge in Late Antiquity: The Talmud Yerushalmi and Roman Law Codes," in P. Schäfer, *The Talmud Yerushalmi in Graeco-Roman Culture I*, 582–641.

Hirshman, M., *A Rivalry of Genius: Jewish and Christian Biblical Interpretation* (Albany: SUNY Press, 1996).

Hock, R., and E. O'Neil, eds., *The Chreia in Ancient Rhetoric*, vol. 1: *The Progymnasmata* (Atlanta: Scholars Press, 1986).

Hoenig, S., "Dorshe Halakot in Pesher Nahum," *Journal of Biblical Literature* 83 (1964), 119–138.

Horbury, W., et al., eds., *The Cambridge History of Judaism. Volume Three. The Early Roman Period* (Cambridge: Cambridge University Press, 1999).

Horsely, R. A., *Galilee: History, Politics, People* (Valley Forge, PA: Trinity Press International, 1995).

Houtman, A., *Mishnah and Tosefta: A Synoptic Comparison of the Tractates Berakhot and Shebiit* (Tübingen: J. C. B. Mohr [Paul Siebeck], 1996).

Jacobs, L., "Halakhah le-Mosheh mi-Sinai," *Encyclopaedia Judaica* (Jerusalem: Keter, 1972), vol. 7, p. 167.

Jacobson, A., *The First Gospel: An Introduction to Q* (Sonoma, CA: Polebridge, 1992).

Jaffee, M., "Deciphering Mishnaic Lists: A Form-Analytical Approach," in W. Green, ed., *Approaches to Ancient Judaism*, vol. 3 (Chico, CA: Scholars Press, 1981), 19–34.

——, trans., *The Talmud of Babylonia. 26. Tractate Horayot* (Atlanta: Scholars Press, 1987).

——, "The Taqqanah in Rabbinic Literature: Jurisprudence and the Construction of Rabbinic Memory," *Journal of Jewish Studies* 41 (1990), 204–225.

——, "How Much 'Orality' in Oral Torah? New Perspectives on the Composition and Transmission of Early Rabbinic Tradition," *Shofar* 10 (1992), 53–72.

——, "*Halakhah* in Early Rabbinic Judaism: Innovation Beyond Exegesis, Tradition Before the Oral Torah," in M. Williams et al., *Innovation in Religious Traditions: Essays in the Interpretation of Religious Change* (Berlin & New York: Mouton de Gruyter, 1992), 109–142.

——, "Writing and Rabbinic Oral Tradition: On Mishnaic Narrative, Lists and Mnemonics," *Journal of Jewish Thought and Philosophy* 4 (1994), 123–146.

——, "*Halakhah* as Primordial Tradition: A Gadamarian Dialogue with Early Rabbinic Memory and Jurisprudence," in S. Kepnes, ed., *Interpreting Judaism in a Postmodern Age* (New York & London: New York University Press, 1996), 85–117.

——, "A Rabbinic Ontology of the Written and Spoken Word: On Discipleship, Transformative Knowledge, and the Living Texts of Oral Torah," *Journal of the American Academy of Religion* 65 (1997), 525–549.

——, "The Oral-Cultural Context of the Talmud Yerushalmi: Greco-Roman Rhetorical Paideia, Discipleship, and the Concept of Oral Torah," in P. Schäfer, *The Talmud Yerushalmi and Graeco-Roman Culture I*, 27–61.

——, "Oral Tradition in the Writings of Rabbinic Oral Torah," *Oral Tradition* 14 (1999), 3–32.

Kaatz, S., *Die Mündliche Lehre und Ihr Dogma*, vol. 1 (Leipzig: M. W. Kaufman, 1922), vol. 2 (Berlin: M. Poppelauer, 1923).

Kalmin, R., *Sages, Stories, Authors, and Editors in Rabbinic Babylonia* (Atlanta: Scholars Press, 1994).

——, *The Sage in Jewish Society of Late Antiquity* (London & New York: Routledge, 1999).

Kampen, J., and M. Bernstein, eds., *Reading 4QMMT: New Perspectives on Qumran Law and History* (Atlanta: Scholars Press, 1996).

Kanter, S., *Rabban Gamaliel II: The Legal Traditions* (Chico, CA: Scholars Press, 1980).

Kaplan, J., *The Redaction of the Babylonian Talmud* (New York: Bloch, 1933).

Kelber, W., "Sayings Collection and Sayings Gospel: A Study in the Clustering Management of Knowledge," *Language and Communication* 9 (1989), 213–24.

——, *The Oral and the Written Gospel: The Hermeneutics of Speaking and Writing in the Synoptic Tradition, Mark, Paul, and Q*, Foreword by W. J. Ong (repr. Bloomington & Indianapolis: Indiana University Press, 1997).

——, "Jesus and Tradition: Words in Time, Words in Space," in J. Dewey, *Semeia* 65, 139–167.

Kennedy, G., *A New History of Classical Rhetoric* (Princeton, NJ: Princeton University, 1994).

Kister, M., *Studies in Avot De-Rabbi Nathan: Text, Redaction, and Interpretation* (Heb.) (Jerusalem: Hebrew University & Yad Izhak Ben-Zvi, 1998).

Kittel, B. P., *The Hymns of Qumran* (Chico, CA: Scholars Press, 1981).

Klein, S., *The Book of Jewish Settlement* (Heb.) (Jerusalem: Bialik, 1939).

Kloppenborg, J., *The Formation of Q: Trajectories in Ancient Wisdom Collections* (Philadelphia: Fortress, 1987).

Kloppenborg, J., et al., *Q Thomas Reader* (Sonoma, CA: Polegridge, 1990).

Kohut, A., ed., *Aruch Completum Sive Lexicon Vocabula et Res, Quae in Libris Targumicis, Talmudicis et Midraschicis*, Vols. 1–9 (repr. nd, n.p.).

Kosovsky, M., *Concordance to the Talmud Yerushalmi*, Vols. 1–6 (Jerusalem: Israel Academy of Sciences and Humanities & Jewish Theological Seminary of America, 1979–1995).

Kraemer, D., "On the Reliability of the Attributions in the Babylonian Talmud," *Hebrew Union College Annual* 60 (1989), 175–190.

Kraft, R., and G. Nickelsburg, eds., *Early Judaism and Its Modern Interpreters* (Atlanta: Scholars Press, 1986).

Lachs, S. T., *A Rabbinic Commentary on the New Testament* (Hoboken, NJ & New York: KTAV and Anti-Defamation League of Bnai Brith, 1987).

Lapin, H., *Early Rabbinic Civil Law and the Social History of Roman Galilee: A Study of Mishnah Tractate Bab'a Meṣi'a'* (Atlanta: Scholars Press, 1995).

——, "Rabbi," in D. Freedman, *The Anchor Bible Dictionary*, vol. 5, pp. 600–602.

Lauterbach, J., *Rabbinic Essays* (Cincinnati: Hebrew Union College, 1951).

Leiman, S. Z., *The Canonization of Hebrew Scripture: The Talmudic and Midrashic Evidence*. 2nd ed. (New Haven: Connecticut Academy of Arts and Sciences, 1991).

Lerner, M., "The Tractate Avot," in S. Safrai, *The Literature of the Sages*, 263–276.

——, "The External Tractates," in S. Safrai, *The Literature of the Sages*, 367–403.

Levenson, J., "The Sources of Torah: Psalm 119 and the Modes of Revelation in Second Temple Judaism," in P. Miller et al., eds., *Ancient Israelite Religion* (Philadelphia: Fortress Press, 1987), 559–574.

Levine, L. I., ed., *The Synagogue in Late Antiquity* (Philadelphia: American Schools of Oriental Research, 1987).

——, "The Second Temple Synagogue," in idem, *The Synagogue in Late Antiquity*, 7–31.

——, ed., *The Galilee in Late Antiquity* (New York & Jerusalem: Jewish Theological Seminary of America, 1992).

Levinson, B. M., *Deuteronomy and the Hermeneutics of Legal Innovation* (New York & Oxford: Oxford University Press, 1997).

Lewin, B., ed., *Iggeret Rav Sherira Gaon: The Spanish Text and the French Text* (Haifa: Itzokofsky, 1921).

Lieberman, S., *Tosefet Rishonim. A Commentary Based Upon Manuscripts of the Tosefta and Works of the Rishonim and Midrashim and Rare Editions*, vols. 3–4 (Heb.) (Jerusalem: 1939).

——, *Greek in Jewish Palestine: Studies in the Life and Manners of Jewish Palestine in the II–IV Centuries* C.E. (New York: Jewish Theological Seminary of America, 1942).

——, *Hellenism in Jewish Palestine: Studies in the Literary Transmission, Beliefs, and Manners of Palestine in the I Century* B.C.E.–IV *Century* C.E. (New York: Jewish Theological Seminary of America, 1950).

——, "The Discipline in the So-Called Dead Sea Manual of Discipline," *Journal of Biblical Literature* 71 (1951), 199–206.

——, *Tosefta Ki-fshuta: A Comprehensive Commentary on the Tosefta*, vols. 1–10 (Heb.) (New York: Jewish Theological Seminary of America, 1955–1988).

——, *HaYerushalmi Kiphshuto: A Commentary. Part One. Vol. I: Shabbath, 'Erubin, Pesahim*. (Heb.) 2nd ed. (New York & Jerusalem: Jewish Theological Seminary of America, 1995).

Lord, A. B., *The Singer of Tales* (Cambridge, MA: Harvard University Press, 1960).

Marrou, H., *A History of Education in Antiquity* (London: Sheed & Ward, 1956).

Martin, M., *The Scribal Character of the Dead Sea Scrolls*, vols. 1–2 (Louvain: Publications Universitaires & Institut Orientaliste, 1958).

Martinez, F., "The Origins of the Essene Movement and of the Qumran Sect," in idem and J. Barrera, eds., *The People of the Dead Sea Scrolls: Their Writings, Beliefs, and Practices* (Leiden: E. J. Brill, 1995), 77–96.

Mason, S., "Philosophia as a Group-Designation in Graeco-Roman Society, Judaism, and Early Christianity," (1990) http://www.Lehigh.edu/pub/listserv/ioudaios-l/Articles/smphilos.

——, *Flavius Josephus on the Pharisees: A Composition-Critical Study* (Leiden: E. J. Brill, 1991).

Mason, S., and T. Robinson, eds., *An Early Christian Reader* (Toronto: Canadian Scholars Press, 1990).

McGuire, M., "Letters and Letter Carriers in Ancient Antiquity," *Classical World* 53 (1960), 148–199.

Meade, D. G., *Pseudonymity and Canon: An Investigation into the Relationship of Authorship and Authority in Jewish and Earliest Christian Tradition* (Grand Rapids, MI: Eerdman's, 1987).

Melammed, E., *Introductory Comments on the Talmudic Literature* (Heb.) (Jerusalem: Tel Aviv University & Bar Ilan University, 1963).

——, *The Relationship of the Halakhic Midrashim to the Mishnah and Tosefta* (Heb.) (Jerusalem: Melammed, 1967).

Meshorer, Y., *Ancient Jewish Coinage, Vol. 1. Persian Period Through Hasmonaeans* (Dix Hills, NJ: Amphora Books, 1982).

Metso, S., *The Textual Development of the Qumran Community Rule* (Leiden: E. J. Brill, 1997).

Meyers, E., ed., *The Oxford Encyclopedia of Archeology in the Near East*, vols. 1–6 (New York & Oxford: Oxford University Press, 1997).

Moore, G., *Judaism in the First Centuries of the Christian Era: The Age of the Tannaim*, vols. 1–3 (repr. Peabody, MA: Hendrickson Publishers, 1997).

Mulder, M., ed., *Mikra: Text, Translation, Reading and Interpretation of the Hebrew Bible in Ancient Judaism and Early Christianity* (Assen/Maastricht: Van Gorcum & Philadelphia: Fortress Press, 1988).

Naeh, S., "Structure and Division of the Midrash Torat HaKohanim (A): Scrolls" (Heb.), *Tarbiz* 66 (1997), 483–515.

Nelson, D., *Textuality and Talmud Torah: Issues of Early Rabbinic Written and Oral Transmission of Tradition as Exemplified in the Mekhilta of Rabbi Shimon b. Yohai* (Hebrew Union College Dissertation, 1999).

Neusner, J., *The Rabbinic Traditions About the Pharisees Before 70*, vols. I–III (Leiden: E. J. Brill, 1971).

——, "The Written Tradition in the Pre-Rabbinic Period," *Journal for the Study of Judaism* (1973), 56–65.

——, *A History of the Mishnaic Law of Purities*, vols. 1–22 (Leiden: E. J. Brill, 1975–1978).

——, "Oral Torah and Oral Tradition: Defining the Problematic," in idem, *Method and Meaning in Ancient Judaism* (Missoula, MT: Scholars Press, 1979), 59–75.

——, *From Politics to Piety: The Emergence of Pharisaic Judaism*. 2nd ed. (New York: KTAV, 1979).

——, "The Formation of Rabbinic Judaism: Yavneh (Jamnia) from A.D. 70 to 100," in W. Haase, ed., *Aufstieg und Niedergang der Römischen Welt II*, 19.2 (Berlin: Walter de Gruyter, 1979), 3–42.

——, *A History of the Mishnaic Law of Holy Things, Part Six* (Leiden: E. J. Brill, 1980).

——, *Judaism: The Evidence of the Mishnah* (Chicago & London: University of Chicago Press, 1981).

——, *A History of the Mishnaic Law of Appointed Times, Parts One–Six* (Leiden, E. J. Brill, 1981–1983).

——, *Midrash in Context: Exegesis in Formative Judaism* (Philadelphia: Fortress Press, 1983).

——, *Torah: From Scroll to Symbol in Formative Judaism* (Philadelphia: Fortress Press, 1985).

——, *Judaism and Christianity in the Age of Constantine: History, Messiah, Israel, and the Initial Confrontation* (Chicago: University of Chicago, 1987).

——, *The Oral Tradition in Judaism: The Case of the Mishnah* (New York & London: Garland Publishing, 1987).

——, *The Mishnah: An Introduction* (Northvale, NJ: Jason Aronson, 1989).

——, *The Tosefta: An Introduction* (Atlanta: Scholars Press, 1992).

——, *Judaic Law from Jesus to the Mishnah* (Atlanta: Scholars Press, 1993).

——, *Introduction to Rabbinic Literature* (New York: Doubleday, 1994).

——, "Evaluating the Attributions of Sayings to Named Sages in the Rabbinic Literature," *Journal for the Study of Judaism* 26 (1995), 93–111.

——, *What, Exactly, Did the Sages Mean by "the Oral Torah"? An Inductive Answer to the Question of Rabbinic Judaism* (Atlanta: Scholars Press, 1999).

Niditch, S., *Oral World and Written Word: Ancient Israelite Literature* (Louisville, KY: Westiminster John Knox Press, 1966).

Nitzan, B., *Qumran Prayer and Religious Poetry* (Leiden: E. J. Brill, 1994).

Nock, A., *Conversion: The Old and New in Religion from Alexander the Great to Augustine of Hippo* (London: Oxford University Press, 1933).

Östborn, G., *Cult and Canon: A Study in the Canonization of the Old Testament* (Uppsala: A. B. Lundequistska & Leipzig: Otto Harrassowitz, 1950).

Olbricht, T., "Delivery and Memory," in S. Porter, ed., *Handbook of Classical Rhetoric in the Hellenistic Period 330 B.C.–A.D. 400* (Leiden: E. J. Brill, 1997).

Olrik, A., "Epic Laws of the Folktale," in A. Dundes, ed., *The Study of Folklore* (Englewood Cliffs, NJ: Prentice Hall, 1965), 129–141.

Olyan, S., "Ben Sira's Relationship to the Priesthood," *Harvard Theological Review* 80 (1987), 261–286.

Ong, W., *Orality and Literacy: The Technologizing of the Word* (repr. London & New York: Routledge, 1988).

Parry, A., ed., *The Making of Homeric Verse: The Collected Papers of Milman Parry* (Oxford: Clarendon Press, 1971).

Poirier, J., "Why Did the Pharisees Wash Their Hands?" *Journal of Jewish Studies* 47 (1996), 219–233.

Pospisil, L., *Anthropology of Law: A Comparative Theory* (New York: Harper & Row, 1971).

Propp, V., *Morphology of the Folktale*, trans. L. Scott (Austin: University of Texas Press, 1968).

Pryke, E., *Redactional Style in the Markan Gospel: A Study of Syntax and Vocabulary as Guides to Redaction in Mark* (Cambridge: Cambridge University Press, 1978).

Rabin, C., *Qumran Studies* (New York: Schocken, 1975).

Reichman, Ronen, *Mishna und Sifra: Ein Literarkritischer Vergleich Paralleler Überlieferungen* (Tübingen: Mohr Siebeck, 1998).

Rendtorff, R., *The Old Testament: An Introduction* (Philadelphia: Fortress Press, 1986).

Renteln, A., and A. Dundes, eds., *Folk Law*, vols. 1–2 (Madison: University of Wisconsin Press, 1995).

Rivkin, E., *A Hidden Revolution: The Pharisees' Search for the Kingdom Within* (Nashville: Abingdon, 1978).

Robbins, V., "Oral, Rhetorical, and Literary Cultures: A Response," J. Dewey, *Semeia* 65, 75–91.

——, "Writing as a Rhetorical Act in Plutarch and the Gospels," in D. Watson, ed., *Persuasive Artistry: Studies in New Testament Rhetoric* (Sheffield: JSOT, 1991), 157–186.

——, "Progymnasmatic Rhetorical Composition and Pre-Gospel Traditions: A New Approach," in C. Focant, ed., *The Synoptic Gospels: Source Criticism and the New Literary Criticism* (Leuven: Leuven University Press, 1993), 111–147.

——, "Rhetoric and Culture: Exploring Types of Cultural Rhetoric in a Text," in S. Porter and T. Olbricht, *Rhetoric and the New Testament* (Sheffield: Sheffield Academic, 1993), 443–463.

Roth, J. *The Halakhic Process: A Systemic Analysis* (New York: Jewish Theological Seminary of America, 1986).

Rozental, A., "Oral Torah and Torah From Sinai—Theory and Practice" (Heb.), in D. Rozental and M. Bar-Asher, eds., *Talmudic Studies*, vol. 2 (Jerusalem: Magnes Press, 1994), 448–487.

Saenger, P., "Silent Reading: Its Impact on Late Medieval Script and Society," *Viator* 13 (1982), 367–414.

Safrai, S., ed., *The Literature of the Sages, First Part: Oral Tora, Halakha, Mishna, Tosefta, Talmud, External Tractates* (Assen/Maastricht: Van Gorcum and Philadelphia: Fortress Press, 1987).

——, "Oral Tora," in idem, *The Literature of the Sages*, 35–119.

Saldarini, A., *Scholastic Rabbinism: A Literary Study of the Fathers According to Rabbi Nathan* (Chico, CA: Scholars Press, 1982).

——, *Pharisees, Scribes, and Sadducees in Palestinian Society: A Sociological Approach* (Wilmington, DE: M. Glazer, 1988).

——, "Pharisees," in D. Freedman, *The Anchor Bible Dictionary*, vol. 5, 289–303.

Sanders, E., *Jewish Law from Jesus to the Mishnah: Five Studies* (London & Philadelphia: SCM & Trinity, 1990).

Sanders, J. A., *Torah and Canon* (Philadelphia: Fortress Press, 1972).

Sanders, J. T., *Schismatics, Sectarians, Dissidents, Deviants: The First One Hundred Years of Jewish–Christian Relations* (Valley Forge, PA: Trinity Press International, 1993).

Sandmel, S., *Philo's Place in Judaism: A Study of Conceptions of Abraham in Jewish Literature* (New York: KTAV, 1971).

Sarason, R., *A History of the Mishnaic Law of Agriculture. Section 3. A Study of Tractate Demai. Part One* (Leiden: E. J. Brill, 1979).

Schäfer, P., "Das Dogma von der Mündlichen Torah," in idem, *Studien zur Geschichte und Theologie des Rabbinischen Judentums* (Leiden: E. J. Brill, 1978), 153–197.

——, ed., *The Talmud Yerushalmi and Graeco-Roman Culture, I* (Tübingen: Mohr Siebeck, 1998).

Schams, C., *Jewish Scribes in the Second-Temple Period* (Sheffield: Sheffield Academic Press, 1998).

Schiffman, L., *The Halakhah at Qumran* (Leiden: E. J. Brill, 1975).

——, *Sectarian Law in the Dead Sea Scrolls: Courts, Testimony, and the Penal Code* (Chico, CA: Scholars Press, 1983).

——, "Pharisees and Sadducees in Pesher Nahum," in M. Brettler and M. Fishbane, eds., *Minhah le-Nahum: Biblical and Other Studies Presented to Nahum M. Sarna in Honour of His 70th Birthday* (Sheffield: JSOT, 1993), 272–290.

——, "Was the Mishnah Written? The Answer of Rav Sherira Gaon," in G. Sed-Rajna, *Rashi 1040–1990: Hommage a Ephraim E. Urbach* (Paris: Editions du Cerf, 1993), 213–218.

——, *Reclaiming the Dead Sea Scrolls.* Foreword by C. Potok (Philadelphia & Jerusalem: Jewish Publication Society, 1994).

Schlüter, M., *Auf Welche Weise Wurde die Mishna geschrieben?* (Tübingen: J. C. B. Mohr [Paul Siebeck], 1993).

Schürer, E., *The Jewish People in the Age of Jesus Christ*, vols. 1–3. Rev. and ed. G. Vermes et al. (Edinburgh: T & T Clark, 1973–1987).

Schulz, F., *History of Roman Legal Science* (Oxford: Oxford University Press, 1946).

Schwabe, M., "On the Jewish and Greco-Roman Schools in the Days of the Mishnah and the Talmud" (Heb.), *Tarbiz* 21 (1949), 112–123.

Schwartz, D., "Josephus and Nicolaus on the Pharisees," *Journal for the Study of Judaism* 14 (1983), 157–171.

——, "MMT, Josephus, and the Pharisees," in J. Kampen and M. Bernstein, *Reading 4QMMT*, 67–80.

Schwartz, S., *Josephus and Judaean Politics* (Leiden: E. J. Brill, 1990).

Segal, B-Z, *Mishnaic Geography* (Heb.) (Jerusalem: Institute of Mishnaic Research, 1969).

Segert, S., "Observations on the Poetic Structures of the Songs of the Sabbath Sacrifice," *Revue de Qumran* 13 (1988), 215–224.

Shavit, Y., "The 'Qumran Library' in the Light of the Attitude Towards Books and Libraries in the Second Temple Period," in M. Wise et al., *Methods of Investigation*, 299–315.

Shinan, A., "Aggadic Literature Between Oral Recitation and Written Tradition" (Heb.), *Jerusalem Studies in Jewish Folklore* 1 (1981), 44–60.

Small, J., *Wax Tablets of the Mind: Cognitive Studies of Memory and Literacy in Classical Antiquity* (London & New York: Routledge, 1997).

Smith, J., "Sacred Persistence: Toward a Redescription of Canon," in J. Smith, *Imagining Religion: From Babylon to Jonestown* (Chicago: University of Chicago Press, 1982), 36–52.

Smith, M., "Palestinian Judaism in the First Century," in M. Davis, ed., *Israel: Its Role in Civilization* (New York: Harper & Row, 1956), 67–81.

——, "The Dead Sea Sect in Relation to Ancient Judaism," *New Testament Studies* 7 (1960), 347–360.

——, *Palestinian Parties and Politics that Shaped the Old Testament* (New York & London: Columbia University Press, 1971).

Snyder, H., *Teachers, Texts, and Students: Textual Peformance and Patterns of Authority in Greco-Roman Schools* (Yale University Dissertation, 1998).

Sokoloff, M., *A Dictionary of Jewish Palestinian Aramaic of the Byzantine Period* (Ramat Gan: Bar Ilan University Press, 1990).

Staal, F., *Rules Without Meaning: Ritual, Mantras and the Human Sciences* (New York: Peter Lang, 1989).

Stemberger, G., *Introduction to the Talmud and Midrash*, 2nd ed. Trans. and ed. M. Bockmuehl (Edinburgh: T & T Clark, 1995).

——, *Jewish Contemporaries of Jesus: Pharisees, Sadducees, Essenes* (Minneapolis: Fortress, 1995).

Stern, D., *Parables in Midrash: Narrative and Exegesis in Rabbinic Literature* (Cambridge, MA, & London: Harvard University Press, 1991).

Stern, S., "Attribution and Authorship in the Babylonian Talmud," *Journal of Jewish Studies* 45 (1994), 28–51.

——, "The Concept of Authorship in the Babylonian Talmud," *Journal of Jewish Studies* 46 (1995), 183–195.

Sternberg, M., *The Poetics of Biblical Narrative: Ideological Literature and the Drama of Reading* (Bloomington: Indiana University Press, 1987).

Stolz, B., and R. Shannon, eds., *Oral Literature and the Formula* (Ann Arbor: University of Michigan, 1976).

Stone, M., ed., *Jewish Writings of the Second Temple Period: Apocrypha, Pseudepigrapha, Qumran Sectarian Writings, Philo, Josephus* (Assen: Van Gorcum; Philadelphia: Fortress Press, 1984).

Strack, H., and G. Stemberger, *Introduction to Talmud and Midrash* (Edinburgh: T & T Clark, 1991).

Suter, D. W., *Tradition and Composition in the Parables of Enoch* (Missoula, MT: Scholars Press, 1979).

Swartz, M., *Scholastic Magic: Ritual and Revelation in Early Jewish Mysticism* (Princeton, NJ: Princeton University Press, 1996).

Talmon, S., "The Calendar of the Covenanters of the Judean Desert," in idem, *The World of Qumran from Within* (Jerusalem: Magnes Press and Leiden: E. J. Brill, 1989), 147–185.

———, "Oral Tradition and Written Transmission, or the Heard and the Seen Word in Judaism of the Second Temple Period," in H. Wansbrough, *Jesus and the Oral Gospel Tradition*, 121–158.

Tomson, P., *Paul and the Jewish Law: Halakha in the Letters of the Apostle to the Gentiles* (Assen/Maastricht: Van Gorcum; Minneapolis: Fortress, 1990).

Tov, E., *Textual Criticism of the Hebrew Bible* (Assen/Maastricht: Van Gorcum; Philadelphia: Fortress Press, 1992).

———, "Scribal Practices Reflected in the Paleo-Hebrew Texts from the Judean Desert," *Scripta Classica Israelica* 15 (1996), 268–273.

———, "The Scribes of the Texts Found in the Judean Desert," in C. Evans and S. Talmon, eds., *The Quest for Context and Meaning: Studies in Biblical Intertextuality in Honor of James A. Sanders* (Leiden: E. J. Brill, 1998), 131–152.

———, "Scribal Practices Reflected in Texts from the Judaean Desert," in P. Flint and J. VanderKam, *The Dead Sea Scrolls After Fifty Years*, vol. 1, 405–429.

Trocme, E., *The Formation of the Gospel According to Mark* (Philadelphia: Westminster, 1975).

Urbach, E., *The Halakhah: Its Sources and Development* (Jerusalem: Massada, 1986).

Valantasis, R., *Spiritual Guides of the Third Century: A Semiotic Study of the Guide–Disciple Relationship in Christianity, Neoplatonism, Hermetism, and Gnosticism* (Minneapolis: Fortress Press, 1991).

van der Horst, P., "Two Notes on Hellenistic Lore in Early Rabbinic Literature," *Jewish Studies Quarterly* 1 (1993–94), 252–262.

VanderKam, J., *Enoch and the Growth of the Apocalyptic Tradition* (Washington, DC: Catholic Biblical Association of America, 1984).

———, *The Dead Sea Scrolls Today* (Grand Rapids, MI: William B. Eerdmans, 1994).

Vansina, J., *Oral Tradition*, trans. H. Wright (Hammondsworth: Penguin, 1973).

Visotzky, B., *Fathers of the World: Essays in Rabbinic and Patristic Literatures* (Tübingen: J.C.B. Mohr [Paul Siebeck], 1995).

Wacholder, B., "A Qumran Attack on the Oral Exegesis? The Phrase *'šr btlmwd šqrm* in 4Q Pesher Nahum," *Revue de Qumran* 5 (1964–66), 575–578.

Wansbrough, H., ed., *Jesus and the Oral Gospel Tradition* (Sheffield: Sheffield Academic Press, 1991).

Ward, R., "Pauline Voice and Presence as Strategic Communication," J. Dewey, *Semeia* 65, 95–107.

Wasserstein, A., "Greek Language and Philosophy in the Early Rabbinic Academies," in G. Abramson and T. Parfitt, eds., *Jewish Education and Learning* (Switzerland: Harwood Academic Publishers, 1994).

Weingreen, J., "Oral Torah and Written Records," in F. Bruce and E. Rupp, eds., *Holy Book and Holy Tradition* (Grand Rapids, MI: William B. Eerdmans, 1968).

Weiss-Halivni, D., *Sources and Traditions* (Heb.), vols. 1–2 (Jerusalem: Jewish Theological Seminary of America, 1975).

——, *Midrash, Mishnah, and Gemara: The Jewish Predilection for Justified Law* (Cambridge, MA, & London: Harvard University Press, 1986).

Wilken, R., "Collegia, Philosophical Schools, and Theology," in S. Benko and J. O'Rourke, eds., *The Catacombs and the Colloseum* (Valley Forge, PA: Judson, 1971), 268–291.

Williams, D., "Josephus or Nicolaus on the Pharisees?" *Revue des Etudes Juives* 156 (1997), 43–58.

Wise, M., et al., eds., *Methods of Investigation of the Dead Sea Scrolls and the Khirbet Qumran Site* (New York: New York Academy of Sciences, 1994).

Wright III, B., "'Fear the Lord and Honor the Priest': Ben Sira as Defender of the Jerusalem Priesthood," in P. Beentjes, ed., *The Book of Ben Sira in Modern Research: Proceedings of the First International Ben Sira Conference* (Berlin & New York: Walter de Gruyter, 1997), 189–222.

Yassif, E., "Traces of Folk-Traditions of the Second Temple Period in Rabbinic Literature," *Journal of Jewish Studies* 39 (1988), 212–233.

Zeidman, R., "An Introduction to the Genesis and Nature of Tosefta, The Chameleon of Rabbinic Literature," in H. Fox and T. Meacham, *Introducing Tosefta*, pp. 73–97.

Zlotnick, D., *The Iron Pillar Mishnah: Redaction, Form, and Intent* (Jerusalem: Bialik Institute, 1988).

Zussman, Y., "The Inscription in the Synagogue at Rehob," in L. Levine, ed., *Ancient Synagogues Revealed* (Detroit: Wayne State University Press, 1982).

——, "The Study Tradition and Text Tradition of the Talmud Yerushalmi: Clarifying the Texts of Yerushalmi Sheqalim" (Heb.), in E. Urbach, ed., *Studies in Talmudic Literature: A Celebration of the 80th Birthday of Saul Lieberman, 8–9 Sivan, 5738* (Jerusalem: Israel Academy of Sciences, 1983), 12–76.

——, "Research in the History of the Halakhah and the Scrolls of the Judean Desert: Preliminary Talmudic Reflections on 4QMMT," *Tarbiz* 49 (1990), 111–76.

Index of Citations

Flavius Josephus, Against
   Apion
1.167: 178n30
2:104–108: 197n24

Flavius Josephus,
   Antiquities of the Jews
3:38: 165n11
4:302–304: 165n11
5:61: 165n11
12:11–18: 171n59
13:171–173: 178n33
13:288–298: 53, 178n33
13:295–298: 50–52
13:377–383: 42
13:408: 42
13:410–415: 42
15:370–371: 52
17:41: 52
17:41–45: 178n33
18:12: 52
18:12–15: 178n33
18:14: 45

Flavius Josephus, Life
10–12: 178n33
12: 41
189–198: 178n33
190–191: 52

Flavius Josephus, The
   Jewish War
1:92–98: 42
1:107–114: 178n33
1:110–111: 51
1:113: 42
2:162: 52
2:162–166: 178n33
2:163: 45

Hermogenes of Tarsus,
   Progymnasmata
7,16–8,8: 132

Philo of Alexandria, Life of
   Moses
2:37: 25

Philo of Alexandria, On
   Abraham
275: 193n35

Philostratus, Lives of the
   Sophists
490: 207n64
541: 129

Theon of Alexandria,
   Progymnasmata
201, 17–20: 130
207, 1–5: 130
210, 8–10: 130
210, 19–24: 131
211, 5–11: 131

RABBINIC LITERATURE

Mishnah

Avot
1:1ff.: 48, 55, 183n6
1:1: 84
1:1–2:8: 84
1:4–12: 80
1:6: 155
1:10: 53
1:12: 53
1:13: 69
2:8: 56
3:7–8: 185n18
3:13: 186n30
3:18: 190n8
5:5: 197n25
6:1: 68
6:9: 183n8

Bava Metzia
2:11: 148
7:8: 192n28

Bava Qamma
8:4: 181n60

Berakhot
1:1: 174n28
1:3: 77
8:23: 48

Bikkurim
3:2–6: 196n14
3:3: 197n23

Demai
2:2–3: 57–58, 181n64

Eduyyot
1:3: 185n25
1:5: 95
1:5–6: 75, 79
5:7: 68
8:7: 8

Eruvin
3:2: 198n36
6:2: 52
9:1–10:15: 107
10:10–14: 106–108

Gittin
5:6: 187n36
6:7: 73

Hagigah
1:8: 85–86, 93, 95, 100,
   190n9
2:2: 80
2:7: 179n46, 180n54

Hallah
1:1: 198

Hullin
9:1: 181n57

Horayot
1:1: 76
3:8: 183n6

Kelim
13:7: 183n8
15:16: 180n56

Keritot
3:9: 75

Ketubot
5:3: 187n36

Maaserot
1:5–8: 106

Makhshirin
6:7: 193n32

Makkot
1:6: 180n48

Megillah
3:5: 80
4:3: 174n27

General Index

Abraham, 95–97
aggadah, 88–90, 97, 135, 145
Associates (*haverim*), 57–59, 181n63, 182n65
authority
  prophetic, 23–27, 29–30, 32, 61
  rabbinic, 67, 79–88, 93–96, 98
  scribal, 20–27, 29, 61, 66, 93–96
  scriptural, 24–26, 51
  traditional, 44, 51–53, 60–61, 83, 94, 98
Avtalion, 53

books
  oral origins of, 11, 18–27, 28–30, 32, 38
  social functions of, 16–19

canon, scriptural, 18–19, 22–23, 25, 29, 163n3, 163n5, 170nn47–48
chreia, 130–133, 139, 147
codex, 16
composition, oral and written, 5–6, 9–10, 18–19, 36–37, 100–125, 138–140, 195n7
curriculum pericope, 88–92

discipleship
  Greco-Roman, 12, 128–129. 147
  rabbinic, 12, 58–60, 72, 126–128, 147–152, 155–156
  Second Temple period, 147
divrei soferim, 92–99, 192n28, 192n30
dorshei halaqot, 40, 41–44

epic, oral, 10, 103
Ezra, 24–25, 117

halakhah
  as modality of tradition, 43–44, 48, 70, 72–83, 85–99, 135, 142–143, 149, 151 187n37, 187n42, 188n55, 190n8
  Mosaic, 79–83, 98–100, 142, 192n28
  pre-exilic, 80–82
  Second Temple period, 80–83
Hillel, 48, 79–81, 84, 133

Jesus of Nazareth, 44–47, 60, 65

Libraries, ancient, 15–16, 165n11
list-making, 106–111
literacy in antiquity, 11, 15–20, 164nn7–8

masoret, 73
memorization, 3–5, 17–18, 68–72, 101, 103, 105–106, 109, 124–146, 130–132, 140
midrash, 72, 88–90, 97
mishnah (*matnyta*), 4–5, 67–70, 73, 84, 90, 106, 145, 194n2
mistoryn/mysterion, 146
mnemonics, 109–111, 130–140
Moses, 3–5, 24, 79–80, 82–85, 89–91, 96, 98–99, 144–146, 156

narrative, 103–106, 113–124

orality, ideological formulations of, 9–11, 15–27, 84–99, 140–147, 175n2, 201n70

paideia, 147, 152
Paul of Tarsus, 40, 45–46, 52

237

performance, oral, 5–6, 8, 11–12, 15–18, 26,
    30, 36–37, 60–61, 92, 105–106, 124–125,
    127–131, 133–136, 140–141, 148–151
Pharisees, 30, 38–61, 175n2, 176n3, 179n46,
    180n48
    in Christian literature, 40, 44–50
    in Josephus, 40–41, 50–52
    in Qumranian literature, 40–44
    in rabbinic literature, 41, 52–60
pinax/pinqas, 141–142
Progymnasmata, 130–132, 136–139
pseudepigraphy, 23–25, 170n51, 171nn52–53

Q source, 46–47, 49
qabbalah, 73
Qumran sect, 21–22, 30–32, 40, 60, 172nn5–
    7, 181n63

Rabban Gamaliel (I and II), 52–82, 91,
    191n23
Rabban Shimon b. Gamaliel, 52
Rabban Yohanan b. Zakkai, 55–56, 69, 72,
    80, 84, 119
Rabbi Aqiva, 3–4, 68, 71, 74–75, 91–92, 103,
    114–115
Rabbi Yehudah the Patriarch, 4, 68, 84, 127
Rabbi Yohanan b. Nappaha, 126, 128, 142–
    144, 148–150, 153–155
Reading, performative, 8–9, 18–20, 25–27,
    28–36, 68, 101–102, 124–125, 165n9,
    165n16, 166n19, 175n44
Repeated Tradition, 3–4, 67, 69–70, 72,
    126, 142–143, 145–146, 153–154
Revelation, Sinaitic, 3–4, 24–26, 95–96, 98,
    100, 127, 152–154
rhetoric
    Greco-Roman, 128–132
    Rabbinic, 128–129, 132–140
Righteous Teacher, 31, 37

Sadducees, 44, 46, 51–52, 55–56, 65, 115
Sages
    early rabbinic, 30, 53–60, 79–83, 97
    Galilean Amoraic, 7, 97, 99, 102, 126–
        128, 133–135, 144–156
Scribes
    cultural world of, 6–7, 15–20, 28–30, 66
    functions of, 7, 17, 20–21, 65, 167n28
    lay, 21–22, 169n41
    priestly, 20–24, 169n40

rabbinic, 66, 101–102, 111, 183,nn7–8
in Second Temple period, 7, 11, 20–27,
    30, 133, 168n30
training of, 15–18, 20–21, 136, 166n22,
    168nn34–35, 173n22
words of (*divrei soferim*), 92–99, 192n28,
    192n30
scrolls, as storage media, 16–18, 165n13,
    166n14
Shammai, 48, 79–81, 133
Shemaiah, 53
Shimon b. Kosiva, 77–78
Smooth Things, Expounders of (*dorshei
    halaqot*), 40, 41–44
Sophists, 129–130

talmud, 88, 97, 145
Torah
    essence of, 85–87, 93, 98
    Mosaic, 18, 21, 24, 37, 51, 80, 83–89, 95–
        96, 98, 142–144, 154, 156
    Oral and Written, 5, 9, 39, 51, 54, 84, 90,
        92, 98, 127, 142, 146, 162n6, 183n9,
        188n55, 189n4
    revelation of, 3, 11, 45–46, 84–85
    study of, 3–4, 22, 32–36, 67–72, 77–78,
        83, 92, 140–146. 148–151. 154–156
Torah in the Mouth/in Script, 5, 7–10, 67,
    84, 91–92, 99, 102, 127, 146, 151–152,
    154–156, 163n14, 193n39
Tosefta
    in relation to Mishnah, 57–58, 70, 76–
        77, 82, 86–87, 96–97, 112–124, 137–
        140, 157–159, 181n64, 202n6
Tradition
    of the fathers/ancestors, 45, 47–48, 51, 83
    hermeneutical functions of, 5–6, 10, 28–
        29, 88–92
    oral, 3–6, 9–11, 19–20, 24–25, 30, 41, 43, 45,
        49–50, 53–54, 60, 77, 91, 97–99, 101,
        109, 124, 154, 162nn6–10, 185n25,
        195n7, 196$\frac{5}{10}$, 201n70, 204n35
    oral-formulaic, 5–6, 44, 66–67, 70–71,
        105–111
    oral-literary, 7–10, 37–38, 44, 60–61,67, 0,
        86, 88–89, 100–102, 128–132, 162n13
    oral-performative, 5–6, 8–10, 11, 26, 29–
        30, 34–36,60–61, 67, 69, 83, 85, 92,
        94–95, 102, 106, 111–112, 116, 120, 126,
        130–132, 142, 146, 152

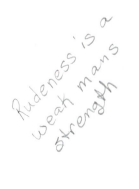

Printed in the United States
36405LVS00001B/16